THE BIG BOOK OF SELF PROMOTION

Bell
PI/DA

THE BIG BOOK OF SELF PROMOTION

Introduction by
PELEG TOP and ILISE BENUN

Edited by
SUZANNA MW STEPHENS

COLLINS DESIGN
An Imprint of HarperCollins*Publishers*

THE BIG BOOK OF SELF-PROMOTION

HarperCollins books may be purchased for educational, business, or sales promotional use. For information, please write: Special Markets Department, HarperCollins*Publishers*, 10 East 53rd Street, New York, NY 10022.

First Edition

First published in 2009 by:
Collins Design
An Imprint of HarperCollins*Publishers*
10 East 53rd Street
New York, NY 10022
Tel: (212) 207-7000
Fax: (212) 207-7654
collinsdesign@harpercollins.com
www.harpercollins.com

Distributed throughout the world by:
HarperCollins*Publishers*
10 East 53rd Street
New York, NY 10022
Fax: (212) 207-7654

Jacket and book design by Anderson Design Group, Nashville, TN
www.AndersonDesignGroup.com

Page design and additional photography by

Designs on You!

Anthony & Suzanna Stephens
www.designs-on-you.net

Case studies written by Eve Bohakel Lee.
www.editoreve.com

Library of Congress Control Number: 2008933500

ISBN: 978-0-06-169169-0

Produced by Crescent Hill Books, Louisville, KY.
www.CrescentHillBooks.com

Printed in China by Everbest Printing Company.

First Printing, 2009

TABLE OF CONTENTS

THE BIG BOOK OF SELF PROMOTION

"Promoting yourself and your services puts you in the driver's seat to choose who you work with."

Self-promotion often gets a bad rap, but that's because most people don't understand exactly what it is.

You see, it's not bragging, as many creative professionals seem to believe. (They're the ones whose mothers told them not to brag.)

And it doesn't have to be sleazy or slimy or pushy or aggressive, even if that's your experience when someone is promoting themselves to you.

It's not even really about tooting your own horn, although there are times when that's called for.

In a word, self-promotion is freedom, because promoting yourself and your services puts you in the driver's seat to choose who you work with, instead of being at the mercy of whomever chooses you.

INTRODUCTION

"In a world of often boring cookie-cutter work, your own self-promotional campaign can be a very satisfying creative outlet."

Here's how. When you promote yourself and your services consistently and with a clear message, and when that message corresponds to the needs of your market, here's what happens: A pipeline full of prospects starts knocking on your door, calling on the phone, sending e-mail, visiting your Web site, clamoring to work with you. That's where the freedom comes in. Instead of being overwhelmed by all the attention, you are free to calmly review your options and carefully choose which projects and clients fit best with the personal and professional goals you are aiming to achieve.

There's another type of freedom to be had as well. Your own self-promotion campaign is your chance to be free of the constraints imposed by client work. Although you may find it challenging to create your own marketing materials—whether it's a Web site, brochure, or mailing piece—rarely do you have the opportunity to bring your true creativity into your commercial work.

But when it's for you, there's no formula to follow, no one controlling the message, no committee of non-creatives second-guessing you, telling you it's too edgy or too loud. You can be as humorous, as silly, as colorful (or as dark) as you want—as long as it is appropriate for your market. (Remember, this is a marketing piece and one of the goals is to convey the message, "We can help you.")

In a world of often boring cookie-cutter work, your own self-promotional campaign can be a very satisfying creative outlet. That much is evident from the excellent examples featured in this book.

Beyond freedom, self-promotion is a way to reach out to the world. You can (and should) use your marketing to build relationships and stay in touch with the people who need your services. The goal of your campaign should be to start a conversation with your clients and prospects. With your very first outreach—whether you send first or call first—you are inviting them into a conversation about collaboration. Don't dismay if they don't respond immediately, and don't give up. Persistence and consistency are the keys to success. Your goal is to be there—in their face, in their inbox—when their need arises, and it may take a couple of months or even a couple of years. But when it happens, the dialogue begins.

That dialogue can take many forms, as you will see in the collection of work featured in this book. But by staying in touch and continuing to reach out, you send a message that says, "I am reliable. I am consistent. You can depend on me."

"By staying in touch and continuing to reach out, you send a message that says, 'I am reliable. I am consistent. You can depend on me.'"

So here are some tips on how to create self-promotional materials that will get that dialogue going, sooner rather than later:

- Keep a calendar or schedule for your own self-promotion; then follow it. You should be reaching out to your network quarterly at the minimum, monthly at the maximum.
- Make it simple. Don't overthink it, don't complicate it. Do what you do for clients: Come up with the clearest message, then get it out the door. It will do no good sitting in a box in your office.
- Collaborate with other creatives. You don't have to do this alone. Designers, writers, photographers, illustrators all have similar markets and complementary services. You can help each other and yourselves by promoting together. Consider trading with a local printer. You provide creative services in exchange for printing to help offset the cost. They may need to be in touch with the same prospects too.
- Personalize it. Take advantage of the latest technology: Digital printing makes it easy and not too expensive to personalize promotional pieces for each prospect.
- Make it useful. Too many self-promotional items end up in the trash; don't let yours join them. Create something that is useful to your clients and prospects. Something they may want to hold on to, maybe even put on their desk, so your name and brand is always in their view—just in case a need arises.
- Don't forget your contact information. It happens more often than you'd think: You get so wrapped up in the creative aspect of your promotional piece that you forget the basics, like your phone number or Web address. Be sure it's on every element of your piece.
- Follow up. If you expect to send out one mailing—even a fabulous one—and have people flocking to your door as a result, you need to readjust your expectations. One fabulous mailing does not a successful business make. It's just the beginning of the conversation. Don't leave the ball in their court. You need a system in place to follow up, which should include phone calls to your very best prospects.

The marketplace is flooded with many companies who offer similar services to yours. But, as is evident in this book, the people and companies who promote themselves in a creative way stand out from the crowd and they're the ones who get the best projects.

The collection of work in this book proves that there are endless possibilities to creating self-promotion materials. We hope that browsing through these pages of promotional ideas will inspire and motivate you to promote yourself too.

Peleg Top & Ilise Benun
Co-Founders, Marketing-Mentor
www.marketing-mentor.com

"Self-promotion is all about spreading the good word about your talents. It builds your reputation and credibility, it sets you apart from other design firms, and it distinguishes you with your clients and prospects."

• • • • • • • •

Bryn Mooth
Editor, *HOW Magazine*

From the Editor
(and occasional commentator)

● ● ● ● ● ● ● ●

After thirteen years of involvement in the production of books featuring collections of the best graphic design in the country—and even the world—I can say without hesitation the most interesting designs are self promotions. These mailers, freebies, posters, and gifts are often sent to us for inclusion in an upcoming volume of graphics. Their arrival in our office consistenty elicits "Did you see this? This is cool!" We immediately lay claim to those that really command our attention. I keep them. The staff keeps them. Friends who wander by the office want to keep them. (I give the most humorous ones as stocking stuffers; they are the highlight of the family Christmas party!)

Suffice it to say, they are kept.

At this very moment, on (or in) my desk alone I have a necklace, a couple of staplers, a calendar, two commemorative tins, and a favorite coffee cup...I have a dresser drawer full of regularly-worn t-shirts promoting OTHER design firms...I have amazing art books that were produced as portfolios...I have a computer game that's a glorified version of "Pong," but the graphics make it seem like something new...I have a "Magic 8-Ball"...I have a View-Master...I have pop-up cards...I have absolutely useless items that are so visually interesting I can't part with them—all garnered from past self promo submissions. Great promotional examples like these make the recipient want to keep them. And in keeping them, the owner has a constant reminder of the creative firm that produced them.

This book is filled with "keepers"—very impressive examples of promotion. Many were done in-house, many were done for clients, but each speaks directly of the organization or individual that is the topic of the campaign.

Obviously the size, texture, printing, or production techniques are an integral part of any design. These qualities aren't always apparent when a three-dimensional piece is represented by a two-dimensional photograph.

Some of the particularly elaborate submissions were chosen for in-depth explanation. These are highlighted on two-page spreads in every chapter. Eve Bohakel Lee contacted and interviewed individuals at each respective firm in order to clearly communicate the thinking and production processes involved in creating these promo packages. Her text beautifully complements the images chosen to showcase the promotions.

Anderson Design Group in Nashville, Tennessse, developed a visually exciting jacket, color scheme, and design template so we could present the submitted work in a format that would display it without detracting from it.

Additional photography and page layout was completed or directed by Anthony B. Stephens, my husband and business partner. Compiling the materials for a book this size is a massive undertaking and his design sense and organization skills are invaluable.

Credit for the concept of *The Big Book of Self-Promotion* goes to Nancy Heinonen at Crescent Hill Books. She also deserves accolades for keeping all components involved in the production of a(nother!) book moving in tandem and focused on our collective goal.

Many thanks to Peleg Top and Ilise Benun, co-founder of *Marketing-Mentor* (www.marketing-mentor.com), who have written an exceptionally insightful and interesting introduction explaining exactly what a promotion is and what it should do. (Samples from Top Design's series of calendar promotions, pages 316 - 319, are proof positive of the validity of their observations.) They've also included steps that will guide you in creating your own successful self-promo!

A self-promotion can be an expression of personal and professional creativity. It allows the designer to ignore the constraints a client may often impose. It is an entity that says, "Look what I can do!" It should also indicate, "Give me a chance. I can do it for you, too." In this book you will see hundreds of examples of what designers can do...and can do for you, too.

Enjoy!

Suzanne Stephens

It's All About . . .

You

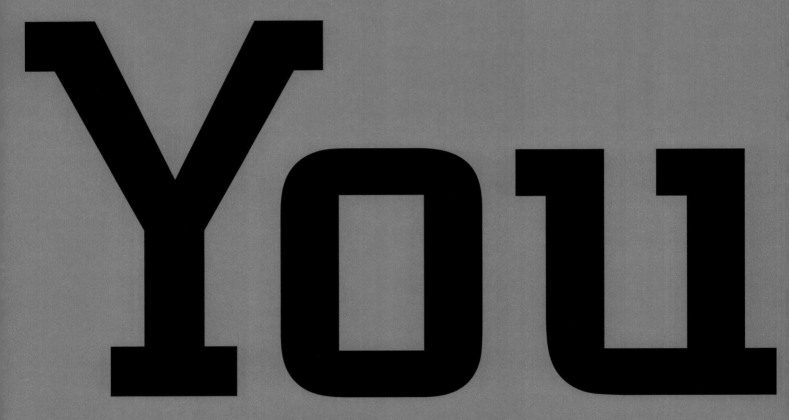

Self-Promotion by Designers and Design Firms

Brady Communications – Pittsburgh, Pennsylvania
Designers : John Brady, Erica Brinker, Tracey Roman, Kevin Polonofsky, Tony Redd, Jeff Beavers, Kat Wintersteen, Alice Benninger, Paul Semonik, Lia Osle, Dan Yazvac
Client : Brady Communications

biz-R – Totnes, England
Designers : Blair Thomson, Paul Warren
Client : biz-R

Reactor – Kansas City, Missouri
Designers : Clifton Alexander, Chase Wilson
Client : Reactor

Sports cards collectors will fully appreciate this nod to a "pop-up of your favorite athlete." Reactor obviously values team players.

Handle with Care
'Twas The Night Before...
DEADLINE
AT LEVINE & ASSOCIATES
Like FedEx, the mailman, or UPS Brown,
No rain, snow or protest would dare slow us down.
The elves, they retreated, like a sea they did part.
A holiday miracle made way for our art!
So with twenty-two hands and eleven warm hearts,
Goodwill to all, peace on earth we impart.
If you haven't yet guessed, here's one final clue...
...the card we created that night was for you!

Levine & Associates, Inc. – Washington, D.C.
Designers : Greg Sitzmann, Lena Markley, Megan Riordan, Kerry McCutcheon
Client : Levine & Associates, Inc.

Octavo Designs – Frederick, Maryland
Designers : Sue Hough, Mark Burrier
Client : Octavo Designs

CANDY
CANDY
Taste our Creative Flavor!

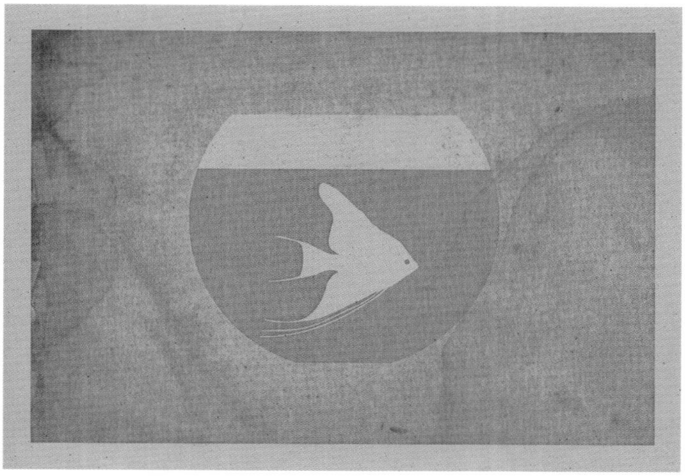

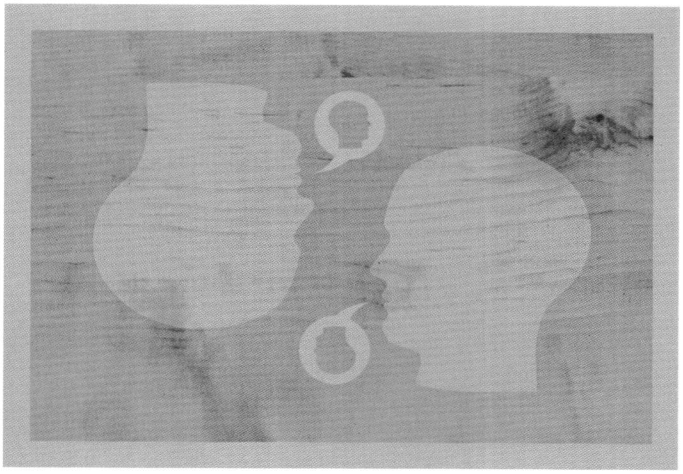

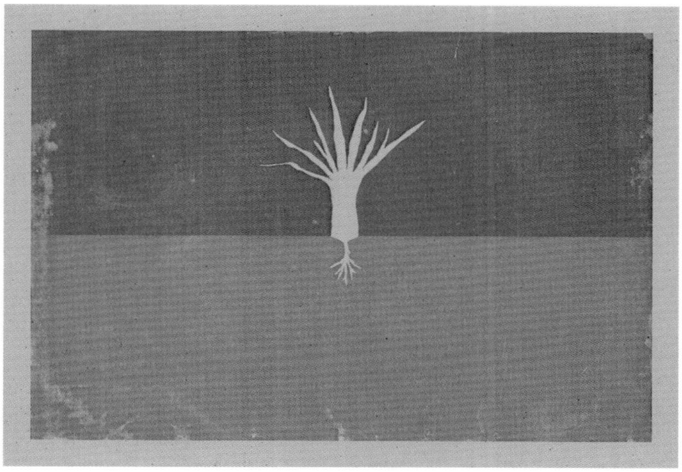

EP designworks – Bettendorf, Iowa
Designer : Eugene Phillips
Client : EP designworks

This die-cut cover opens to reveal a spiral-bound book. Inside, each "page" is a four-color pocket that holds numerous samples of the design firm's work.

Coalesce Marketing & Design, Inc. – Appleton, Wisconsin
Designers : Lisa Piikkila, Michael Gehrman, Michelle Richard
Client : Coalesce Marketing & Design, Inc.

Joven Orozco Design – Newport Beach, California
Designers : Joven Orozco, Kenneth Lim
Client : Joven Orozco Design

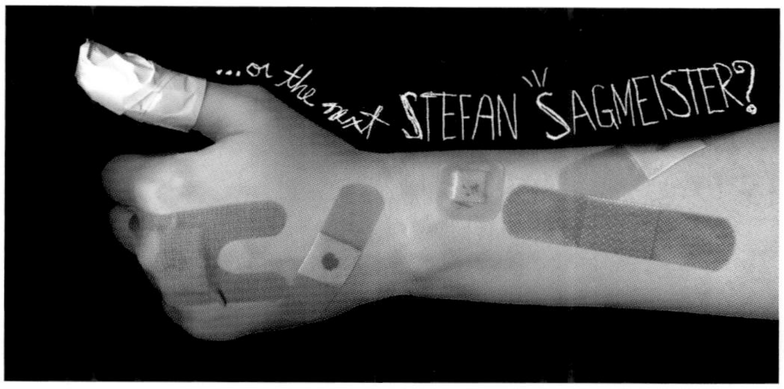
...or the next STEFAN SAGMEISTER?

Am I...

Am I...

Hire me and find out.
Elizabeth Maplesden Graphic Design
215–932–0548 · emdash@att.net

...the next Bradbury Thompson?

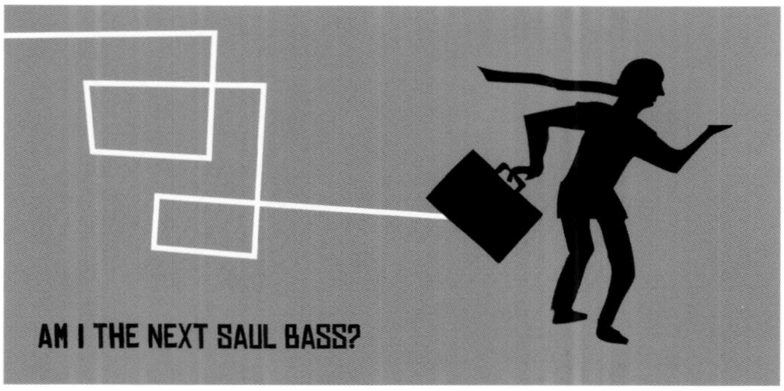
AM I THE NEXT SAUL BASS?

EMdash Design – Yardley, Pennsylvania
Designer : Elizabeth Maplesden
Client : EMdash Design

Sayles Graphic Design – Des Moines, Iowa
Designers : John Sayles, Bridget Drendel
Client : Kansas City Advertising Federation

john sayles & sheree clark of sayles graphic design speak to:
advertising club of kansas city | thursday, september 6, 2007 | 5:30 p.m.
JOHN SAYLES & SHEREE CLARK
GO THE EXTRA MILE
KC AD CLUB
kansas city, missouri
IOWA
KC 195 mi
SOUTH 35
far from the design centers of either coast, sayles graphic design is cruising along from their unlikely location in des moines, iowa. founded in 1985 by john sayles and sheree clark, the company has a client list that reads more like that of a madison avenue shop, including saks fifth avenue, mca records, united airlines and verizon wireless.
our way or the highway
www.kcadclub.com | 816-822-0300

Using a skateboard as a means of advertising is a bold statement about a firm's image and client demographic. Specific illustration styles show the variety of creativity available when contracting a project.

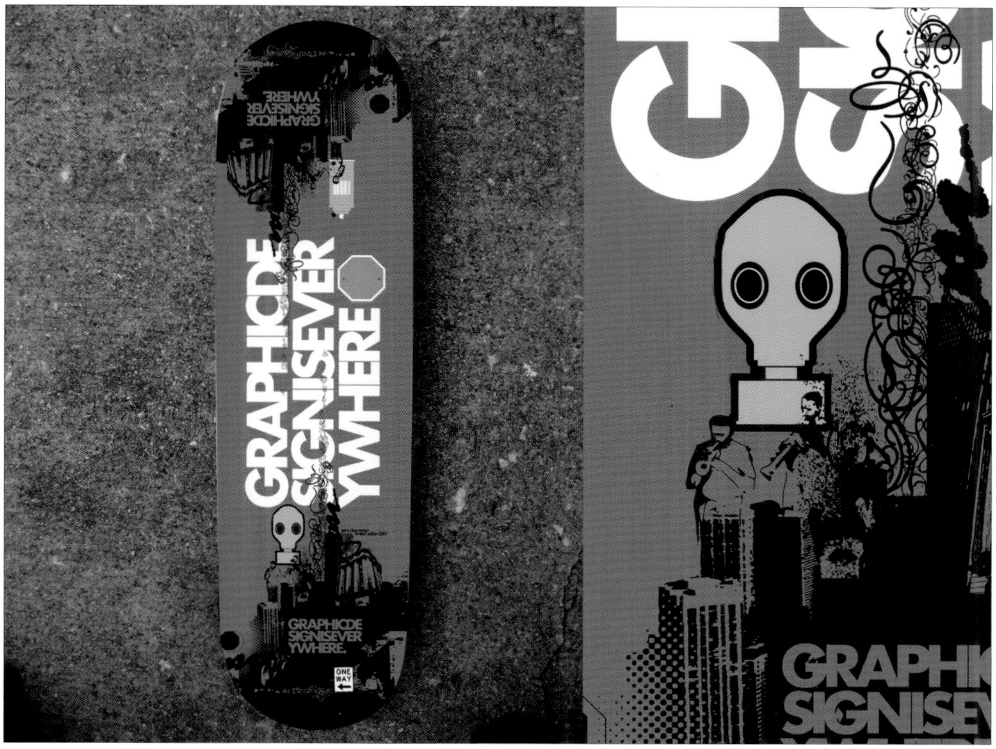

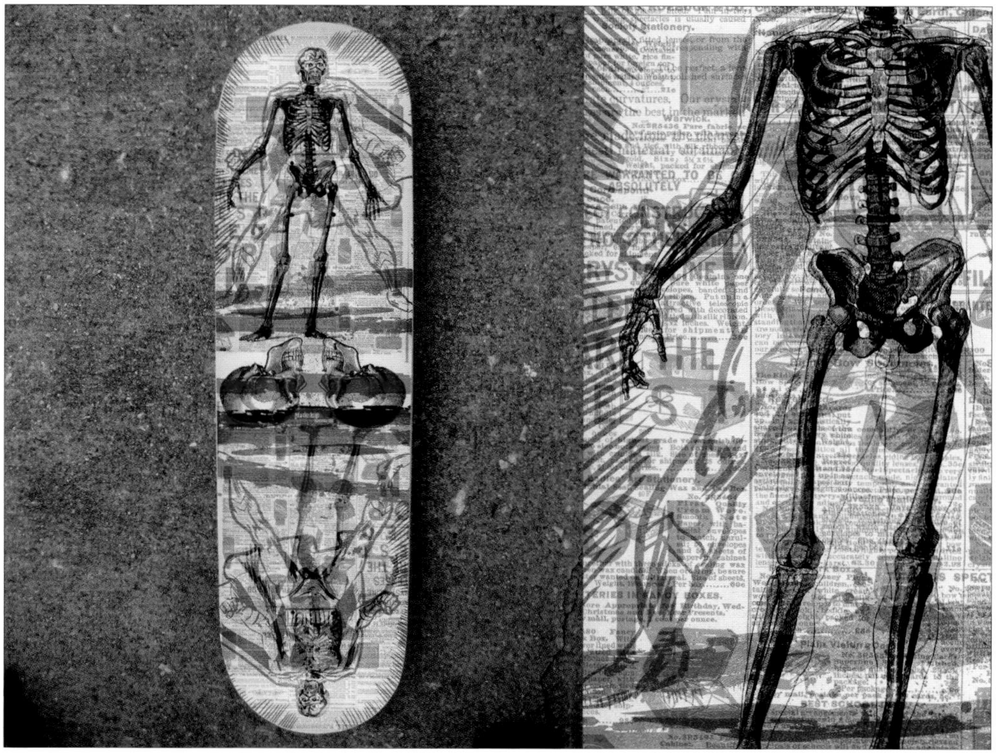

Get A Clue Design – Hickory, North Carolina
Designer : Matt Pfahlert
Client : Get A Clue Design

dig
"Levi Strauss & Co. has worked with 3 Dogz for over three years on various projects, with great success. They quickly adapted to understanding our target group for each of the brands, created great design concepts, all while meeting very tight timelines. Their commitment to working with Levi's without compromise is greatly appreciated, and I look forward to future successes with them."
Gilles Thibeault LEVI STRAUSS & CO.
www.3dogz.com

3 Dogz Creative Inc. – Toronto, Canada
Designers : Dave Gouveia, Chris Elkerton, Roberta Judge, Ryan Broadbent
Client : 3 Dogz Creative Inc.

CHRISTOPH HITZ-ILLUSTRATION.COM (845) 626 7730

Hitz-illustration.com (845) 626 7730

Hitz Studio – Kerhonkson, New York
Designer : Christopher Hitz
Client : Christopher Hitz

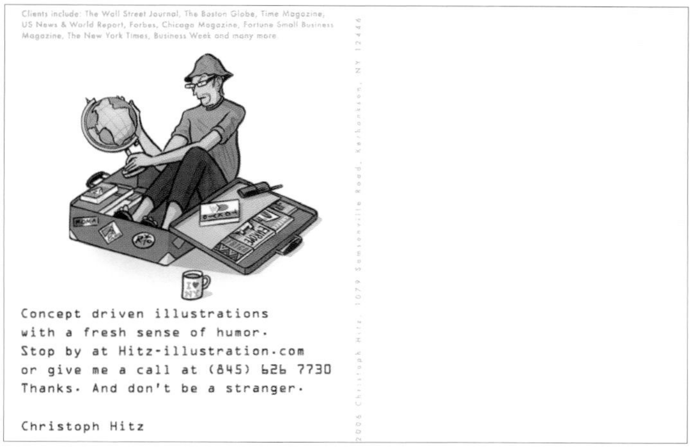
Clients include: The Wall Street Journal, The Boston Globe, Time Magazine, US News & World Report, Forbes, Chicago Magazine, Fortune Small Business Magazine, The New York Times, Business Week and many more
Concept driven illustrations
with a fresh sense of humor.
Stop by at Hitz-illustration.com
or give me a call at (845) 626 7730
Thanks. And don't be a stranger.
Christoph Hitz

Studio 33 Design – South Pasadena, California
Designer : Cynthia J. Holmes
Client : Studio 33 Design

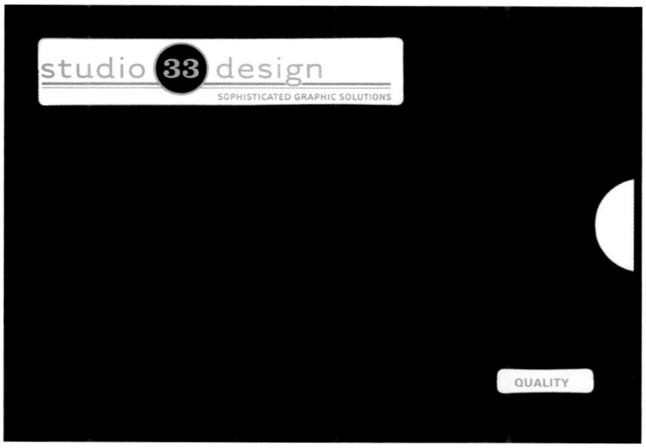
studio 33 design
SOPHISTICATED GRAPHIC SOLUTIONS
QUALITY

Instead of sending a basic promotional postcard, Studio 33 Design places its card in a slide-out envelope. This physically involves the viewer when the information is removed from its housing.

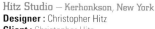

studio 33 design
SOPHISTICATED GRAPHIC SOLUTIONS
At Studio 33 Design
quality is our first priority!
626.799.0246
www.studio33design.com
Now at our NEW location:
710 Arroyo Drive Suite 1
South Pasadena, CA 91030
T 626.799.0246 F 626.799.3814
Services we offer:
• Branding & Identity
• Marketing Collateral
• Packaging
• Annual Reports
• Architectural Signage
• Advertising
• Book Design
• Photography
INTEGRITY RELIABILITY FRESH IDEAS CREATIVITY ELEGANCE QUALITY
Call us today and let us show you how we can use these attributes to benefit your business.

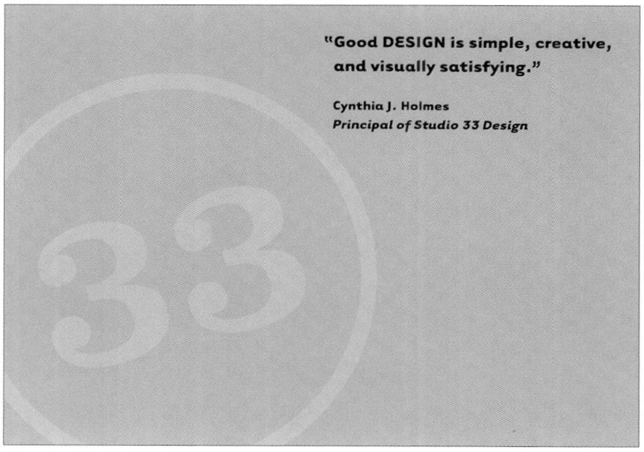
"Good DESIGN is simple, creative, and visually satisfying."
Cynthia J. Holmes
Principal of Studio 33 Design
33

laura tallardy illustration 212 475 0440

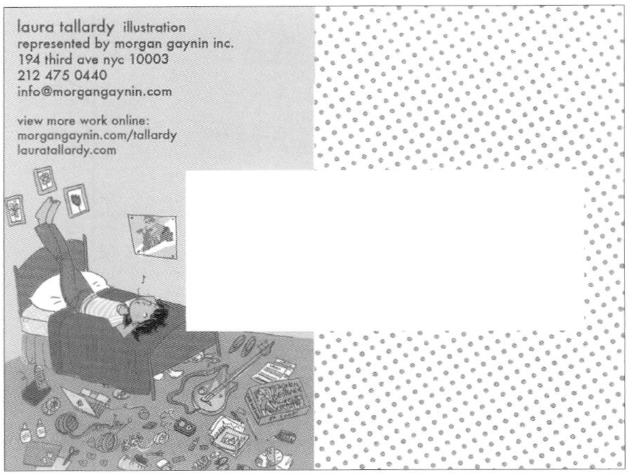
laura tallardy illustration
represented by morgan gaynin inc.
194 third ave nyc 10003
212 475 0440
info@morgangaynin.com
view more work online:
morgangaynin.com/tallardy
lauratallardy.com

laura tallardy illustration 212 475 0440

laura tallardy illustration
represented by morgan gaynin inc.
212 475 0440
info@morgangaynin.com
view more work online:
morgangaynin.com/tallardy
lauratallardy.com
morgan gaynin inc.
194 third ave nyc 10003

Morgan Gaynin, Inc. – New York, New York
Designer : Laura Tallardy
Client : Laura Tallardy

Right-Hemisphere Laboratory – Littleton, Colorado
Designer : Rich Barry
Client : Right-Hemisphere Laboratory

Erin Mauterer
Bluewater Advertising & Design
732-922-2269
www.erinm.com
erin@erinm.com
"Albert's Lucky Day" ©2008erinmauterer

Bluewater Advertising & Design – Ocean, New Jersey
Designer : Erin Marie Mauterer
Client : Bluewater Advertising & Design

Black Eye Design – Montreal, Canada
Designer : Michel Vrana
Client : Black Eye Design

Design 446 – Manasquan, New Jersey
Designer : Brian Stern
Client : Design 446

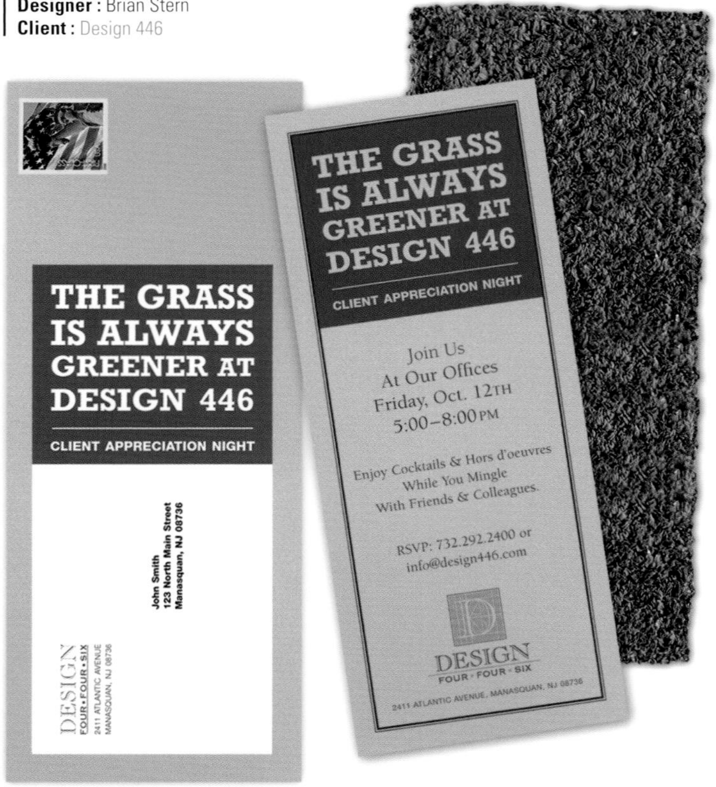

If an item from a promotional campaign is something the potential client keeps, it may well be a regular reminder of the soliciting firm and its good ideas.

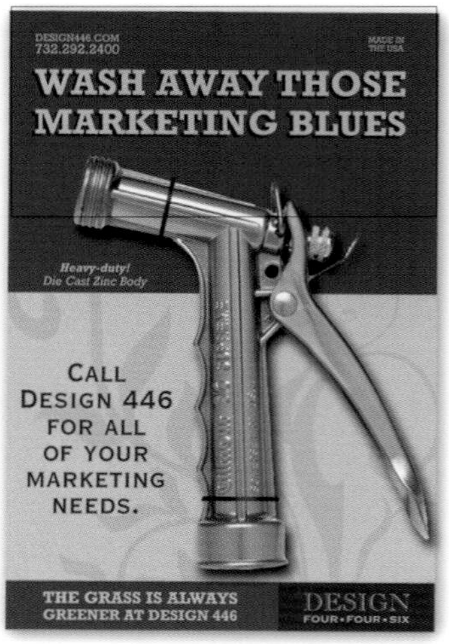

Chase Wilson
CF-24

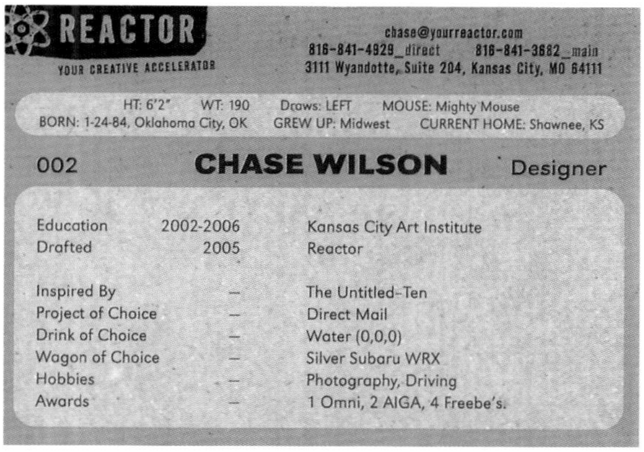
REACTOR
YOUR CREATIVE ACCELERATOR
chase@yourreactor.com
816-841-4929_direct 816-841-3682_main
3111 Wyandotte, Suite 204, Kansas City, MO 64111
HT: 6'2" WT: 190 Draws: LEFT MOUSE: Mighty Mouse
BORN: 1-24-84, Oklahoma City, OK GREW UP: Midwest CURRENT HOME: Shawnee, KS
002 CHASE WILSON Designer
Education 2002-2006 Kansas City Art Institute
Drafted 2005 Reactor
Inspired By – The Untitled-Ten
Project of Choice – Direct Mail
Drink of Choice – Water (0,0,0)
Wagon of Choice – Silver Subaru WRX
Hobbies – Photography, Driving
Awards – 1 Omni, 2 AIGA, 4 Freebe's.

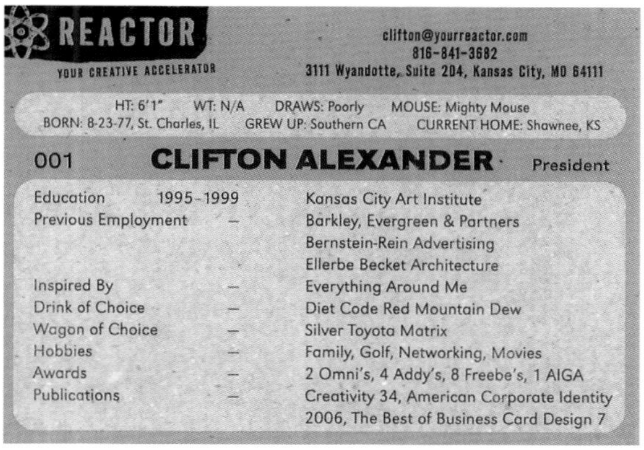
REACTOR
YOUR CREATIVE ACCELERATOR
clifton@yourreactor.com
816-841-3682
3111 Wyandotte, Suite 204, Kansas City, MO 64111
HT: 6'1" WT: N/A DRAWS: Poorly MOUSE: Mighty Mouse
BORN: 8-23-77, St. Charles, IL GREW UP: Southern CA CURRENT HOME: Shawnee, KS
001 CLIFTON ALEXANDER President
Education 1995-1999 Kansas City Art Institute
Previous Employment – Barkley, Evergreen & Partners
Bernstein-Rein Advertising
Ellerbe Becket Architecture
Inspired By – Everything Around Me
Drink of Choice – Diet Code Red Mountain Dew
Wagon of Choice – Silver Toyota Matrix
Hobbies – Family, Golf, Networking, Movies
Awards – 2 Omni's, 4 Addy's, 8 Freebe's, 1 AIGA
Publications – Creativity 34, American Corporate Identity 2006, The Best of Business Card Design 7

Athletics
8
1B-8
REACTOR
Clifton Alexander

Reactor – Kansas City, Missouri
Designers : Clifton Alexander, Chase Wilson
Client : Reactor

Infinite Studio – Albisola, Italy
Designer : Fabio Berruti
Client : Infinite Studio

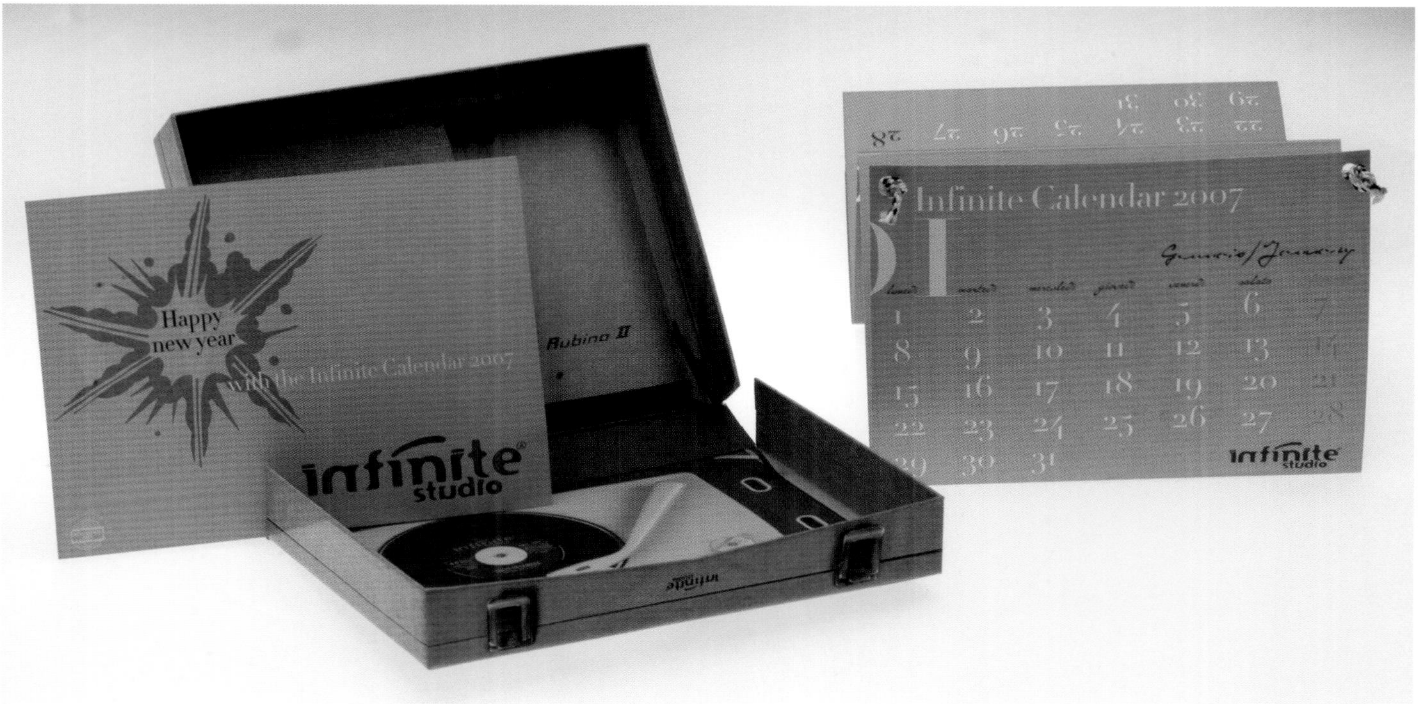

Sue Todd Illustration – Toronto, Canada
Designer : Sue Todd
Client : Sue Todd Illustration

Insight Marketing Design
– Sioux Falls, South Dakota
Designers : Doug Moss, Wanda Goodman
Client : Insight Marketing Design

Reinforcing the creative firm in the mind of the client, the gift itself possesses a visual reference to the firm's name. Inviting the recipient to take a break for a fun couple of minutes results in a mobile that will surely be hung in the office.

Hatch Design — San Francisco, California
Designers : Katie Jain, Joel Templin, Eszter T. Clark, Lisa Pemrick
Client : Hatch Design

3 Dogz Creative, Inc. – Toronto, Canada
Designers : Dave Gouveia, Chris Elkerton, Roberta Judge, Ryan Broadbent
Client : 3 Dogz Creative, Inc.

A desk planner distributed by USA TODAY is chock full of the pictorial graphs for which they are so well known. Each is strategically placed, mindful of the relationship between topic and date.

USA TODAY Brand Marketing – McLean, Virginia
Designer : Scott Ament
Client : USA TODAY Brand Marketing

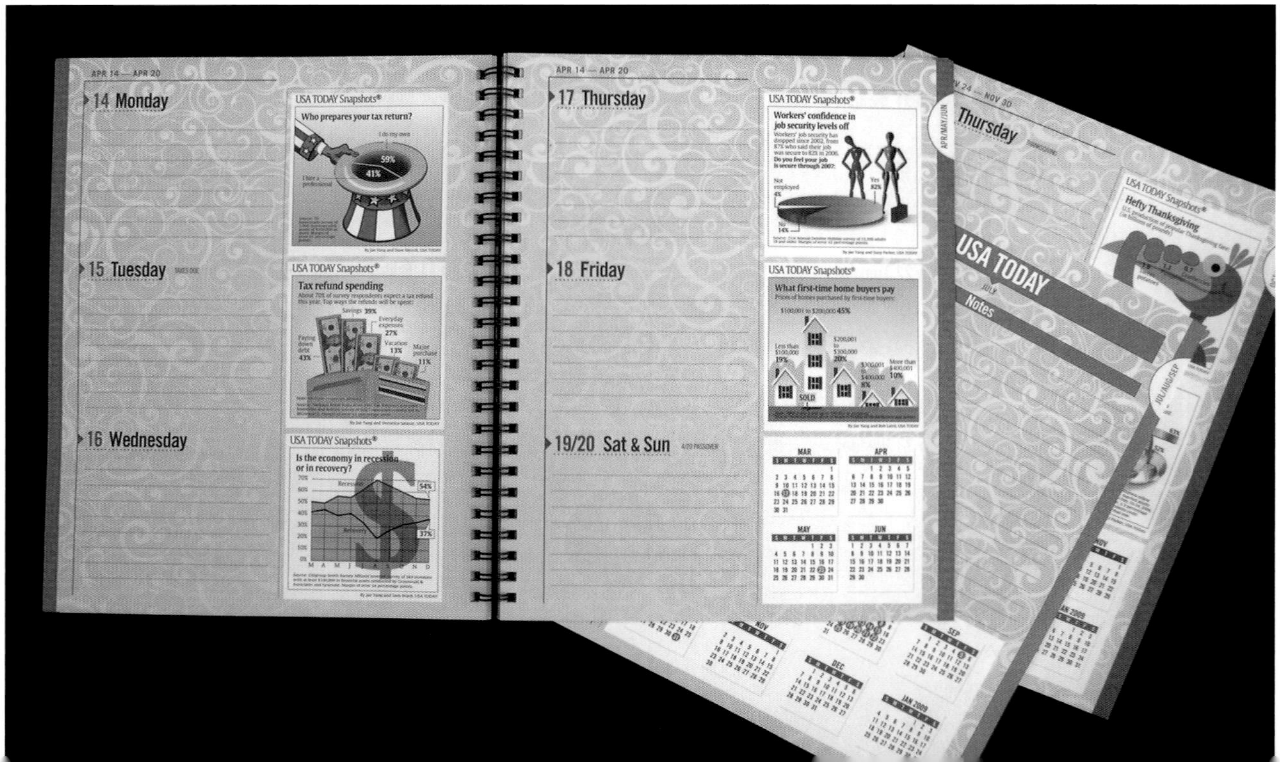

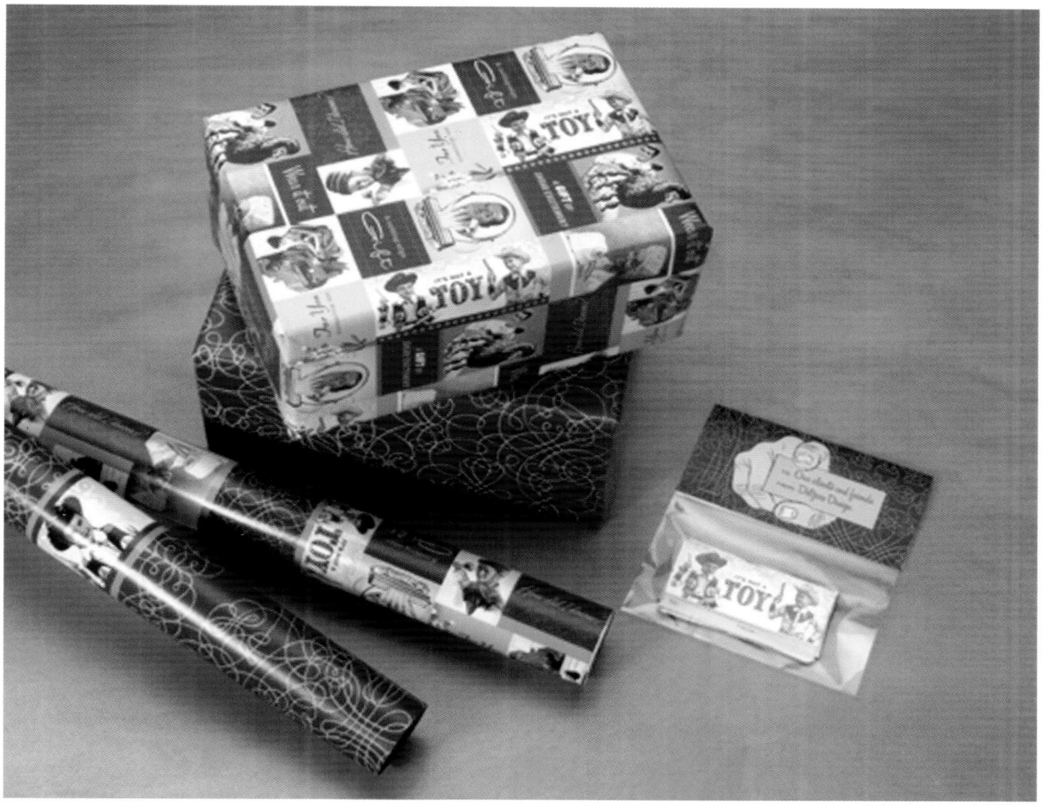

Dotzero Design – Portland, Oregon
Designers : Karen Wippich, Jon Wippich
Client : Dotzero Design

2creativo – Barcelona, Spain
Designers : 2creativo Team
Client : 2creativo

If he seems
out of this world...
there's a good
chance he is!

Why is it AFTER you leave them,
they get a great job,
lose weight,
dress so much better,
finally style their hair,
and just look so damned good?

Bruno,
I don't think we're in
California anymore.
corny....

Wishing you a very
GOTHIC
Halloween
www.jillbell.com

Good girls
go to heaven;
Bad girls go
everywhere

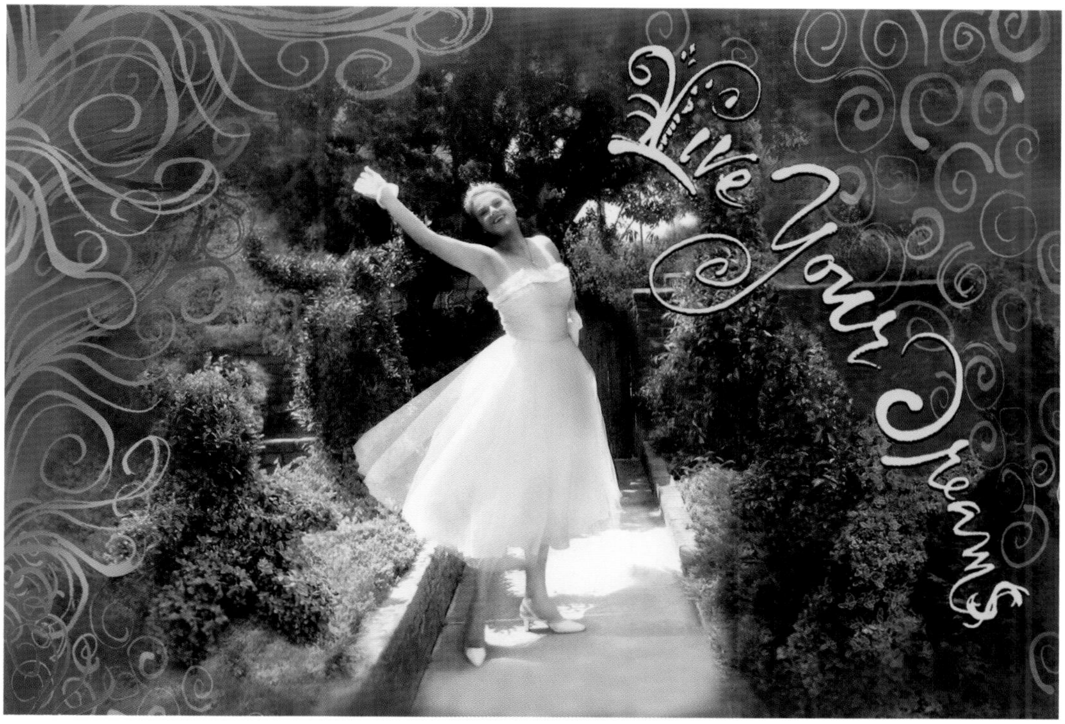

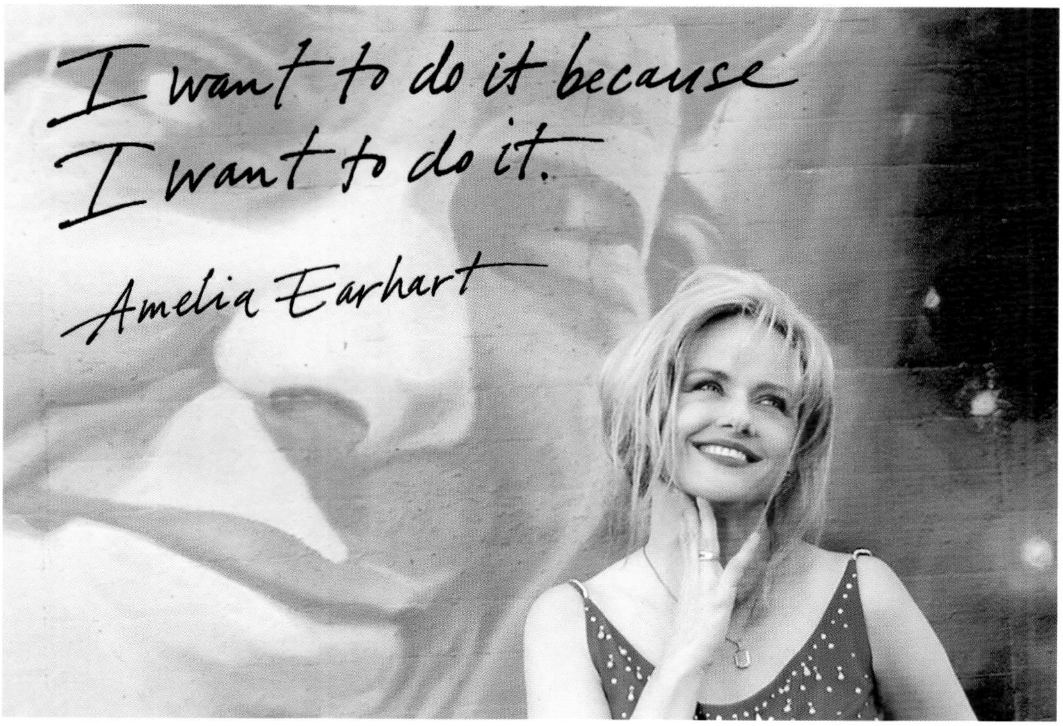

Jill Bell Brandlettering – Leawood, Kansas
Designer : Jill Bell
Client : Jill Bell Brandlettering

Morgan Gaynin, Inc. — New York, New York
Designer : Valeria Petrone
Client : Valeria Petrone

Lucie M. Rice Illustration — Nashville, Tennessee
Designer : Lucie Rice
Client : Lucie M. Rice Illustration

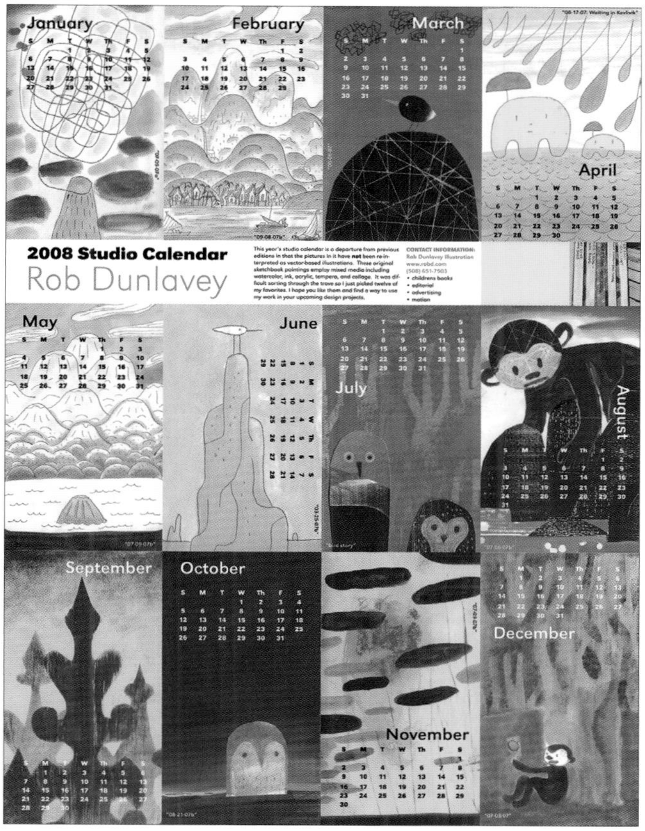

Rob Dunlavey Illustration – South Natick, Massachusetts
Designer : Rob Dunlavey
Client : Rob Dunlavey Illustration

alison beebe :: gum :: mixed media

NOVEMBER

S	M	T	W	T	F	S
						1
2	3	4	5	6	7	8
9	10	11	12	13	14	15
16	17	18	19	20	21	22
23	24	25	26	27	28	29
30						

Curiosity Group – Portland, Oregon
Designers : Curiosity Group Design Team
Client : Curiosity Group

jamal qutub :: how to skate :: digital media

JUNE

S	M	T	W	T	F	S
1	2	3	4	5	6	7
8	9	10	11	12	13	14
15	16	17	18	19	20	21
22	23	24	25	26	27	28
29	30					

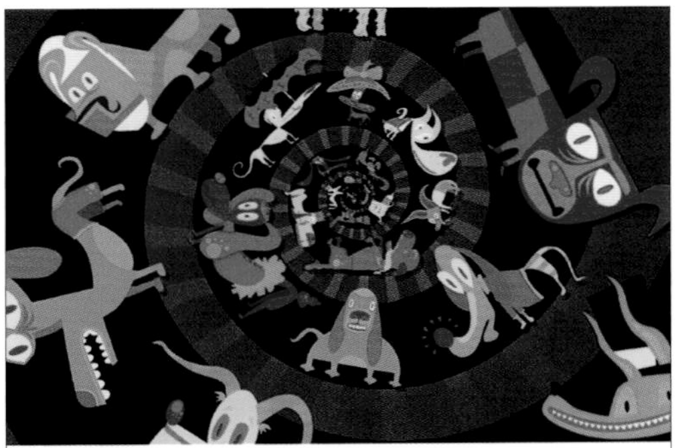

tim may :: dog daze :: digital media

MARCH

S	M	T	W	T	F	S
						1
2	3	4	5	6	7	8
9	10	11	12	13	14	15
16	17	18	19	20	21	22
23	24	25	26	27	28	29
30	31					

alison beebe :: stagnant floating :: oil painting

AUGUST

S	M	T	W	T	F	S
					1	2
3	4	5	6	7	8	9
10	11	12	13	14	15	16
17	18	19	20	21	22	23
24	25	26	27	28	29	30
31						

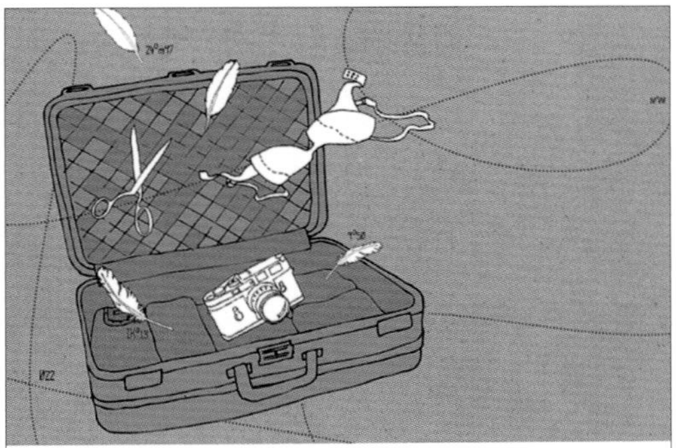

ada mayer :: teaspoon :: mixed media

JULY

S	M	T	W	T	F	S
		1	2	3	4	5
6	7	8	9	10	11	12
13	14	15	16	17	18	19
20	21	22	23	24	25	26
27	28	29	30	31		

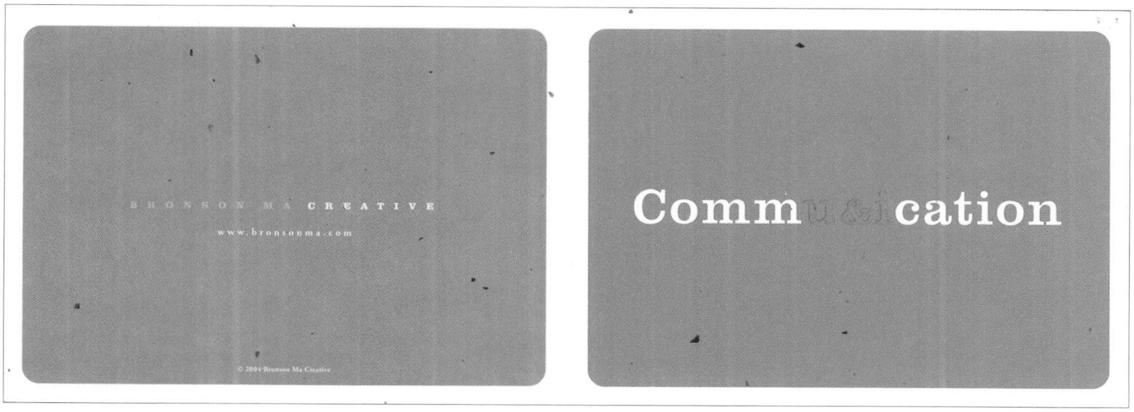

Bronson Ma Creative – San Antonio, Texas
Designer : Bronson Ma
Client : Bronson Ma Creative

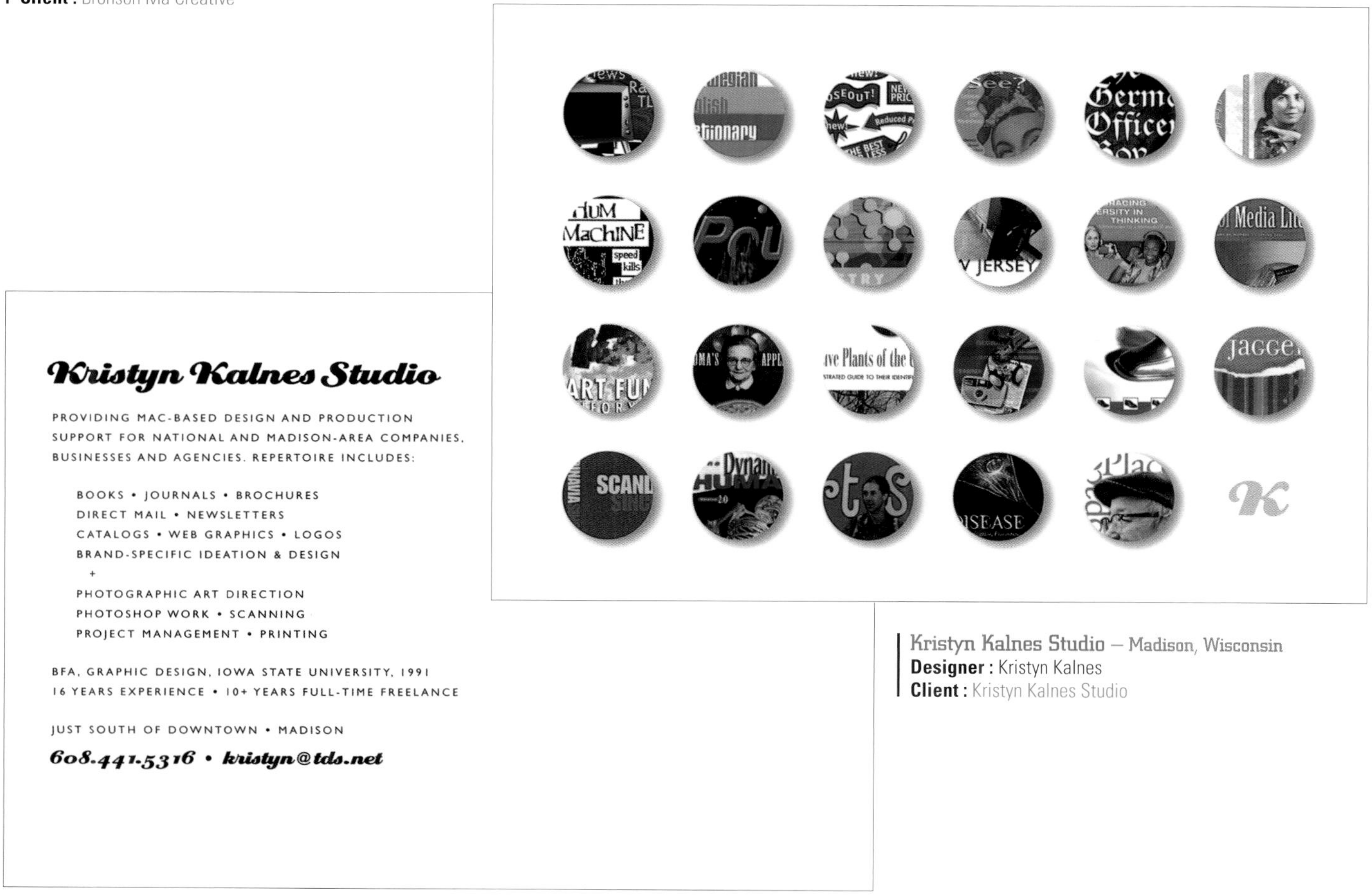

Kristyn Kalnes Studio
PROVIDING MAC-BASED DESIGN AND PRODUCTION SUPPORT FOR NATIONAL AND MADISON-AREA COMPANIES, BUSINESSES AND AGENCIES. REPERTOIRE INCLUDES:
BOOKS • JOURNALS • BROCHURES
DIRECT MAIL • NEWSLETTERS
CATALOGS • WEB GRAPHICS • LOGOS
BRAND-SPECIFIC IDEATION & DESIGN
+
PHOTOGRAPHIC ART DIRECTION
PHOTOSHOP WORK • SCANNING
PROJECT MANAGEMENT • PRINTING
BFA, GRAPHIC DESIGN, IOWA STATE UNIVERSITY, 1991
16 YEARS EXPERIENCE • 10+ YEARS FULL-TIME FREELANCE
JUST SOUTH OF DOWNTOWN • MADISON
608.441.5316 • kristyn@tds.net

Kristyn Kalnes Studio – Madison, Wisconsin
Designer : Kristyn Kalnes
Client : Kristyn Kalnes Studio

mexico
CITY
mexico
BIENVENI
Hecho a
Mano

mexico
CITY
mexico

MAR DEL PLATA

Porteño greeting:
Alex...
you've gained
weight.
Nestor...
you've aged!
CRUZ DE MALTA
taxi ezeiza

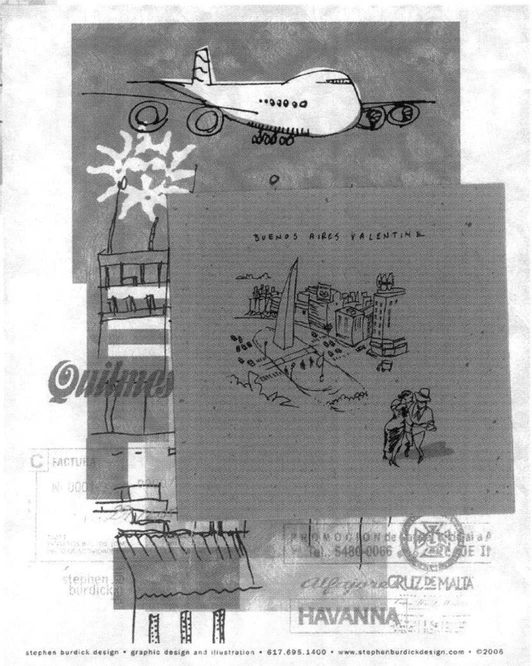

Stephen Burdick Design – Boston, Massachusetts
Designer : Stephen Burdick
Client : Stephen Burdick Design

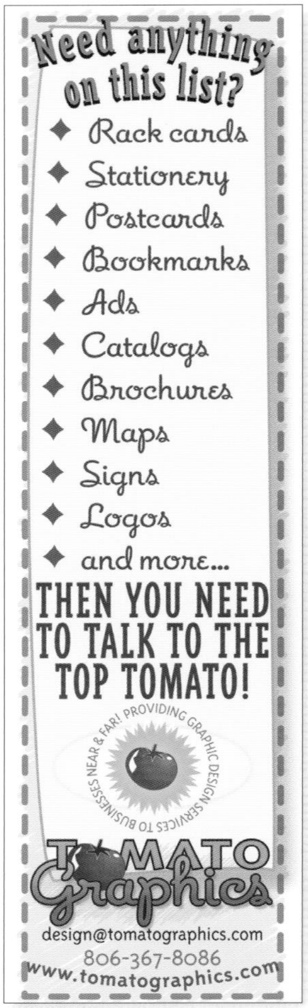
Need anything on this list?
Rack cards
Stationery
Postcards
Bookmarks
Ads
Catalogs
Brochures
Maps
Signs
Logos
and more...
THEN YOU NEED TO TALK TO THE TOP TOMATO!
PROVIDING GRAPHIC DESIGN SERVICES TO BUSINESSES NEAR & FAR!
TOMATO Graphics
design@tomatographics.com
806-367-8086
www.tomatographics.com

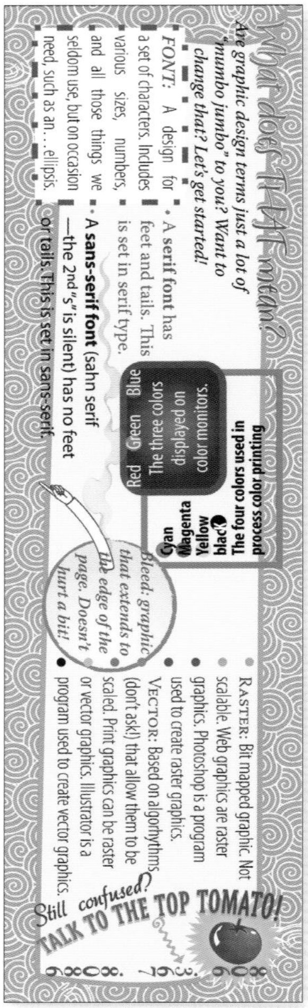

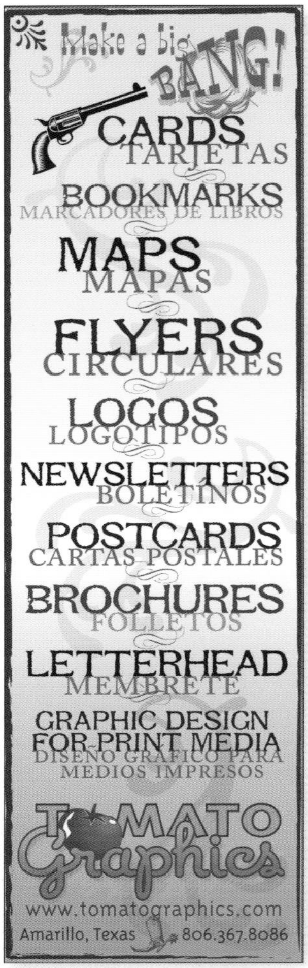
Make a big BANG!
CARDS
TARJETAS
BOOKMARKS
MARCADORES DE LIBROS
MAPS
MAPAS
FLYERS
CIRCULARES
LOGOS
LOGOTIPOS
NEWSLETTERS
BOLETINOS
POSTCARDS
CARTAS POSTALES
BROCHURES
FOLLETOS
LETTERHEAD
MEMBRETE
GRAPHIC DESIGN FOR PRINT MEDIA
DISEÑO GRÁFICO PARA MEDIOS IMPRESOS
TOMATO Graphics
www.tomatographics.com
Amarillo, Texas 806.367.8086

Tomato Graphics – Amarillo, Texas
Designer : Rock Langston
Client : Tomato Graphics

INSPIRATION ✦ CREATIVITY ✦ PEACE
GODDESS OF
infinite bliss
HEALTH ✦ SPIRITUALITY ✦ CLARITY

dezinegirl creative studio, LLC – San Diego, California
Designer : Pam Brown
Client : dezinegirl creative studio, LLC

dezinegirl creative studio
the lifestyle branding source
5752 Oberlin Drive, Suite 106
San Diego, CA 92121
email | pam@dezinegirlcreative.com
office phone | 858.350.4527
Your Tarot Card reading for this month:
The Goddess of Infinite Bliss reveals
a greater brand awareness and
increased profits for your business
by creating a powerful alignment
with dezinegirl creative studio, who will
illuminate and revitalize your brand identity.
Contact us to find out how!
www.dezinegirlcreative.com
creating design for your lifestyle
travel leisure fitness well being
FREE ESTIMATES!

Morgan Gaynin, Inc. – New York, New York
Designer : Shannon Brady
Client : Shannon Brady

A monthly postcard campaign isn't too intrusive on the recipient and offers a consistent reminder of your talent.

The Partners — London, England
Designers : Robert Ball, Jack Renwick
Client : The Partners

Octavo Designs – Frederick, Maryland
Designers : Sue Hough, Mark Burrier, Seth Glass
Client : Octavo Designs

"Branding" in more than one sense of the word, these temporary tattoos are a fun freebie.

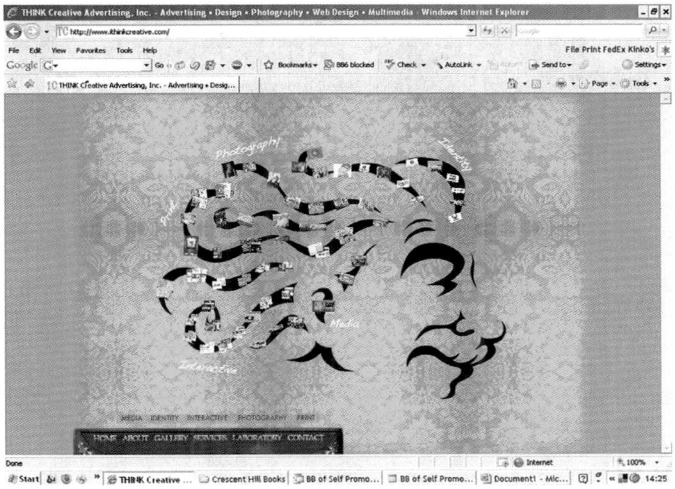

Th!nkCreative Advertising – St. Cloud, Minnesota
Designers : Kevin Ehlinger, Chris Hanson-Ehlinger, Travis Totz, Nick Pelton
Client : Th!nkCreative Advertising

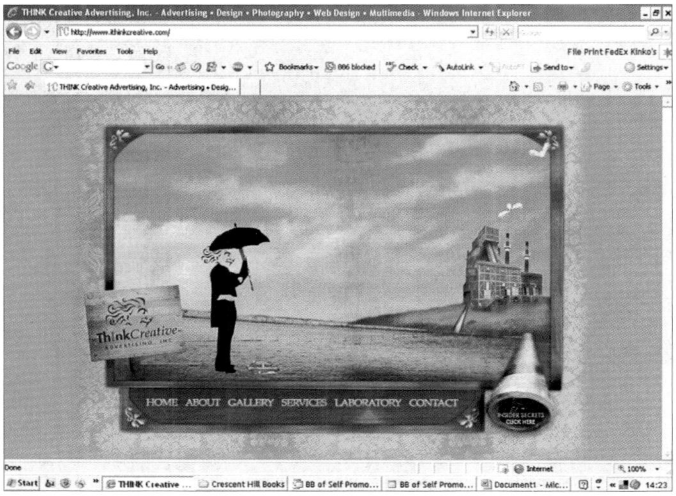

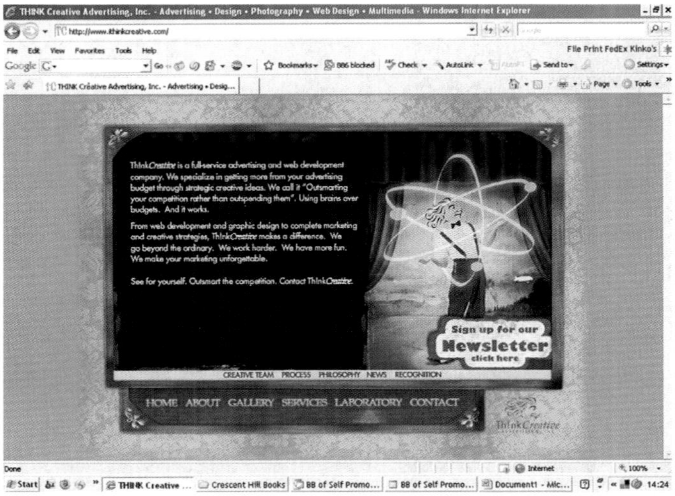

yellobee
b Thankful
Thank you. (Now spread the word.)
Thank you for being part of our great success throughout the years. In appreciation, we've enclosed our little b thankful postcard set. So when your team pulls an all nighter to deliver a spectacular idea, or your boss sends you packing on a ridiculously long vacation, or someone hands you a fantastic new account, now many thanks are at hand.
yellobee
STUDIO
Thank you for the meeting.
Thank you for your time.
WORK
Thank you for your hard work.
Thank you for your flexibility.
JANUARY

Yellobee Studio – Atlanta, Georgia
Designers : Alison Scheel, Jeff Walton, Florencia Banfi
Client : Yellobee Studio

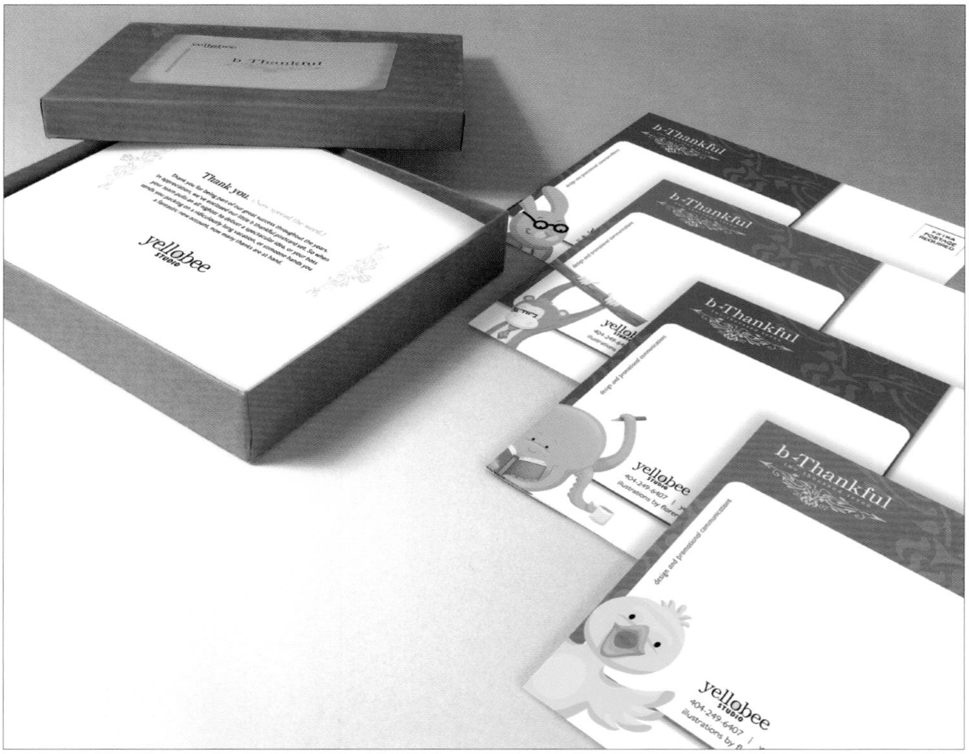
b Thankful
yellobee
STUDIO
404-249-6407

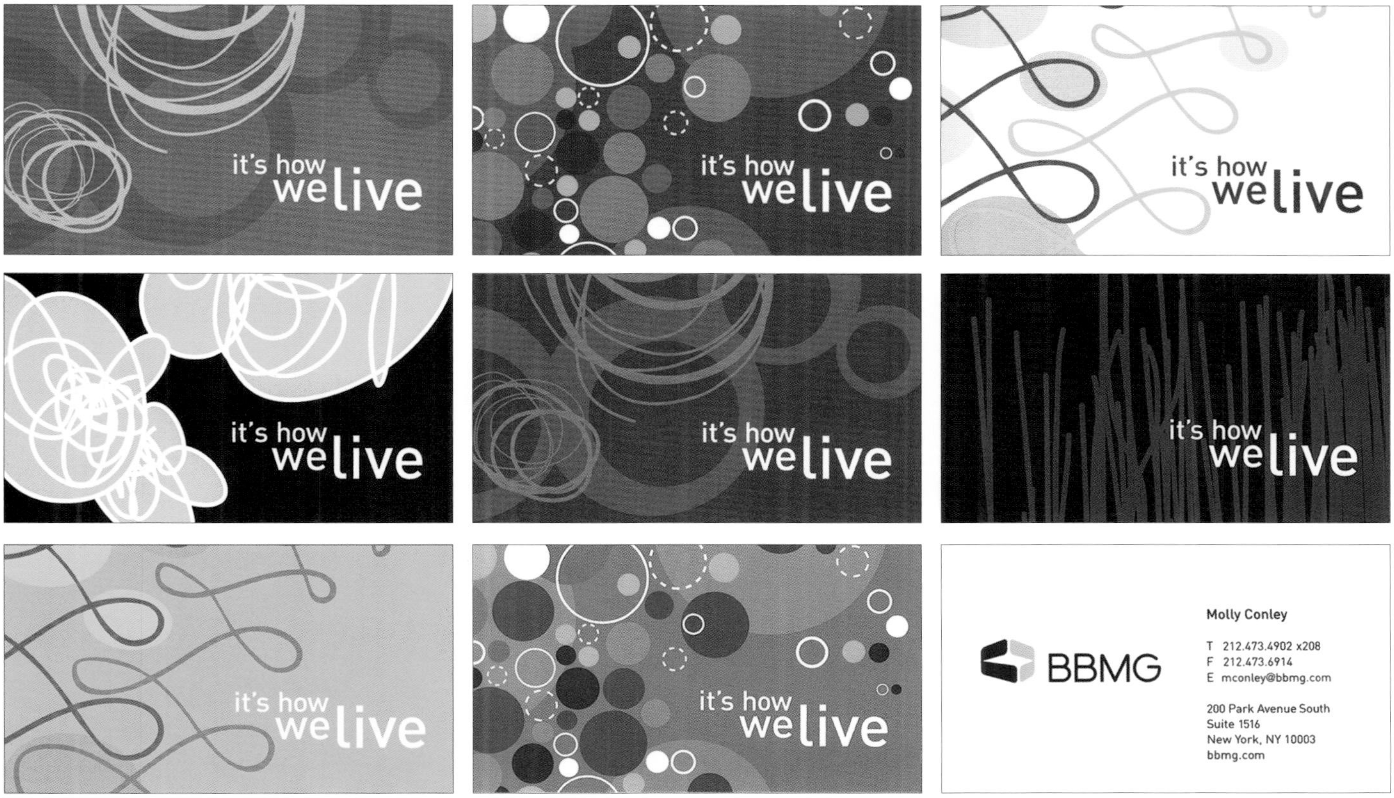

BBMG – New York, New York
Designers : Molly Conley, Scott Ketchum
Client : BBMG

A series of business cards can be like a mini portfolio showing a variety of artistic styles while offering the cohesiveness of a marketing campaign. Remember to leave more than one!

Are you tired of getting clobbered by the competition?
NUKE EM!
ATOMIC Design
Design & advertising is competitive. There's no point in getting mad, so get even. Better yet, kick butt and take names. A public service message from Atomic Design. Making the world safe for powerful communication, one design at a time. 817.939.2445

Atomic Design – Crowley, Texas
Designer : Lewis Glaser
Client : Atomic Design

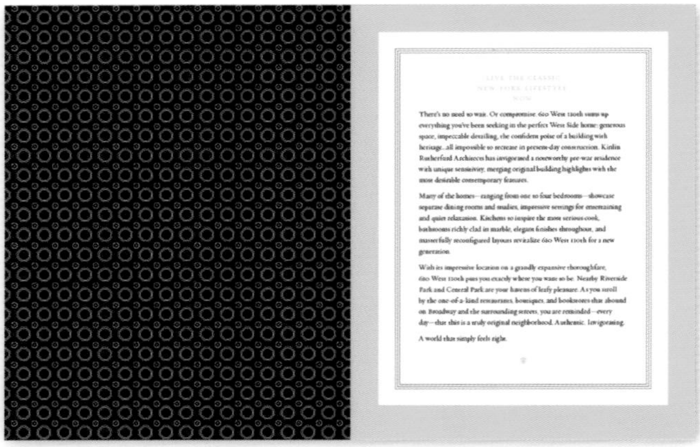

LIVE THE CLASSIC
NEW YORK LIFESTYLE
NOW

There's no need to wait. Or compromise. 610 West 110th sums up everything you've been seeking in the perfect West Side home: generous space, impeccable detailing, the confident poise of a building with heritage...all impossible to recreate in present-day construction. Kinlin Rutherfurd Architects has invigorated a noteworthy pre-war residence with unique sensitivity, merging original building highlights with the most desirable contemporary features.

Many of the homes—ranging from one to four bedrooms—showcase separate dining rooms and studies, impressive settings for entertaining and quiet relaxation. Kitchens to inspire the most serious cook, bathrooms richly clad in marble, elegant finishes throughout, and masterfully reconfigured layouts revitalize 610 West 110th for a new generation.

With its impressive location on a grandly expansive thoroughfare, 610 West 110th puts you exactly where you want to be. Nearby Riverside Park and Central Park are your havens of leafy pleasure. As you stroll by the one-of-a-kind restaurants, boutiques, and bookstores that abound on Broadway and the surrounding streets, you are reminded—every day—that this is a truly original neighborhood. Authentic. Invigorating.

A world that simply feels right.

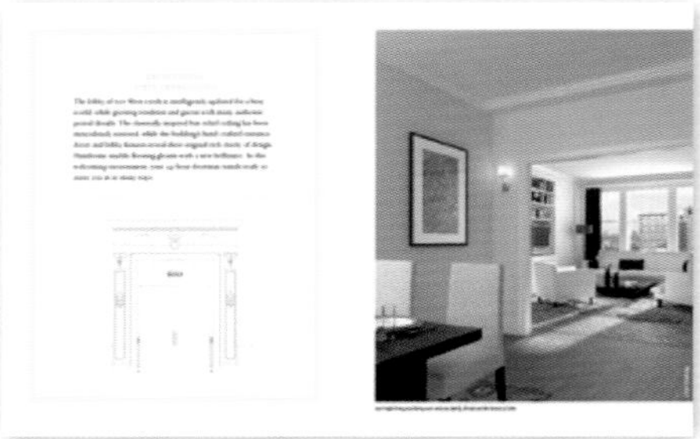

And Partners – New York, New York
Designers : And Partners Design Team
Client : And Partners

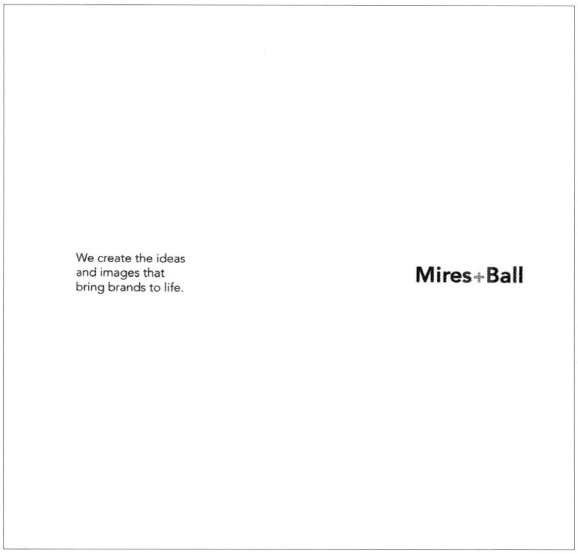
We create the ideas
and images that
bring brands to life.
Mires+Ball

MiresBall – San Diego, California
Designers : John Ball, Miguel Perez, Rachel Thomas
Client : MiresBall

jill bell
LITTLE BOOK OF LOGOS

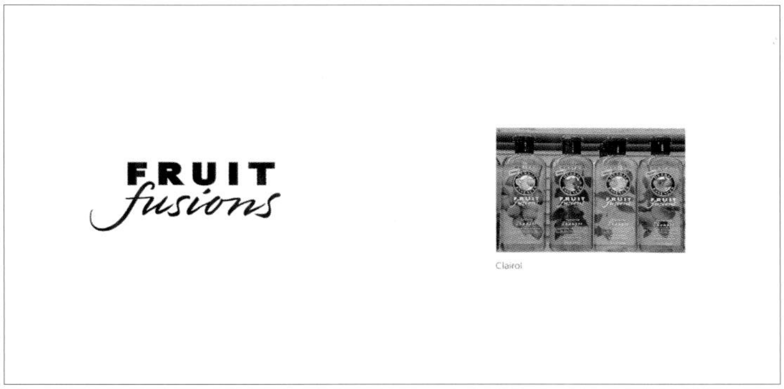

Jill Bell Brandlettering – Leawood, Kansas
Designer : Jill Bell
Client : Jill Bell Brandlettering

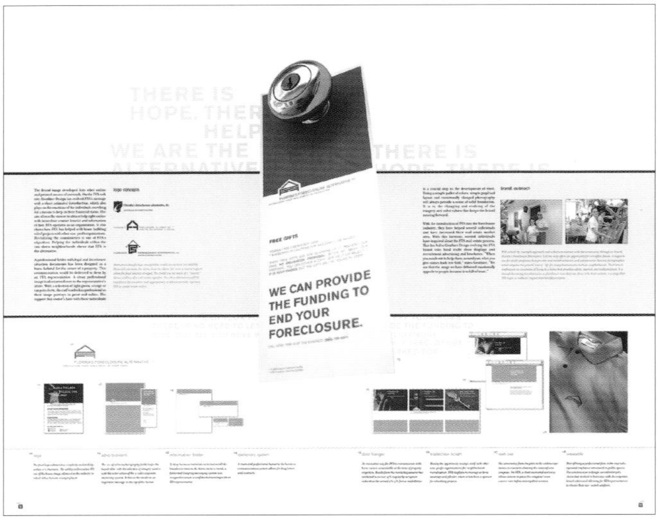
WE CAN PROVIDE THE FUNDING TO END YOUR FORECLOSURE.

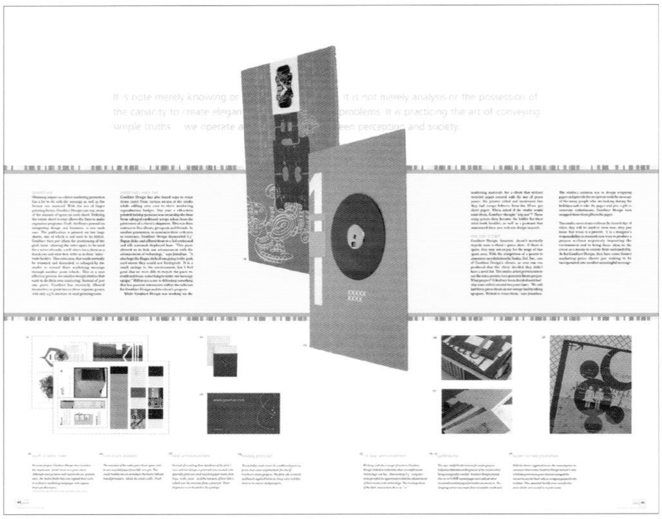

Gouthier Design: A Brand Collective – New York, New York
Designers : Gouthier Design Creative Team
Client : Gouthier Design: A Brand Collective

graft

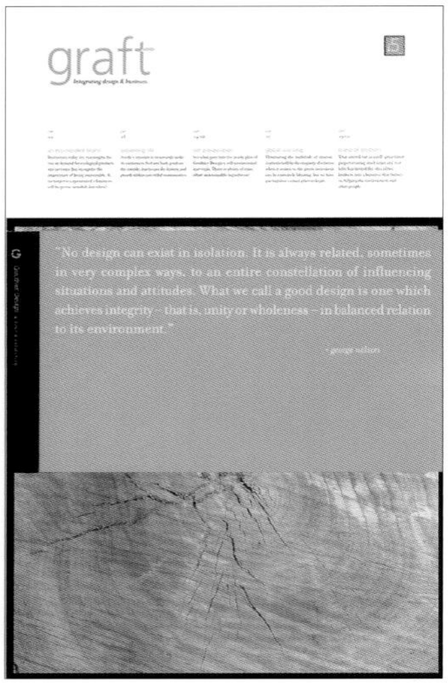
graft
"No design can exist in isolation. It is always related, sometimes in very complex ways, to an entire constellation of influencing situations and attitudes. What we call a good design is one which achieves integrity – that is, unity or wholeness – in balanced relation to its environment."

YOU'VE WORKED HARD. You have a great product or service customers appreciate. You just need more customers. Trouble is about 25% of your success deals with having a good product or service, the remaining 75% deals with how well and how often you tell people about it.
MARKETING IS ABOUT ENERGY. You take action in hopes of generating an equal or greater reaction. When your advertising lacks energy so do your returns.
TH!NK CREATIVE specializes in getting more from your advertising through strategic creative ideas. We go BEYOND THE ORDINARY. We WORK HARDER. We HAVE MORE FUN. We make your marketing UNFORGETTABLE. And along the way we build your brand, give it energy, and create action that generates reaction.
SEE FOR YOURSELF.
OUTSMART THE COMPETITION.
CALL TH!NK CREATIVE TODAY.
Th!nkCreative ADVERTISING, INC
www.OutsmartTheCompetition.com
320.259.9400
FREE INITIAL CONSULTATION
WE WANT TO WORK FOR YOU!
EXPLORE OUR WEBSITE AND REGISTER TO WIN
$500 OFF YOUR NEXT WEB DESIGN, BRAND IDENTITY, OR ADVERTISING PROJECT
GO TO www.OutsmartTheCompetition.com/500now
HURRY, LIMITED TIME OFFER!
ADVERTISING • DESIGN • PHOTOGRAPHY • WEB DESIGN
MULTIMEDIA • BRAND DEVELOPMENT • MARKETING STRATEGY
THINKCREATIVE ADVERTISING, INC.
813 W. SAINT GERMAIN ST.
ST CLOUD, MN 56301
PRSRT STD
U.S. POSTAGE
PAID
Brainerd, MN
Permit No. 472

Th!nkCreative Advertising – St. Cloud, Minnesota
Designers : Kevin Ehlinger, Chris Hanson-Ehlinger, Travis Totz
Client : Th!nkCreative Advertising

GET HAPPY.
OUTSMART THE COMPETITION.

BIGGER RETURNS.
OUTSMART THE COMPETITION.

ENERGY=REACTION.
OUTSMART THE COMPETITION.

POSSIBILITIES.
OUTSMART THE COMPETITION.

The ghosted image of the Wolf logo was printed with an off-line tinted silver varnish on black textured 80# stock. In addition, the "Randi Wolf" logotype and text were engraved in a metallic copper mixed with PMS 732U.

The inserts were digitally printed on both sides of a coated stock, then laminated to stiffen and protect them. Digital printing allows small quantities which can be updated periodically.

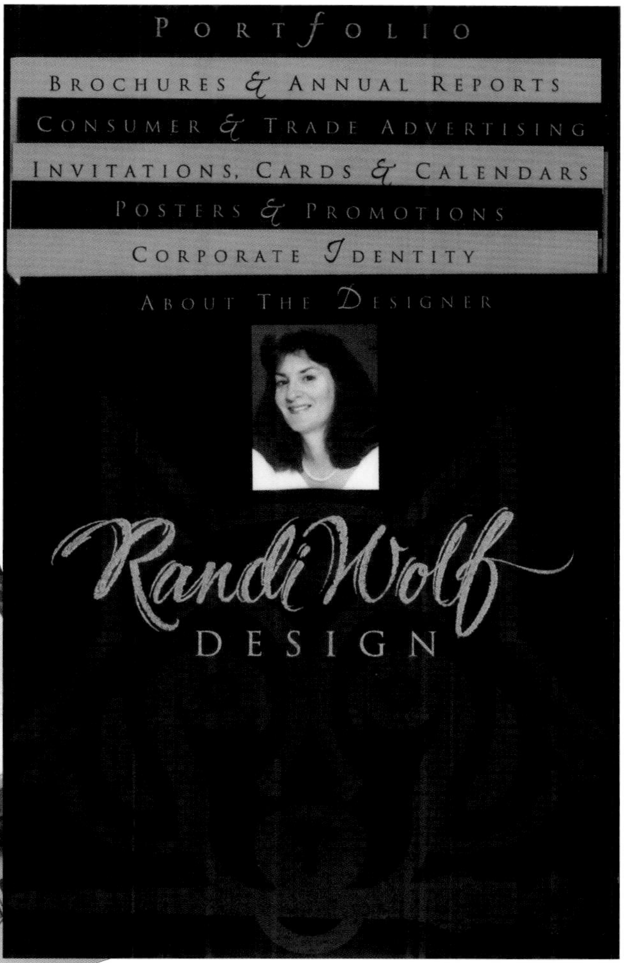
Portfolio
Brochures & Annual Reports
Consumer & Trade Advertising
Invitations, Cards & Calendars
Posters & Promotions
Corporate Identity
About the Designer
Randi Wolf
Design

Corporate Identity
Corporate Identity
Old Market Street

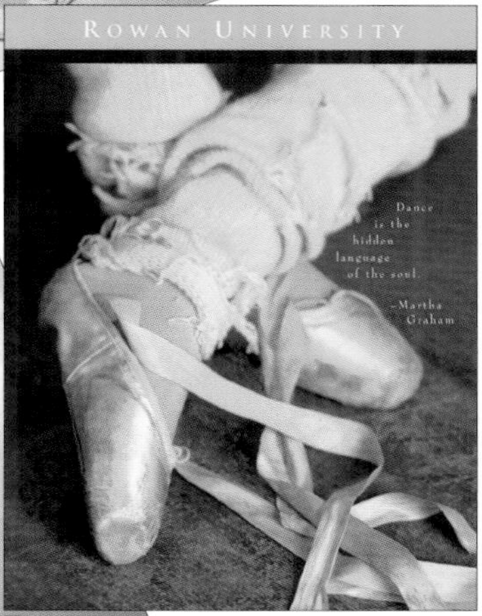
Rowan University
Dance
is the
hidden
language
of the soul.
-Martha
Graham

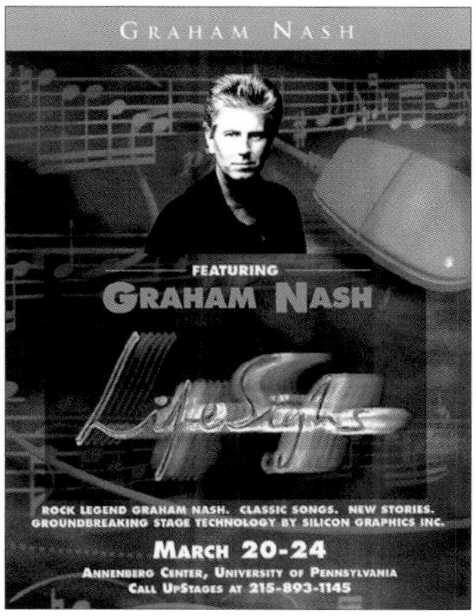
Graham Nash
Featuring
Graham Nash
Rock legend Graham Nash. Classic songs. New stories.
Groundbreaking stage technology by Silicon Graphics Inc.
March 20-24
Annenberg Center, University of Pennsylvania
Call UpStages at 215-893-1145

Randi Wolf
Design

Randi Wolf
Design

Randi Wolf Design
20th
Anniversary
'08
of Design Excellence
In celebration of my 20th Anniversary, I have designed a "Trivial Pursuit" game for you to play. Flip through the cards. See how many you can answer correctly!
Thanks to clients like you, during these past 20 years, my pursuit of creative excellence has been anything but trivial. Thank you for your appreciation and support.

Randi Wolf Design – Glassboro, New Jersey
Designer : Randi Wolf
Client : Randi Wolf

BBMG'S TOP FIVE
RHETT MILLER SONGS
"Our Love"
"Come Around"
"Fireflies"
"Question"
"This Is What I Do"
RHETT MILLER'S TOP FIVE RULES FOR WRITING GREAT POP SONGS
Don't overthink your plot
Find the uncommon in the common
Get in touch with your inner beauty and your inner tragedy
Let your hero off the hook from saving the world
Expect your characters to take on a life of their own

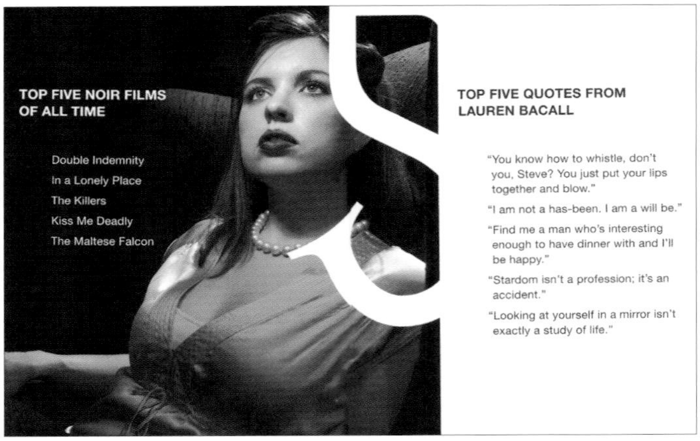
TOP FIVE NOIR FILMS
OF ALL TIME
Double Indemnity
In a Lonely Place
The Killers
Kiss Me Deadly
The Maltese Falcon
TOP FIVE QUOTES FROM
LAUREN BACALL
"You know how to whistle, don't you, Steve? You just put your lips together and blow."
"I am not a has-been. I am a will be."
"Find me a man who's interesting enough to have dinner with and I'll be happy."
"Stardom isn't a profession; it's an accident."
"Looking at yourself in a mirror isn't exactly a study of life."

TOP FIVE WESTERNS OF ALL TIME
Treasure of Sierra Madre
The Outlaw Josey Wales
Unforgiven
High Noon
They Call Me Trinity
TOP FIVE HONKY-TONKS IN
OR NEAR AUSTIN, TEXAS
The Broken Spoke
The Continental Club
Ginny's Little Longhorn
Club 21
Gruene Hall

BBMG – New York, New York
Designers : Scott Ketchum, Molly Conley, Sayaka Ito
Client : BBMG

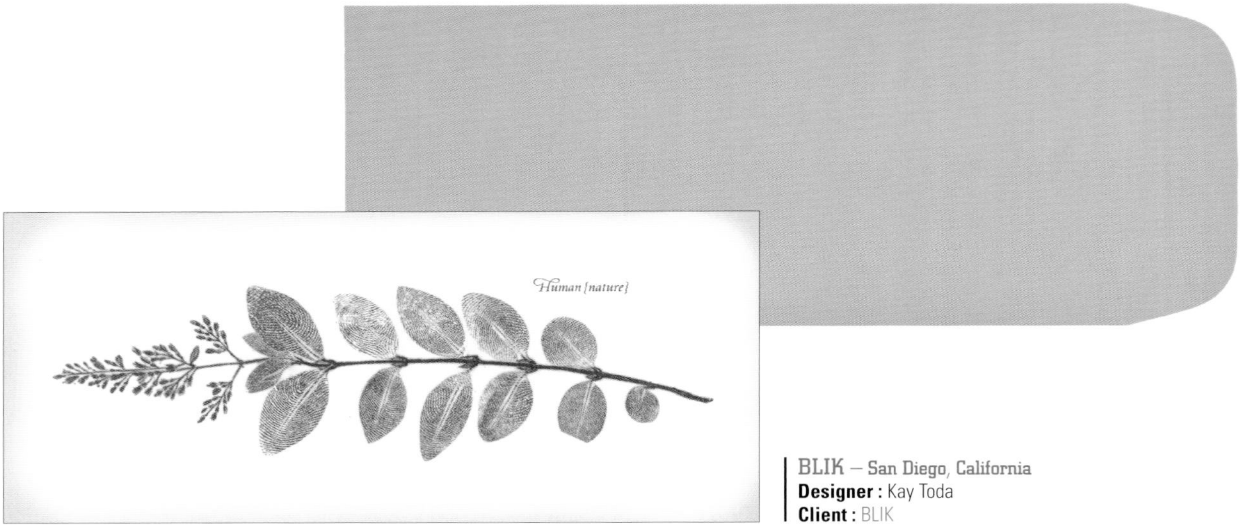
Human {nature}

BLIK – San Diego, California
Designer : Kay Toda
Client : BLIK

Human {Nature}. At Blik we believe the two are inextricably connected to one another. For more than 23 years, organizations have come to rely on us to deliver communication programs that connect people to ideas and experiences in smart, sustainable ways. We build enduring marketplace relationships for our clients. Ones that are thoughtful, moving and timeless in their expression.
Discover how Blik can help define the unique human nature of your business.
Contact us today at 619.234.4434 or online at www.tylerblik.com
blik
Recycled

The concept of human nature is conveyed here beautifully using fingerprints in place of leaf veins.

design hoch drei GmbH + Co. KG – Stuttgart, Germany
Designers : Susanne Wacker, Sabine Avenz, Thoroten Grimm
Client : design hoch drei

If a number evokes good times, it's got to be the German word for twenty-five: fünfundzwanzig. "To the American eye it has 'fun' in it—twice!" says Hayden Schoen, a designer at Seattle's Hornall Anderson, who, along with design director Mark Popich, developed a unique theme for the firm's twenty-fifth anniversary celebration. "We thought about how hard it is to pronounce and how much fun we could have with it."

"We wanted to have a big party and invite clients to thank them—people who work with us and used to work with us but have gone on to bigger things," says Popich. "We're twenty-five years old, but it seemed a bit too self-congratulatory." The anniversary took place in October, lending itself to an Oktoberfest theme—but with a twist. "It's a designer Oktoberfest, so it had to be more than oompa bands and sausages."

But, as with all good Oktoberfests, the beer flowed freely. "We had clients in the craft beer brand alliance for whom we'd done packaging for a few years, so we thought, 'Here's a way to include our clients,'" Popich adds. Along with beer vendors Widmer and Redhook, Hornall Anderson hosted about seven hundred employees, former employees, clients and prospective clients. Popich recalls the tenth anniversary party: "It was at the Museum of Flight, people wore ties, very classy. It was more serious, more formal, as if to say, 'We've arrived, we're a force to be reckoned with.' Twenty-five years? We're probably going to make it, so let's have some fun."

"A party we'd like to go to," agrees Schoen.

The event, held on two floors at Hornall Anderson's headquarters, took steps to actually enforce attendees' fun. "We rearranged the conference rooms to make lounges; one had a Wii with a bowling game on it," says Popich. "There are five wings in the office, and each one had a bar." Specialized lettering on the street-level doors directed attendees to the site for one night only. "One of our interns slept in the conference room to take it down the next morning," says Schoen. But was the intern really sleeping or passed out? "No comment," Popich says.

From the theme to the site to the invitations, one design element took an everyday symbol and put in a hilarious context. "We started out doing the international pictograms to show where the bathrooms and food were," says Popich. "Then we took the German highway signs and decided to blow it out and have fun." The result was a collection of traffic sign-inspired figures in very irreverent poses—throwing up, partaking in drinking games, urinating into a potted plant (and missing), disrobing and sitting on the office copier, to name a few. It wasn't just the designers who had all the fun with the figures, either. "We had a companywide coaster competition," says Popich. "Everyone designed a coaster, then we chose twenty-five winners. It was a good way to meet people, because you wanted to collect the whole set."

Hornall Anderson – **Seattle, Washington**
Designers : Mark Popich, Hayden Schoen, Kalani Gregoire
Client : Hornall Anderson

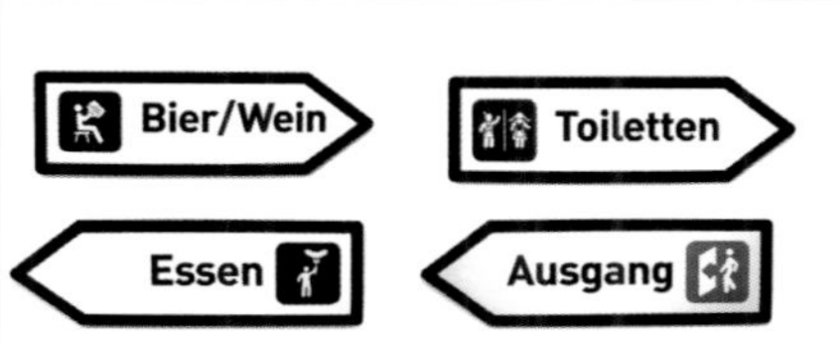

Even without collecting the coasters, another souvenir was something even a teetotaler could love. Explains Popich: "We had these posters that we printed up using an old Vandercook letterpress machine. The day before the party we printed up beer steins out of letterforms using brown ink, then at the party we used yellow ink so people could 'fill up' their steins and have this great poster to take home."

While Hornall Anderson's employees look at their stein posters, Popich has no immediate plans for the next milestone. "We're still recovering!" he says. "We've got to get some time to figure out how to tap it." And although the "designer Oktoberfest" was a hit, people largely behaved themselves, keeping the furniture clean and leaving the greenery unmolested. "I was hoping we'd see someone in lederhosen," admits Popich, "but designers tend not to stray too much from the black turtleneck."

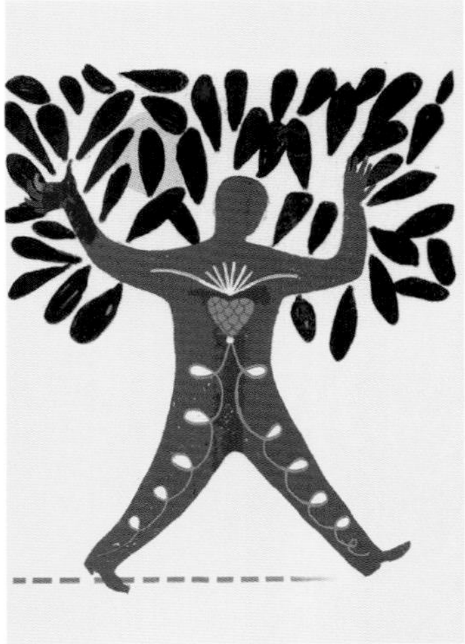

Morgan Gaynin, Inc. – New York, New York
Designer : Beppe Giacabbe
Client : Beppe Giacabbe

Jill Bell Brandlettering – Leawood, Kansas
Designer : Jill Bell
Client : Jill Bell Brandlettering

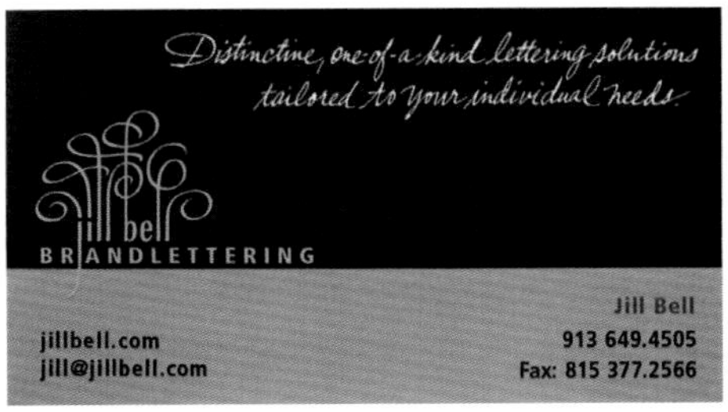

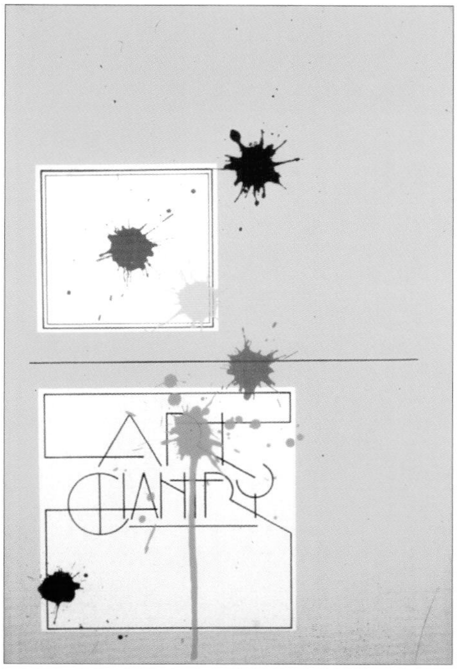

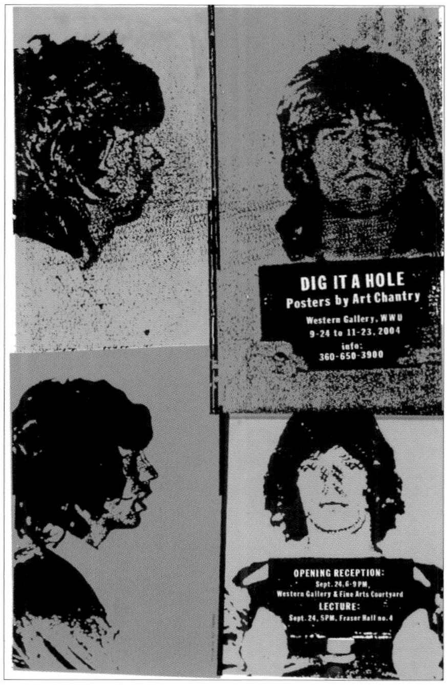

Art Chantry — Tacoma, Washington
Client: Art Chantry
(continued on next spread)

There's no better way to show the audience what they can expect at a public exhibition than to give them a peek at the promo poster.

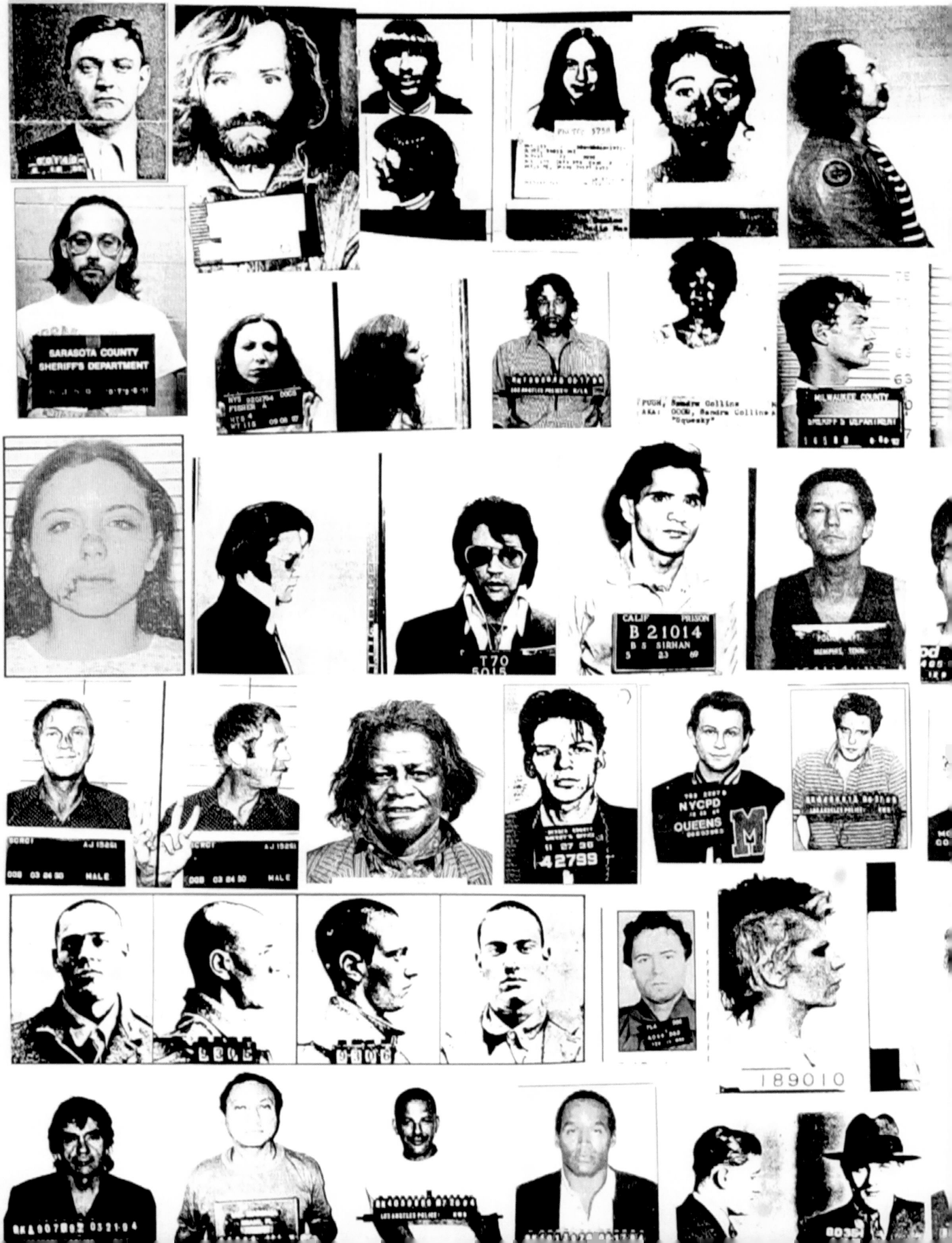
SARASOTA COUNTY
SHERIFF'S DEPARTMENT
PUGH, Sandra Collins
AKA: GOOD, Sandra Collins
"Squeaky"
MILWAUKEE COUNTY
SHERIFF'S DEPARTMENT
CALIF PRISON
B 21014
B S SIRHAN
5 23 69
T70
5015
NYCPD
QUEENS
M
42799
DOB 03 04 30 MALE
189010

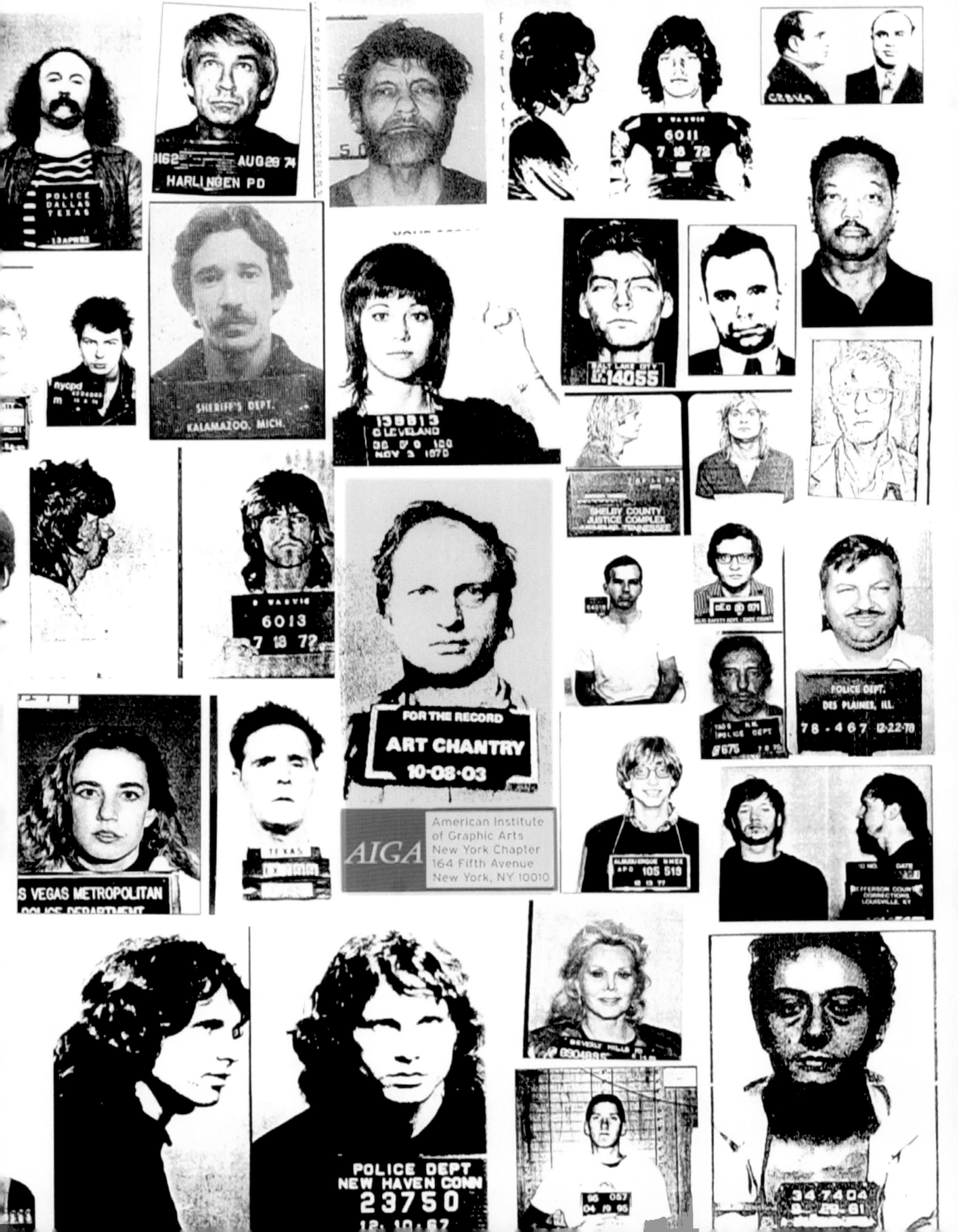
POLICE DALLAS TEXAS
AUG 29 74
HARLINGEN PD
6011
7 18 72
SHERIFF'S DEPT.
KALAMAZOO, MICH.
CLEVELAND
NOV 3 1970
14055
SHELBY COUNTY
JUSTICE COMPLEX
6013
7 18 72
FOR THE RECORD
ART CHANTRY
10-08-03
AIGA
American Institute
of Graphic Arts
New York Chapter
164 Fifth Avenue
New York, NY 10010
POLICE DEPT.
DES PLAINES, ILL.
78-467 12-22-78
S VEGAS METROPOLITAN
TEXAS
105 519
POLICE DEPT
NEW HAVEN CONN
23750
347404

Anderson Design Group, Inc. – Nashville, Tennessee
Designer : Joel Anderson
Client : Anderson Design Group, Inc.

To promote a new logo, Anderson Design utilized it in the patterns for a variety of giveaways. The agency collected the items and presented them in gift bags to clients at an elaborate open house.

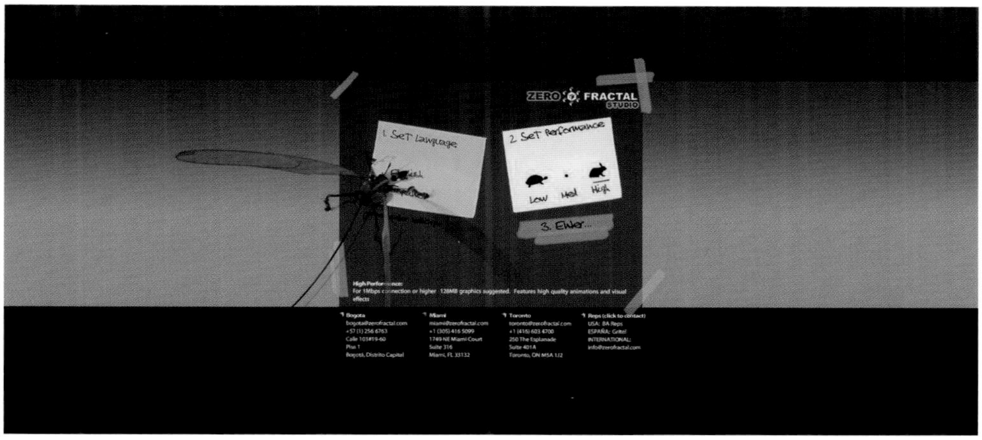

Zerofractal Studio – Toronto, Canada
Designers : Alejandro Gonzalez, Eduardo Smith, Jose Uribe, Paul Kuhne, Jairo Gonzalez, Alejandro Galindo, Libero Floriani, Dian Zuluaga, Grace Mojica
Client : Zerofractal Studio

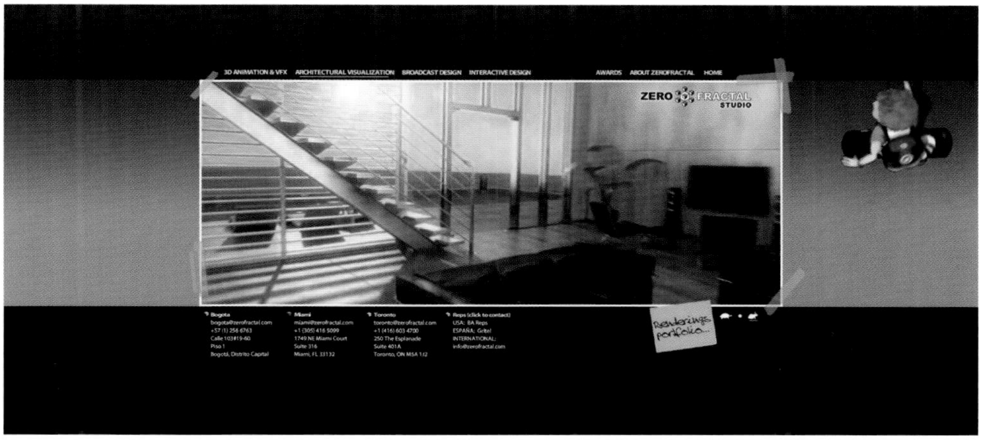

Calagraphic Design
– Elkins Park, Pennsylvania
Designer : Ronald J. Cala II
Client : www.cafepress.com/calagraphic

Anthem Worldwide – San Francisco, California
Designers : Philip VanDusen, Chris Toner, Lisa Toner, Bill Braznell
Client : Peet's Coffee

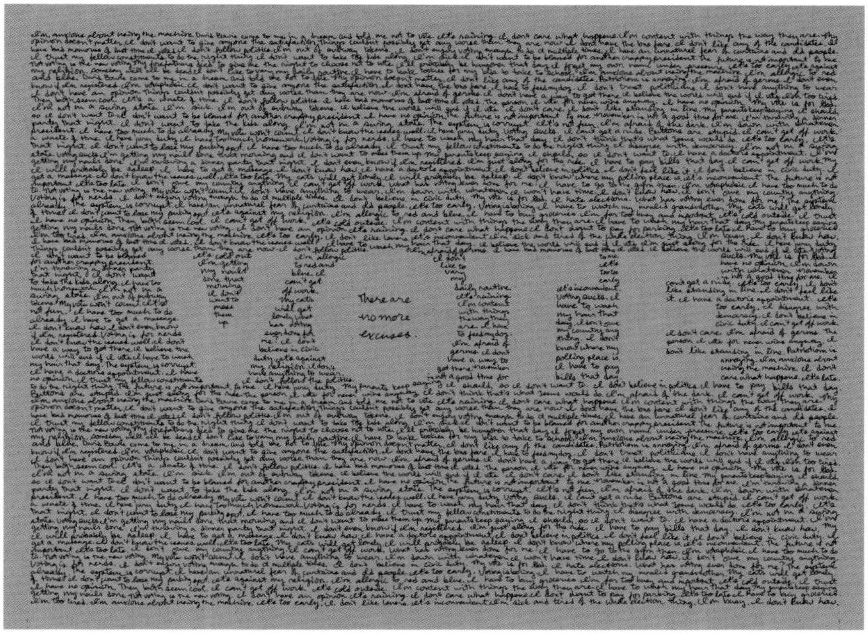

Somewhat Awesome Design – Elkins Park, Pennsylvania
Designers : Ronald J. Cala II, Kaite Hatz
Client : Somewhat Awesome Design

DESIGN about TOWN – San Francisco, California
Designers : Solana Crawford, Ezequiel Frelli, Lucas Oliveros
Client : DESIGN about TOWN

BETH
IS
READY FOR
PRIMETIME
V.O.:
On the internet, any time is primetime. See more work at www. elizabethmaplesden .com
V.O.:
Ready to be excellent.
THIS IS
BETH MAPLESDEN
SPEAKING FOR
BETH
IS
READY FOR
PRIMETIME...
ULTRA SUPER MEGA
DOPPLER TRACKER RADAR
V.O.:
...but soon she decided she was ready for more. She was...

EMdash Design – Yardley, Pennsylvania
Designer : Elizabeth Maplesden
Client : EMdash Design

Housed in a spiral-bound booklet, each page shows us why "Beth is Ready for Primetime" as we view her on various television and computer screens throughout.

michael wright
FRESH marketing

Group Fifty-Five Marketing – Detroit, Michigan
Designers : Jeannette Gutierrez, Heather Sowinski
Client : Group Fifty-Five Marketing

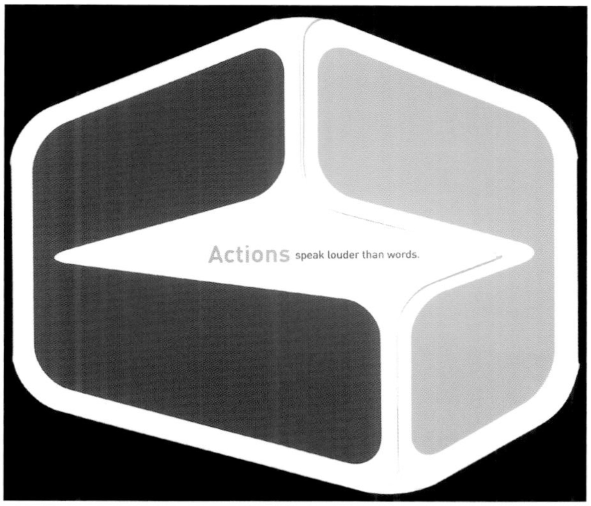
Actions speak louder than words.

BBMG – New York, New York
Designers : Molly Conley, Scott Ketchum
Client : BBMG

BBMG IT'S HOW WE LIVE GRANT
Dream big. Do good. Live well.
When we align our values with our actions,
great things can happen.
Introducing the BBMG It's How We Live Grant, a $100,000 package of in-kind marketing services to create and launch a breakthrough cause marketing campaign for a visionary nonprofit and its corporate partner.
Bring us your dreams, goals and commitment, and we'll create the strategy, message and campaign to make it happen. After all, bold ideas need passionate champions.
Learn more at ItsHowWeLive.com
Deadline for submissions is July 31, 2006.

A Blue Moon Arts – Tulsa, Oklahoma
Designer : Kathy Piersall
Client : A Blue Moon Arts

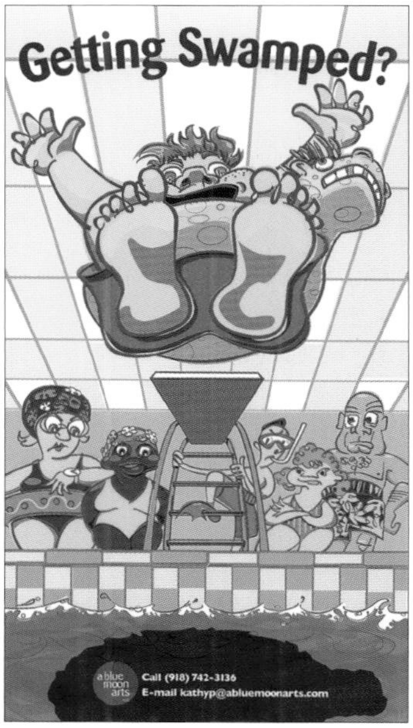

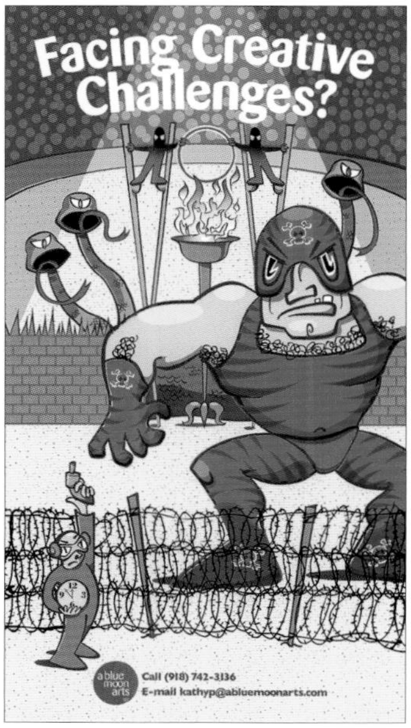

Simpatico Design Studio, LLC – **Alexandria, Virginia**
Designers : Amy Simpson, Dave Simpson
Client : Simpatico Design Studio, LLC

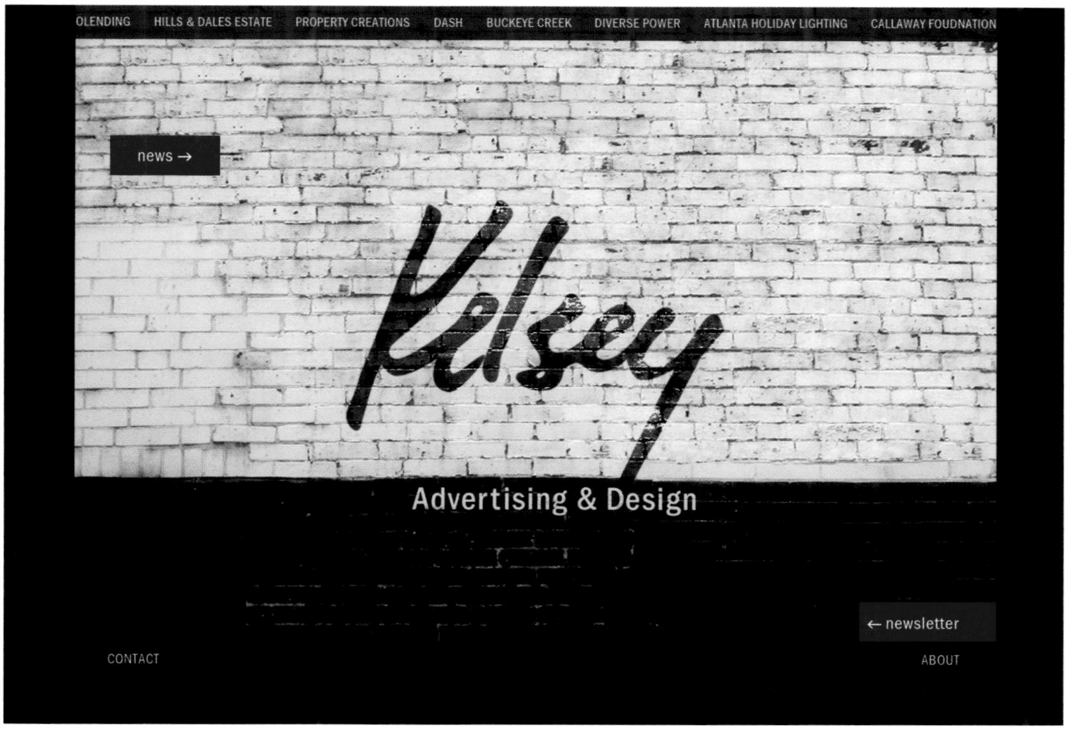
OLENDING
HILLS & DALES ESTATE
PROPERTY CREATIONS
DASH
BUCKEYE CREEK
DIVERSE POWER
ATLANTA HOLIDAY LIGHTING
CALLAWAY FOUDNATION
news →
Kelsey
Advertising & Design
← newsletter
CONTACT
ABOUT

Kelsey Advertising & Design – LaGrange, Georgia
Designers : Brant Kelsey, Niki Studdard, Brian Handley
Client : Kelsey Advertising & Design

Glitschka Studios – Salem, Oregon
Designer : Von Glitschka
Client : Glitschka Studios

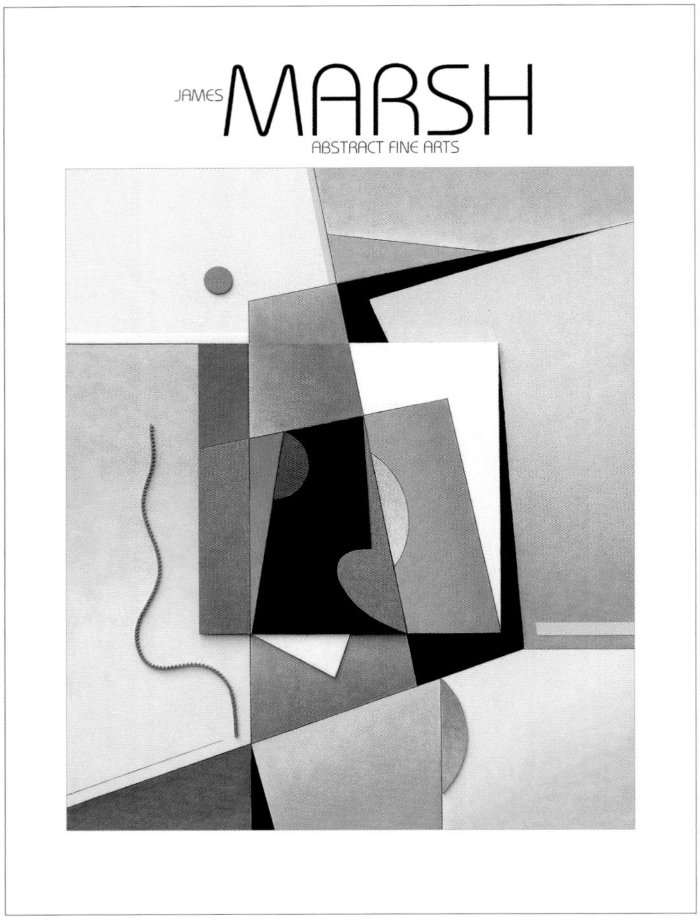

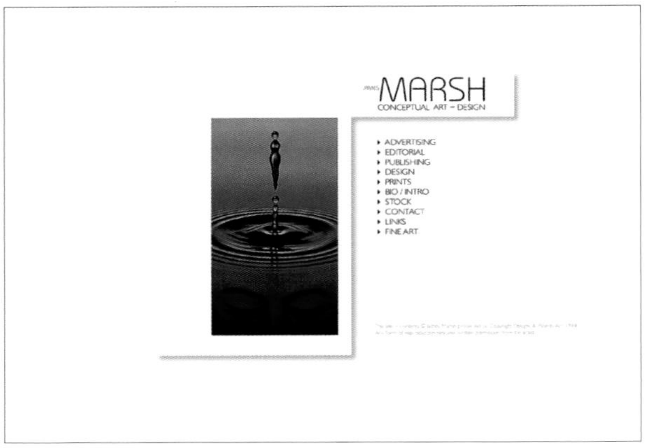

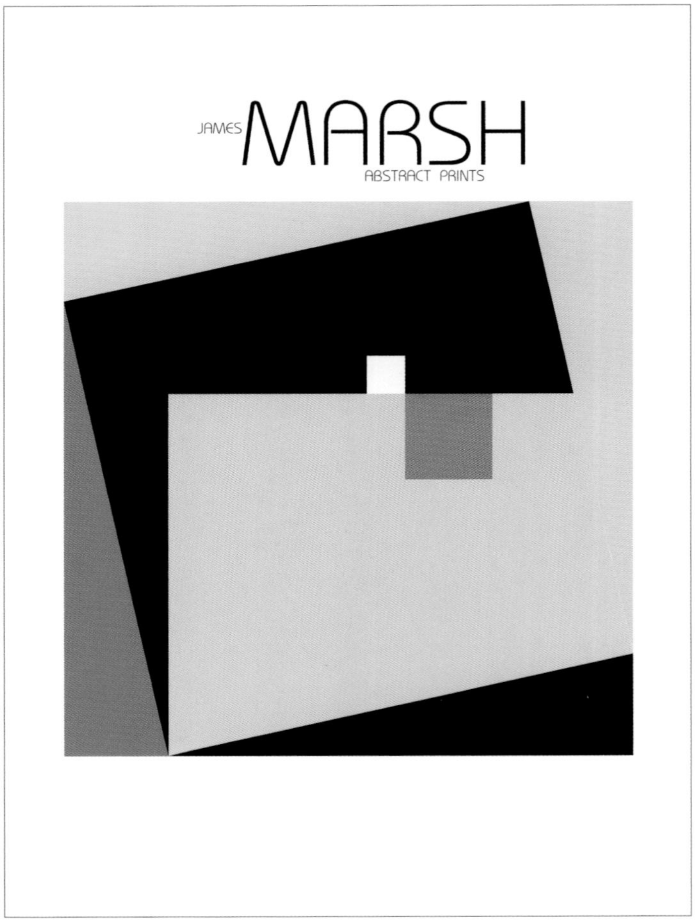

James Marsh Design – Hythe, England
Designer : James Marsh
Client : James Marsh

HOW
MANY
designers
DO YOU
NEED
who are...

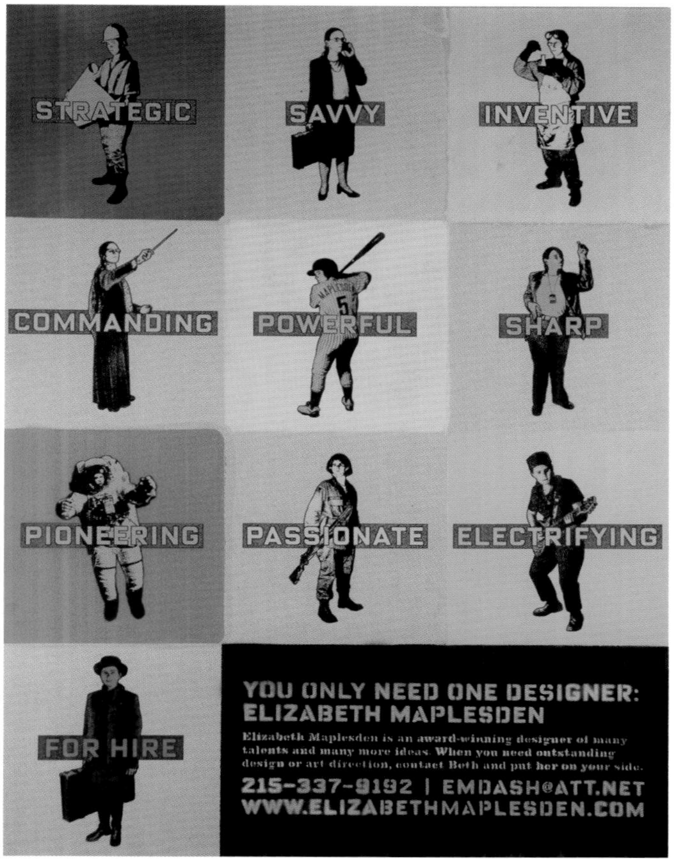
STRATEGIC
SAVVY
INVENTIVE
COMMANDING
POWERFUL
SHARP
PIONEERING
PASSIONATE
ELECTRIFYING
FOR HIRE
YOU ONLY NEED ONE DESIGNER:
ELIZABETH MAPLESDEN
Elizabeth Maplesden is an award-winning designer of many talents and many more ideas. When you need outstanding design or art direction, contact Beth and put her on your side.
215-337-9192 | EMDASH@ATT.NET
WWW.ELIZABETHMAPLESDEN.COM

Using bright colors and strong imagery, this foldout poster graphically displays all the qualities of the only designer you'll ever need.

EMdash Design – Yardley, Pennsylvania
Designer : Elizabeth Maplesden
Client : EMdash Design

January '08
FEBRUARY
DECEMBER '07
2008 ~ 366 days
A LUCKY LEAP YEAR

Crawford Design – Chagrin Falls, Ohio
Designer : Alison Crawford
Client : Crawford Design

An In-Depth Look at: ROCK, PAPER, SCISSORS

Celebrating the twentieth anniversary of Lawrenceville, Georgia's Rock, Paper, Scissors design studio, owner Cindy Sutt and her art director daughter, Amanda, wanted to make the event—and their new digs—something to remember. "It's our third location in the past twenty years," says Cindy, who also serves as the firm's managing creative director, "so we decided to put this whole thing together."

To this end, the pair designed a series of drink coasters that also served as invitations to a cocktail party at the studio, which is part of a one-hundred-year-old building in the Atlanta suburb. After distributing the invitations to business associates, clients, and the local community members in what Amanda brightly describes as "very shiny copper envelopes," the Sutts allowed invitees to get a look at Rock, Paper, Scissors' design vision literally from the inside out. "We renovated an old building—sixteen thousand square feet—from the early 1900s," says Cindy, "and our studio is part of it. So the city fathers were very supportive."

The offices themselves look more like a cozy apartment than an advertising studio. "It has a very homey feel to it," says Cindy. "That's our hallmark as a company—for clients to come in and sit down and be comfortable. It's a very warm and inviting environment." The one hundred fifty attendees also got a first look at the harmony between the new studio environment and the rest of the Rock, Paper, Scissors brand. Along with the commemorative coasters, mugs, and pens, the Web site and direct mail pieces got a redesign with muted hues based on Rock, Paper, Scissors' old, boldly colored scheme. "It matches our office," says Amanda.

Within that office, a twenty-first century attitude prevails. "We're going a bit paperless," Amanda says. "Instead of printing envelopes, we're using mailing labels to stick on envelopes [of any size]." The Sutts skipped ordering new letterhead, too. "We print it in-house, or send e-mails"—PDFs or letterhead templates—"to cut down on paperwork back and forth. We want to be smarter about how business works today, and show our clients that you don't have to do new business cards every time you move." Adds Cindy: "We've really adapted e-newsletters to keep our clients up to date."

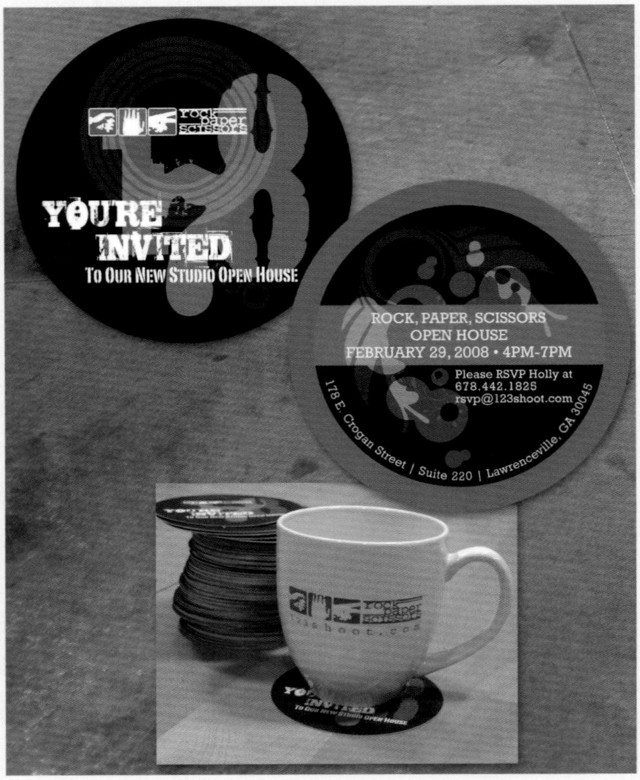

Rock, Paper, Scissors – Lawrenceville, Georgia
Designers : Cindy Sutt, Amanda Sutt, Nicole Hopkins, Ting Low
Client : Rock, Paper, Scissors

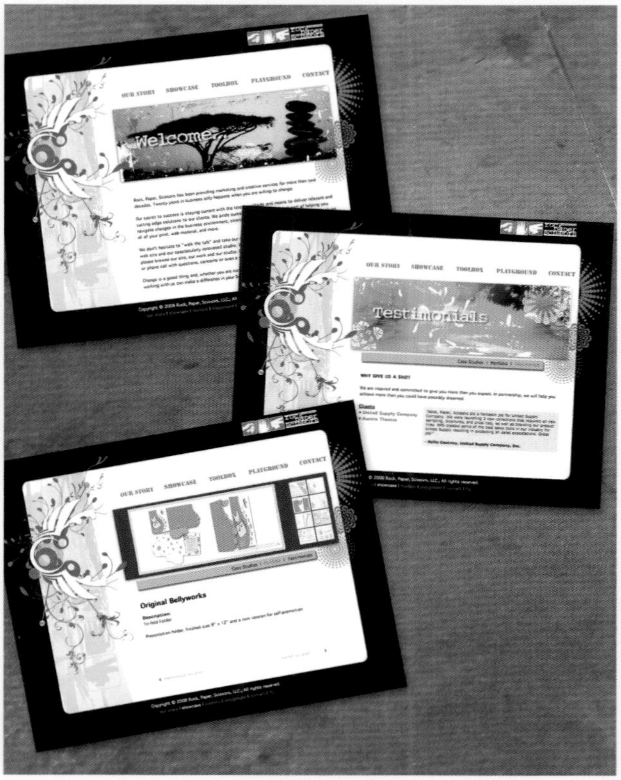

The electronic correspondence is anything but boring. The Web site, for example, prominently features a brand-new, recurring motif of sophisticated swirls echoed in the cocktail party invitations/coasters. "Our new site was our kicking off point," says Cindy. "We went from a completely Flash site. We'd timed it to be launched at our new move, so it was good."

As for the site itself, the URL—123shoot.com—maintains a sense of playfulness born of convenience and necessity. "It's easy to remember. It helps over the phone, being so simple," says Amanda. But that's only part of it, as Cindy explains: "RockPaperScissors.com was taken, rps.com was taken. But when you're playing Rock, Paper, Scissors—you know, '1-2-3, shoot.'"

Karoo Design – Southampton, England
Designers : Danelle Macaulay, Ryan Edwards, Karen Ellis
Client : Karoo Design

Soloflight Design Studio – Roswell, Georgia
Designers : Renee Solomon, Michelle Ducayet, Adrianne Kimbell, Kerry McCaughn
Client : Soloflight Design Studio

Delivered in a shiny silver metal box, the lively orange contents are a striking contrast. Full of items with a common theme—luggage tags, notebook/journal, airport iconography—it all reminds the client of Soloflight Design.

Group Fifty-Five Marketing – Detroit, Michigan
Designers : Heather Sowinski, Stacey Shires
Client : Group Fifty-Five Marketing

Calagraphic Design – Elkins Park, Pennsylvania
Designer : Ronald J. Cala II
Client : Art Making Machine Studios

2008 Art Calendar
JM Design Studio, Inc
April
August
September
October
November
December
The Artwork presented in this calendar was painted from scratch using natural media brushes, a digital pen and a pressure sensitive Wacom™ tablet.
Joshua Miller, the artist and owner of JM Design Studio, has spent over 10 years developing the skills to paint in this surrealistic way.
For more information about the artwork, or to purchase a fine art giclée, visit www.jmstudio.us
JM Design
© Copyright 2007 JM Design Studio, Inc. www.jmdesign.us

JM Design Studio, Inc. – Lake Forth, Florida
Designers : Joshua Miller, Dacia Miller
Client : JM Design Studio, Inc.

RDormann Design – Milltown, New Jersey
Designer : Roger Dormann
Client : RDormann Design

NAUGHTY OR NICE

Sophisticated and simple, silver metallic engraving on blue metallic cover stock belies this holiday card's humorous interior.

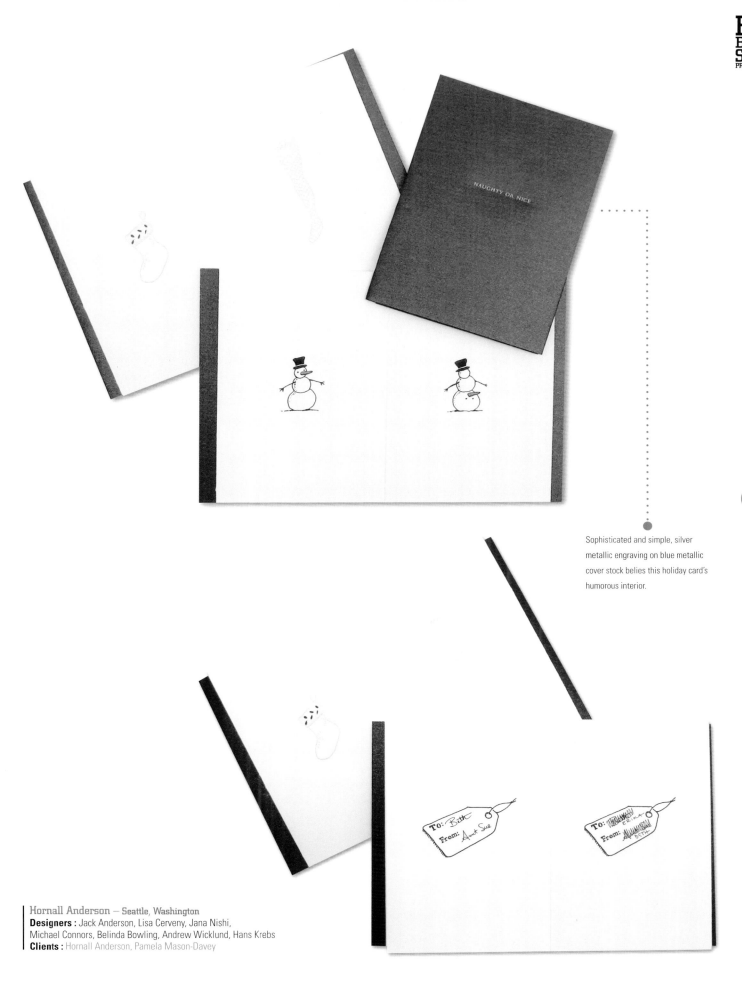

To: Beth
From: Aunt Sue
To:
From:

Hornall Anderson – Seattle, Washington
Designers : Jack Anderson, Lisa Cerveny, Jana Nishi, Michael Connors, Belinda Bowling, Andrew Wicklund, Hans Krebs
Clients : Hornall Anderson, Pamela Mason-Davey

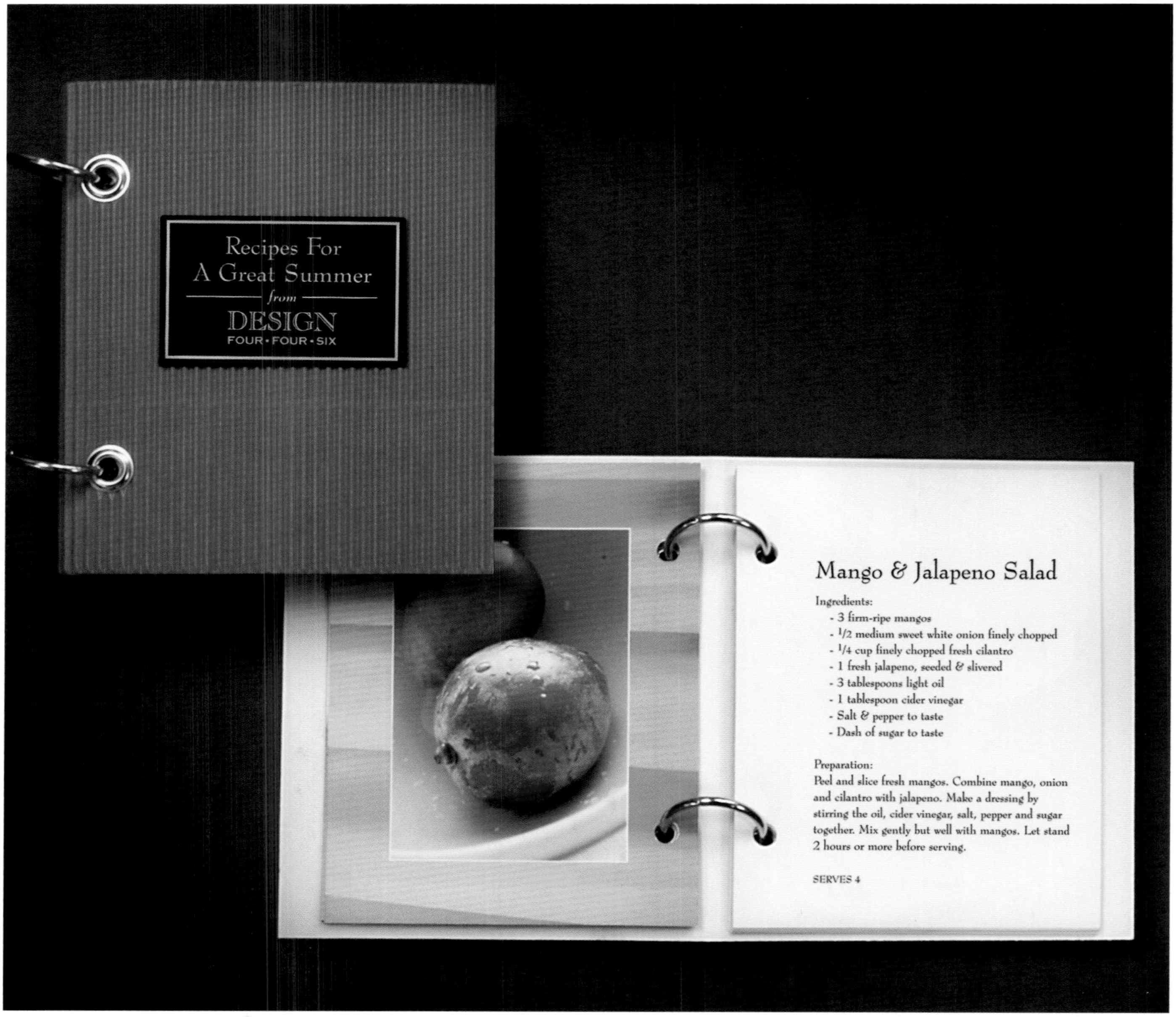
Recipes For
A Great Summer
from
DESIGN
FOUR • FOUR • SIX
Mango & Jalapeno Salad
Ingredients:
- 3 firm-ripe mangos
- 1/2 medium sweet white onion finely chopped
- 1/4 cup finely chopped fresh cilantro
- 1 fresh jalapeno, seeded & slivered
- 3 tablespoons light oil
- 1 tablespoon cider vinegar
- Salt & pepper to taste
- Dash of sugar to taste
Preparation:
Peel and slice fresh mangos. Combine mango, onion and cilantro with jalapeno. Make a dressing by stirring the oil, cider vinegar, salt, pepper and sugar together. Mix gently but well with mangos. Let stand 2 hours or more before serving.
SERVES 4

Design 446 – Manasquan, New Jersey
Designer : Brian Stern
Client : Design 446

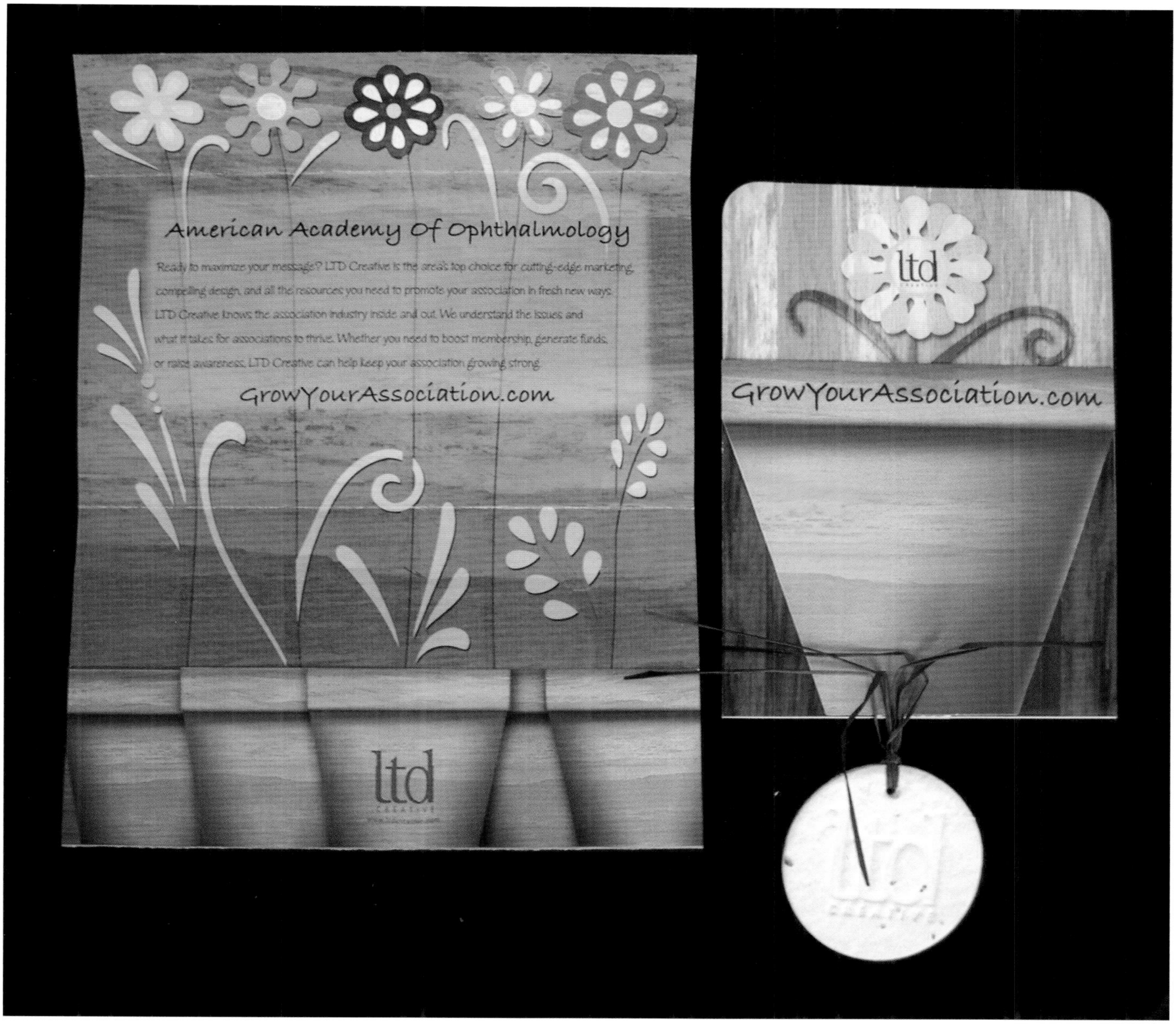
American Academy Of Ophthalmology
Ready to maximize your message? LTD Creative is the area's top choice for cutting-edge marketing, compelling design, and all the resources you need to promote your association in fresh new ways. LTD Creative knows the association industry inside and out. We understand the issues and what it takes for associations to thrive. Whether you need to boost membership, generate funds, or raise awareness, LTD Creative can help keep your association growing strong.
GrowYourAssociation.com
ltd
ltd
GrowYourAssociation.com
LTD

LTD Creative – Frederick, Maryland
Designers: Timothy Finnen, Louanne Welgoss
Client: LTD Creative

This mailer, the theme of which is "Grow Your Association," is punctuated with a natural, biodegradable disk embedded with forget-me-not seeds. Soak it, plant it—and LTD Creative will have grown its association with you!

[maul:tasche]
sag, was sache ist!"

design hoch drei GmbH + Co. KG – Stuttgart, Germany
Designers : Wolfram Schäffer, Susanne Wacker, Marcus Wichmann
Client : design hoch drei

»WER KOMMT FRÜHER ODER SCHRÖDER? ICH MERKEL NOCH NICHTS, ANGELA.«
[maul:tasche]
»wenn immer nur Politiker reden, verstehen wir bald gar nichts mehr!«
»Politik ist mehr als der Spielraum
die Wirtschaft
lässt.«
»RAN AN DEN DIÄTEN SPECK«
»WIR MÖCHTEN DIE GRENZEN DES MÖGLICHEN KENNEN. JETZT UND NICHT ERST NACH DER WAHL.«
964

SHE CONTEMPLATED MANY THINGS WHILE SHE WAITED FOR HIM TO POOP.

BUTTERFLIES LOVED HER AS MUCH AS SHE LOVED THEM.

Kelly-Anne Leyman Design – East Norriton, Pennsylvania
Client : Kelly-Anne Leyman Design

SHE FINALLY FIGURED OUT HOW TO PREVENT PRUNEY TOES

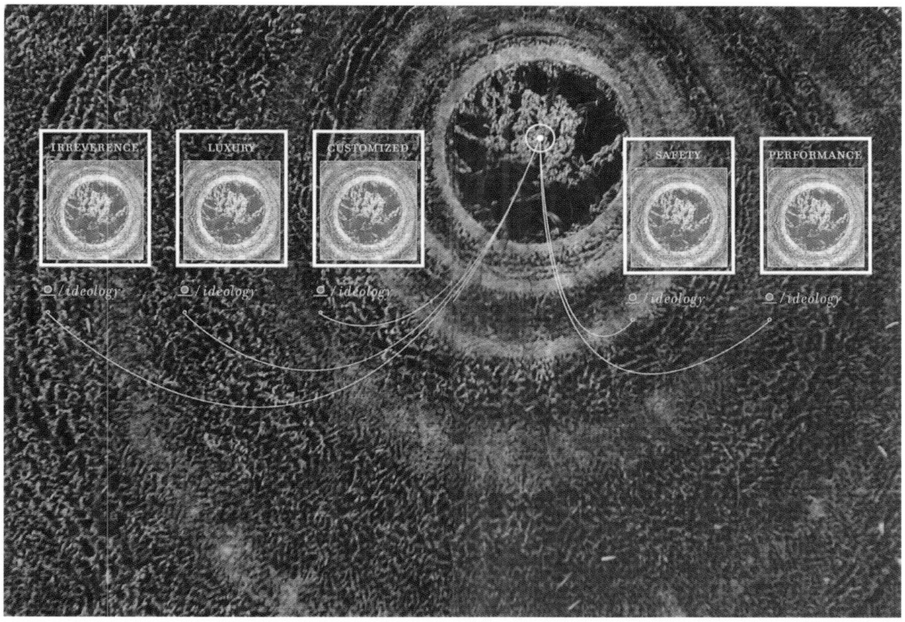

Gouthier Design: A Brand Collective
– New York, New York
Designers : Gouthier Design Creative Team
Client : Gouthier Design: A Brand Collective

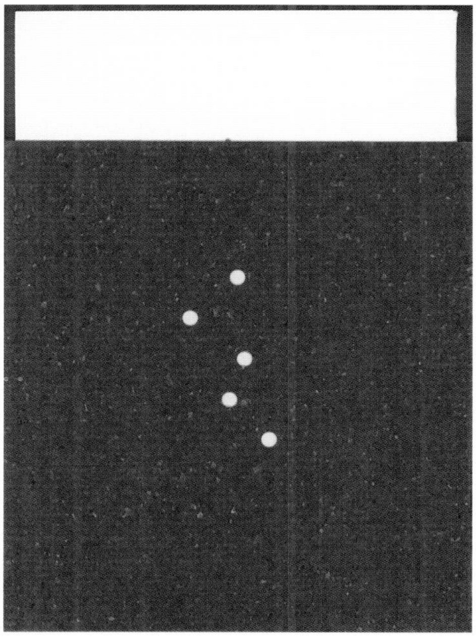

The envelope features five small die-cut dots, representative of our five senses and the design firm's five areas of expertise, to give the recipient an inside peek and create curiosity about the contents.

biz-R — Totnes, England
Designers : Blair Thomson, Claire Gregory
Client : biz-R

MDG Strategic Branding — Holliston, Massachusetts
Designers : Mike Eaton, Kris Greene, Tim Merry
Client : MDG Strategic Branding

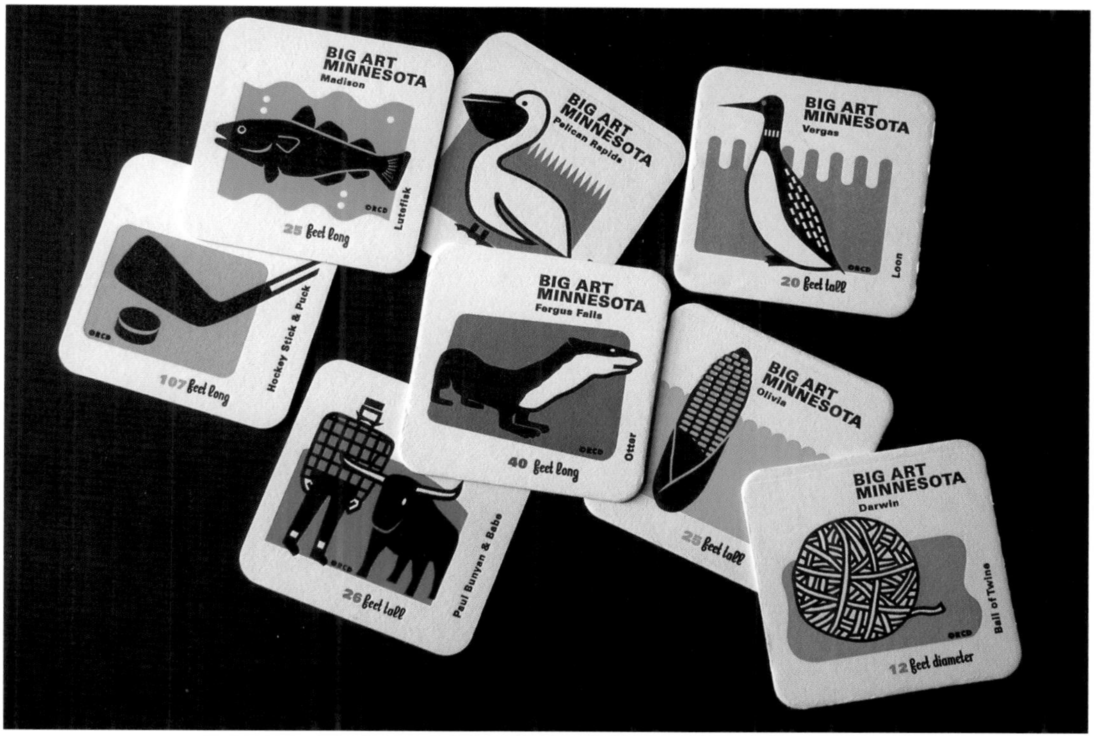

Rubin Cordaro Design – Minneapolis, Minnesota
Designers : Jim Cordaro, Bruce Rubin
Client : Rubin Cordaro Design

Contact Jupiter – St-Eustache, Canada
Designers : Yvan Meunier, C.R.E.E.—Alain Salesse, Oliver Mielenz
Client : Contact Jupiter

Bill Weber
CREATIVITY AT WORK

HOW TO BE AN INVOLVED PARENT ■ TOYS & GAMES THAT TEACH
FIGHTING DRUGS ■ COMPLETE CULTURAL CALENDAR OF EVENTS
Parents & Kids Directory
ANNUAL EDUCATION ISSUE
Partnership For The Future
P U B L I S H I N G
People gather around special interests like children, hobbies, and business. Marketers succeed when they serve these communities with the right mix of editorial, advertising, and circulation strategy.
Bill Weber has been the guiding force behind many successful communities – in print, online, and out in the real world.
Facing page: Parents & Kids Directory, New York's first local parenting magazine (publisher)
This page (top to bottom): Marquee, NJ Theatre programs (publisher)
Parents Datebook & Planner, school fund-raising product (publisher)
Corporate Image, business magazine insert on design and advertising (publisher)
ParentAge, newsletter for new parents over 35 (consultant)
The Dinosaur Times, newstand comic (consultant)
Motion Picture TV & Theatre Directory (general manager)
Weber's Internet Sourcebook, directory (concept)
Children's Entertainment Business (concept)
Archive (general manager)
Keep Peace Visible, art annual (concept)
Marquee
1992
Corporate Image
"A baby? ...at your age?"
KEEP PEACE VISIBLE
13

Bill Weber Studios – New York, New York
Designer : Bill Weber
Client : Bill Weber Studios

Melanie Marder Parks – Red Hook, New York
Designer : Melanie Marder Parks
Client : Melanie Marder Parks

Melanie Marder Parks
Illustration
Beacon Bridge
HUDS
RIVE
Beaco
845~758~0656
www.melaniemarderparks.com
melaniemarderparks@msn.com

IF SLEEK+LIVELY
DESIGNS ARE WHAT YOU SEEK
JILL'S GOT YOUR TICKET
jill LYNN design

Initials, inc.
Fall-Winter 2007
CATALOG DESIGN

DOES YOUR LIFE NEED A LAXATIVE?
Dr. Fred's PRACTICAL PRESCRIPTIONS FOR HAPPINESS
FRED BRODER, Ph.D.
DOES
YOUR LIFE
NEED A
LAXATIVE
?
Dr. Fred's
PRACTICAL
PRESCRIPTIONS FOR
HAPPINESS
FRED BRODER, Ph.D.
BOOK DESIGN

Jill Lynn Design – Atlanta, Georgia
Designer : Jill Anderson
Client : Jill Lynn Design

Self-promotional samples of Jill Lynn Design's work show a variety of work including catalog, book, invitation, and package design.

SPARK COLLEGE
THE UNOFFICIAL
COLLEGE
GUIDE TO
HARVARD
WITH
MURDER
OR . . . EVERYTHING YOU EVER WANTED TO KNOW
ABOUT HARVARD BUT WERE TOO AFRAID TO ASK.
DEAD
This book has not been endorsed by Harvard University.
BOOK DESIGN

OH, THE WEATHER OUTSIDE IS FRIGHTFUL,
BUT BOWLING WILL BE SO DELIGHTFUL,
AND SINCE IT'S HOLIDAY PARTY TIME,
LET US BOWL,
LET US BOWL,
LET US BOWL!
SPARKNOTES
8 LANES OF BOWLING AT
CHELSEA PIERS
23RD STREET AND WESTSIDE HIGHWAY
DRINKS & SNACKS BEER, WINE, SODA, CHIPS & SALSA,
CHEESE & CRACKERS, MINI QUESADILLAS, AND QUICHE!
TUESDAY,
DECEMBER
13
2005
4:30 P.M.
–TO–
6:30 P.M.
PLEASE ARRIVE
BY 4:00 P.M.
INVITATION DESIGN

BELOVED!
Amen
BODY BUTTER
PACKAGING DESIGN

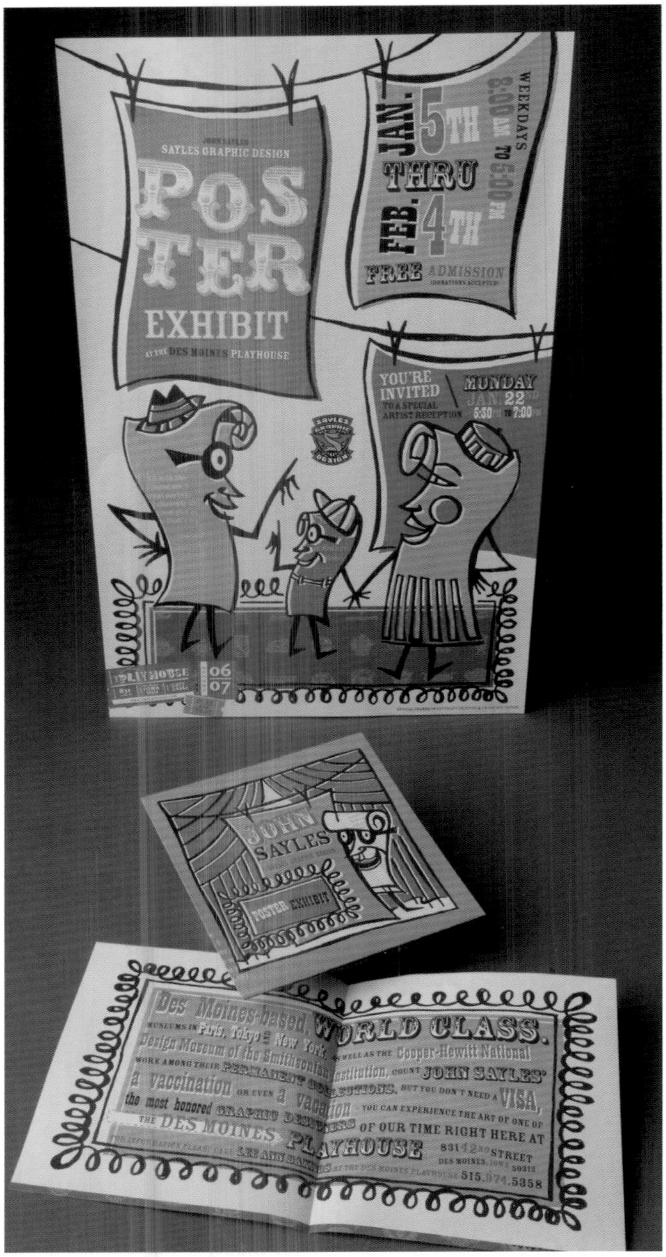

Sayles Graphic Design – Des Moines, Iowa
Designer : John Sayles
Client : Sayles Graphic Design

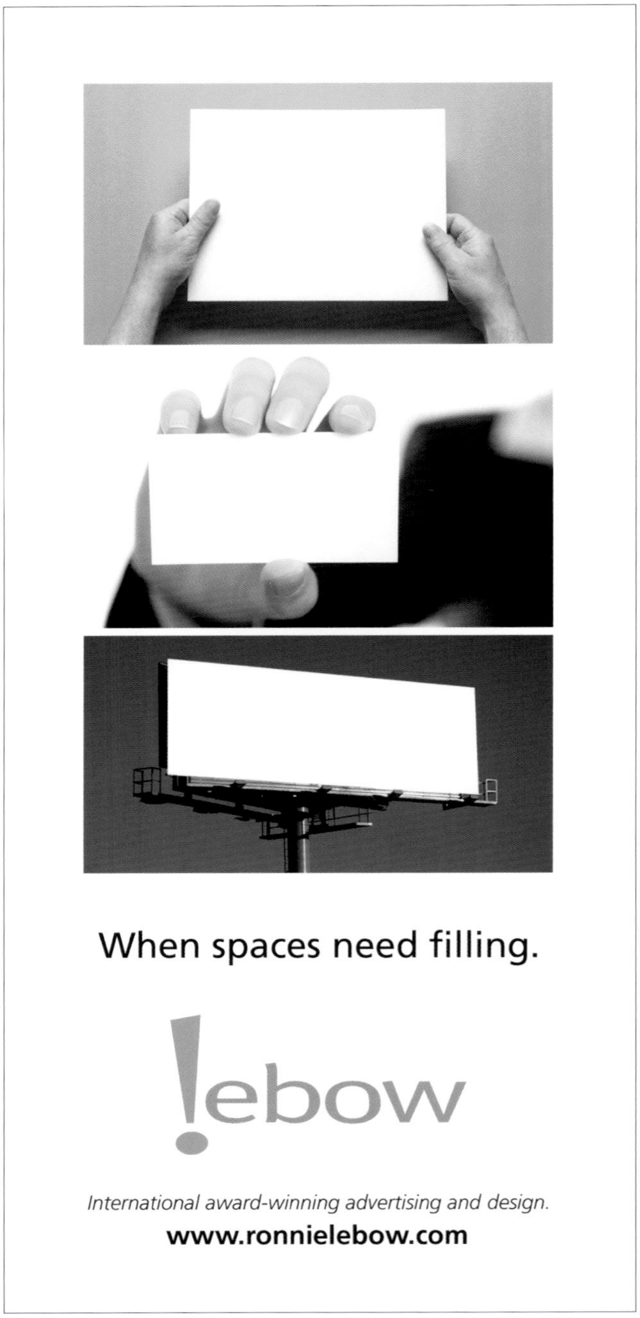
When spaces need filling.
!ebow
International award-winning advertising and design.
www.ronnielebow.com

Lebow – Toronto, Canada
Designer : Ronnie Lebow
Client : Lebow

NOTE: No human beings were harmed in the production or research of this project.

CDI Studios – **Las Vegas, Nevada**
Designers : Brian Felgar, Victoria Hart, Aaron Moses, Tracy Brockhouse, Dan McElhattan III, Eddie Roberts, Natasha Khachatourians
Client : CDI Studios

Alexander Egger/Satellites Mistaken for Stars – Vienna, Austria
Client : Alexander Egger/Satellites Mistaken for Stars

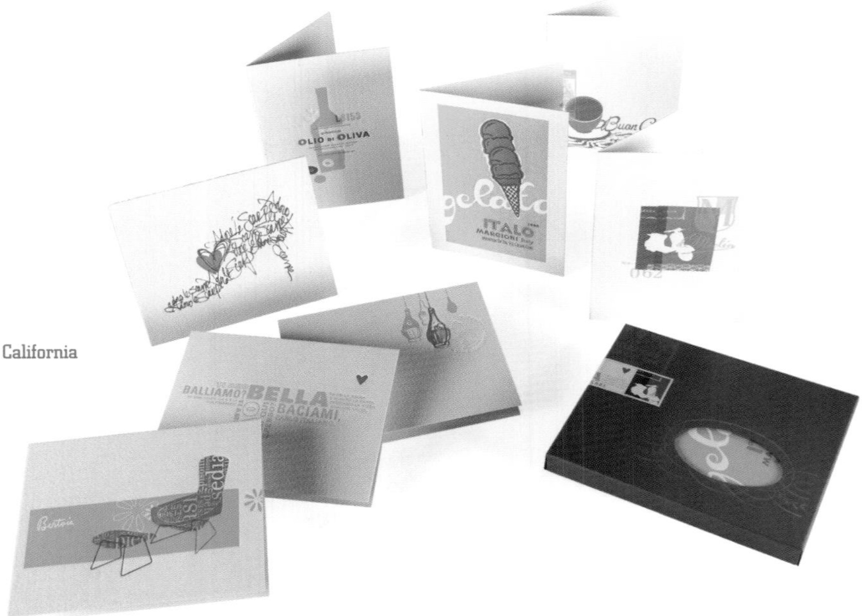

Miriello Grafico – San Diego, California
Designer : Dennis Garcia
Client : Miriello Grafico

Gouthier Design: A Brand Collective – New York, New York
Designers : Gouthier Design Creative Team
Client : Gouthier Design: A Brand Collective

A fresh green apple included in this package creates a memorable (and tasty) connection between the promotion and the design firm's location.

veronica hebard
HEBSANDFISH.COM

mink
kink
Veronica Hebard
illustration
fashion + editorial + design
wink
HEBSANDFISH.COM

DEADLINES GOT YOU WORRIED?
NOBODY DRAWS FASTER THAN
ANDY FISH
ILLUSTRATOR
FOR HIRE
See Deadlines Met!
Worries disappear Instantly!
TECHNICOLOR
Check out more at
HebsandFish.com
508.208.4707

Hebsandfish.com – Worcester, Massachusetts
Client : Hebs and Fish

Insight Marketing Design – Sioux Falls, South Dakota
Designers : Doug Moss, Clara Jacob
Client : Insight Marketing Design

Adults and children alike would love to receive any volume of this series of beautifully illustrated and cleverly written Christmas tales.

a classic
christmas tail
2
so on christmas eve,
we won't have
any
light."

MDG INC
STRATEGIC BRANDING & DESIGN

MDG Strategic Branding – Holliston, Massachusetts
Designers : Kris Green, Tim Merry, Mike Eaton
Client : MDG Strategic Branding

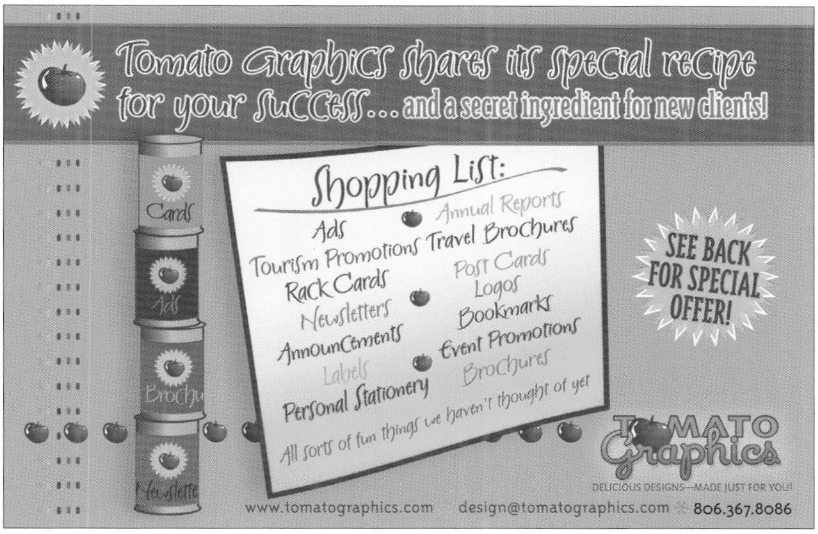
Tomato Graphics shares its special recipe for your success… and a secret ingredient for new clients!
Shopping List:
Ads
Annual Reports
Tourism Promotions
Travel Brochures
Rack Cards
Post Cards
Logos
Newsletters
Bookmarks
Announcements
Event Promotions
Labels
Brochures
Personal Stationery
All sorts of fun things we haven't thought of yet
SEE BACK FOR SPECIAL OFFER!
Cards
Ads
Brochu
Newslette
TOMATO Graphics
DELICIOUS DESIGNS—MADE JUST FOR YOU!
www.tomatographics.com design@tomatographics.com 806.367.8086

Tomato Graphics – Amarillo, Texas
Designer : Rock Langston
Client : Tomato Graphics

Tomato Graphics' Recipe for Success
3/4 c. creativity
1/2 c. design experience
1/4 c. patience
Pinch of humor...
DIRECTIONS:
Always use only the finest ingredients: Start with a great designer.
Have her whip up a tantalizing logo. Add an enticing color palette.
Assemble spicy text and snappy copy. Combine with tasty graphics.
Carefully blend the above ingredients to make delicious design treats to promote your business or event.
Share with everyone. Enjoy the results!
SERVES 10 TO 10,000
Recipe for Success Secret Ingredient for New Clients:
Projects commissioned before June 15, 2007 will receive 15% off design fees. Printing costs not included.
TOMATO Graphics
DELICIOUS DESIGNS—MADE JUST FOR YOU!
www.tomatographics.com design@tomatographics.com 806.367.8086

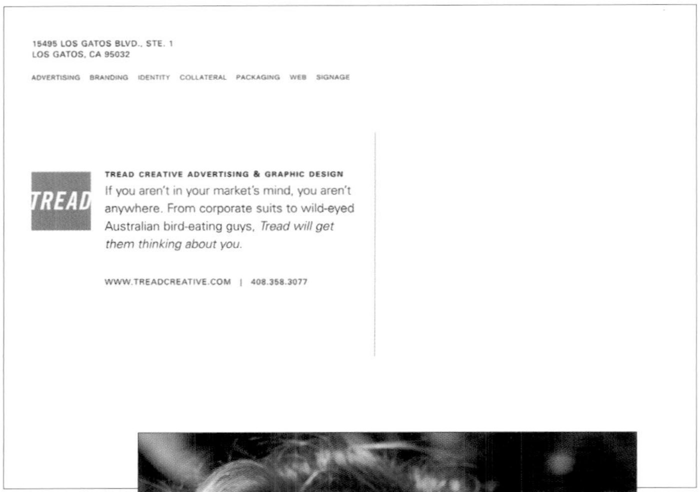
15495 LOS GATOS BLVD., STE. 1
LOS GATOS, CA 95032
ADVERTISING BRANDING IDENTITY COLLATERAL PACKAGING WEB SIGNAGE
TREAD
TREAD CREATIVE ADVERTISING & GRAPHIC DESIGN
If you aren't in your market's mind, you aren't anywhere. From corporate suits to wild-eyed Australian bird-eating guys, *Tread will get them thinking about you.*
WWW.TREADCREATIVE.COM | 408.358.3077

Tread Creative – Los Gatos, California
Designers : Phil Mowery, Achille Bigliardi
Client : Tread Creative

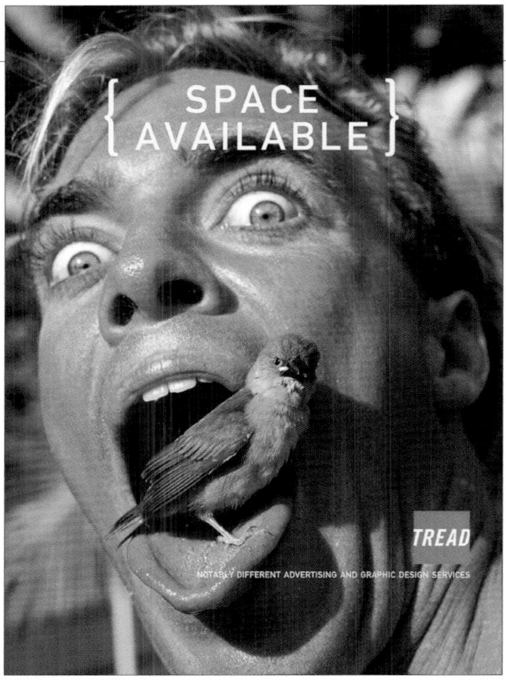

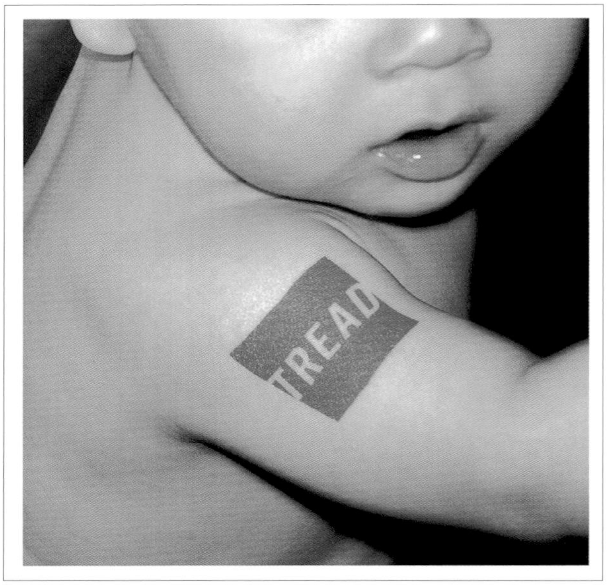

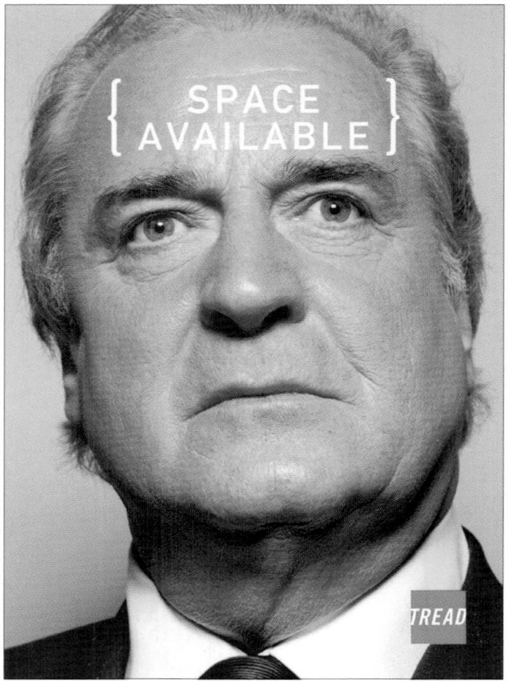

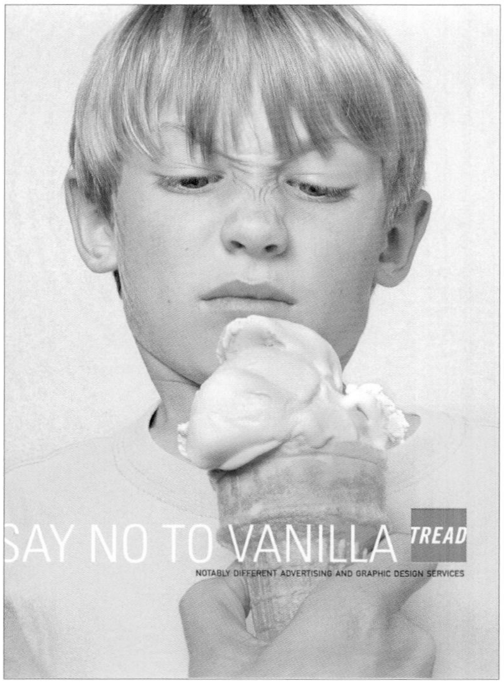

design hoch drei GmbH + Co. KG – Stuttgart, Germany
Designers : Wolfram Schäffer, Susanne Wacker, Marcus Wichmann
Client : design hoch drei

If you are what you eat, those who want to be "brave," "happy," or "imaginative" only need to munch these Springerle cookies. These traditional Christmas cookies, impressed with various words highlighting desirable personality traits, are packed separately in cardboard boxes and then hand delivered.

xo Create! – Alpharetta, Georgia
Designers : xo Create! Team
Client : xo Create!

Katie Cusack Illustration – Columbus, Ohio
Client : Katie Cusack

1. Target Audience
2. Coffee
3. Process
4. Creative Mix
5. Guitar
6. Peddle Power
LOVE
7. Collaboration
8. Recycling
9. Reward
10. Macintosh
11. Beats
12. Multi-tasking
12. Bad Presentations
11. Milking It
10. Selling Out
9. Sales Calls
8. Wasted Energy
7. Slow Turnaround
HATE
6. Boundaries
5. Waste
4. Sitting
3. The Cold
2. Cutting Corners
1. Copy Cats

Carbon Studio – **Cardiff, Wales**
Designers : Tom Tribe, Mike Clague
Client : Carbon Studio

This almost reads as a personal ad or a brief list of personality traits for a dating service. What better way to see if you and the client are compatible?

Anderson Design Group, Inc. – Nashville, Tennessee
Designers : Joel Anderson, Kristi Carter Smith
Client : Anderson Design Group, Inc.

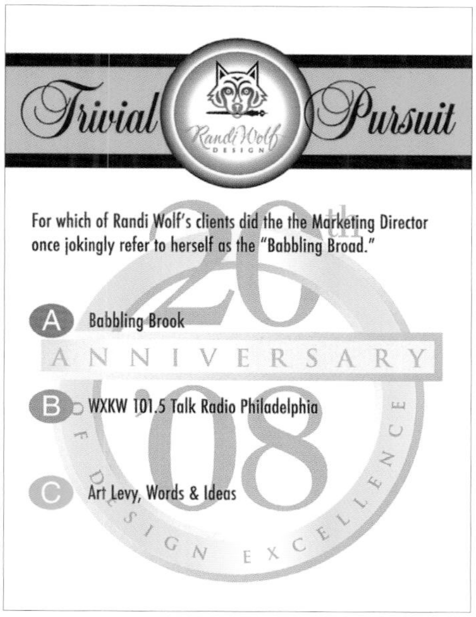

Trivial Pursuit
Randi Wolf DESIGN
For what financial client did Randi Wolf show that perhaps money does grow on trees?
For what client did Randi Wolf art direct a photo with her own cat, Cocoa Puff, for the client's full page ad?
For which of Randi Wolf's clients did the the Marketing Director once jokingly refer to herself as the "Babbling Broad."
20th ANNIVERSARY '08 OF DESIGN EXCELLENCE
A Oak Leaf Financial, LLC
B Prudent Management Associates
C PNC Bank
A Joe Stone's Hardwood Floors
B Maggie's Mice
C Purina Cat Chow
A Babbling Brook
B WXKW 101.5 Talk Radio Philadelphia
C Art Levy, Words & Ideas

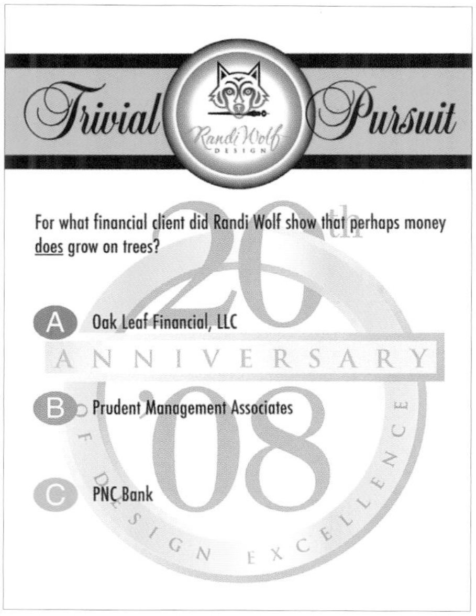

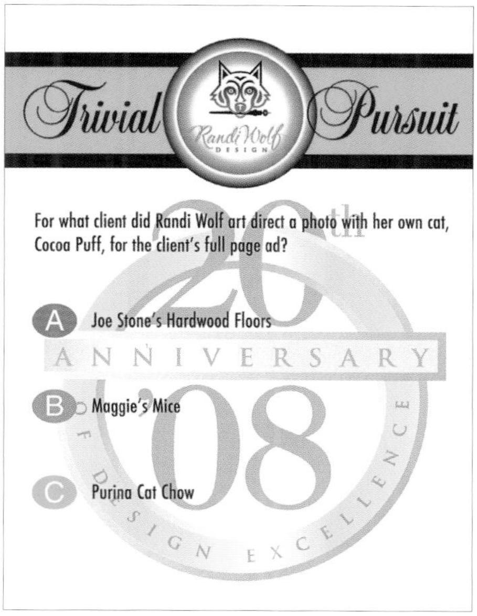

Randi Wolf Design – Glassboro, New Jersey
Designer : Randi Wolf
Client : Randi Wolf Design

Roycroft Design – Boston, Massachusetts
Designers : Jennifer Roycroft, Emily Chionchio
Client : Roycroft Design

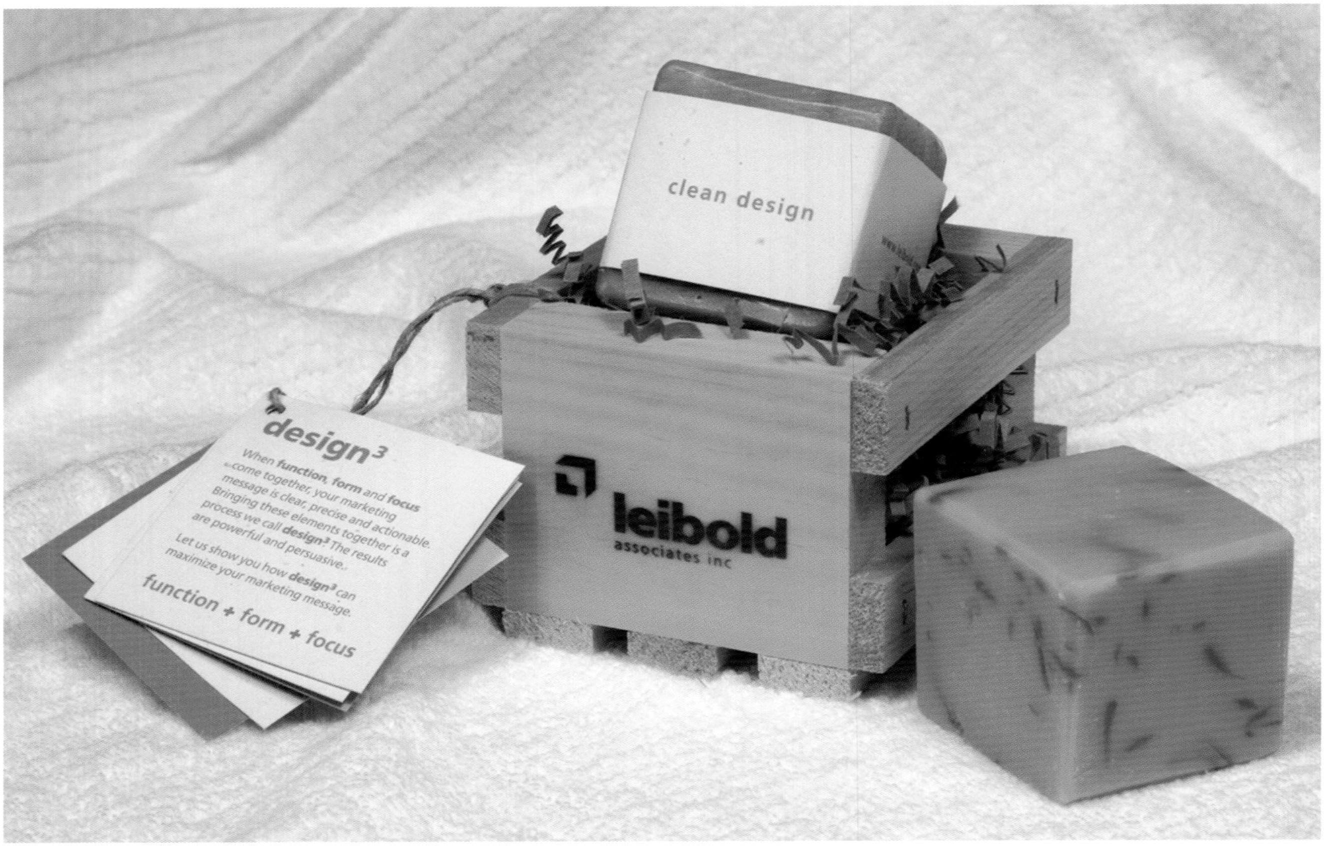
clean design
design³
When function, form and focus come together, your marketing message is clear, precise and actionable. Bringing these elements together is a process we call design³. The results are powerful and persuasive.
Let us show you how design³ can maximize your marketing message.
function + form + focus
leibold
associates inc

Leibold Associates, Inc. – **Neenah, Wisconsin**
Designers : Chad Fulwiler, Jane Oliver, Ryan Wienandt, Jason Harttert, Therese Joanis, Greg Madson
Client : Leibold Associates, Inc.

Leibold's Clean Design promotion relies on the delightfully-scented, handmade soaps that are sent in small custom crates. Accompanying cards of information explain the firm's goals and process: function + form + focus. They call it "design³" and visually represent it in the promo's dominant shapes.

leibold

Leibold Associates, Inc.
– **Neenah, Wisconsin**
Designers : Chad Fulwiler, Jane Oliver, Ryan Wienandt, Jason Harttert, Therese Joanis, Greg Madson
Client : Leibold Associates, Inc.

FUN…Colorful office supplies and The Guy in Brown! This firm obviously knows what you need and then delivers.

Leibold Associates, Inc. – Neenah, Wisconsin
Designers : Chad Fulwiler, Jane Oliver, Therese Joanis
Client : Leibold Associates, Inc.

Leibold Associates, Inc. – Neenah, Wisconsin
Designer : Mark Vanden Berg
Client : Leibold Associates, Inc.

These hand-silkscreened card sets come four to a bag. Utilizing a variety of styles and images, they are printed in pairs so each one can share ink colors with another design.

Dotzero Design — Portland, Oregon
Designers : Karen Wippich, Jon Wippich, Courtenay Hamiester
Client : Dotzero Design

Synthetic Infatuation – St. Paul, Minnesota
Designers : Lucas Buick, Ryan Dorshorst
Client : Synthetic Infatuation

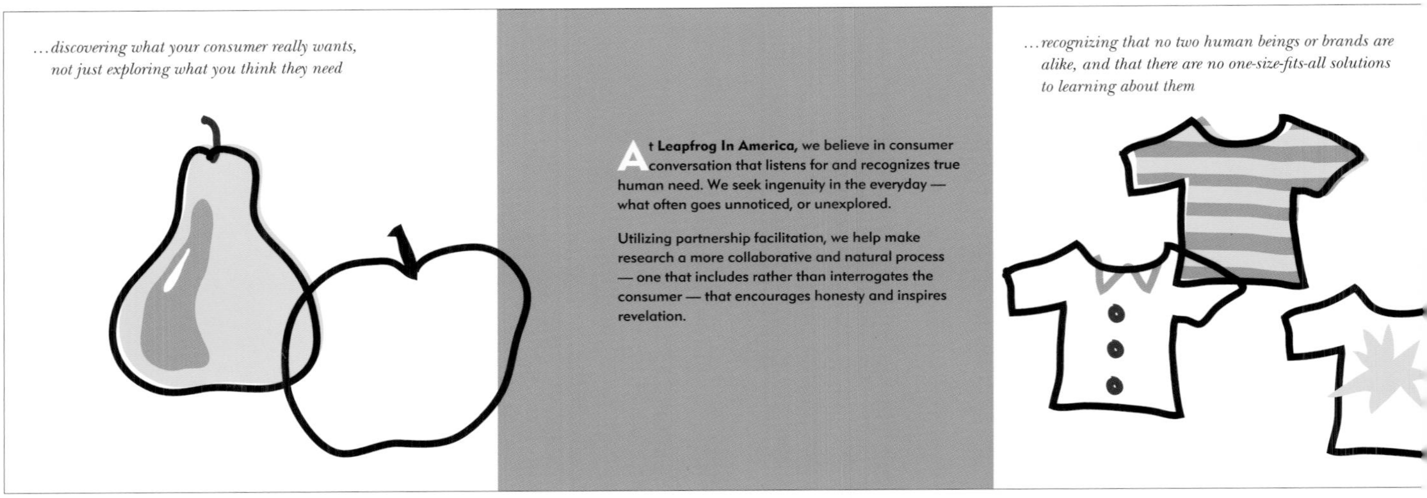
...discovering what your consumer really wants, not just exploring what you think they need
At Leapfrog In America, we believe in consumer conversation that listens for and recognizes true human need. We seek ingenuity in the everyday — what often goes unnoticed, or unexplored.
Utilizing partnership facilitation, we help make research a more collaborative and natural process — one that includes rather than interrogates the consumer — that encourages honesty and inspires revelation.
...recognizing that no two human beings or brands are alike, and that there are no one-size-fits-all solutions to learning about them

Aaron Design, Inc. – New York, New York
Designer: Stephanie Aaron
Client: Aaron Design, Inc.

48 Flower Mandalas
David J. Bookbinder

Phototransformations – Beverly, Massachusetts
Designer: David J. Bookbinder
Client: Phototransformations

We resist "tools", preferring to identify the combination of approaches and techniques that will provide the most useful and novel information. The search is most productive when it's not only designed for a particular challenge, but is open and flexible, able to nimbly change course if necessary. Leapfrog In America has even designed new, individualized approaches to help more traditional, well-known brands get at what's unknown.
...finding out how a brand can occupy a particular space... and earn the right to stand apart from the others.
Often, creating a unique space for a brand just means helping it find and courageously own its human-ness. At Leapfrog In America we seek, at all times, the human involvement of the people who are crucial to a brand's success — not just its consumers but its creators and caretakers.
Extended workshop sessions, using environments and intuitive approaches designed to meet the objectives and needs of each project, have helped recent clients make clear and exciting progress on their brands.

Jacob Tyler Creative Group – San Diego, California
Designers : Les Kollegian, Mo Saad, Jodi White
Client : Jacob Tyler Creative Group

gemini
Publicité Stratégie Marketing
Ici vos défis deviennent des réalités
DESIGN,
PUBLICITÉ et MARKETING,
COMMUNICATION
• Planification stratégique et gestion de la marque
• Plan de communication et marketing
• Conception et gestion de campagnes publicitaires
• Graphisme
• Packaging - Design d'emballage et de produits
• Services d'imprimerie
• Publicité TV
• Objets promotionnels
MARKETING INTERNET,
SITE WEB et APPLICATIONS D'AFFAIRES
• Analyse, conception et développement de solutions Web
• Programmation Web
Îles de la Madeleine, Québec : [418] 986-2545
Moncton, Nouveau-Brunswick : [506] 855-2545
info@gemini3d.com
www.gemini3d.com

Gemini 3D – Cap-aux-Meules, Canada
Designers : Dany Bouffard, Daniel Bouffard, Nancy Thorne
Client : Gemini 3D

www.loredanastudio.com – New York, New York
Designer : Loredana Sanginlians
Client : Image Rave

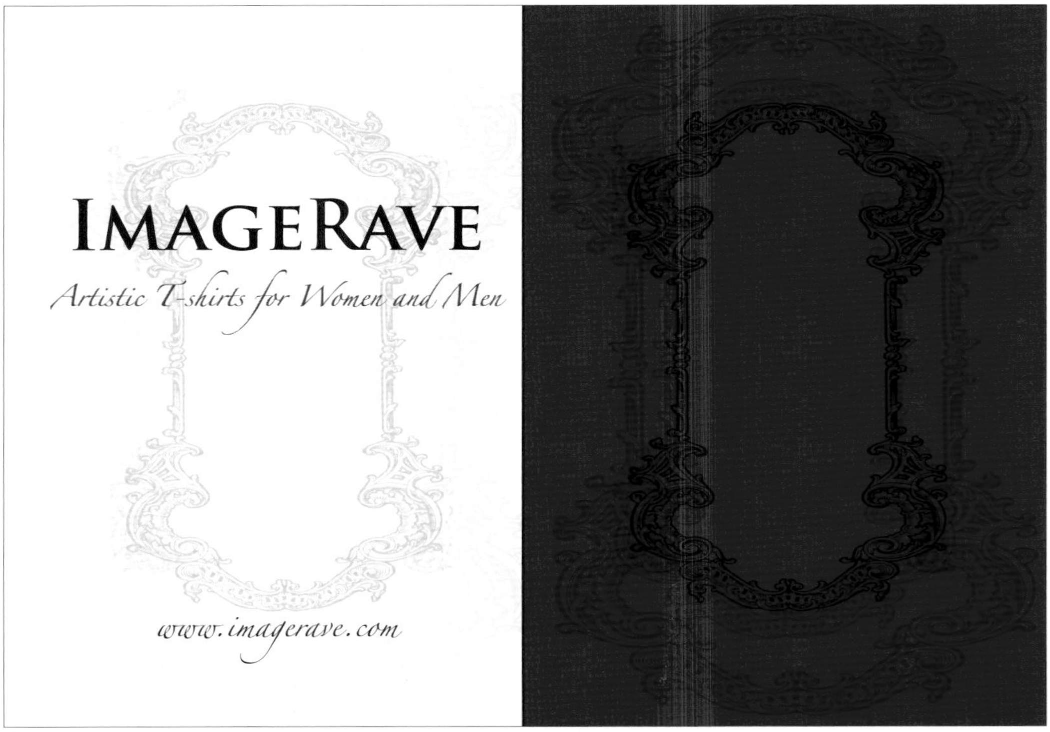
IMAGERAVE
Artistic T-shirts for Women and Men
www.imagerave.com

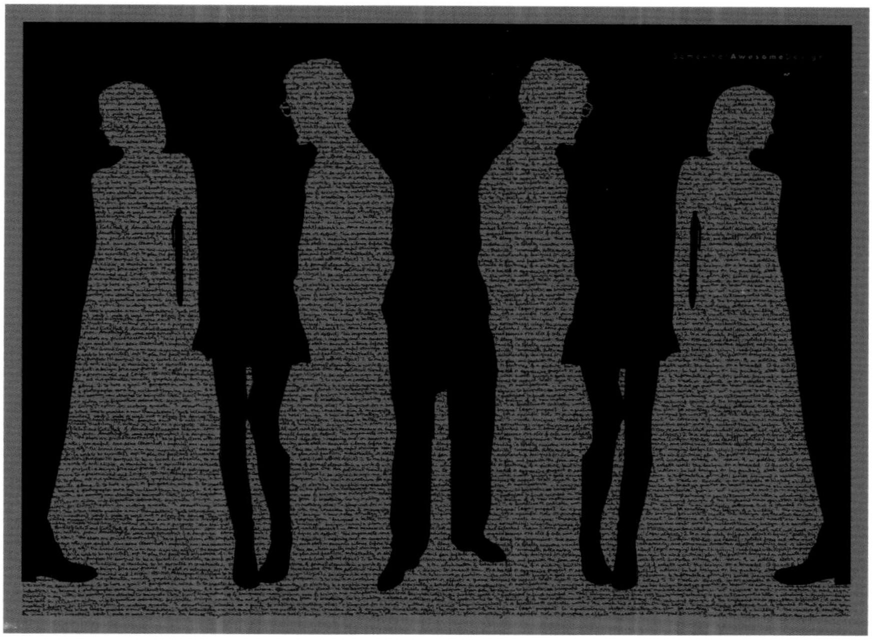

Somewhat Awesome Design – Elkins Park, Pennsylvania
Designers : Ronald J. Cala II, Katie Hatz
Client : Somewhat Awesome Design

2creativo – Barcelona, Spain
Designers : 2creativo Team
Client : 2creativo

2creativo produced this card/note holder from several colors of felt. With the goal of creating a memorable gift, the successful result contrasts nicely with the typical cold, hard-edged items usually found on a desk.

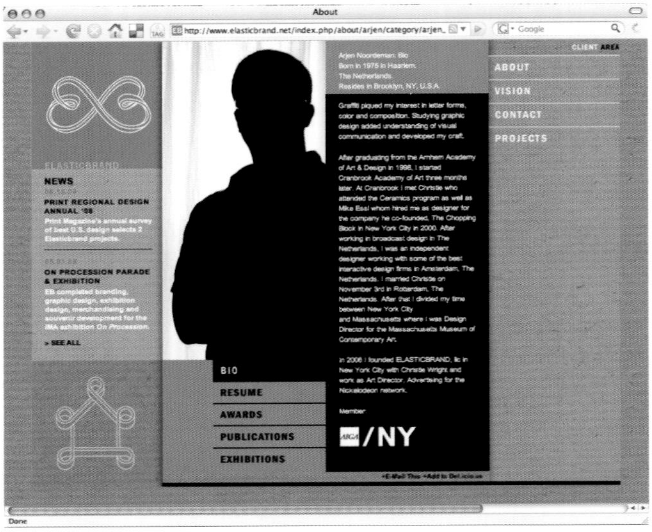

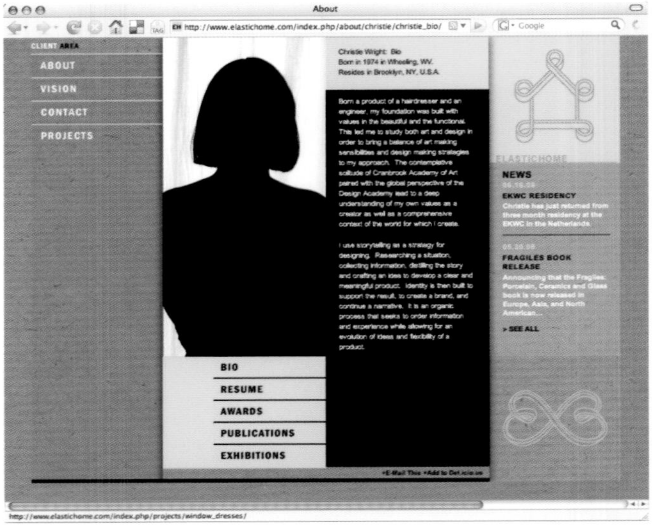

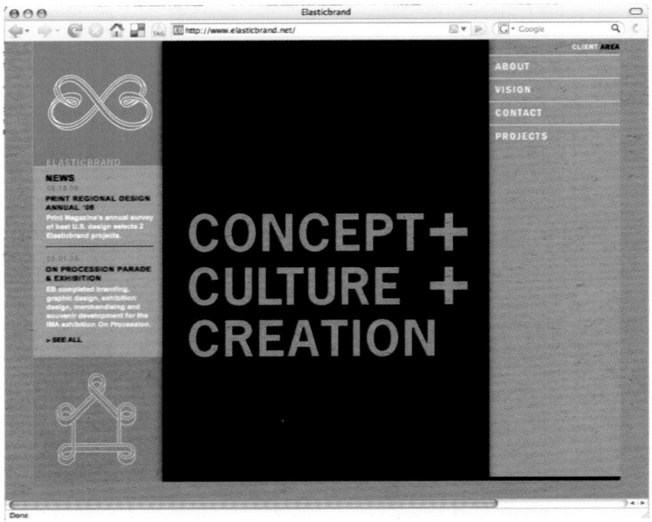

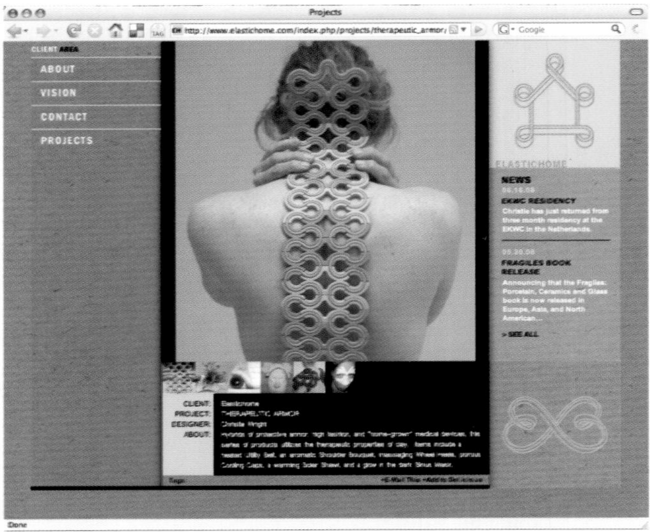

Elasticbrand, LLC – Brooklyn, New York
Designers : Arjen Noordeman, Christie Wright
Client : Elasticbrand, LLC

Andrij Shevchenko – Berdyansk, Ukraine
Designer : Andrij Shevchenko
Client : Andrij Shevchenko

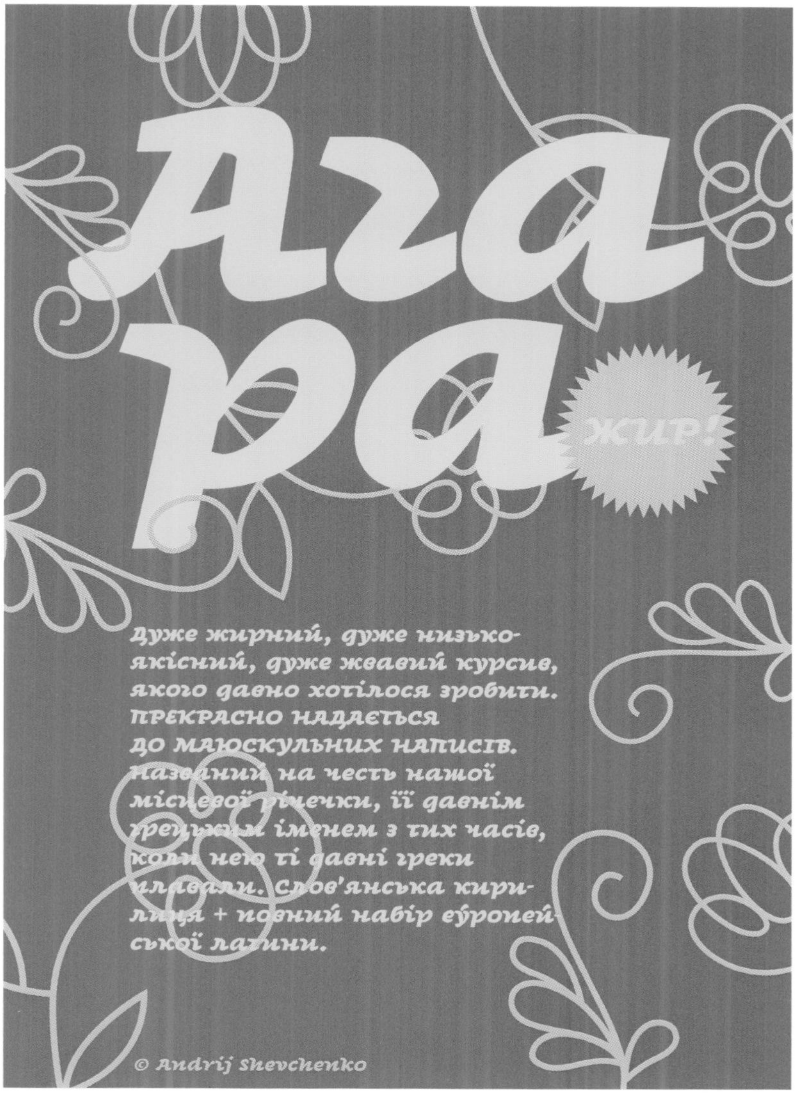
Агара
жир!
дуже жирний, дуже низько-
якісний, дуже жвавий курсив,
якого давно хотілося зробити.
ПРЕКРАСНО НАДАЄТЬСЯ
ДО МАЮСКУЛЬНИХ НАПИСІВ.
Названий на честь нашої
місцевої річечки, її давнім
грецьким іменем з тих часів,
коли нею ті давні греки
плавали. Слов'янська кири-
лиця + повний набір європей-
ської латини.
© Andrij Shevchenko

This poster promoting a new display type shows its subject's readability by using it as the body copy. With free-flowing letters, the Agarsky font, was named after the Berda River,—known as Agara at the time the ancient Greeks sailed on it.

When OrangeSeed moved—transplanted their roots—they increased their staff and office space. To announce the change they sent notebooks, "Watch Us Move, See Us Grow," that included flip-scene animation in the bottom right corner of each page.

OrangeSeed Design – Minneapolis, Minnesota
Designers : Damien Wolf, Kelly Munson, Eddie Ulrich
Client : OrangeSeed Design

Passing Notes, Inc. – Oakland, California
Designer : Abbie Planas Gong
Client : Passing Notes, Inc.

j. riley creative LLC – Houston, Texas
Designer : Julie Riley
Client : j. riley creative LLC

A SIP OF
Holiday Cheer
TEXAS PECAN COFFEE
A roasted blend of the finest coffee beans
with delicious Texas Pecans.

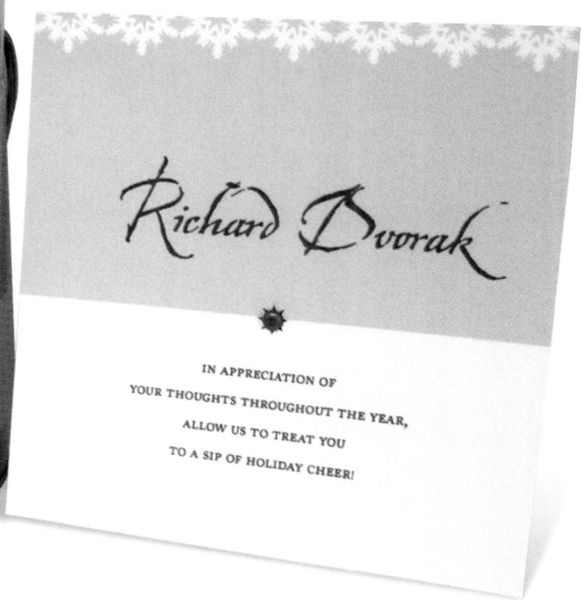
Richard Dvorak
IN APPRECIATION OF
YOUR THOUGHTS THROUGHOUT THE YEAR,
ALLOW US TO TREAT YOU
TO A SIP OF HOLIDAY CHEER!

La nature s'éveille...
gemini
... et notre créativité déborde au delà des frontières
de la communication conventionnelle
Ici vos défis deviennent des réalités
DESIGN,
PUBLICITÉ et MARKETING,
COMMUNICATION,
• Planification stratégique et gestion de la marque
• Plan de communication et marketing
• Conception et gestion de campagnes publicitaires
• Graphisme
• Packaging - Design d'emballage et de produits
• Services d'imprimerie
• Publicité TV
• Objets promotionnels
SITE WEB et APPLICATIONS D'AFFAIRES
• Analyse, conception et développement de solutions Web
• Programmation Web
Moncton, Nouveau-Brunswick : [506] 855-2545
Îles de la Madeleine, Québec : [418] 986-2545
info@gemini3d.com
www.gemini3d.com
La nature s'éveille...
gemini

Gemini 3D – Quebec, Canada
Designers : Dany Bouffard, Daniel Bouffard, Nancy Thorne
Client : Gemini 3D

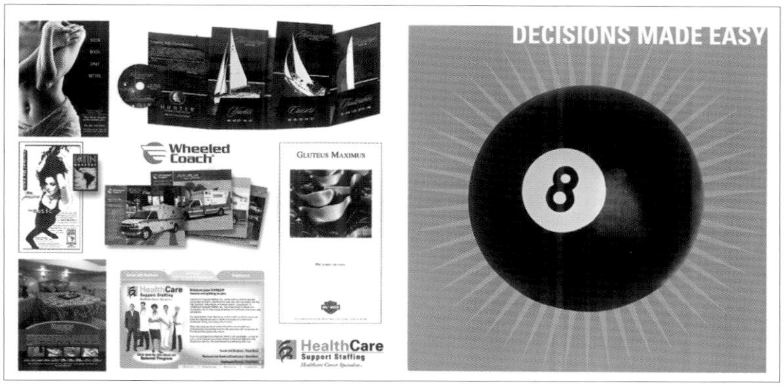
DECISIONS MADE EASY
Wheeled Coach
GLUTEUS MAXIMUS
HealthCare
Support Staffing

A less expensive campaign than buying and mailing actual Magic 8-Balls, this layered card offers the same kind of fun and interaction. Turn the wheel at the top of the card and your answer appears in the die-cut area below—*You May Rely On It.*

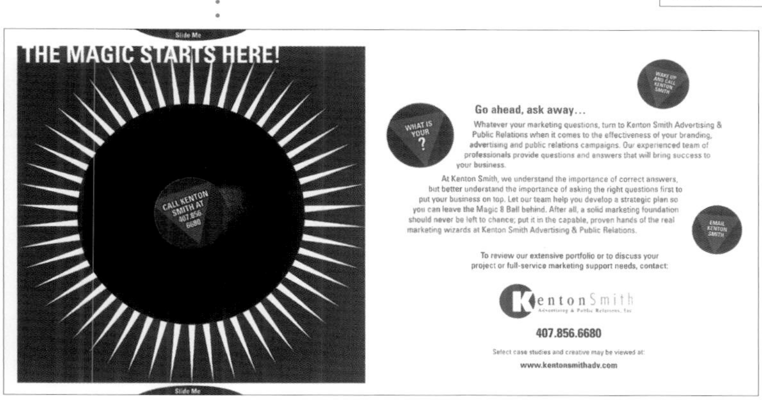
Slide Me
THE MAGIC STARTS HERE!
CALL KENTON SMITH AT 407.856.6680
WHAT IS YOUR ?
WAKE UP AND CALL KENTON SMITH
Go ahead, ask away...
Whatever your marketing questions, turn to Kenton Smith Advertising & Public Relations when it comes to the effectiveness of your branding, advertising and public relations campaigns. Our experienced team of professionals provide questions and answers that will bring success to your business.
At Kenton Smith, we understand the importance of correct answers, but better understand the importance of asking the right questions first to put your business on top. Let our team help you develop a strategic plan so you can leave the Magic 8 Ball behind. After all, a solid marketing foundation should never be left to chance; put it in the capable, proven hands of the real marketing wizards at Kenton Smith Advertising & Public Relations.
EMAIL KENTON SMITH
To review our extensive portfolio or to discuss your project or full-service marketing support needs, contact:
KentonSmith
407.856.6680
Select case studies and creative may be viewed at:
www.kentonsmithadv.com
Slide Me

Kenton Smith Advertising & Public Relations, Inc. – Orlando, Florida
Designers : Wanda Kenton Smith, Mark Kellum, Scott Saylor, Danielle Watson
Client : Kenton Smith Advertising & Public Relations, Inc.

Stephen Burdick Design – Boston, Massachusetts
Designer : Stephen Burdick
Client : Stephen Burdick Design

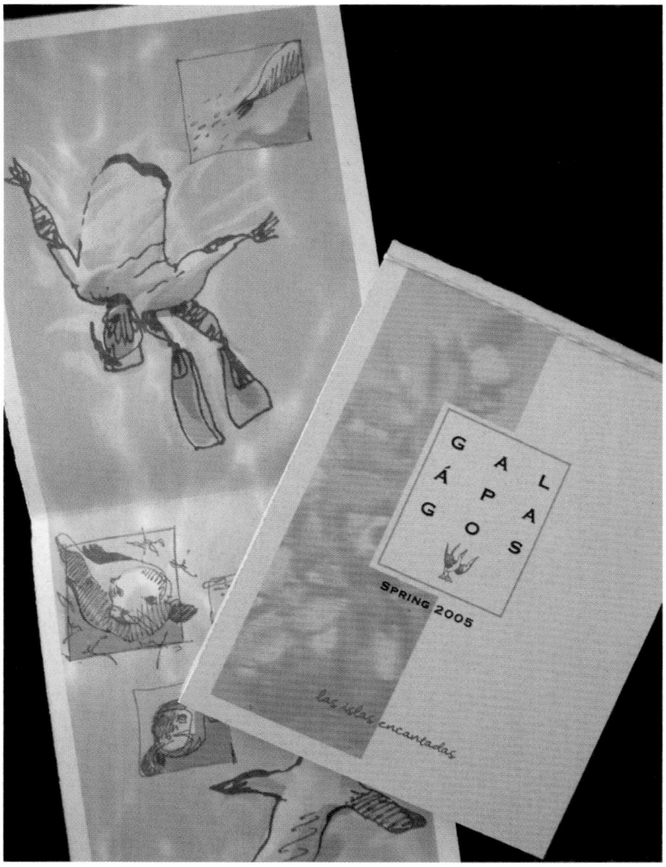
GALÁPAGOS
SPRING 2005
las islas encantadas

Rule29 Creative, Inc. – Geneva, Illinois
Designers : Justin Ahrens, Kerri Liu, Kara Merrick
Client : Rule29 Creative, Inc.

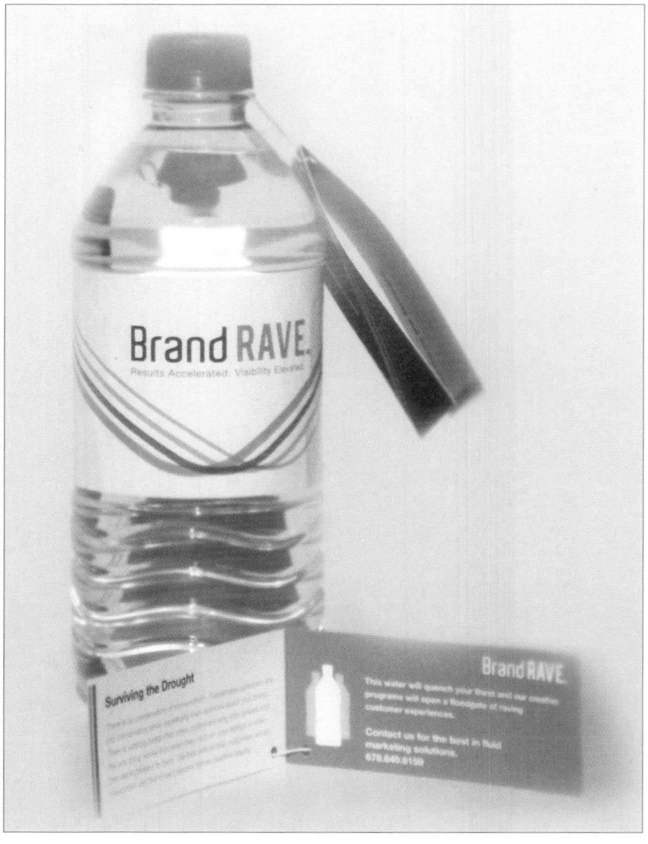

Brand RAVE, Inc. – Atlanta, Georgia
Designers : Ray Killebrew, Chris Manning
Client : Brand RAVE, Inc.

Crawford Design — Chagrin Falls, Ohio
Designer : Alison Crawford
Client : Crawford Design

Get A Clue Design – Hickory, North Carolina
Designer : Matt Pfahlert
Client : Get A Clue Design

GET A CLUE
DESIGN STUDIO

Michelle Roberts Design — Barneveld, New York
Designer : Michelle Roberts
Client : Michelle Roberts Design

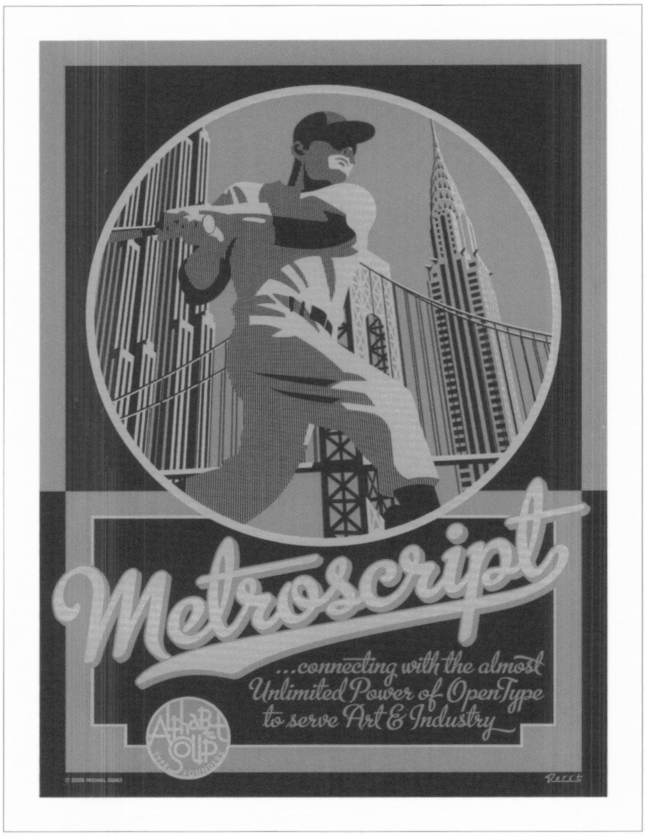

Michael Doret Graphic Design — Hollywood, California
Designer : Michael Doret
Client : Alphabet Soup Type Founders

Avive Design — Portland, Oregon
Designer : Lia Miternique
Client : Avive Design

THE CENTER FOR THERAPY THROUGH THE ARTS, THE ART STUDIO
THE 15TH CREATIVE CONFECTIONS PREMIER DESSERT COMPETITION
CRAWFORD AUTO-AVIATION MUSEUM
OCTOBER 28, 2006

Crawford Design – Chagrin Falls, Ohio
Designers : Alison Crawford
Client : Crawford Design

Vellum envelopes and raffia-stitched binding add a complementary, tactile quality to this fall promotion with a natural flavor.

Zunda Group, LLC – South Norwalk, Connecticut
Designers : Charles Zunda, Todd Nickel, Siri Korsgren, Dan Price, Maija Rieskstins-Rutens, Lauren Millar, Doug Pashley
Client : Zunda Group, LLC

These bottles were produced in observance of Zunda Group's twenty-fifth anniversary. Eight different design team members created their own version of the celebration and mailed clients different designs randomly. The hang-tag front showed all the variations and some clients traded amongst themselves to get a bottle that attracted them personally.

avive design
avive design

Avive Design – Portland, Oregon
Designer : Lia Miternique
Client : Avive Design

FINAL FANTASY XII
WE HELP YOU
MAKE A BIG
IMPRESSION
FINAL FANTASY XII BANNERS CLIENT: SQUARE ENIX
NEED SIGNAGE A STOREY TALL AND A BUILDING WIDE?
NO PROBLEM. OUR EXPERT ARTISTS AND RETOUCHERS
MAKE SHORT WORK OF EVEN THE BIGGEST PROJECTS.
STUDIO
QED
INC.
DESIGN & MARKETING SOLUTIONS

Studio QED, Inc. – San Mateo, California
Designer : Steven Wright
Client : Studio QED, Inc.

qed details
SEPTEMBER, 2007
VOLUME ONE, NUMBER THREE
1.3
FEATURE:
STAND
Specialty packaging
PlayStation.2
WILD ARMS 5
qed details
THE NEWSLETTER OF STUDIO QED, INC. DESIGN AND MARKETING AGENCY
APRIL, 2008
VOLUME TWO, NUMBER ONE
2.1
FEATURE:
The BEST of BOTH WORLDS
Creating SYNERGY with integrated ONLINE and TRADITIONAL promotions
BOMBERMAN LIVE
DON'T PULL YOUR PUNCHES.
VICTORIOUS BOXERS REVOLUTION
your path to victory contains many obstacles
Let us know what you'd like to achieve with your next ad campaign, and we'd be happy to help you exceed your expectations!
WWW.STUDIOQED.COM
650.804.6564

Studio QED, Inc. – San Mateo, California
Designer : Steven Wright
Client : Studio QED, Inc.

Roycroft Design – Boston, Massachusetts
Designers : Jennifer Roycroft, Kaitlin Imwalle
Client : Roycroft Design

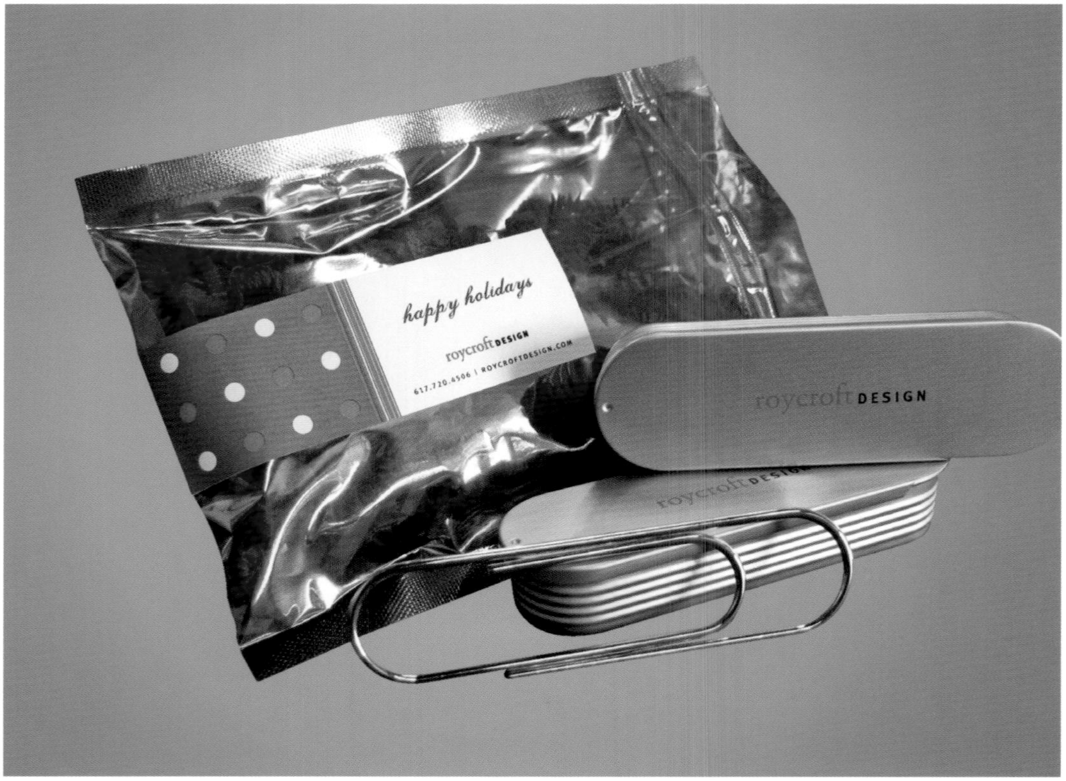
happy holidays
roycroftDESIGN
617.720.6506 | ROYCROFTDESIGN.COM
roycroftDESIGN
roycroftDESIGN

Krug Creative — Asheville, North Carolina
Designers : Emily Chaplin Krug, Brooke Thomas
Client : Krug Creative

EBD — Denver, Colorado
Designers : Ellen Bruss, Gabe Re
Client : EBD

An In-Depth Look at: FACTOR DESIGN

San Francisco's Factor Design knows how to make an impression, and in doing so seeks to engage clients with a vision as ambitious as theirs. "In a world where everyone is using the Web and digital media, our Promo Box is something a client can touch and feel and hold in their hands," says creative director Jeff Zwerner. "It says a lot about how we do things and about our commitment. People like to experience opening things, then they'll call and say, 'Oh my God, that box!'"

The light blue, handcrafted boxes feature a company brochure and an ever-changing assortment of portfolio cards and case studies about what Factor Design has done for some of its clients. "The cards are mostly visual, without any story on them," says Zwerner. "The front and back are portfolio samples." The brochure, divided into three sections, showcases the company's signature values. "We do three things: launching companies and products, renewing brands, and what we call envisioning exercises—that is to say, prototyping. So the brochure shows our vision about launching, renewing, and envisioning. It's how we speak of ourselves."

This identity goes back to an involved self-examination leading to a place from where Factor Design could find and pursue its best clients. "About three years ago we underwent our own positioning exercise," says Zwerner. "Other companies do logos, corporate collateral, [address] problems that they help the client solve. We didn't like that." What Zwerner does like is cultivating nascent relationships. "Most of our work is referrals," he says. "It's rare to send the boxes to someone who doesn't know us."

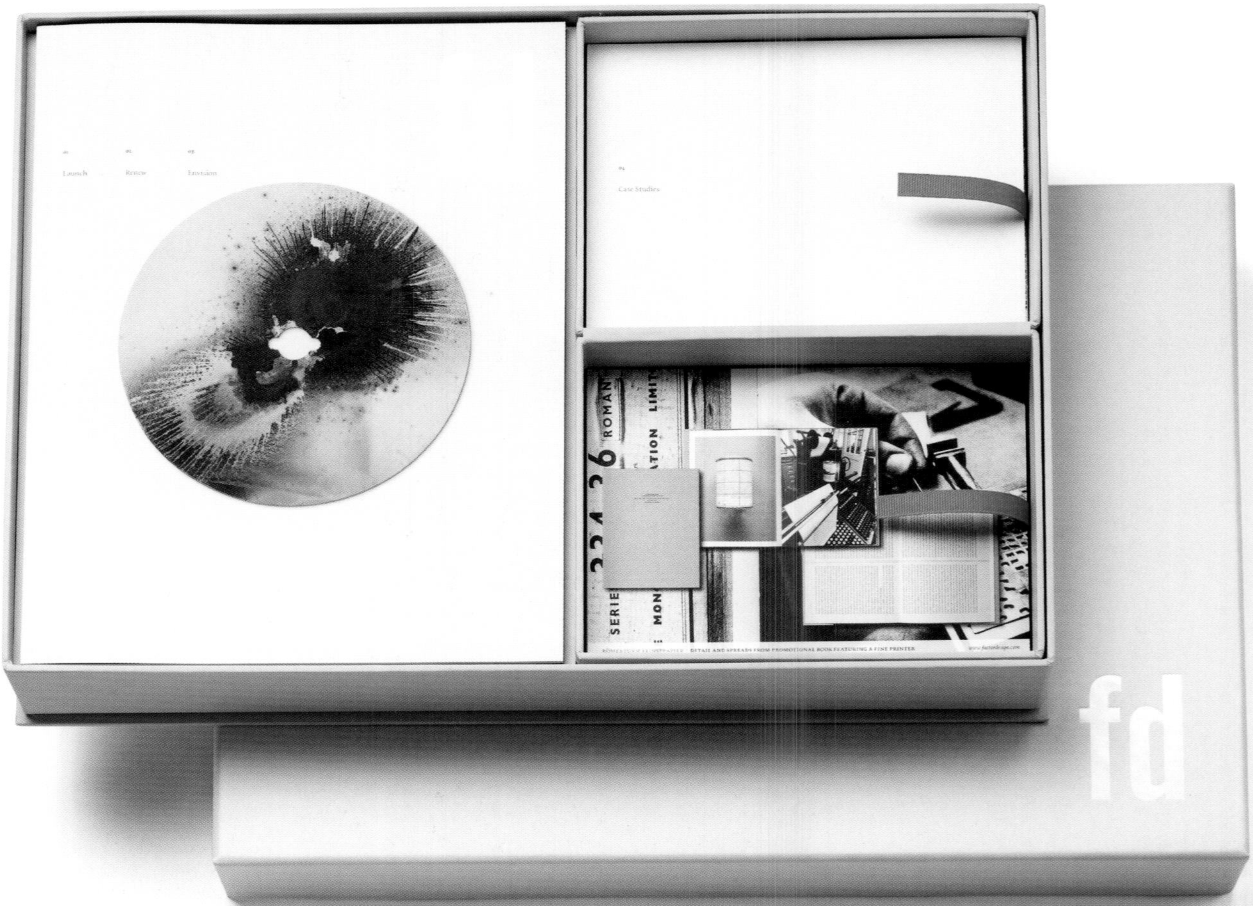

Even if a stranger were to receive a Promo Box—which has a very simple exterior but for a foil-stamped FD logo—that person wouldn't remain a stranger for long. "The real purpose is to go after the top design-driven companies in the world," Zwerner says, adding that the Promo Box strategy "works great." Upon seeing, holding, and opening the box, he says, "everybody thinks it's incredibly beautiful and expensive—which it is. If they're not disciplined in developing content and prepared to create things equally as perfect, they'll know that. If they're not ready, that's good—it's not a good alignment of values. Clients need someone to take them there, and that's us. [The right client will say,] 'I want our company and our business to be represented this way.'"

Factor Design – San Francisco, California
Designers : Jeff Zwerner, Gabe Campodonico, Craig Williamson, Kara Nichols, Doug Adesko, Peter Belanger, Dwight Eschliman, Bertrand Lagros de Langeron
Client : Factor Design

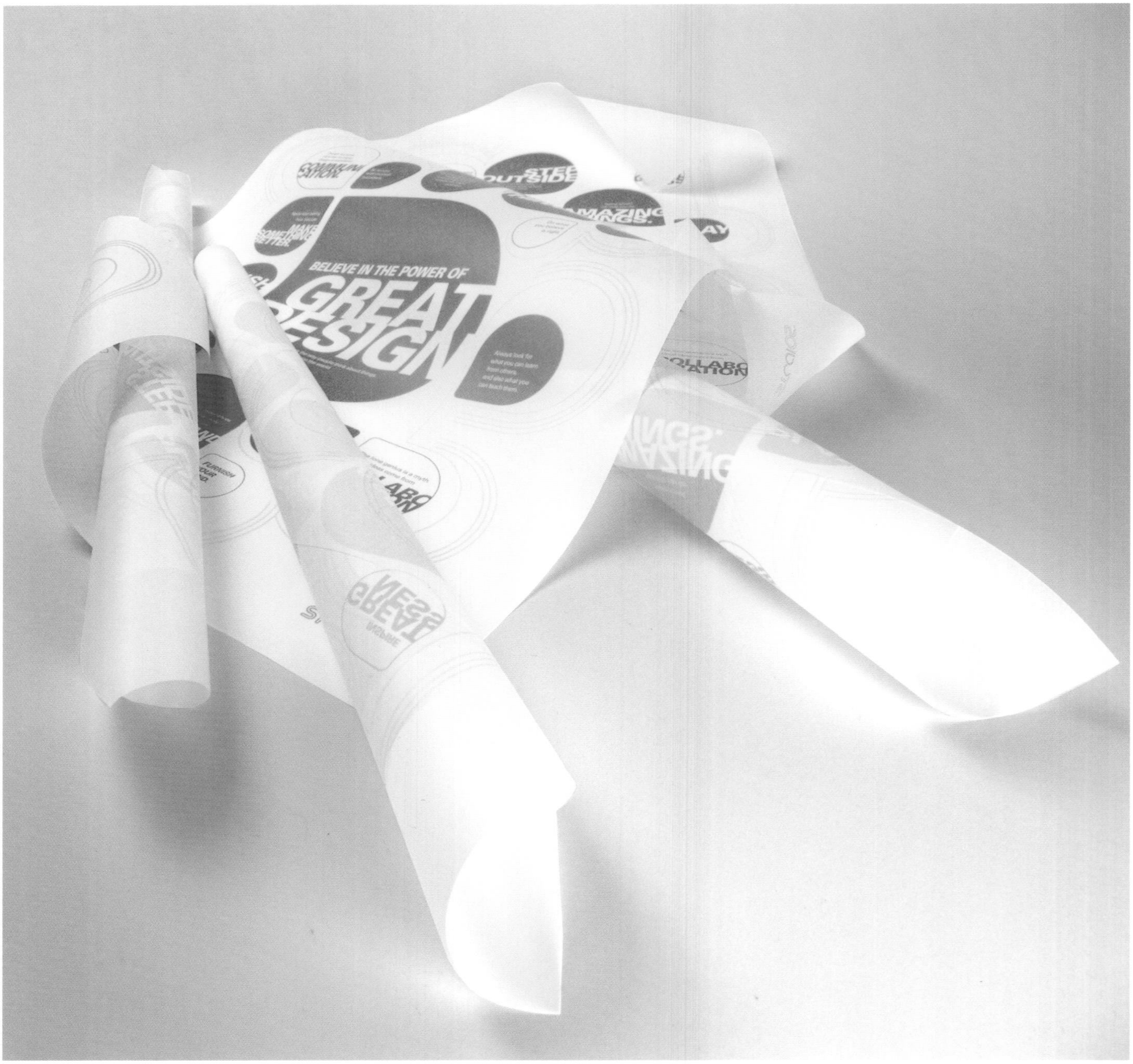

CDI Studios – Las Vegas, Nevada
Designers : Brian Felgar, Victoria Hart
Client : CDI Studios

This business-card sized promo grew out of finding some plastic magnifying glasses at a novelty/closeout store. The cards were professionally printed and drilled to accommodate the beaded chain. Dotzero sourced small envelopes, then rubber-stamped them with their logo. It was all assembled in-house. A few of the cards were held out from being drilled and worked well as business cards for the firm.

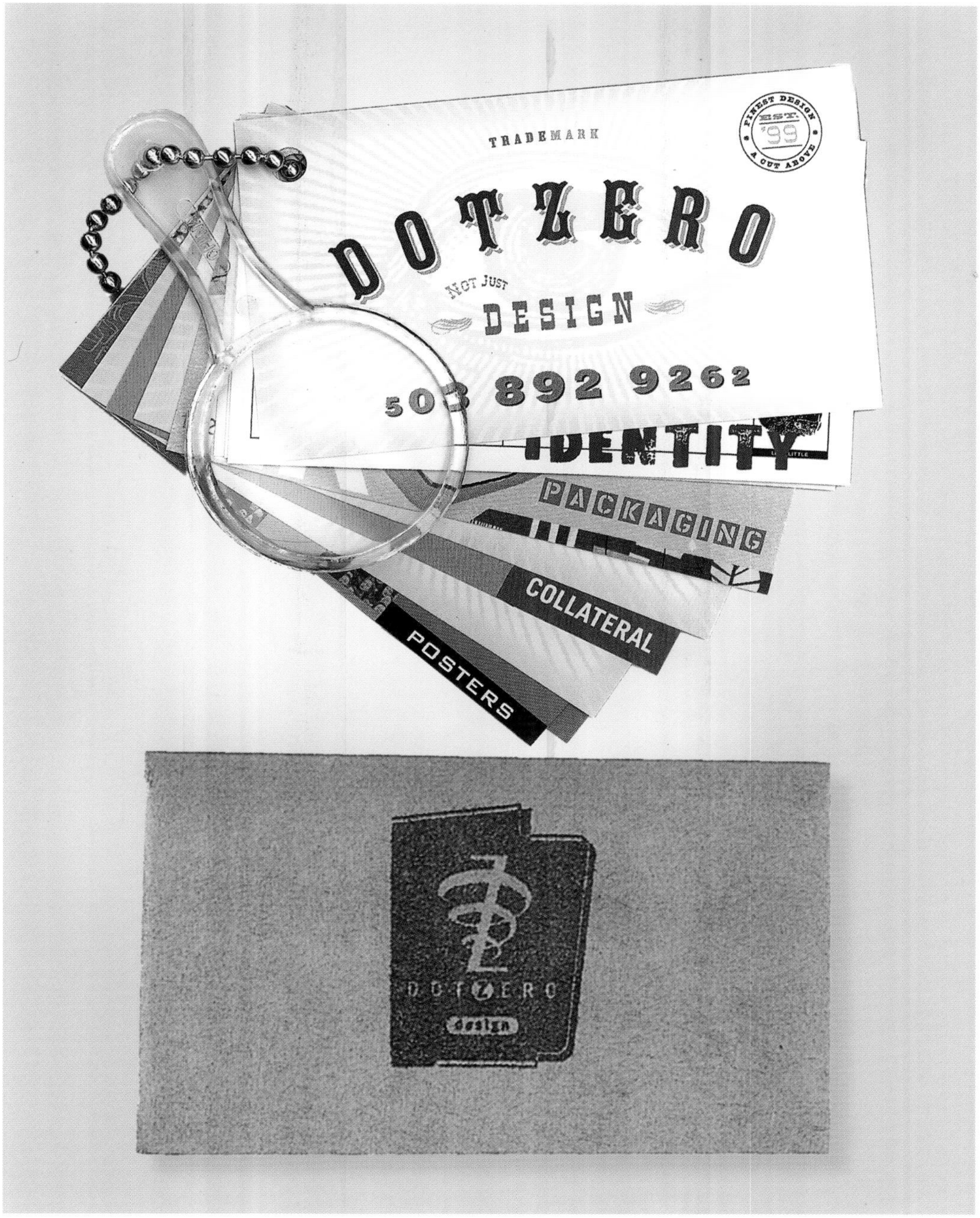

Dotzero Design — Portland, Oregon
Designers : Karen Wippich, Jon Wippich
Client : Dotzero Design

Roycroft Design – Boston, Massachusetts
Designer : Jennifer Roycroft
Client : Roycroft Design

IE Design + Communications – Hermosa Beach, California
Designer : Marcie Carson
Client : IE Design + Communications

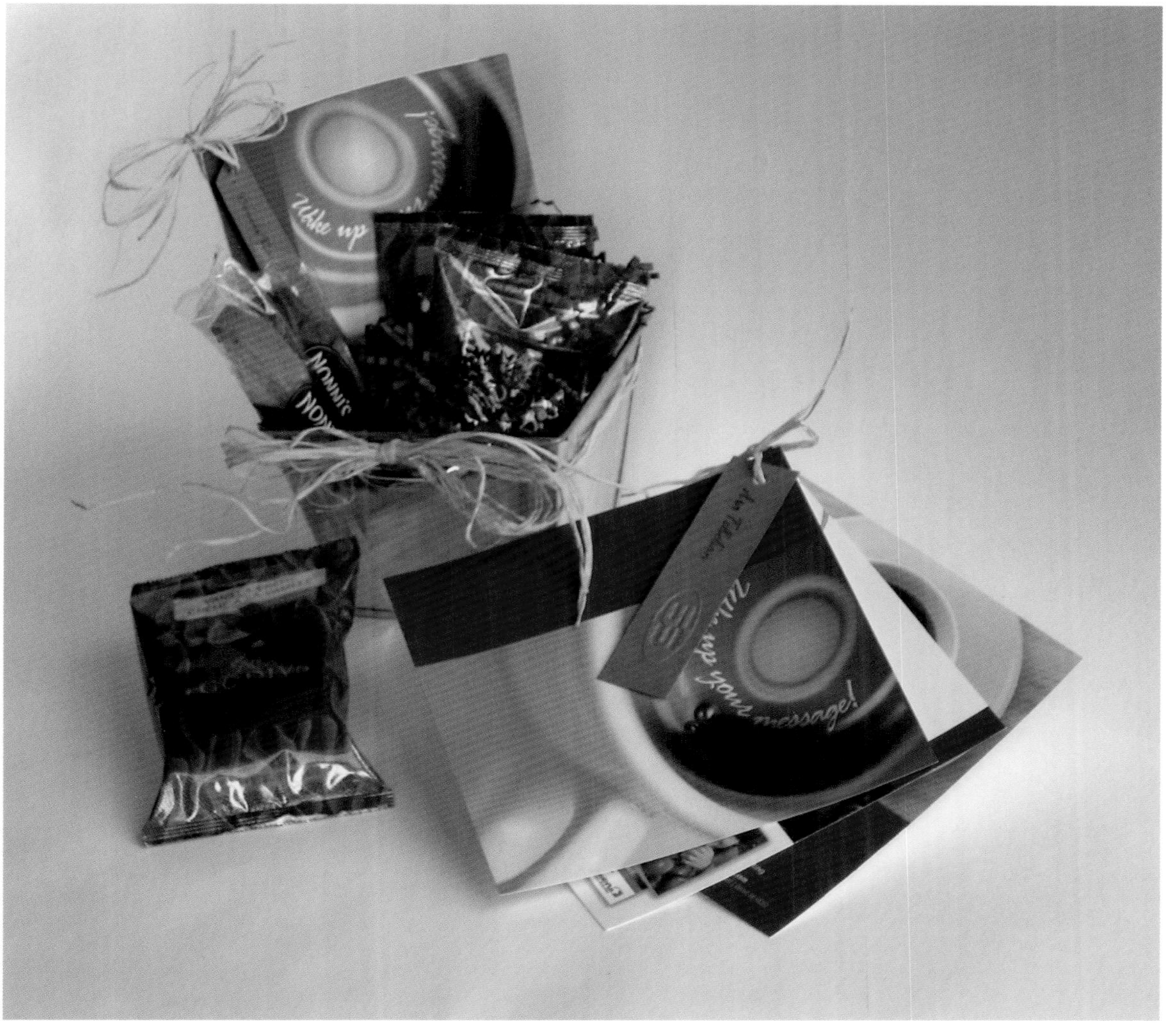

Group Fifty-Five Marketing – Detroit, Michigan
Designers : Heather Sowinski, Stacey Shires
Client : Group Fifty-Five Marketing

Anderson Design Group – Nashville, Tennessee
Designers : Wayne Brezinka, Emily Keafer, Kristi Carter Smith
Client : Paper Monkeys (a division of Anderson Design Group)

Thinking of you
It's not always hard
MARRIAGE.
To GROW...
to compromise.
Challenging each other
to become
BETTER PEOPLE.
Together,
taking stock in life...
DISCARDS
HIGH VOLTAGE
VACANT
There are no bad days.
GET WELL SOON!
TO MY EX,
I STILL
THINK
OF YOU...
Oh, the Places You'll Go!
Listen here...
you flat-hair, big-assed
Tupperware snatching wench!
Happy Birthday
GRAB YOUR BALLS

elf design, inc. – Belmont, California
Designer : Erin Ferree
Client : elf design, inc.

Michael Doret Graphic Design – Hollywood, California
Designer : Michael Doret
Client : Alphabet Soup Type Founders

Striking graphics and colors are the very personality of this piece. No gradient or shading was used, but there's an undeniable visual energy created by the design —a valuable lesson for photo manipulation addicts.

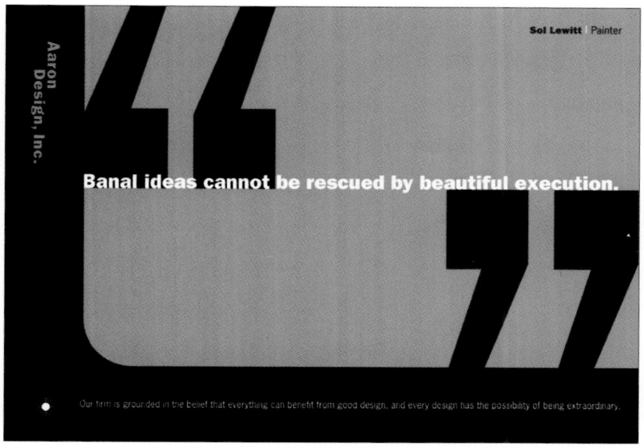
Aaron Design, Inc.
Sol Lewitt | Painter
Banal ideas cannot be rescued by beautiful execution.
Our firm is grounded in the belief that everything can benefit from good design, and every design has the possibility of being extraordinary.

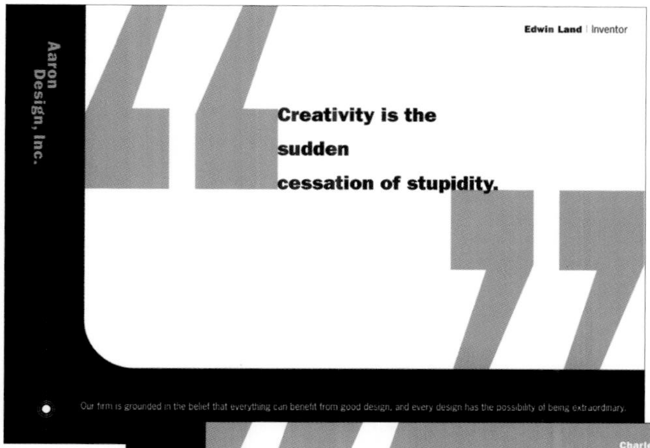
Aaron Design, Inc.
Edwin Land | Inventor
Creativity is the sudden cessation of stupidity.
Our firm is grounded in the belief that everything can benefit from good design, and every design has the possibility of being extraordinary.

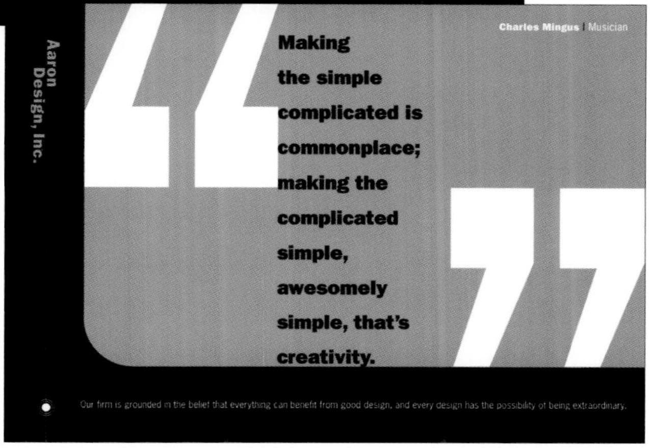
Aaron Design, Inc.
Charles Mingus | Musician
Making the simple complicated is commonplace; making the complicated simple, awesomely simple, that's creativity.
Our firm is grounded in the belief that everything can benefit from good design, and every design has the possibility of being extraordinary.

Aaron Design, Inc. – New York, New York
Designer : Stephanie Aaron
Client : Aaron Design, Inc.

Dotzero Design – Portland, Oregon
Designers : Karen Wippich, Jon Wippich
Client : Dotzero Design

It's All About . . .

Them

Promotions for Paying Clients

Factor Design – San Francisco, California
Designers : Tim Guy, Craig Williamson, Gabe Campodonico, Sandbox Studio
Client : Sandbox Studio

Arriving as printed flat sheets, these Chinese zodiac animals include basic instructions so anyone with a little patience can produce a fanciful work of art.

Curiosity Group – Portland, Oregon
Designers : Yvonne Perez Emerson, Casey Burns
Client : HP Activity Center

Curiosity Group – Portland, Oregon
Designers : Ada Mayer, Sean Garrison, Robb Sturtcman, Nate Currie
Client : HP/Dreamworks

Joven Orozco Design – Newport Beach, California
Designers : Joven Orozco, Kenneth Lim
Client : El Rey Theatre

Srijan Advertising – Indore, India
Designers : Nitin Sarkar, Pranav
Client : Naidunia News & Networks

Hindustan Ka Dil
Hamare Paas Hai
THE HEART IS WITH US.
After sequential success sagas of Raipur & Bilaspur launches, the historical Jabalpur launch has made our profound presence in 'Dil of Hindustan'.
NaiDunia, the most trusted and honored media brand of Madhya Pradesh & Chhattisgarh, now has an expanded readership base too.
WE COVER M.P. - C.G. 100%
नईदुनिया
• INDORE • GWALIOR • JABALPUR • RAIPUR • BILASPUR • BHOPAL •
NaiDunia News & Network Pvt. Ltd., 60/1, Babu Labhchand Chhajlani Marg, Indore (M.P.) - 452 009
Tel.: 0731-2763111-14, 3011000, E-mail: response@naidunia.com www.naidunia.com

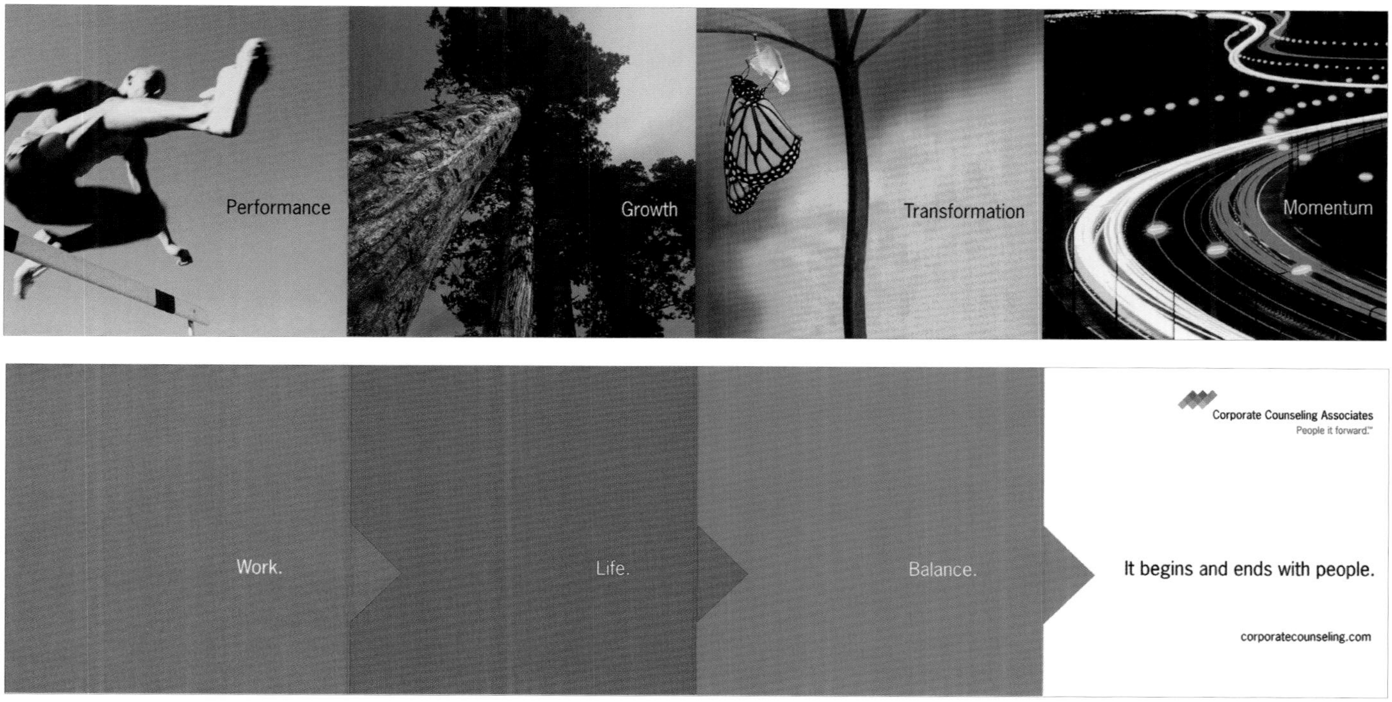
Performance
Growth
Transformation
Momentum
Corporate Counseling Associates
People it forward.™
Work.
Life.
Balance.
It begins and ends with people.
corporatecounseling.com

BBMG – New York, New York
Designers : Mitch Baranowski, Scott Ketchum, Maria Marromatis
Client : Corporate Counseling Associates

Karoo Design – Hampshire, England
Designer : Danelle Macaulay

Associating an iconic image (brick) with the business of a client (property development) is a powerful marketing tool. Taking the concept an impressive extra step is offering a brick that opens to reveal valuable information.

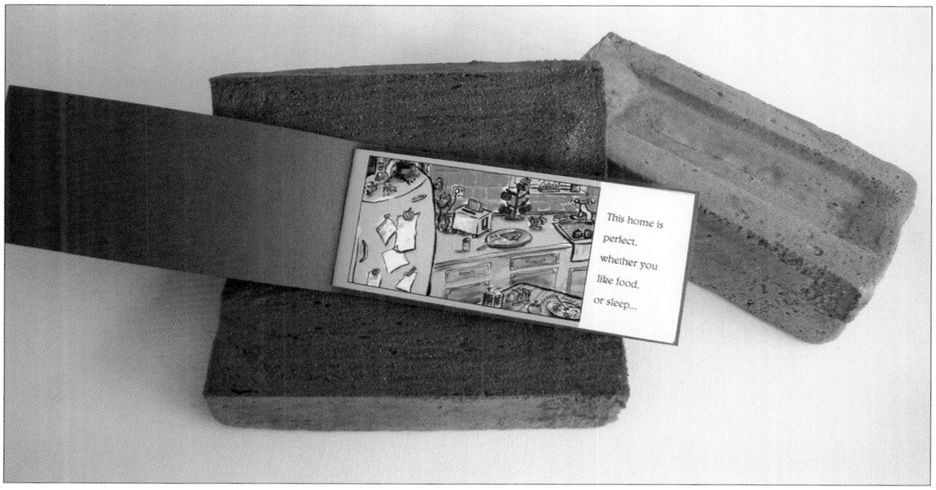

An In-Depth Look at: PRO TEC INTERNATIONAL

When it comes to playing music, the clarinet isn't exactly rock and roll. That's why PRO TEC, a musical instrument equipment manufacturer in Fullerton, California, introduced the Dolce Amaro sisters for a line of instrument cases for girls who reject the image of classical music as all drawing rooms and dullness.

PRO TEC's vice president, Christina Oh, found inspiration at a department store. "I was in a group exhibition of Asian-Pacific artists at Nordstrom," says designer Grace Chen, who heads Oakland-based design firm Softpill. "Christina saw it and found me that way." Oh not only licensed the characters and dubbed the trio the Dolce Amaro sisters—"bittersweet" in Italian—but worked with Chen to create a story based on their own experiences as would-be child prodigies.

"I used to play music as well, and we talked about how we're both victims of parental instigation," Chen says. Oh designed the bags—which feature a pattern reading, "I play the way I do because I can"—for young kids, which, due to the nature of the instruments themselves, most often strike a chord with budding female musicians. "Those instruments—violin, flute, and clarinet—are the most popular ones with girls, and most of the time the lessons are instigated by their parents. We're playing off that sentiment—semi-not-so-sweet characters."

Oh reviewed Chen's portfolio and selected her band from about twenty characters, then worked with Chen to make musicians out of the trio. "Usually companies want me to draw more positive, smiling, wholesome characters, and this was different. I didn't do the traditional classical music poses," says Chen of her characters, Clara (clarinet), Fiona (flute), and Viola (violin), diminutive females with wicked attitudes and candy-colored hair that would make even the freewheeling Mozart envious. "The [PRO TEC] site says that the girls 'prefer jam sessions to lessons and like to perform the classics from Bach to rock,' but you can tell from their expressions that there's something else going on. Especially the one playing clarinet—*Oh, do I really have to?* She's kind of dragging it."

Girls aren't the only ones who identify with the sisters' mixed emotions about music, torn between dutiful practice and soulful, joyous playing. "I'm told that a lot of guys like the bags but because there are girls on the bags, they're hesitant," says Chen. "So one day there may be Dolce Amaro brothers, or an animal."

Oh concurs. "I definitely started the Dolce Amaro sisters envisioning the possibility of growing the offering," she says. "I wanted to grow the girls to cover other instruments that are somewhat popular but less common for girls—such as the trumpet and sax, percussion, guitar, bass—and I would love to do a line of characters that are kind of crazy and strong, funky, nonhuman, and non-instrument-specific."

"People are drawn to the product because of this particular product line and perhaps buy a more serious product from Protec," Chen says "and instrument bags are pretty boring. People often start playing when they're young, so it totally makes sense to cater to that. And growing up, I always had really cute bags."

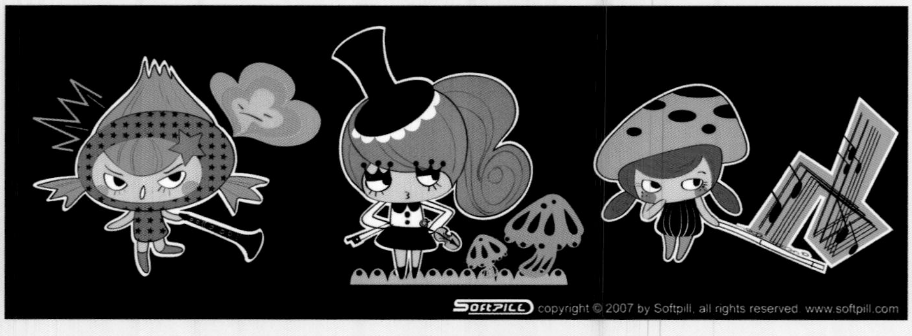

Softpill / PRO TEC International – Oakland, California
Designers: Grace Chen, Christina Oh (PRO TEC)
Client: PRO TEC International

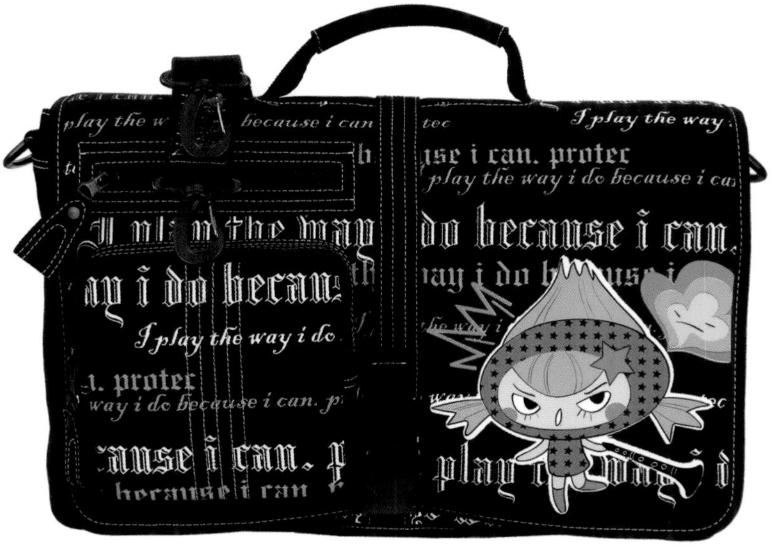
I play the way i do because i can.
ause i can. protec

I play the way i do because i can. protec

I play the way i do because i can.

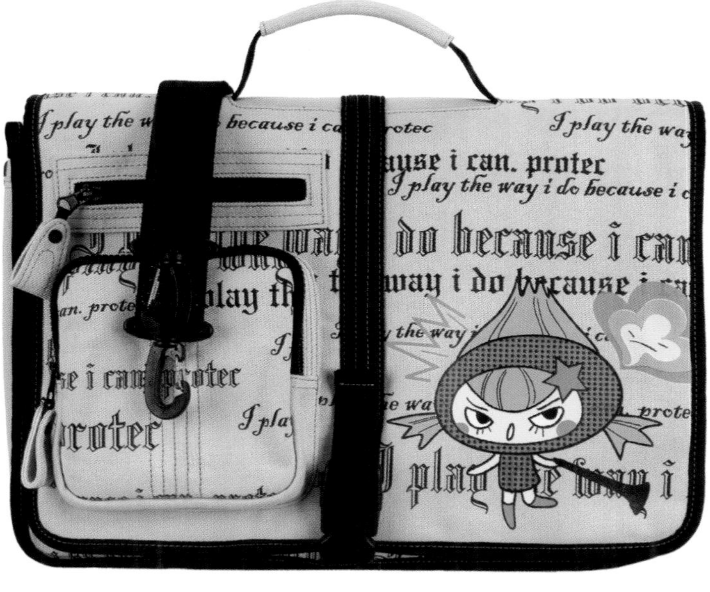
I play the way i do because i c
ause i can. protec

Hull Creative Group – Brookline, Massachusetts
Designers : Caryl H. Hull, Carol Thistle, Chris Klein, Sherman Morss, Pat King Powers, Nicole L. Vecchiotti
Client : Boston Harbor Island Alliance

Studio QED, Inc. – San Mateo, California
Designer : Steven Wright
Client : Square Soft

Anderson Design Group, Inc. – Nashville, Tennessee
Designer : Joel Anderson
Client : Spirit of Nashville

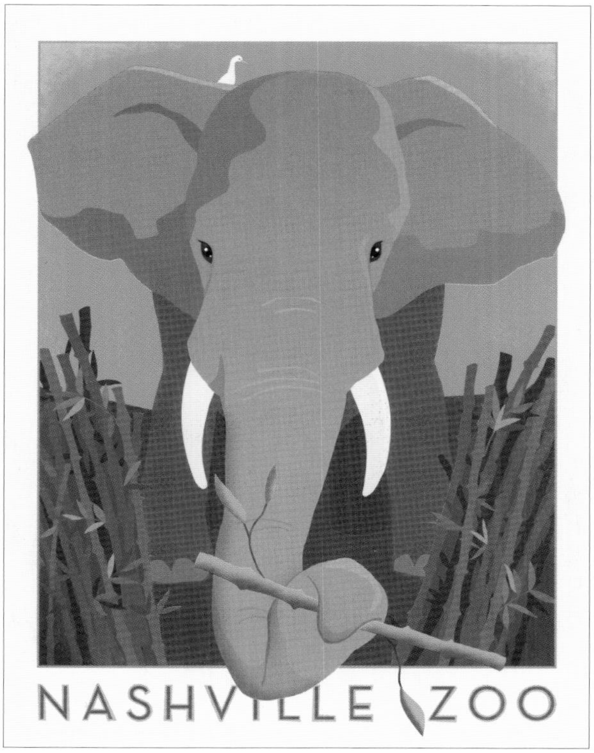

The illustrations in this campaign each break the border of its respective poster—even if only implied, as in the case of the giraffe. This technique adds visual interest and suggests the animals, and their spirit, are too big to contain.

Liquid Pixel Studio – Las Vegas, Nevada
Designer : Yana Beylinson
Client : theispot.com

Leibold Associates, Inc. – Neenah, Wisconsin
Designers : Therese Joanis, Greg Madson, Jason Konz
Client : Hills of Hackberry

FIELDturf
of Nevada
HISTORY
PRODUCTS & INSTALLATION
WARRANTY
GOLF
RESIDENTIAL APPLICATIONS
COMMERCIAL APPLICATIONS
LOOKS LIKE GRASS...
FEELS LIKE GRASS...
PLAYS LIKE GRASS.®

This is a one-piece, accordion-fold brochure. The panel widths widen with each graduated fold, leaving several edges on both sides which can be treated as tabs and printed with topic titles.

Sutton Watkins Advertising – Las Vegas, Nevada
Designers : Jennifer Green, Shari Sutton
Client : Field Turf of Nevada

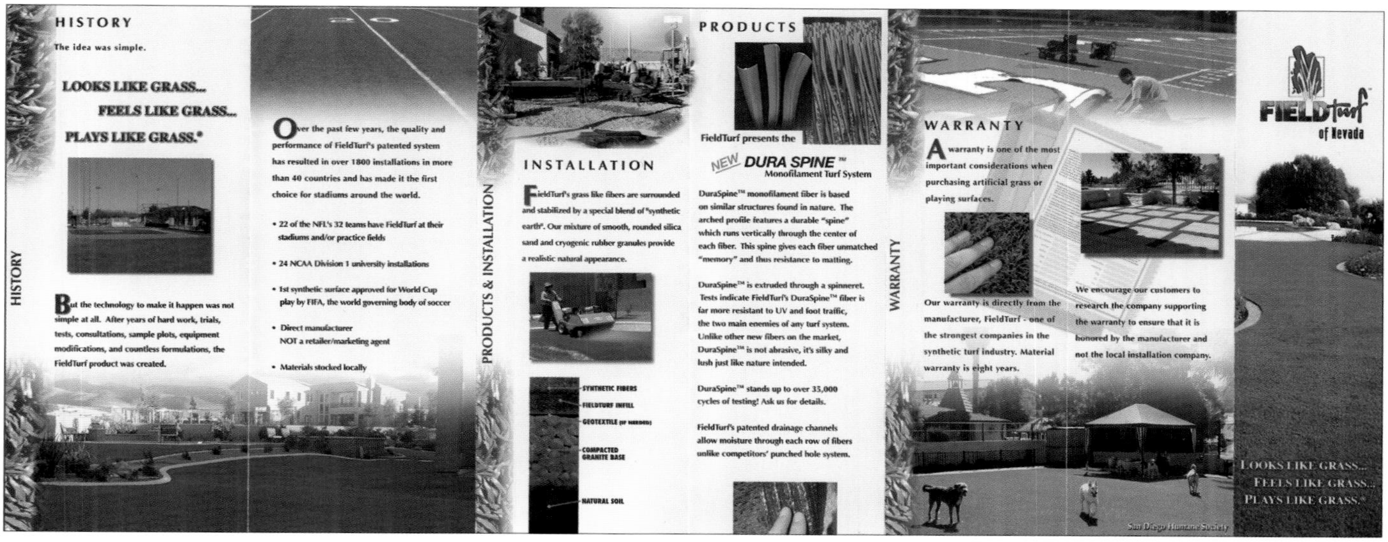
HISTORY
The idea was simple.
LOOKS LIKE GRASS...
FEELS LIKE GRASS...
PLAYS LIKE GRASS.®
But the technology to make it happen was not simple at all. After years of hard work, trials, tests, consultations, sample plots, equipment modifications, and countless formulations, the FieldTurf product was created.
Over the past few years, the quality and performance of FieldTurf's patented system has resulted in over 1800 installations in more than 40 countries and has made it the first choice for stadiums around the world.
• 22 of the NFL's 32 teams have FieldTurf at their stadiums and/or practice fields
• 24 NCAA Division 1 university installations
• 1st synthetic surface approved for World Cup play by FIFA, the world governing body of soccer
• Direct manufacturer NOT a retailer/marketing agent
• Materials stocked locally
PRODUCTS & INSTALLATION
INSTALLATION
FieldTurf's grass like fibers are surrounded and stabilized by a special blend of "synthetic earth". Our mixture of smooth, rounded silica sand and cryogenic rubber granules provide a realistic natural appearance.
SYNTHETIC FIBERS
FIELDTURF INFILL
GEOTEXTILE
COMPACTED GRANITE BASE
NATURAL SOIL
PRODUCTS
FieldTurf presents the
NEW DURA SPINE™
Monofilament Turf System
DuraSpine™ monofilament fiber is based on similar structures found in nature. The arched profile features a durable "spine" which runs vertically through the center of each fiber. This spine gives each fiber unmatched "memory" and thus resistance to matting.
DuraSpine™ is extruded through a spinneret. Tests indicate FieldTurf's DuraSpine™ fiber is far more resistant to UV and foot traffic, the two main enemies of any turf system. Unlike other new fibers on the market, DuraSpine™ is not abrasive, it's silky and lush just like nature intended.
DuraSpine™ stands up to over 35,000 cycles of testing! Ask us for details.
FieldTurf's patented drainage channels allow moisture through each row of fibers unlike competitors' punched hole system.
WARRANTY
A warranty is one of the most important considerations when purchasing artificial grass or playing surfaces.
Our warranty is directly from the manufacturer, FieldTurf - one of the strongest companies in the synthetic turf industry. Material warranty is eight years.
We encourage our customers to research the company supporting the warranty to ensure that it is honored by the manufacturer and not the local installation company.
San Diego Humane Society
FIELDturf
of Nevada
LOOKS LIKE GRASS...
FEELS LIKE GRASS...
PLAYS LIKE GRASS.®

A Turf for all Reasons and all Seasons
COMMERCIAL APPLICATIONS
Step on a FieldTurf of Nevada installation and you'll feel the future of synthetic grass is right at your feet.
Only FieldTurf's patented formulation, construction and installation method succeeds in emulating natural grass. FieldTurf is the ideal alternative to real grass in commercial projects because of the ability to integrate it with natural plant material and hardscapes.
Commercial applications include daycare centers, shopping centers, hotels and resorts, master planned communities, golf course communities, animal shelters, sports parks, athletic fields, high-profile golf courses and surrounding landscape designs within amusement parks and major resorts around the country.
School Playground
Resort Installation
COMMERCIAL APPLICATIONS
RESIDENTIAL APPLICATIONS
FieldTurf is the best low-maintenance and no-water-use alternative to natural lawns and xeriscaping. It's a great alternative for the big and little kids in your family!
BENEFITS
• Saves money
Low maintenance, no watering, mowing or chemicals needed.
• Provides a non-abrasive playing environment
• Enhanced durability
Through a wide range of temperatures
Turf Supplier for:
Pulte Homes KB Homes Centex Homes Lennar Homes
just to name a few!
RESIDENTIAL APPLICATIONS
GOLF
The Natural Approach to Synthetic Turf
Constructed into patterns to simulate natural turf, FieldTurf provides a surface that duplicates the playing conditions of natural turf but eliminates high maintenance and labor costs.
Putting Greens
FieldTurf putting greens have a natural bent-grass playing surface that are installed with the contours and true roll of a professional green. Each blade of FieldTurf emerges from our unique infill just as real grass emerges from the soil. FieldTurf feels like the earth beneath your feet. It is the ultimate all-weather surface with maximum drainage and perfect playability, regardless of season or weather conditions. Field Turf looks, feels and plays like natural grass.
Tour Turf by FieldTurf is the official synthetic Golf turf or both the PGA TOUR and Champions Tour.
GOLF
FIELDturf
of Nevada
Nevada Contractors License #0058117
FieldTurf specializes in the sales and installation of synthetic grass for use in residential and commercial applications and in the design and construction of putting greens, driving ranges, tee lines, cart paths and any other golf applications.
Phone (702) 889-TURF (8873)
Fax: (702) 253-9570
www.fieldturfofnevada.com
www.fieldturf.com

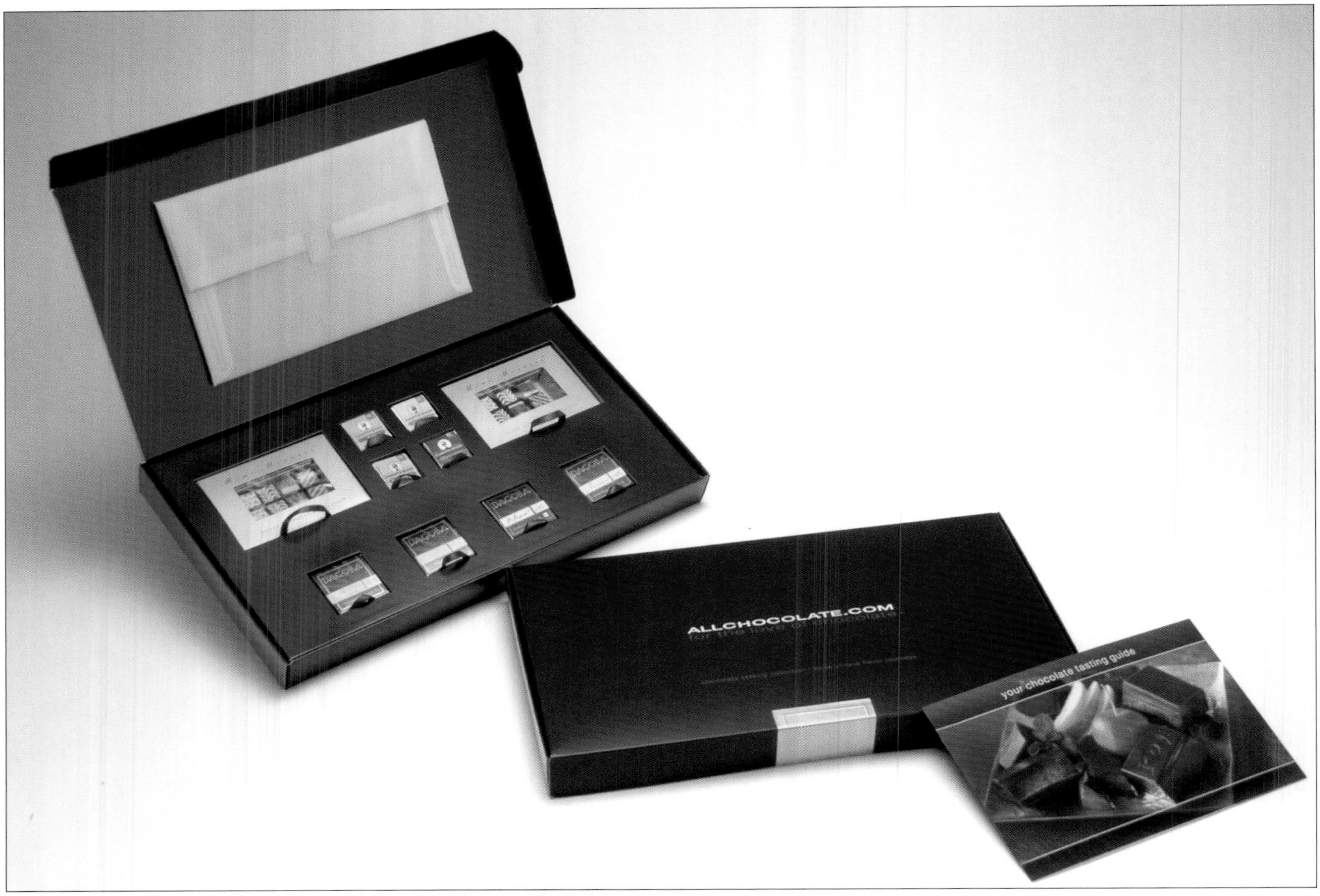

JPL Productions – Harrisburg, Pennsylvania
Designer : Katy Jacobs
Client : The Hershey Company

MiresBall – San Diego, California
Designers : Scott Mires, Gale Spitzley, Bil Zelman, Holly Houk
Client : Taylor Guitars

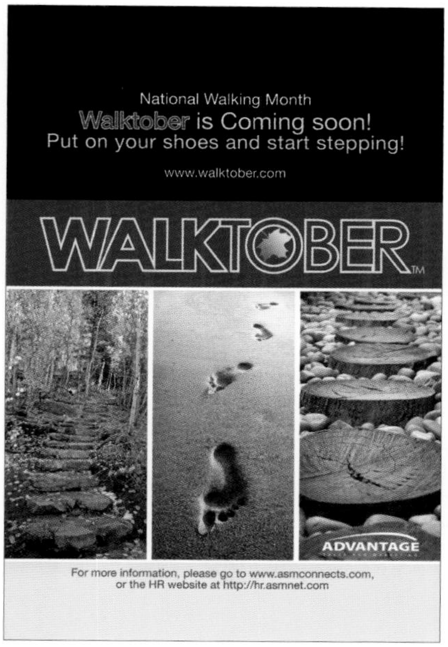
National Walking Month
Walktober is Coming soon!
Put on your shoes and start stepping!
www.walktober.com
WALKTOBER
ADVANTAGE
For more information, please go to www.asmconnects.com,
or the HR website at http://hr.asmnet.com

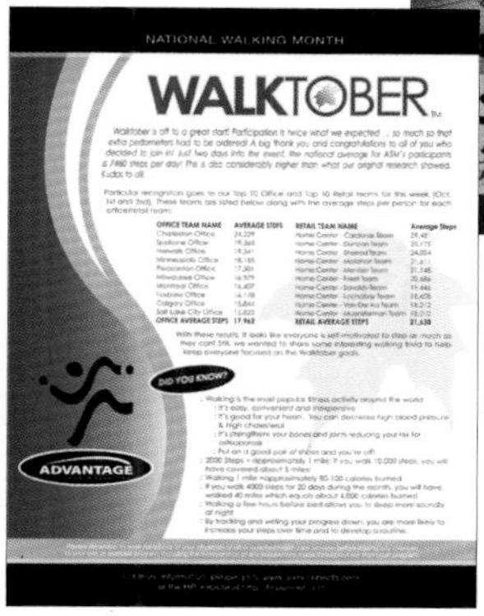
NATIONAL WALKING MONTH
WALKTOBER
DID YOU KNOW?
ADVANTAGE

National Walking Month
ASM
WALKTOBER
2007
Begins Today, October 1st
START STEPPING TODAY!
CONGRATULATIONS TO YOU FOR TAKING AN ACTIVE ROLE IN YOUR FITNESS ACTIVITY LEVEL!

National Walking Month
WALKTOBER
is Coming soon!
Put on your shoes and start stepping!
ADVANTAGE
Advantage Sales and Marketing will be participating in Walktober.
RECEIVE A FREE PEDOMETER WHEN YOU REGISTER.
For more information, please go to www.asmconnects.com,
or the HR website at http://hr.asmnet.com
www.walktober.com

Urban Geko, Inc. – Newport Beach, California
Designer : Monique LeFrancois
Client : Advantage Sales and Marketing

Hansen Design Group – Woodruff, South Carolina
Designers : Sandy Hansen, Ed Zeigler, Paula Angermeier
Client : Craig Gaulden Davis

A completely black cover and band wrap can still offer texture and dimension with black foil stamping and suede-like stock.

top drawer

Sol Design Group – Sacramento, California
Designer : Kelly Cooper Kwoka
Client : Fromthefarm.com

Theyhatemydesign Studio – Yogyakarta, Indonesia
Designers : Theyhatemydesign Studio Team
Client : TOC Shop

Hatch Design – San Francisco, California
Designers : Katie Jain, Joel Templin, Ryan Meis, Lisa Pemrick
Client : AIGA Minnesota

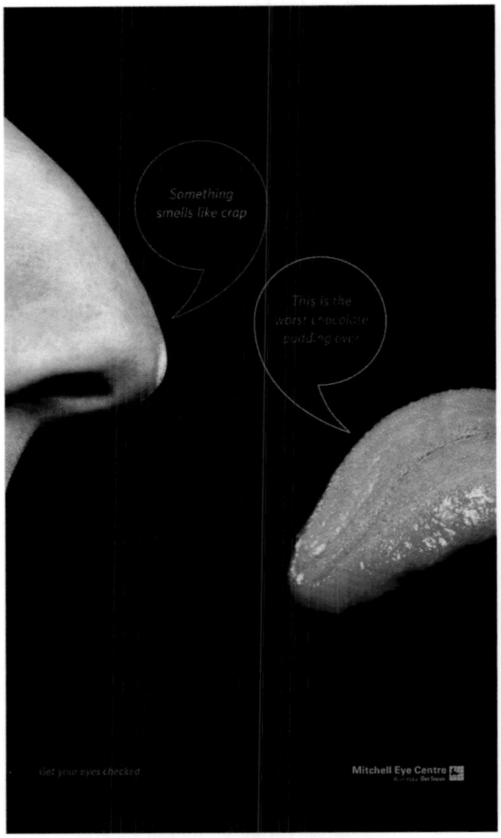
Something smells like crap
This is the worst chocolate pudding ever
Get your eyes checked
Mitchell Eye Centre

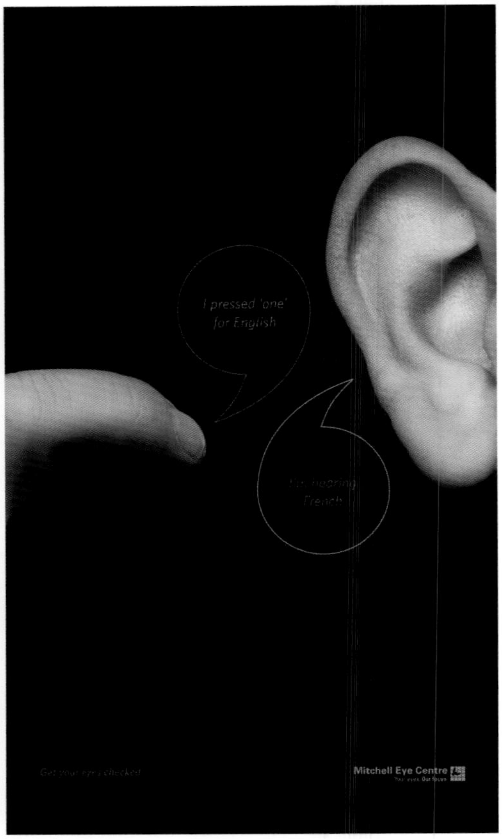
I pressed 'one' for English
Mitchell Eye Centre

WAX – Calgary, Canada
Client : Mitchell Eye Centre

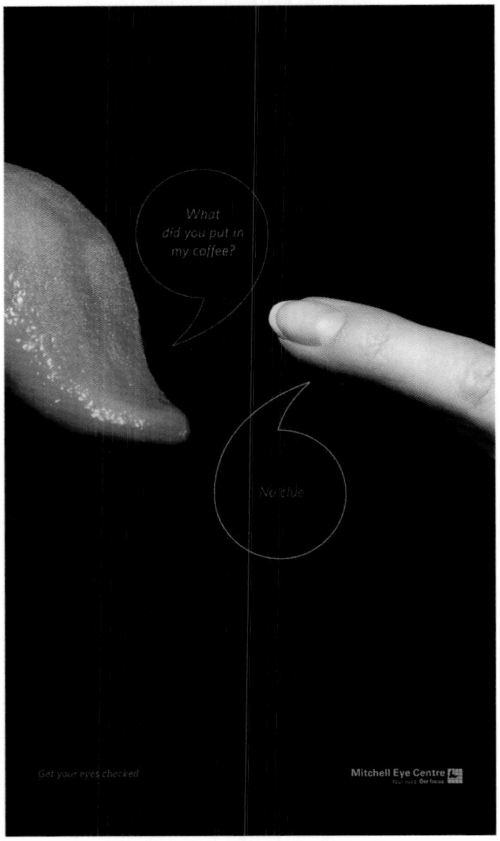
What did you put in my coffee?
No clue
Get your eyes checked
Mitchell Eye Centre

5
Φεστιβάλ
Φαντασίας
Θέρμης
6-7/01/07
ΔΙΑΡΚΕΙΑ 11.00 - 22.00
ΕΙΣΟΔΟΣ ΕΛΕΥΘΕΡΗ
Πολιτιστικό
Κέντρο
Θέρμης
ΤΟΥΡΝΟΥΑ RPG WESTERN: GUN TALE
ΕΠΙΣΗΜΟ ΤΟΥΡΝΟΥΑ MAGIC the GATHERING
ΕΠΙΣΗΜΟ ΤΟΥΡΝΟΥΑ YU-GI-OH!
ΕΠΙΤΡΑΠΕΖΙΑ ΠΑΙΧΝΙΔΙΑ
και άλλα...
rpg_thermi@yahoo.gr

Elixirion – Thessaloniki, Greece
Designers : Michael Sachpazis, Konstantinos Petridis
Client : Liquid Fire Team

Design Management RUFFNEKK Oy – Espoo, Finland
Designer : Mikko Mäkelä
Client : Nokia's Annual Mobile Rules! 2007 Competition

Printed on a transparency to give the impresson of an actual X-ray, the viewer is immediately cued to a healthcare connection.

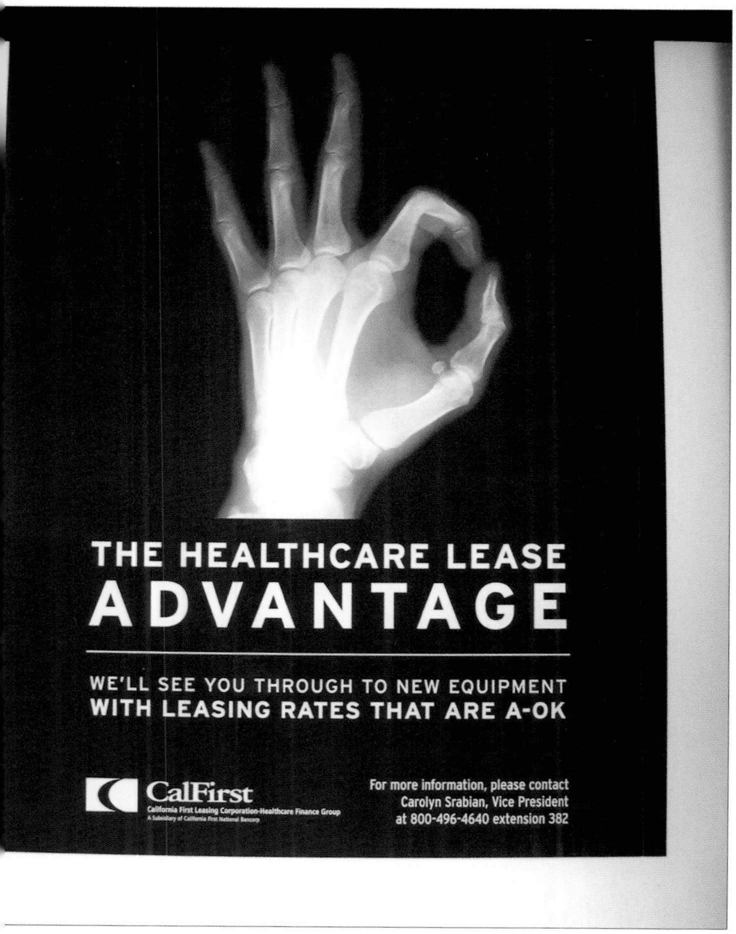

Viadesign – Espoo, Finland
Designers : Scott Pacheco, Stephan Donche
Client : CalFirst Leasing

Drive your sales...
AND MAKE THE GREEN!
HealthPlus
Get Maximum Distance with HealthPlus!
Titleist
THE FEEL GOOD GOLF BALL

Group Fifty-Five Marketing – Detroit, Michigan
Designers : Heather Sowinski, Stacey Shires
Client : HealthPlus of Michigan

Get A Clue Design – Hickory, North Carolina
Designer : Matt Pfahlert
Client : Tony Margherita Management

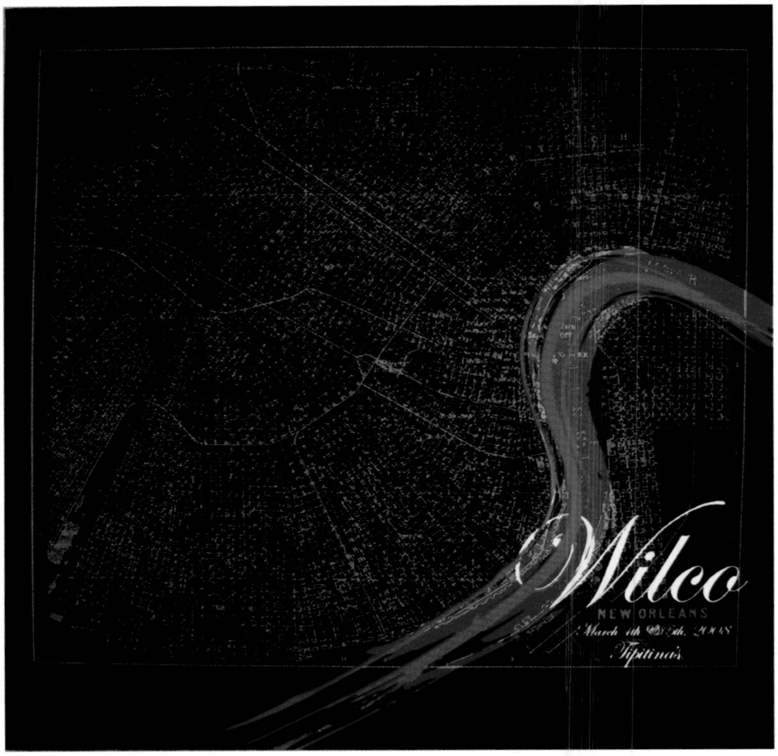
Wilco
NEW ORLEANS

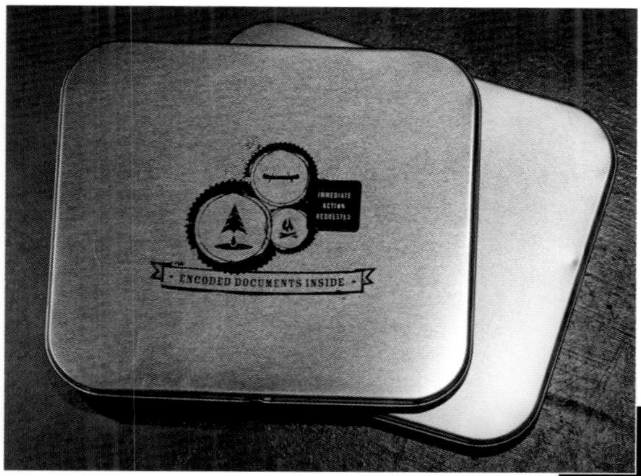
ENCODED DOCUMENTS INSIDE

pierpoint design + branding – Spokane, Washington
Designers : Jesse Pierpoint, Erin Wenz, Jesica Vestal, Jesse Scheller
Client : Kootenai Kids Camp

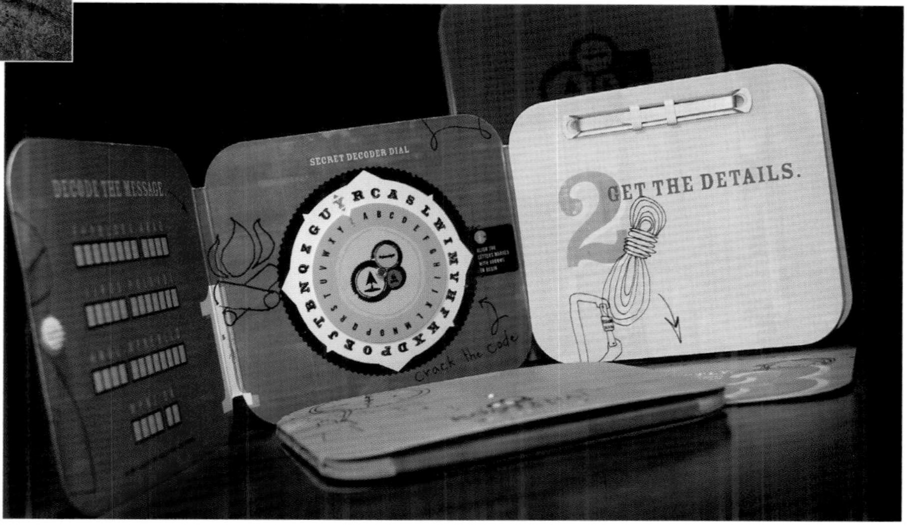
DECODE THE MESSAGE
SECRET DECODER DIAL
crack the code
2
GET THE DETAILS.

Leibold Associates, Inc. – Neenah, Wisconsin
Designers : Chad Fulwiler, Jane Oliver, Nick Maggio
Client : J.J. Keller & Associates, Inc.

NAVIGATE the compliance Roadway
Angela,
join me for lunch
and I'll show you
how I can guide
your way.
BRENDA JOACHIM
J. J. Keller & Associates, Inc.
Since 1953
I will call you
to learn more
about your program.
ANGELA
is your program
100% COMPLIANT?
J. J. Keller's Business Services
Will Get You On The Right Path.

JUMPIN' JUICE & JAVA
the hippest drinks on earth
Jumpin' Juice & Java
26676 #E Portola Pkwy
Foothill Ranch, CA 92610
(949) 916-3555
In the Staples shopping center,
next to Out of the Bleu
Try our
"Pink Passion"
Smoothie!
Also Enjoy:
~ Free WIFI ~ Newspapers ~ Work/study space ~ Games for the kids ~ Flat Screen TVs ~

JUMPIN' JUICE & JAVA
the hippest drinks on earth
Now open in
Foothill Ranch!
Bring this card in and receive a FREE
coffee drink or fresh smoothie
with the purchase of one of equal
or lesser value.
Also Enjoy:
~ Free WIFI ~ Newspapers ~ Work/study space ~ Games for the kids ~ Flat Screen TVs ~

Urban Geko, Inc. – Newport Beach, California
Designer : Reza Widjaja
Client : Jumpin Java

Jill Lynn Design – Atlanta, Georgia
Designer : Jill Anderson
Client : Claudia Colombo

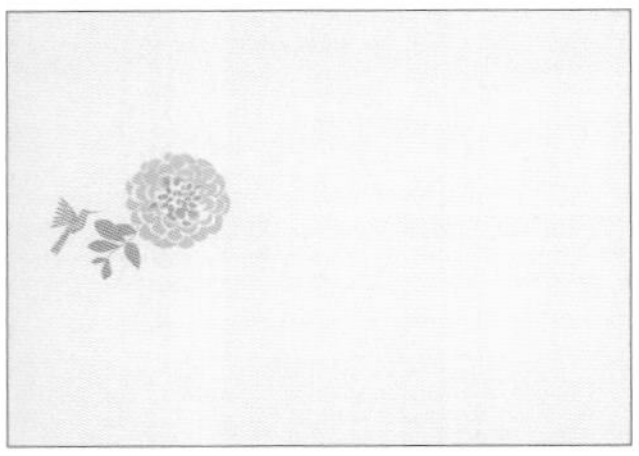

Claudia Colombo &
Franco Monteleone

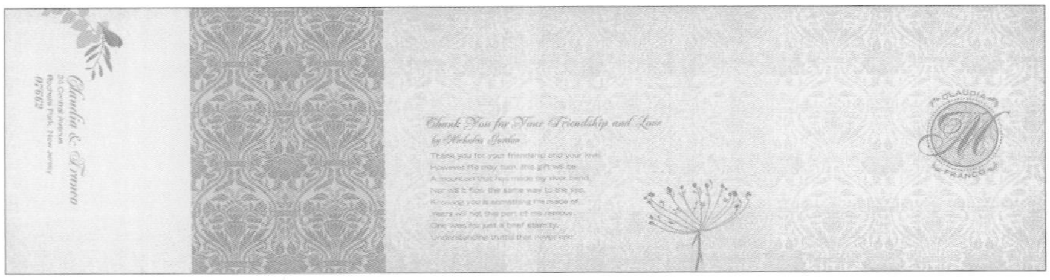

Thank You

A simple bag becomes elegant with a foil-stamped initial cap.

Crawford Design — Chagrin Falls, Ohio
Designer : Alison Crawford
Client : Simply Charming

Get A Clue Design – Hickory, North Carolina
Designer : Matt Pfahlert
Client : Superfly Productions

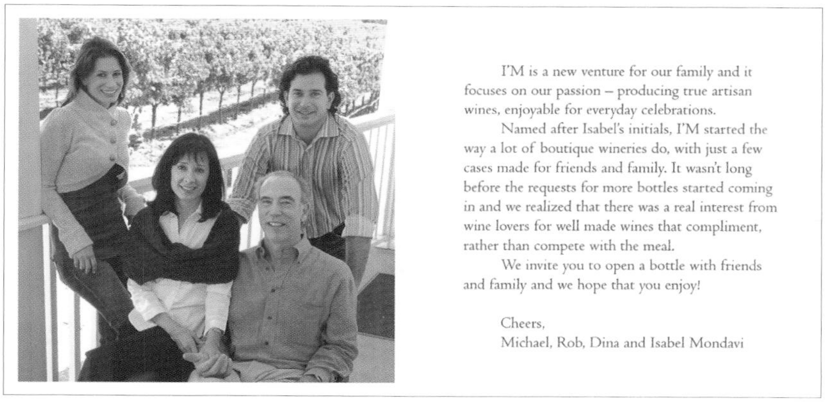
I'M is a new venture for our family and it focuses on our passion – producing true artisan wines, enjoyable for everyday celebrations.
Named after Isabel's initials, I'M started the way a lot of boutique wineries do, with just a few cases made for friends and family. It wasn't long before the requests for more bottles started coming in and we realized that there was a real interest from wine lovers for well made wines that compliment, rather than compete with the meal.
We invite you to open a bottle with friends and family and we hope that you enjoy!
Cheers,
Michael, Rob, Dina and Isabel Mondavi

OUR WINERY & VINEYARDS
We believe first and foremost that great wine starts in the vineyard. The fruit for I'M is sourced from our family's Napa vineyards and from respected growers that our family has longstanding relationships with in Sonoma and Willamette Valley, Oregon.
The wine is made as close as possible to the vineyard sites, allowing for gentle transportation and handling to ensure high quality production. The Rosé and Chardonnay are made at the Folio Winemakers' Studio in Carneros, Napa Valley, and the Pinot Noir is made at the Scott Paul Winery in Willamette Valley, Oregon.

Kendra Spencer Design – Sonoma, California
Designer : Kendra Spencer
Client : Folio Fine Wine Partners

Urban Geko, Inc. – Newport Beach, California
Designer : Reza Widjaja
Client : PJ's Travel

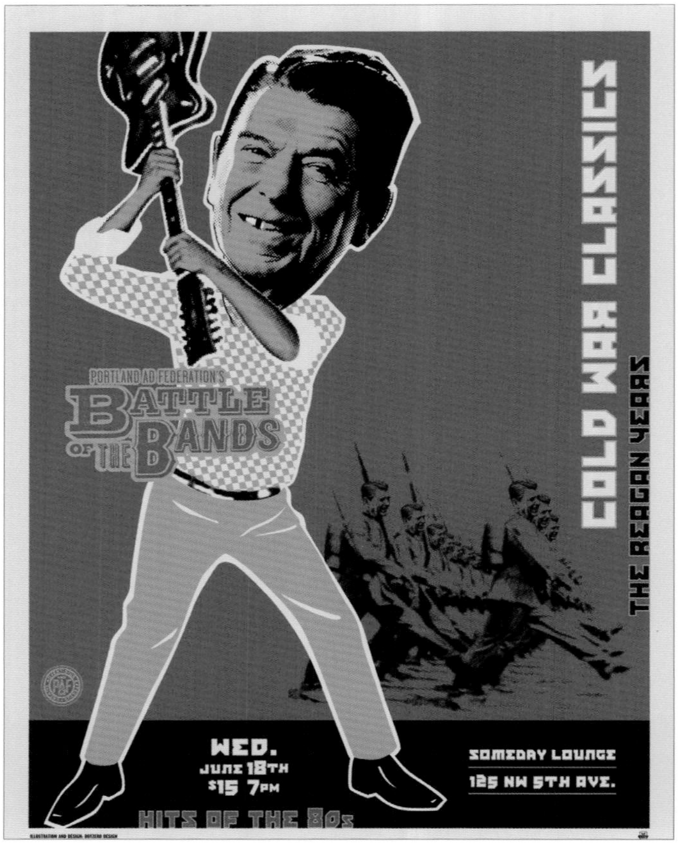

Dotzero Design – Portland, Oregon
Designers : Karen Wippich, Jon Wippich, Mike Terry
Client : Portland PAF

Sue Todd Illustration – Toronto, Canada
Designer : Sue Todd
Client : Waterloo Busker Carnival, City of Waterloo, Ontario

A Grand Opening So Special,
We're Giving You An Ice Cold Introduction.
GET READY FOR A HEAPING HELPING OF FOOD & FUN AT HOME BANK'S GRAND OPENING CELEBRATION, THURSDAY, SEPTEMBER 28.
We're Really Cooking In Crowley
Home HB Bank
REGISTER TO WIN A CAJUN GRILL / MUSIC BY BON VIE / COMEDIAN STEVE SHAW
GUEST CHEFS PATRICK MOULD & JOHN GREENE / GREAT FOOD & ICE COLD BEER
Join us for our grand opening, we promise, you'll be cooking, dancing, winning and laughing — all the way to the bank.
THURSDAY, SEPTEMBER 28 / 5:00PM-8:00PM / 204 N. PARKERSON AVENUE / CROWLEY, LA
FDIC

A Grand Opening So Special,
It's Bringing Tears To Our Eyes.
GET READY FOR A HEAPING HELPING OF FOOD & FUN AT HOME BANK'S GRAND OPENING CELEBRATION, THURSDAY, SEPTEMBER 28.
We're Really Cooking In Crowley
Home HB Bank
REGISTER TO WIN A CAJUN GRILL / MUSIC BY BON VIE / COMEDIAN STEVE SHAW
GUEST CHEFS PATRICK MOULD & JOHN GREENE / GREAT FOOD & ICE COLD BEER
Join us for our grand opening, we promise, you'll be cooking, dancing, winning and laughing — all the way to the bank.
THURSDAY, SEPTEMBER 28 / 5:00PM-8:00PM / 204 N. PARKERSON AVENUE / CROWLEY, LA
FDIC

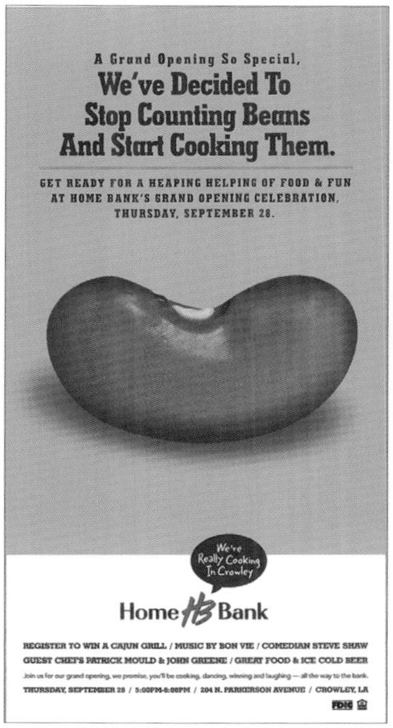
A Grand Opening So Special,
We've Decided To Stop Counting Beans And Start Cooking Them.
GET READY FOR A HEAPING HELPING OF FOOD & FUN AT HOME BANK'S GRAND OPENING CELEBRATION, THURSDAY, SEPTEMBER 28.
We're Really Cooking In Crowley
Home HB Bank
REGISTER TO WIN A CAJUN GRILL / MUSIC BY BON VIE / COMEDIAN STEVE SHAW
GUEST CHEFS PATRICK MOULD & JOHN GREENE / GREAT FOOD & ICE COLD BEER
Join us for our grand opening, we promise, you'll be cooking, dancing, winning and laughing — all the way to the bank.
THURSDAY, SEPTEMBER 28 / 5:00PM-8:00PM / 204 N. PARKERSON AVENUE / CROWLEY, LA
FDIC

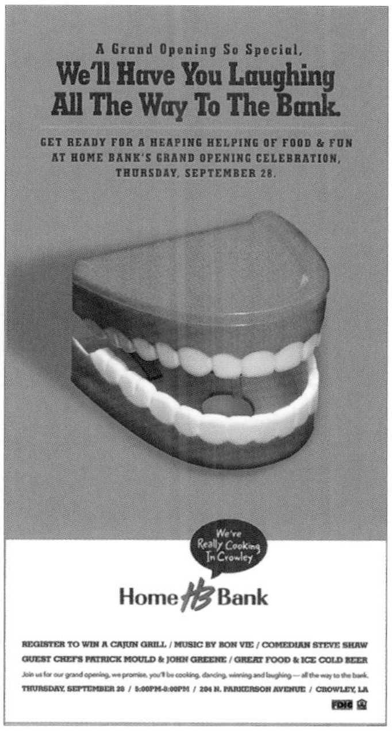
A Grand Opening So Special,
We'll Have You Laughing All The Way To The Bank.
GET READY FOR A HEAPING HELPING OF FOOD & FUN AT HOME BANK'S GRAND OPENING CELEBRATION, THURSDAY, SEPTEMBER 28.
We're Really Cooking In Crowley
Home HB Bank
REGISTER TO WIN A CAJUN GRILL / MUSIC BY BON VIE / COMEDIAN STEVE SHAW
GUEST CHEFS PATRICK MOULD & JOHN GREENE / GREAT FOOD & ICE COLD BEER
THURSDAY, SEPTEMBER 28 / 5:00PM-8:00PM / 204 N. PARKERSON AVENUE / CROWLEY, LA
FDIC

BBR Creative – Lafayette, Louisiana
Designers : Cathi Pavy, Maria Lambert
Client : Home Bank

If someone gives you a set of chattering teeth, your last reaction is to regard the giver as stuffy or unapproachable. This bank obviously wants to let its community know that it is a friendly, welcoming (maybe even fun!) organization.

Direct from Saks
SPECIAL DELIVERY
This just in: over $100 million of new shipments delivered directly from Saks Fifth Avenue at total savings of up to
80% off
Sale begins Wednesday, February 20
Saks Fifth Avenue
OFF 5TH
You Get What You Give
Take 25% off an entire purchase for you and three friends
Hands on the Spring Trends
For Men
Graphic Tees
Classic Polos
Denim
Sunglasses
Woven Shirts
MysteryMoney
Thank You
Note with a
Twist...
30% off any one
Wednesday, February
to Sunday, February

Market Demogra
Customer Profile
Our Purpose
Saks Style. Outlet Prices.
Direction
A little more Saks...
Saks Fifth Avenue
OFF 5TH

Saks Fifth Avenue
OFF 5TH
Saks Style. Outlet Prices

Graham Hanson Design – New York, New York
Designers : Graham Hanson, Dorothy Lin
Client : Saks Fifth Avenue Off 5th

Dotzero Design – Portland, Oregon
Designers : Karen Wippich, Jon Wippich
Client : Courtney Hamiester

Rule29 Creative, Inc. – Geneva, Illinois
Designers : Justin Ahrens, Kerri Liu, Kara Merrick, Brian MacDonald
Client : O'Neil Printing

Urban Geko, Inc. – Newport Beach, California
Designer : Reza Widjaja
Client : Aloha Glow

Corporate identity is created by consistently using the same logo, art, fonts, etc. in a variety of venues. This is a magnet for a business car door, but could easily be translated into a business card.

6
C
12.0
CHEMICAL BONDING
SPARKLING CITRUS + POWDERY SOFT
= a flirtatious alchemy
TOP: Smooth Citrus Cocktail, Tea, Blackberry
MIDDLE: Dewy Peony
BASE: Vetiver, Amber, Powdery Musk
C eau de parfum --- 2.5 OZ/75 ML
AFTER MY OWN HEART
After and before
Today and tomorrow
Sand becoming a wave
What was it I saw at the top of the world
as I fell asleep last night?
I recall putting lilacs in your dreams
You smiled in your sleep
I hear your words like the wind
whispering in my ear
the most enchanting words
after my own heart
BALMY DAYS & SUNDAYS
LYING FACE-UP TO THE SKY, dappled light flickering
THROUGH THE PALE GREEN
OF OVERHEAD BRANCHES
TOP: Freesia, Leafy Greens, Grass
MIDDLE: Honeysuckle, Rose, Mimosa
BASE: Chypre Accent, Musk
b
B eau de parfum --- 2.5 OZ/75 ML

Helena Seo Design – Sunnyvale, California
Designers : Helena Seo, Bill O'Such
Client : Ineke, LLC

Sayles Graphic Design – Des Moines, Iowa
Designer : John Sayles
Client : Des Moines Playhouse

PLAYHOUSE
DES MOINES PLAYHOUSE
ENTERTAINMENT
2 GO
THEATRE WORKSHOPS AND CLASSES
INSIDE
[FOR ALL AGES]
HOW TO VOLUNTEER
ACT NOW
PLAY YOUR PART
CALENDAR OF EVENTS
06 07
TICKET TO FUN!
The Best Christmas Pageant Ever
COMING SOON

Hull Creative Group – Brookline, Massachusetts
Designers : Caryl H. Hull, Carol Thistle, Chris Klein, Sherman Morss, Pat King Powers, Nicole L. Vecchiotti
Client : Boston Harbor Island Alliance

Los Alamos National Laboratory Creative Arts and Services – Los Alamos, New Mexico
Designer : Allen Hopkins
Client : Wellness Center

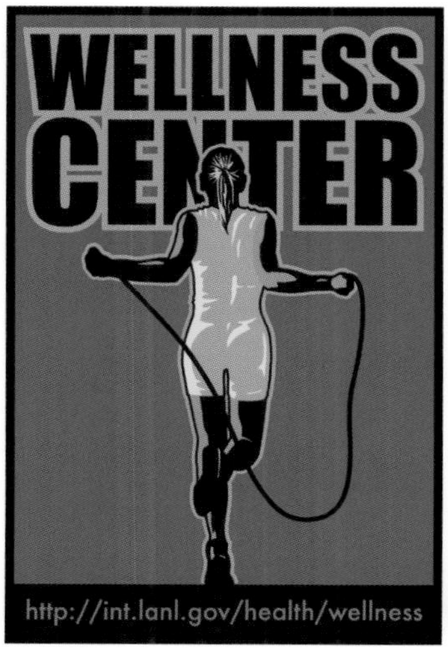

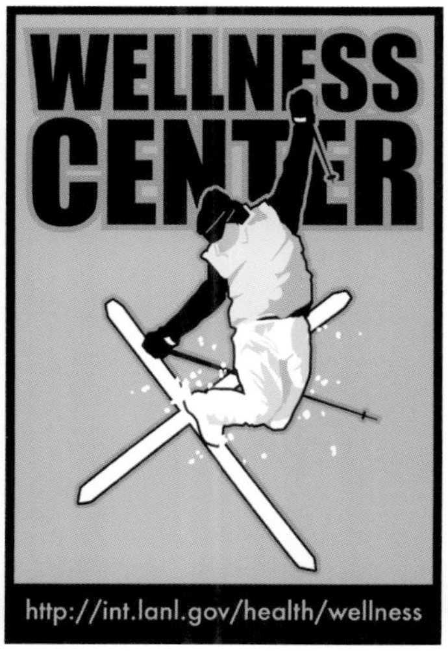

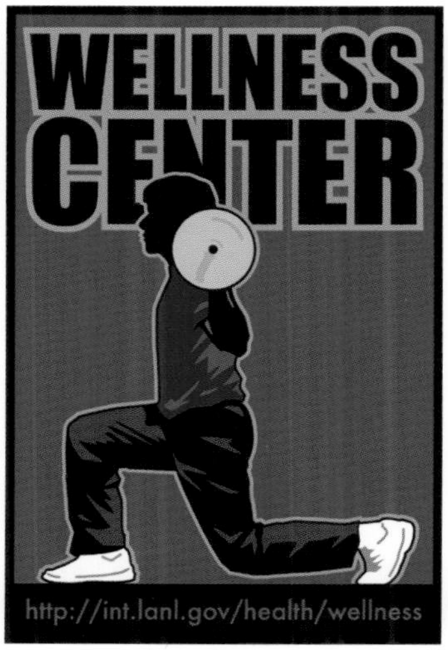

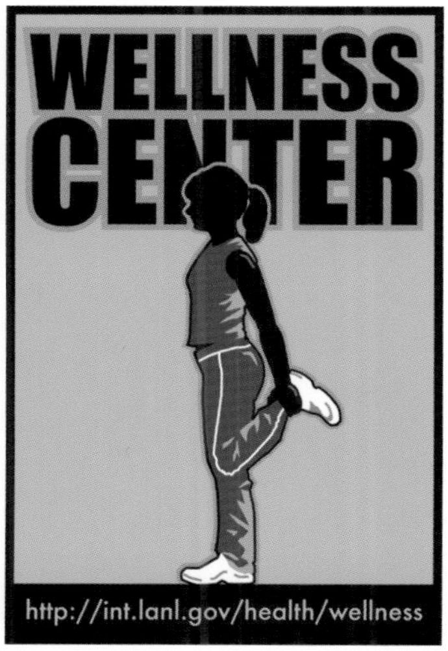

ALPHA
MILL
APARTMENTS
Crosland
It's our place to improve yours.
APARTMENT HOMES

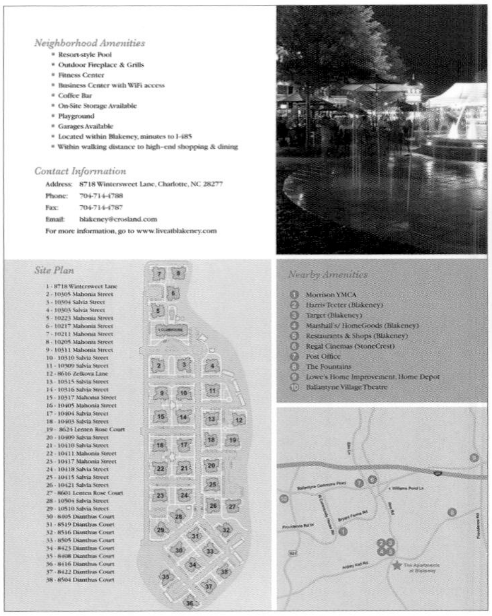
Neighborhood Amenities
Resort-style Pool
Outdoor Fireplace & Grills
Fitness Center
Business Center with WiFi access
Coffee Bar
On-Site Storage Available
Playground
Garages Available
Located within Blakeney, minutes to I-485
Within walking distance to high-end shopping & dining
Contact Information
Address: 8718 Wintersweet Lane, Charlotte, NC 28277
Phone: 704-714-4788
Fax: 704-714-4787
Email: blakeney@crosland.com
For more information, go to www.liveatblakeney.com
Site Plan
Nearby Amenities
1 Morrison YMCA
2 Harris Teeter (Blakeney)
3 Target (Blakeney)
4 Marshall's/ HomeGoods (Blakeney)
5 Restaurants & Shops (Blakeney)
6 Regal Cinemas (StoneCrest)
7 Post Office
8 The Fountains
9 Lowe's Home Improvement, Home Depot
10 Ballantyne Village Theatre

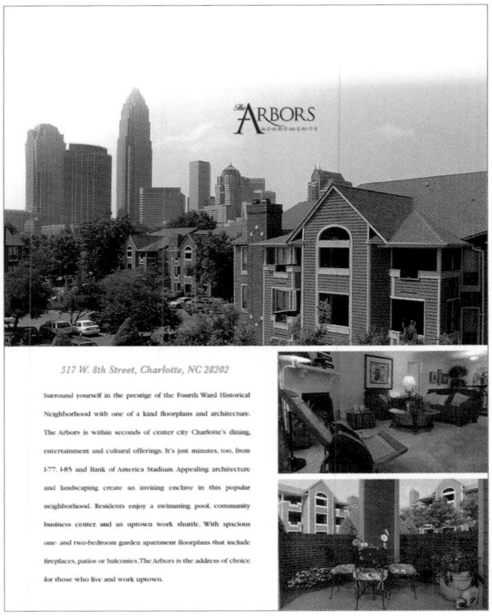
THE ARBORS
APARTMENTS
517 W. 8th Street, Charlotte, NC 28202
Surround yourself in the prestige of the Fourth Ward Historical Neighborhood with one of a kind floorplans and architecture. The Arbors is within seconds of center city Charlotte's dining, entertainment and cultural offerings. It's just minutes, too, from I-77, I-85 and Bank of America Stadium. Appealing architecture and landscaping create an inviting enclave in this popular neighborhood. Residents enjoy a swimming pool, community business center, and an uptown work shuttle. With spacious one- and two-bedroom garden apartment floorplans that include fireplaces, patios or balconies, The Arbors is the address of choice for those who live and work uptown.

Moonlight Creative Group – Charlotte, North Carolina
Designer : Dawn Newsome
Client : Crosland

Sponsored by Gina and John Despres,
Rick Kasten and Arlene and Robert Kogod
The 2007/2008 season
is sponsored by
Donald and Nancy de Laski
LUDWIG VAN BEETHOVEN
world premiere drama
33
VARIATIONS
co-production with Tectonic Theater Project
written and directed by Moisés Kaufman
August 24 through
September 30, 2007
in the Kreeger
arena stage
Molly Smith/Artistic Director 07/08 Season www.arenastage.org

MiresBall – San Diego, California
Designers : Scott Mires, Beth Folkerth, Jody Hewgill
Client : Arena Stage

ENTER
PLAY
SQUARE ENIX
PUSH OUR BUTTONS

Studio QED, Inc. – San Mateo, California
Designers : Steven Wright, Gregory Harsh
Client : Square Enix

FINAL FANTASY VII
ADVENT CHILDREN
Revisit the Fantasy
The most memorable and beloved FINAL FANTASY characters are back in a full-length DVD movie.
The world of Gaia narrowly escaped destruction years ago. Now a new threat, a plague, is spreading quickly, and secluded hero Cloud Strife must again step forward to save his world. This stunning CG animated film realizes the city of Midgar and its inhabitants with detail and clarity never before imagined.

Type E Design – Alexandria, Virginia
Designers : Tipy Taylor, Tina Taylor, Sonia Ourmanova
Client : AOL

This invitation arrives with style and substance. A black box opens to reveal red satin lining. Contents include embossing and debossing effects, die cut materials, heavy card stocks, and an accordion-fold information piece. Interesting text treatments are incorporated into illustrations of movie stars' faces, indicating a more in-depth approach to imagery than traditional press photos.

AOL
STAR
TREATMENT
AGENDA
Arrivals & Hospitality
Welcome Luncheon
Dinner at Wolfgang Puck's CUT
Activities of Preference
"The Night Before" Oscars
Brunch
Leisure Time
Farewell

Tarheel Digital Imaging
A Closer Look
From itsy bitsy one-color business cards
to gargantuan-sized, multi-color brochures,
short-run postcards to multiple-step fulfillment pieces,
we treat every critter with the same care and detail.
We are Tarheel Digital Imaging.
And we are whatever and wherever you need us to be.
That's because we come to you and help you figure out what
you need and the most cost efficient way to get it done.
When challenges arise (and let's face it...they do)
we offer inventive solutions, not pathetic excuses. Then we
deliver it back to you the way you wanted it...done right.
We're not the biggest printer in the Valley,
but we pride ourselves on resourcefulness. So if you've got a
printing challenge that's been bugging you.
Give us a buzz.
602-299-6711
Lotsa Handsus
Okay, perhaps not the prettiest bug on the planet, but he makes up for it
in manual dexterity! And at TDI we have multiple resources to handle virtually all your printing needs.
Big, small, pretty, and...even those slightly ugly ones. So consider yourself in good hands!

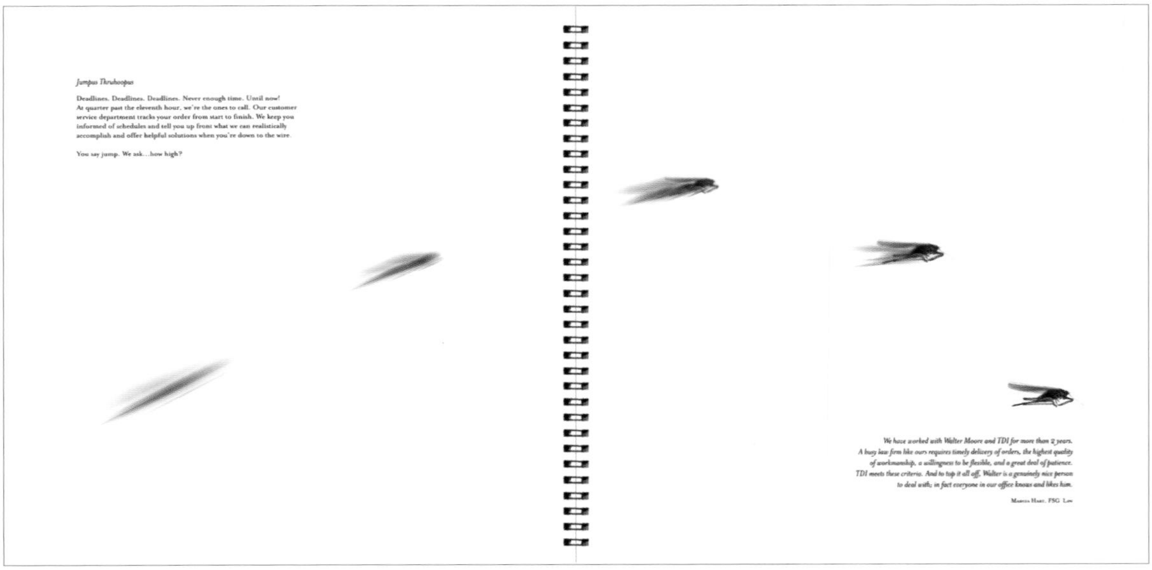
Jumpus Thruhoopus
Deadlines. Deadlines. Deadlines. Never enough time. Until now!
At quarter past the eleventh hour, we're the ones to call. Our customer
service department tracks your order from start to finish. We keep you
informed of schedules and tell you up front what we can realistically
accomplish and offer helpful solutions when you're down to the wire.
You say jump. We ask...how high?
We have worked with Walter Moore and TDI for more than 2 years.
A busy law firm like ours requires timely delivery of orders, the highest quality
of workmanship, a willingness to be flexible, and a great deal of patience.
TDI meets these criteria. And to top it all off, Walter is a genuinely nice person
to deal with; in fact everyone in our office knows and likes him.

We needed 500 full-color newsletters and posters for our annual fund raiser delivered in less than a week.
Tarheel Digital Imaging printed, folded and delivered them to us in vivid, beautiful color on time and for a price I couldn't get anywhere else.
Thanks, Walter. They are stunning!
Multicolorus Beautissimus
Color sells. Whether it's low-cost, short-run color copies or cost-efficient, long-run, 4-color process, we've got the full palette. Small business card runs on on our 2-color presses or full-scale annual reports on our 6-color, 40" Komoris, it's always the same result. Bright, vivid and guaranteed to catch the eye of anyone that flutters by.

Exactium Inregistrationum
Delicate precision. Perfect alignment.
We pride ourselves on taking care of all the details:
- Complete Electronic Imaging
- Pre-Press Flight Checking and Prep
- Direct-to-Plate Equipment
- Color Proofing: Digital Matchprint & Inkjet Proofs
- Complete Software Support
- Multiple Press Options:
- 40" 6-Color Komori with Coater
- 28" 6-Color Komori
- 40" 2-Color Heidelberg
- 36" 2-Color Heidelberg
- 29" 2-Color Heidelberg
We demand strict quality control with full accountability and satisfaction guaranteed. We're not just one of those "fly by night" operations!

Tarheel Digital Imaging
A Collection of Fine Printing Options
We have a vast array of state-of-the-art technological solutions and services to meet your every graphic need:
Copies on Demand
Digital Imaging
Engineering and Oversized Copies
We can produce oversized images up to 36" wide for architectural rendering, site plans, and space plans.
Finishing Services
- Booklet making
- Collating & Stapling
Graphics Solutions
Business Solutions
In addition to talented graphic artists, we can provide your business with solutions in file manipulation. We can edit your digital files, scan your artwork, photos or transparencies, as well as perform digital file transfers to numerous output devices.
Presentation Solutions
- Oversized color copies
- Color transparencies
- Posters and banners
Scanning Solutions
For more information or to get a super quick quote on your next project, buzz on over to:
www.tarheeldigital.com
or call us:
602-299-6711

foxnoggin - thinking design – Phoenix, Arizona
Designer : Neill Fox
Client : Tarheel Digital Imaging

JGA – Southfield, Michigan
Designers : Ken Nisch, Kathi McWilliams, George Vojovski
Client : Lenox Group, Inc.

JGA appeals to a broad range of customers with its specialty designed collateral for Lenox Group's Hoopla store, starting with that which shoppers take home.

MiresBall – San Diego, California
Designers : Scott Mires, Beth Folkerth, Jody Hewgill
Client : Arena Stage

Helena Seo Design – Sunnyvale, California
Client : Minted

The experience of visiting this salon starts when the unique gift card is received. The casual but tasteful card set benefits everyone involved. Michael Christopher is able to promote a professional image by making available to the public well-designed collateral. For the one who chooses to grace a friend with a trip to the salon, the quality packaging, which includes a band of actual grosgrain, suggests the recipient is valuable—as is the gift. Of course, the friend receives an afternoon of pampering!

Crawford Design – Chagrin Falls, Ohio
Designer : Alison Crawford
Client : Michael Christopher Salon

Elixirion – Thessaloniki, Greece
Designers : Michael Sachpazis, Konstantinos Petridis
Client : ESFIPS

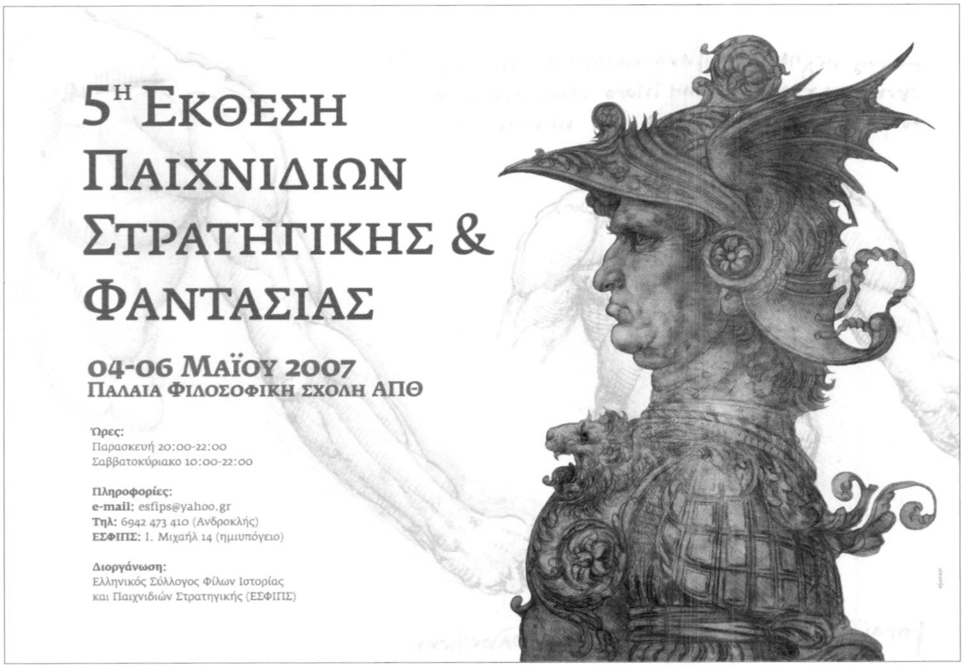

personal best
Healthy businesses depend on it...
DODGER :
WHIP :
WHEN YOU PUT PEOPLE
IN A SMALL BOX,
THINGS GET INTERESTING.

Open Creative Group – Birmingham, Alabama
Designers : April Mraz, Alan Whitley
Client : Oakstone Publishing/Personal Best

Passing Notes, Inc. – Oakland, California
Designer : Abbie Planas Gong
Client : Melanie Mauer Photography

SURF STRONGER

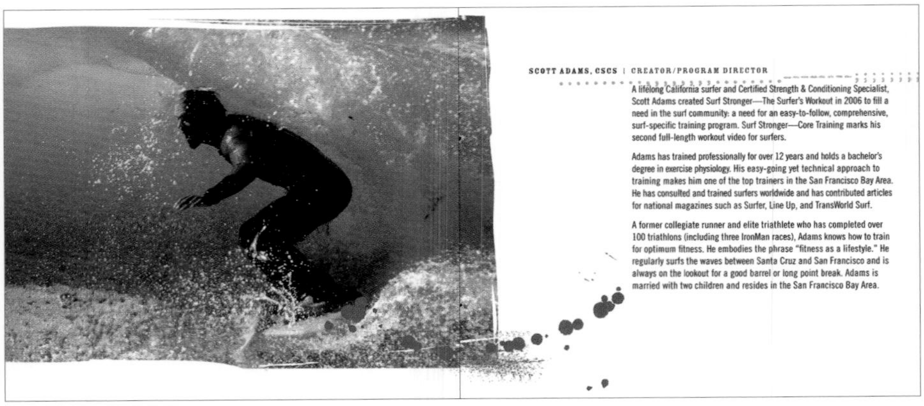
SCOTT ADAMS, CSCS | CREATOR/PROGRAM DIRECTOR
A lifelong California surfer and Certified Strength & Conditioning Specialist, Scott Adams created Surf Stronger—The Surfer's Workout in 2006 to fill a need in the surf community: a need for an easy-to-follow, comprehensive, surf-specific training program. Surf Stronger—Core Training marks his second full-length workout video for surfers.
Adams has trained professionally for over 12 years and holds a bachelor's degree in exercise physiology. His easy-going yet technical approach to training makes him one of the top trainers in the San Francisco Bay Area. He has consulted and trained surfers worldwide and has contributed articles for national magazines such as Surfer, Line Up, and TransWorld Surf.
A former collegiate runner and elite triathlete who has completed over 100 triathlons (including three IronMan races), Adams knows how to train for optimum fitness. He embodies the phrase "fitness as a lifestyle." He regularly surfs the waves between Santa Cruz and San Francisco and is always on the lookout for a good barrel or long point break. Adams is married with two children and resides in the San Francisco Bay Area.

Helena Seo Design
– Sunnyvale, California
Designer : Helena Seo
Client : Surf Stronger

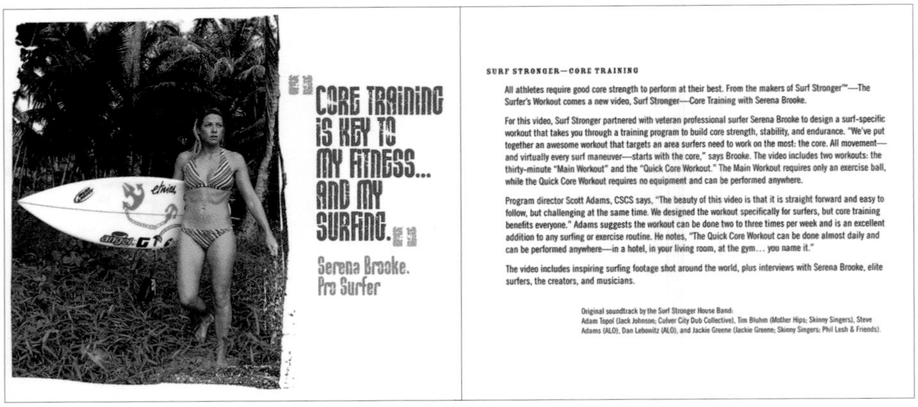
CORE TRAINING IS KEY TO MY FITNESS... AND MY SURFING.
Serena Brooke. Pro Surfer
SURF STRONGER—CORE TRAINING
All athletes require good core strength to perform at their best. From the makers of Surf Stronger™—The Surfer's Workout comes a new video, Surf Stronger—Core Training with Serena Brooke.
For this video, Surf Stronger partnered with veteran professional surfer Serena Brooke to design a surf-specific workout that takes you through a training program to build core strength, stability, and endurance. "We've put together an awesome workout that targets an area surfers need to work on the most: the core. All movement—and virtually every surf maneuver—starts with the core," says Brooke. The video includes two workouts: the thirty-minute "Main Workout" and the "Quick Core Workout." The Main Workout requires only an exercise ball, while the Quick Core Workout requires no equipment and can be performed anywhere.
Program director Scott Adams, CSCS says, "The beauty of this video is that it is straight forward and easy to follow, but challenging at the same time. We designed the workout specifically for surfers, but core training benefits everyone." Adams suggests the workout can be done two to three times per week and is an excellent addition to any surfing or exercise routine. He notes, "The Quick Core Workout can be done almost daily and can be performed anywhere—in a hotel, in your living room, at the gym... you name it."
The video includes inspiring surfing footage shot around the world, plus interviews with Serena Brooke, elite surfers, the creators, and musicians.
Original soundtrack by the Surf Stronger House Band:
Adam Topol (Jack Johnson; Culver City Dub Collective), Tim Bluhm (Mother Hips; Skinny Singers), Steve Adams (ALO), Dan Lebowitz (ALO), and Jackie Greene (Jackie Greene; Skinny Singers; Phil Lesh & Friends).

BBR Creative – Lafayette, Louisiana
Designers : Cathi Pavy, Denise Gallagher
Client : Imperial Fire & Casualty

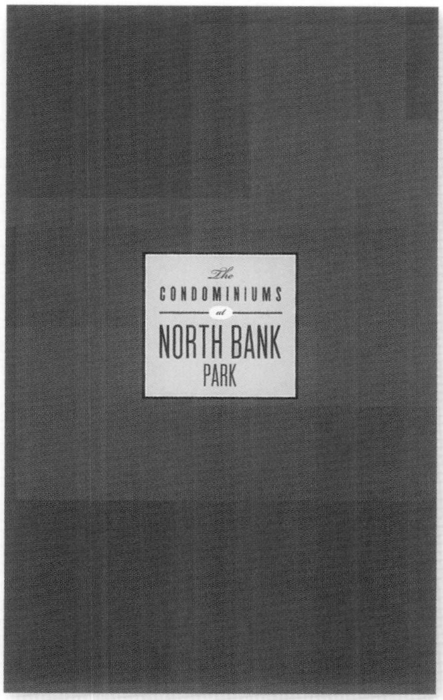
The
CONDOMINIUMS
at
NORTH BANK
PARK

THE HEIGHT OF SOPHISTICATION.
In the center of it all.

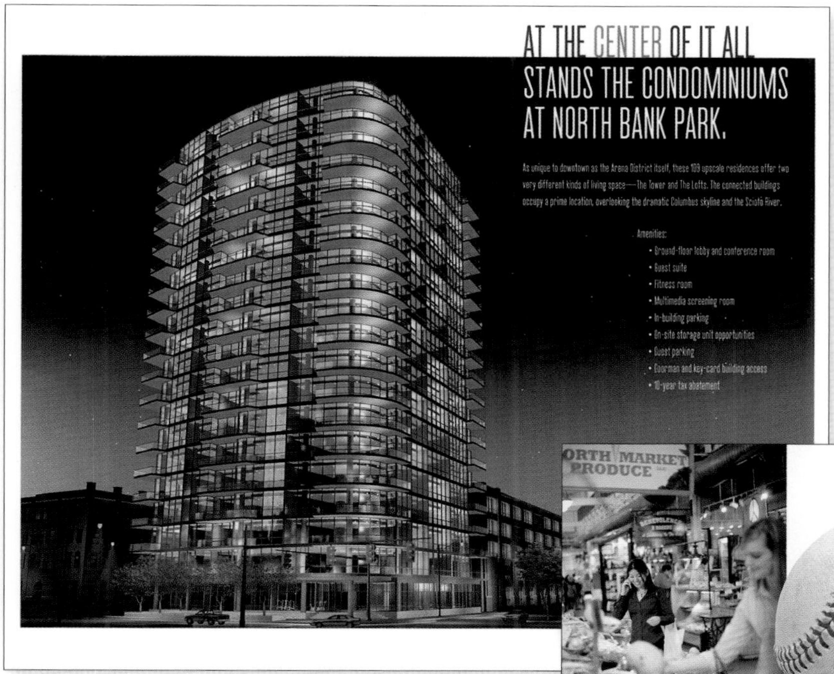
AT THE CENTER OF IT ALL
STANDS THE CONDOMINIUMS
AT NORTH BANK PARK.
As unique to dowtown as the Arena District itself, these 109 upscale residences offer two very different kinds of living space—The Tower and The Lofts. The connected buildings occupy a prime location, overlooking the dramatic Columbus skyline and the Scioto River.
Amenities:
• Ground-floor lobby and conference room
• Guest suite
• Fitness room
• Multimedia screening room
• In-building parking
• On-site storage unit opportunities
• Guest parking
• Doorman and key-card building access
• 10-year tax abatement

Scott Adams Design Associates – Minneapolis, Minnesota
Designers : Scott Adams
Client : Nationwide Realty Investors

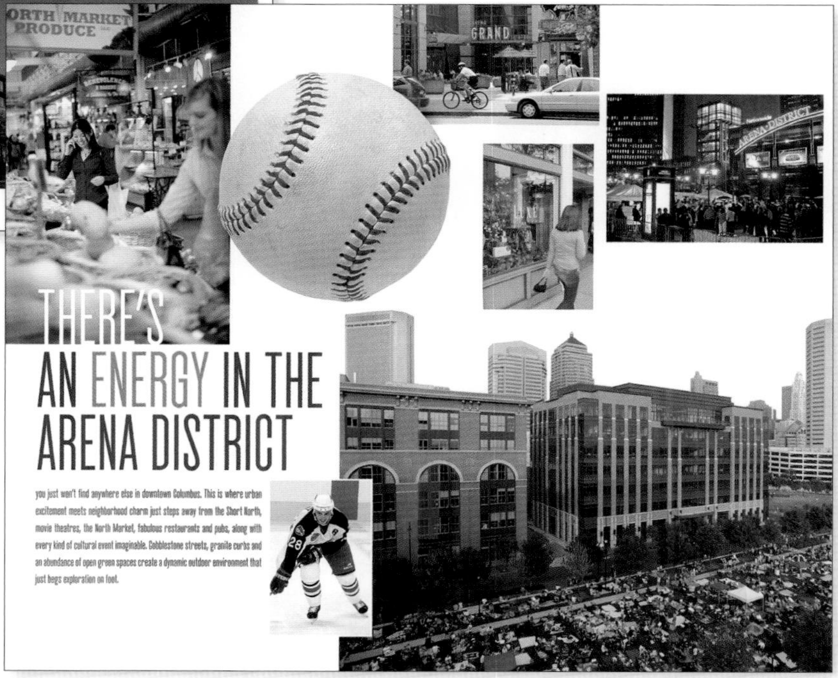
ORTH MARKET
PRODUCE
GRAND
ARENA DISTRICT
THERE'S
AN ENERGY IN THE
ARENA DISTRICT
you just won't find anywhere else in downtown Columbus. This is where urban excitement meets neighborhood charm just steps away from the Short North, movie theatres, the North Market, fabulous restaurants and pubs, along with every kind of cultural event imaginable. Cobblestone streets, granite curbs and an abundance of open green spaces create a dynamic outdoor environment that just begs exploration on foot.

Mad Dog Graphx – Anchorage, Alaska
Designer : Michael Ardaiz
Client : Alaska Stock Images

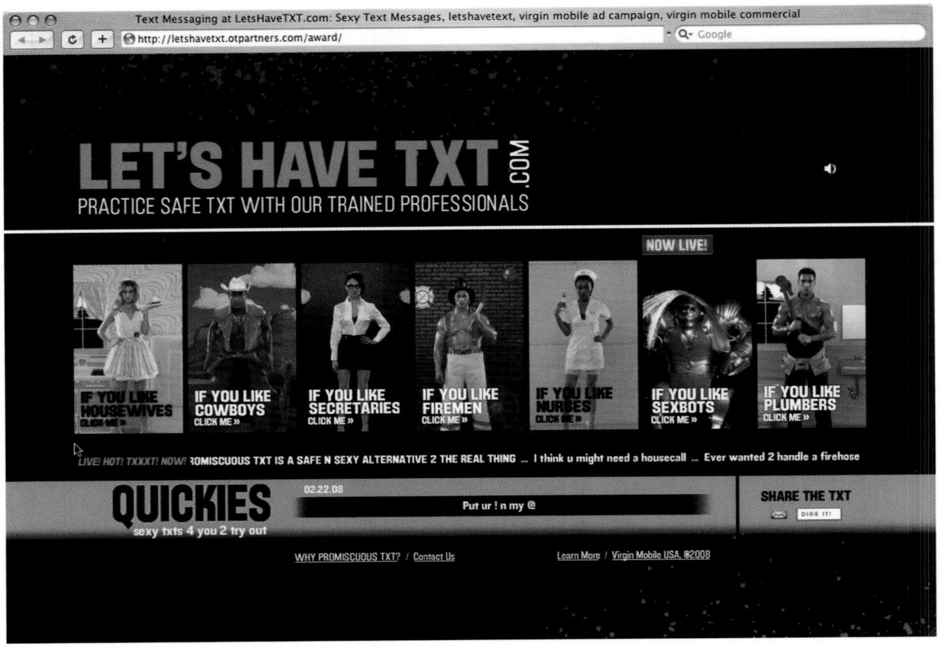
Text Messaging at LetsHaveTXT.com: Sexy Text Messages, letshavetext, virgin mobile ad campaign, virgin mobile commercial
http://letshavetxt.otpartners.com/award/
LET'S HAVE TXT .COM
PRACTICE SAFE TXT WITH OUR TRAINED PROFESSIONALS
NOW LIVE!
IF YOU LIKE HOUSEWIVES
IF YOU LIKE COWBOYS CLICK ME »
IF YOU LIKE SECRETARIES CLICK ME »
IF YOU LIKE FIREMEN CLICK ME »
IF YOU LIKE NURSES
IF YOU LIKE SEXBOTS CLICK ME »
IF YOU LIKE PLUMBERS CLICK ME »
LIVE! HOT! TXXXT! NOW! PROMISCUOUS TXT IS A SAFE N SEXY ALTERNATIVE 2 THE REAL THING ... I think u might need a housecall ... Ever wanted 2 handle a firehose
QUICKIES
sexy txts 4 you 2 try out
02.22.08
Put ur ! n my @
SHARE THE TXT
DIGG IT!
WHY PROMISCUOUS TXT? / Contact Us
Learn More / Virgin Mobile USA. ©2008

McKinney – Durham, North Carolina
Designers : Jonathan Cude, Ellen Steinberg, Jenny Nicholson, Maari Thrall
Client : Virgin Mobile, USA

FAILED DATA BACKUPS CONTINUE TO PLAGUE THE GOOD CITIZENS OF CORPORATE AMERICA...
BUT... THERE IS HOPE!
ONE DRIVE HAS THE POWER...
TO BATTLE EVER GROWING OFFLINE STORAGE COSTS!
KA-POW!
TO MAKE ROOM FOR DOUBLE THE STORAGE CAPACITY!
WHACK
ZAP
TO SHRINK BACKUP WINDOWS WITH A SINGLE DRIVE!
...HMMMM!
WHO IS THIS MYSTERIOUS HERO THAT USES FEWER CARTRIDGES WHILE SAVING FLOOR SPACE?!?
STORAGETEK T10K SAVES THE DAY!
TO REGISTER FOR 1 OF 3 EXCITING PRIZES OR FOR MORE INFO GO TO: WWW.T10KSAVESTHEDAY.COM

foxnoggin - thinking design – Phoenix, Arizona
Designers : Neill Fox, Dan Corredor, Lesley Kitts
Client : StorageTek by Avnet, Inc.

STORAGETEK
PRESERVE TODAY WITH THE TECHNOLOGY OF TOMORROW.
BATTLING THE FORCES OF DATA DISASTER, T10K SAVES THE DAY!
ZAP

Leibold Associates, Inc. – Neenah, Wisconsin
Designers : Jane Oliver, Greg Madson
Client : Wangard Advisors

BBR Creative – Lafayette, Louisiana
Designers : Maria Lambert, Cathi Pavy
Client : BELFOR

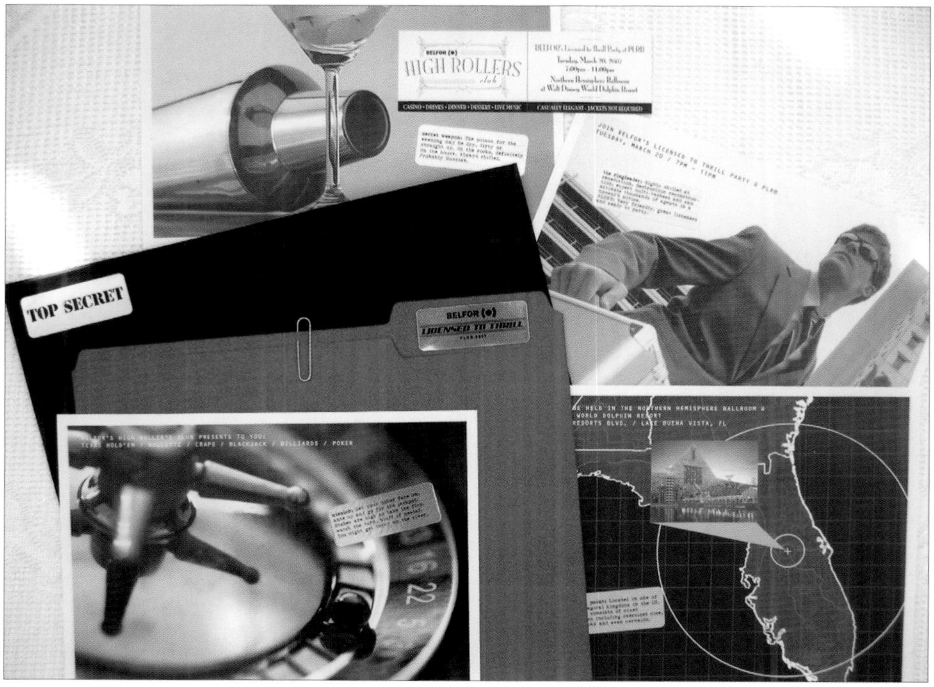

This invitation to a gambling event reads like a dossier for an international agent. By invitation only: sophistication, travel, risk, and excitement...one good game deserves another.

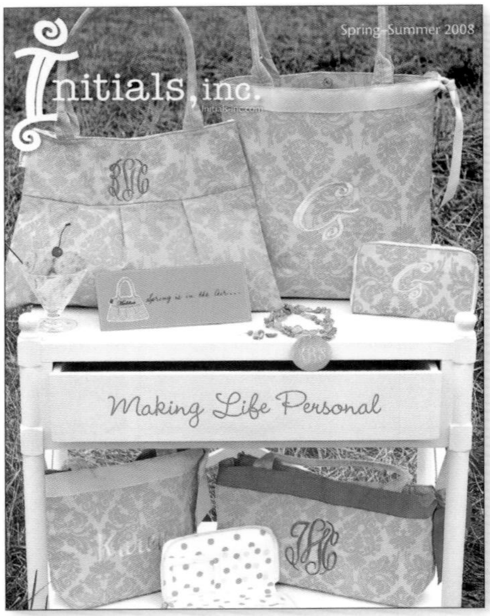

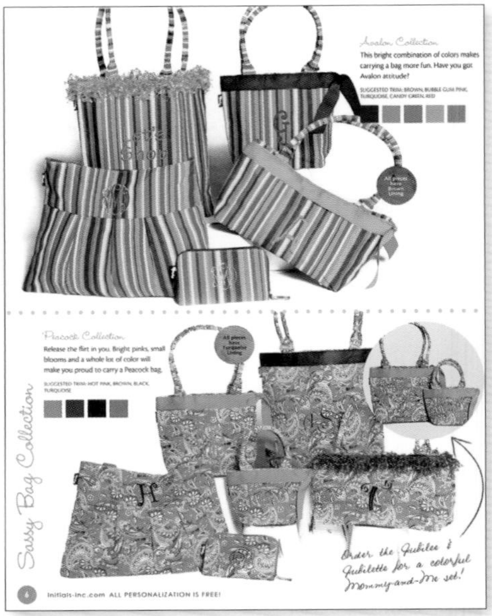

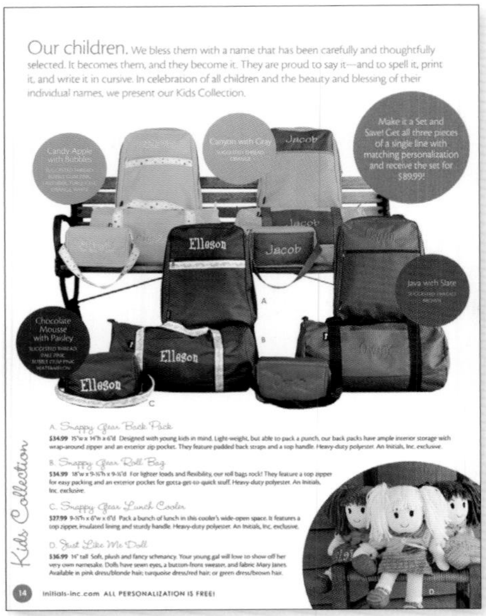

Jill Lynn Design – Atlanta, Georgia
Designer : Jill Anderson
Client : Initials, Inc.

Tell all your friends
Save 10%
Off everything sale

Baker Creative – Groveport, Ohio
Designer : Michele Cuthbert
Client : Moochie + Co.

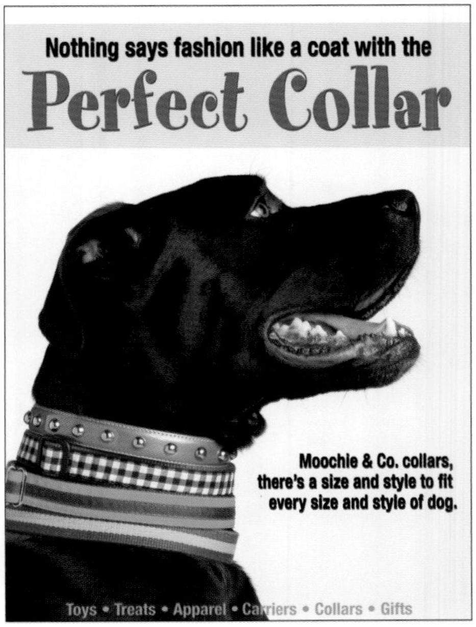

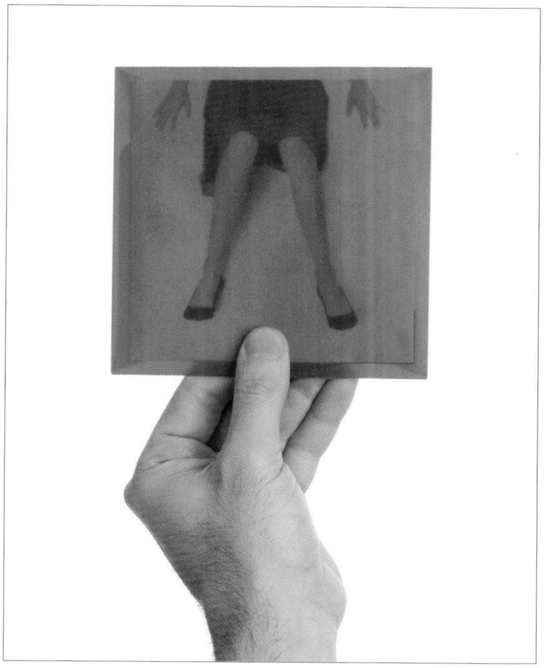

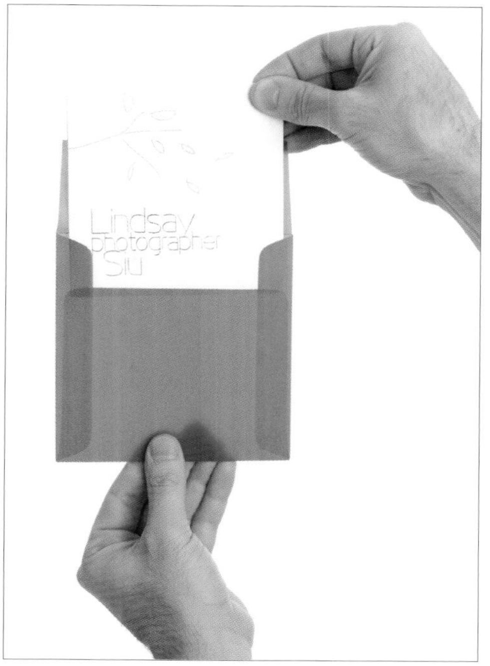

Exhibit A: Design Group – Vancouver, Canada
Designers : Cory Ripley, Lindsay Siu
Client : Lindsay Siu

Greenleaf Media – Madison, Wisconsin
Designer : Mary Walsh
Client : Julie Foster

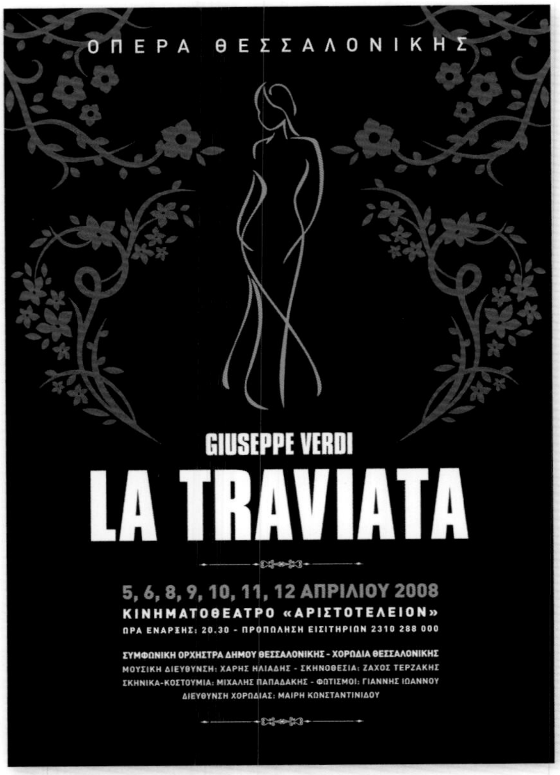

Elixiron – Thessaloniki, Greece
Designer : Michael Sachpazis, Konstantinos Petridis
Client : Opera of Thessaloniki

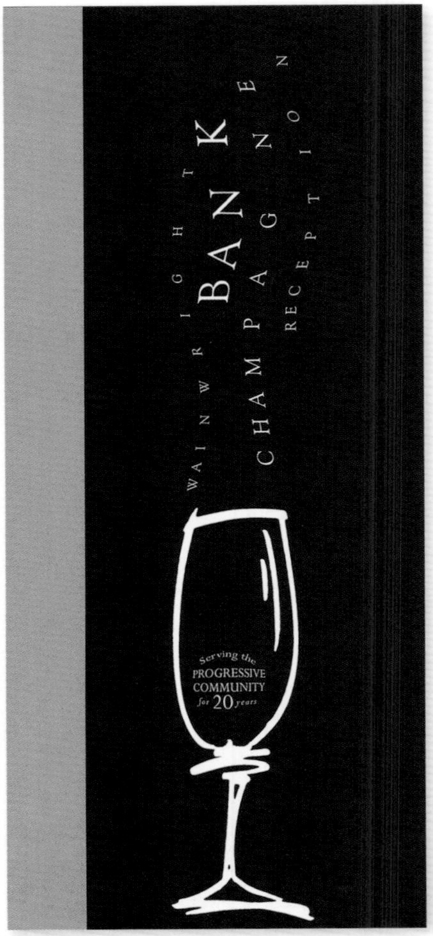

Stephen Burdick Design – Boston, Massachusetts
Designer : Stephen Burdick
Client : Wainwright Bank

Bryan Texas Utilities
Power Pedal
Ride & Stride

Ready to train for a race, but not sure how? Try one of these training schedules. We found them at halhigdon.com, a web site for runners.

5k Training Schedule

Week	S	M	T	W	T	F	S
1	Rest or Run/ Walk	1.5 m run	Rest or Run/ Walk	1.5 m run	Rest	1.5 m run	30-60 min walk
2	Rest or Run/ Walk	1.75 m run	Rest or Run/ Walk	1.5 m run	Rest	1.75 m run	35-60 min walk
3	Rest or Run/ Walk	2 m run	Rest or Run/ Walk	1.5 m run	Rest	2 m run	40-60 min walk
4	Rest or Run/ Walk	2.25 m run	Rest or Run/ Walk	1.5 m run	Rest	2.25 m run	45-60 min walk
5	Rest or Run/ Walk	2.5 m run	Rest or Run/ Walk	2 m run	Rest	2.5 m run	50-60 min walk
6	Rest or Run/ Walk	2.75 m run	Rest or Run/ Walk	2 m run	Rest	2.75 m run	55-60 min walk
7	Rest or Run/ Walk	3 m run	Rest or Run/ Walk	2 m run	Rest	3 m run	60 min walk
8	Rest or Run/ Walk	3 m run	Rest or Run/ Walk	2 m run	Rest	Rest	5k Race

10k Training Schedule

Week	S	M	T	W	T	F	S
1	Stretch/ Strength	2.5 m run	30 min Cross	2 m run + strength	Rest	40 min Cross	3 m run
2	Stretch/ Strength	2.5 m run	30 min Cross	2 m run + strength	Rest	40 min Cross	3.5 m run
3	Stretch/ Strength	2.5 m run	35 min Cross	2 m run + strength	Rest	50 min Cross	4 m run
4	Stretch/ Strength	3 m run	35 min Cross	2 m run + strength	Rest	50 min Cross	4 m run
5	Stretch/ Strength	3 m run	40 min Cross	2 m run + strength	Rest	60 min Cross	4.5 m run
6	Stretch/ Strength	3 m run	40 min Cross	2 m run + strength	Rest	60 min Cross	5 m run
7	Stretch/ Strength	3 m run	45 min Cross	2 m run + strength	Rest	60 min Cross	5.5 m run
8	Stretch/ Strength	3 m run	30 min Cross	2 m run	Rest	Rest	10k Race

powerpedal.com

Bryan Texas Utilities
Power Pedal
Ride & Stride

October 13-14, 2007
Lake Bryan, Texas

15th Annual Event Celebrating
Public Power Week

A portion of the proceeds will benefit
Hospice Brazos Valley.

Mountain Bike Race Events
USA Cycling & Collegiate Categories

Orienteering MTB Race

Kid's Kup Event

5k & 10k Run/Walk

10k, 25k, & 50k Trail Runs

powerpedal.com

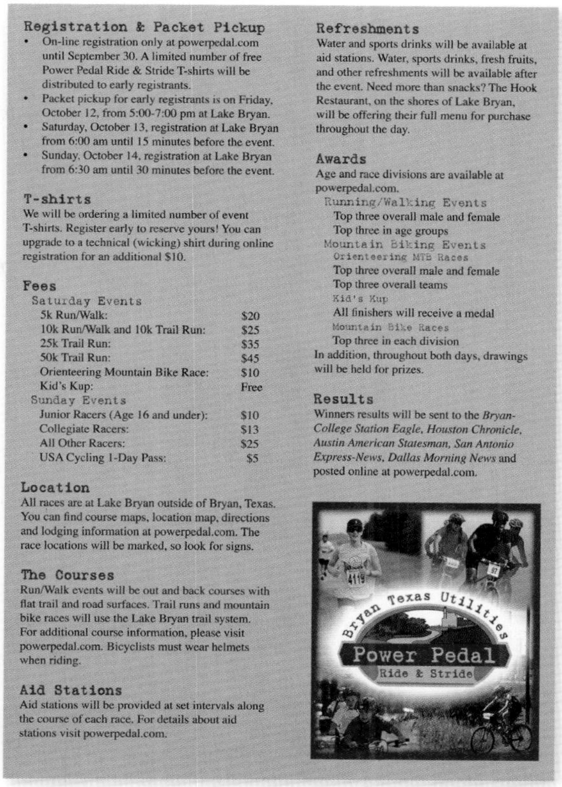

Registration & Packet Pickup

- On-line registration only at powerpedal.com until September 30. A limited number of free Power Pedal Ride & Stride T-shirts will be distributed to early registrants.
- Packet pickup for early registrants is on Friday, October 12, from 5:00-7:00 pm at Lake Bryan.
- Saturday, October 13, registration at Lake Bryan from 6:00 am until 15 minutes before the event.
- Sunday, October 14, registration at Lake Bryan from 6:30 am until 30 minutes before the event.

T-shirts

We will be ordering a limited number of event T-shirts. Register early to reserve yours! You can upgrade to a technical (wicking) shirt during online registration for an additional $10.

Fees

Saturday Events	
5k Run/Walk:	$20
10k Run/Walk and 10k Trail Run:	$25
25k Trail Run:	$35
50k Trail Run:	$45
Orienteering Mountain Bike Race:	$10
Kid's Kup:	Free
Sunday Events	
Junior Racers (Age 16 and under):	$10
Collegiate Racers:	$13
All Other Racers:	$25
USA Cycling 1-Day Pass:	$5

Location

All races are at Lake Bryan outside of Bryan, Texas. You can find course maps, location map, directions and lodging information at powerpedal.com. The race locations will be marked, so look for signs.

The Courses

Run/Walk events will be out and back courses with flat trail and road surfaces. Trail runs and mountain bike races will use the Lake Bryan trail system. For additional course information, please visit powerpedal.com. Bicyclists must wear helmets when riding.

Aid Stations

Aid stations will be provided at set intervals along the course of each race. For details about aid stations visit powerpedal.com.

Refreshments

Water and sports drinks will be available at aid stations. Water, sports drinks, fresh fruits, and other refreshments will be available after the event. Need more than snacks? The Hook Restaurant, on the shores of Lake Bryan, will be offering their full menu for purchase throughout the day.

Awards

Age and race divisions are available at powerpedal.com.

Running/Walking Events
Top three overall male and female
Top three in age groups
Mountain Biking Events
Orienteering MTB Races
Top three overall male and female
Top three overall teams
Kid's Kup
All finishers will receive a medal
Mountain Bike Races
Top three in each division

In addition, throughout both days, drawings will be held for prizes.

Results

Winners results will be sent to the *Bryan-College Station Eagle, Houston Chronicle, Austin American Statesman, San Antonio Express-News, Dallas Morning News* and posted online at powerpedal.com.

Bryan Texas Utilities
Power Pedal
Ride & Stride

Content Solutions – Denton, Texas
Designers : Louellen S. Coker, Brittany Bailey
Client : Bryan Texas Utilities

Mad Dog Graphx – Anchorage, Alaska
Designer : Michael Ardaiz
Client : Alaska Stock Images

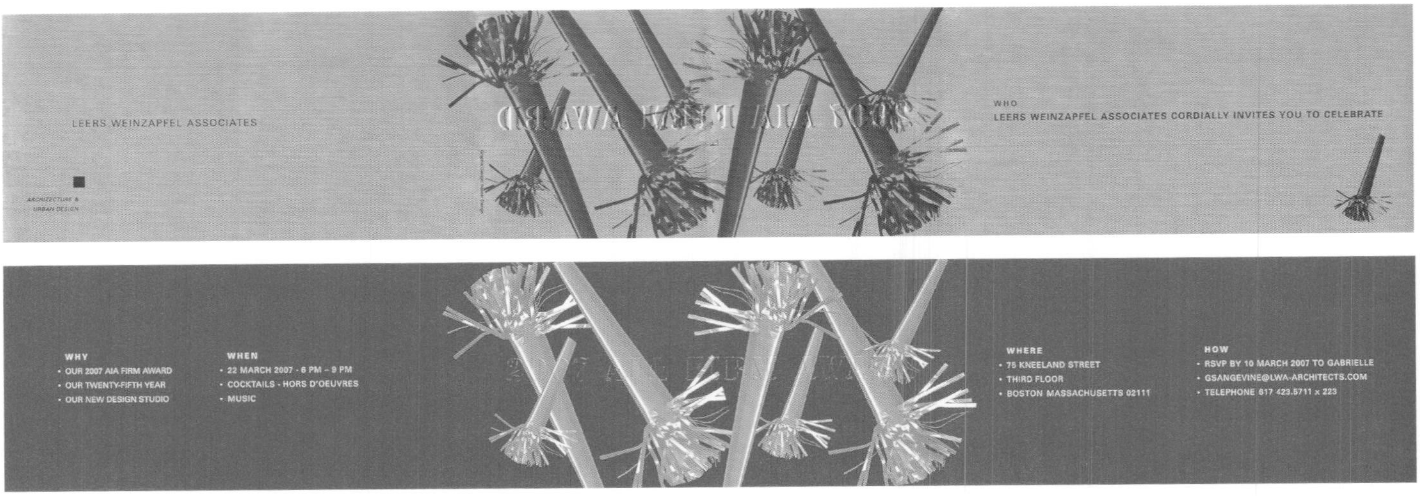
LEERS WEINZAPFEL ASSOCIATES
WHO
LEERS WEINZAPFEL ASSOCIATES CORDIALLY INVITES YOU TO CELEBRATE
WHY
• OUR 2007 AIA FIRM AWARD
• OUR TWENTY-FIFTH YEAR
• OUR NEW DESIGN STUDIO
WHEN
• 22 MARCH 2007 • 6 PM – 9 PM
• COCKTAILS • HORS D'OEUVRES
• MUSIC
WHERE
• 75 KNEELAND STREET
• THIRD FLOOR
• BOSTON MASSACHUSETTS 02111
HOW
• RSVP BY 10 MARCH 2007 TO GABRIELLE
• GSANGEVINE@LWA-ARCHITECTS.COM
• TELEPHONE 617 423.5711 x 223

Nassar Design – Brookline, Massachusetts
Designers : Nelida Nassar, Gabrielle Angevine
Client : Leers Weinzapfel Associates

The Miller Festival is sponsored by Sue and Steve Bralove, John and Linda Derrick, Wendy Farrow Raines, Mark and Merrill Shugoll and Dick and Katie Snowdon.
This production is sponsored by Dr. John W. Layman and David and Peggy Shiffrin.
The 2007/2008 season is sponsored by Donald and Nancy de Laski.
the arthur miller festival
DEATH OF A SALESMAN
by Arthur Miller
directed by Timothy Bond
in repertory with A View from the Bridge
March 14 through May 18, 2008
in the Fichandler
arena stage
Molly Smith/Artistic Director
07/08 Season
www.arenastage.org

MiresBall – San Diego, California
Designers : Scott Mires, Beth Folkerth, Sterling Hundley
Client : Arena Stage

Studio QED, Inc. – San Mateo, California
Designer : Steven Wright
Client : Square Enix

Q – Wiesbaden, Germany
Designers : Zuni Höfer, Kirsten Fabinski, Thilo von Debschitz
Client : arjowiggins fine papers

An In-Depth Look at: KNOXVILLE RACEWAY

Most people may have never heard of tiny Knoxville, Iowa, but it's a giant in the field of sprint racing. Still, Knoxville Raceway didn't have a lot of resources to promote itself, which is why they struck a unique deal with Sayles Graphic Design in Des Moines, about an hour northwest.

"I told them, 'If you're fun to work with, we'll make it work,'" says managing partner Sheree Clark of her first meeting with the track's representative. Actually, the two had met and worked together long before they collaborated on the raceway's rebranding, but that attitude set the tone for their enduring partnership.

"They hired us to do promotions, but then we took it upon ourselves to do a new identity," Clark says of her client, which observes the fiftieth anniversary of its celebrated Knoxville Nationals race in 2010. "They had posters, brochures, and t-shirts, but they did it hodgepodge. We sat down and looked at them to see if there was anything we could get rid of and anything we could expand." Clark and the agency's owner/

designer, John Sayles, also sought to streamline the visual experience, starting with a new logo—and a presence as large as the cars are loud. "In addition to collateral promotions, we also did things like gigantic signs in the grandstand so the television crews have something to look at instead of just smoke and vendors. We wanted to create a real branded experience."

In addition to creating the signs and literature for fans such as brochures and schedules, Sayles also designed t-shirts, which are then compressed into hockey puck-sized capsules for easy distribution to fans. The agency also developed a marketing kit for potential sponsors, consisting of a distinctive Knoxville Raceway box, a t-shirt, and a notebook highlighting three years of "sponsor nights" and their impact on the fans and the overall Knoxville Raceway brand story.

The brand permeates Knoxville, and their sprint car industry is a badge of pride for many residents. Besides the raceway, which calls itself "The Sprint Car Capital of the World," it's also home to the National Sprint Car Hall of Fame & Museum, but since the Knoxville Raceway's dirt track isn't as famous as the Indianapolis Motor Speedway, it has a decidedly lower profile. "They told us, 'Have fun with it, but be respectful of the budget,'" Clark says. So who comes out to watch? "Sprint car fans," she says. "People who come are interested in racing—they may know a driver or someone in the pit crew. Some people are interested in wrecks. The regular season (which runs from early spring to the fall) draws a different crowd than the Knoxville Nationals, but they're definitely positioned for families."

The races may run late and well past the bedtimes of many little ones, Clark acknowledges, but people aren't sitting up nights worrying about whether their partners are to be trusted. "In Iowa, we can do a lot of handshake kinds of deals—you develop a relationship," Clark says. "Knoxville is a town of seventy-seven hundred in a rural state, and the raceway is one of our favorite clients. People there leave their keys in the car and trust that their neighbors will do good business with you. But at the same time, you need to promote their business—you're still trying to get people to come out and pay." The staff at Sayles, too, finds time to take the drive down Highway 5. "I don't go every weekend by any means," says Clark, "but I'll go and drink a beer and hoot and holler at the racing."

Sayles Graphic Design – Des Moines, Iowa
Creatives : John Sayles, Bridget Drendel
Client : Knoxville Raceway

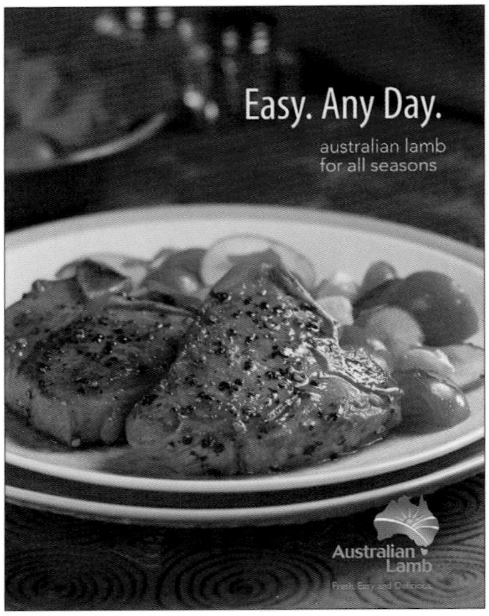
Easy. Any Day.
australian lamb
for all seasons
Australian Lamb

australian lamb niçoise
sliced leg of australian lamb
on cucumber and watercress salad
12 | summer
easy. any day. | 13

Levine & Associates, Inc. – Washington, D.C.
Designer : Maggie Soldano
Client : Australian Lamb

australian lamb loin with zucchini,
walnut and caper couscous

roasted garlic australian lamb leg
with rosemary potatoes
18 | autumn

Australian Lamb hired Levins & Associates to introduce its product to the American market. The result was a cookbook overflowing with photos of the "product" (and of course recipes).

Easy in Winter
You don't have to wait for Valentine's Day to express your love. You don't have to save special gifts for Christmas or Hanukah. And you don't need a New Year to change things up. Adding Australian lamb to your weekly winter menu will keep hearts and kitchens warm on crisp evenings. These healthy, all-natural dishes also let the special someones in your life know just how much you care.
australian lamb marsala
with braised winter squash
easy. any day. | 21

caramelized australian lamb chops
with grilled rosemary carrots

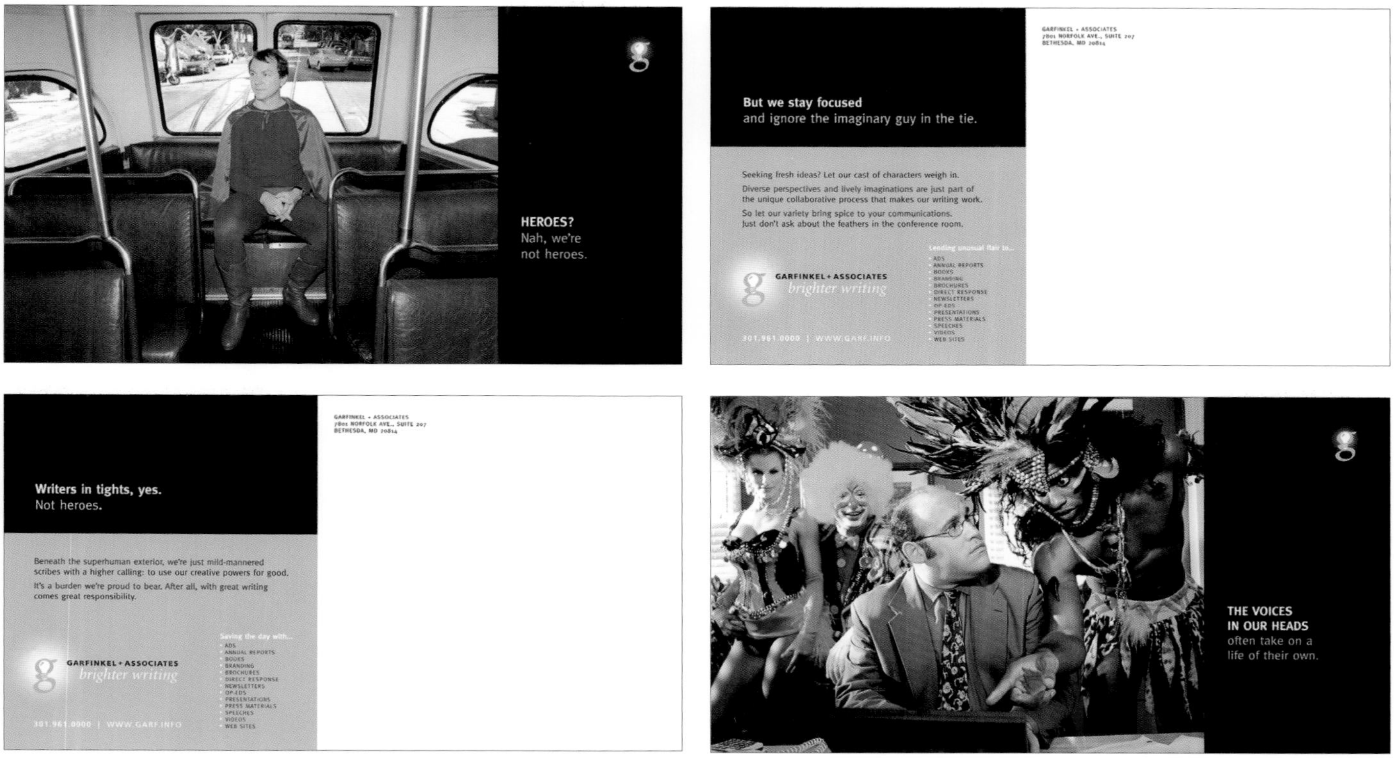
HEROES?
Nah, we're not heroes.
But we stay focused
and ignore the imaginary guy in the tie.
Seeking fresh ideas? Let our cast of characters weigh in.
Diverse perspectives and lively imaginations are just part of the unique collaborative process that makes our writing work.
So let our variety bring spice to your communications.
Just don't ask about the feathers in the conference room.
GARFINKEL + ASSOCIATES
brighter writing
301.961.0000 | WWW.GARF.INFO
Writers in tights, yes.
Not heroes.
Beneath the superhuman exterior, we're just mild-mannered scribes with a higher calling: to use our creative powers for good.
It's a burden we're proud to bear. After all, with great writing comes great responsibility.
GARFINKEL + ASSOCIATES
brighter writing
301.961.0000 | WWW.GARF.INFO
THE VOICES
IN OUR HEADS
often take on a
life of their own.

Levine & Associates, Inc. – Washington, D.C.
Designers : Maggie Soldano, Garfinkel + Associates
Client : Garfinkel + Associates

foxnoggin - thinking design – Phoenix, Arizona
Designers : Neill Fox, Lesley Kitts, Jason Grubb, Jon Balinkie
Client : Camerawerks

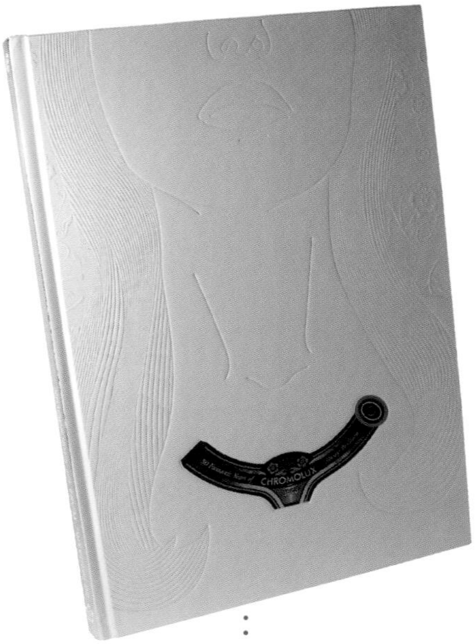

Blind embossing and debossing on the casecover of this book denies the need for additional printing.

Q – Wiesbaden, Germany
Designers : Matthias Frey, Laurenz Nielbock
Client : m-real

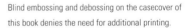

foxnoggin - thinking design – Phoenix, Arizonia
Designers : Neill Fox, Keith Alstrin, Kirsten Sorensen
Client : Reconditioned Systems, Inc.

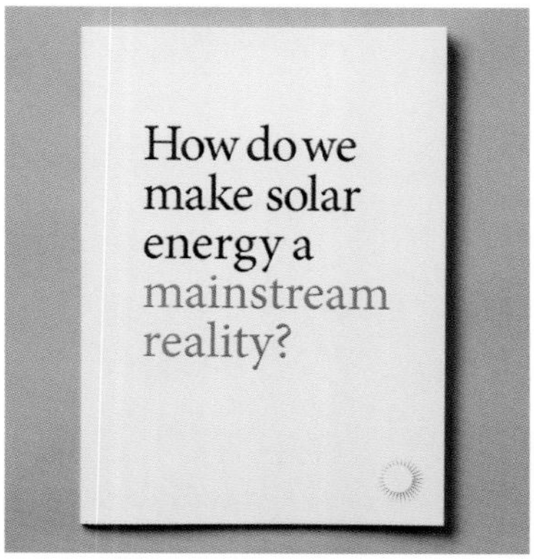
How do we
make solar
energy a
mainstream
reality?

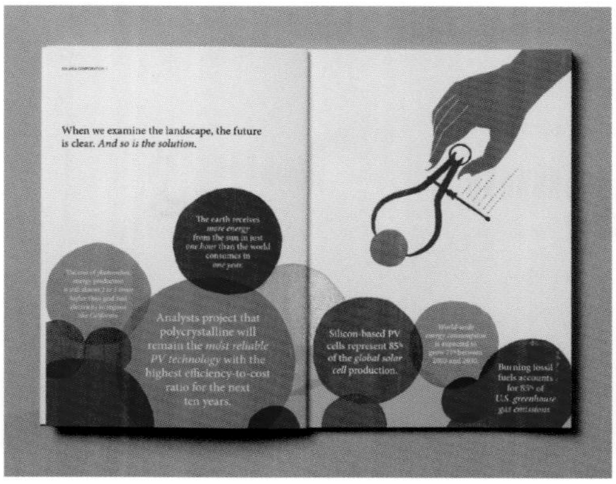

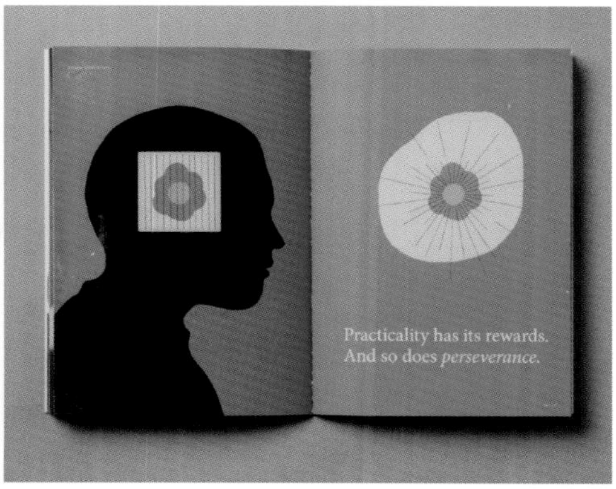

Deep experience in diverse backgrounds has prepared the Solaria team to grow the company from a technology leader to a market leader.

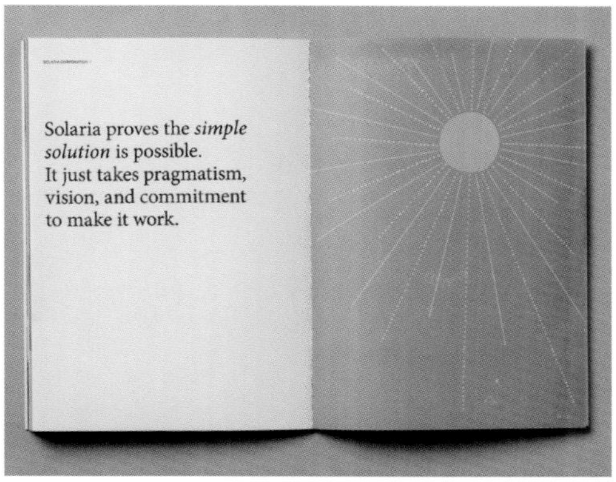
Solaria proves the simple solution is possible.
It just takes pragmatism, vision, and commitment to make it work.

Factor Design – San Francisco, California
Designers : Jeff Zwerner, Tim Guy, Natalie Linden, Chris Silas Neal
Client : The Solaria Corporaton

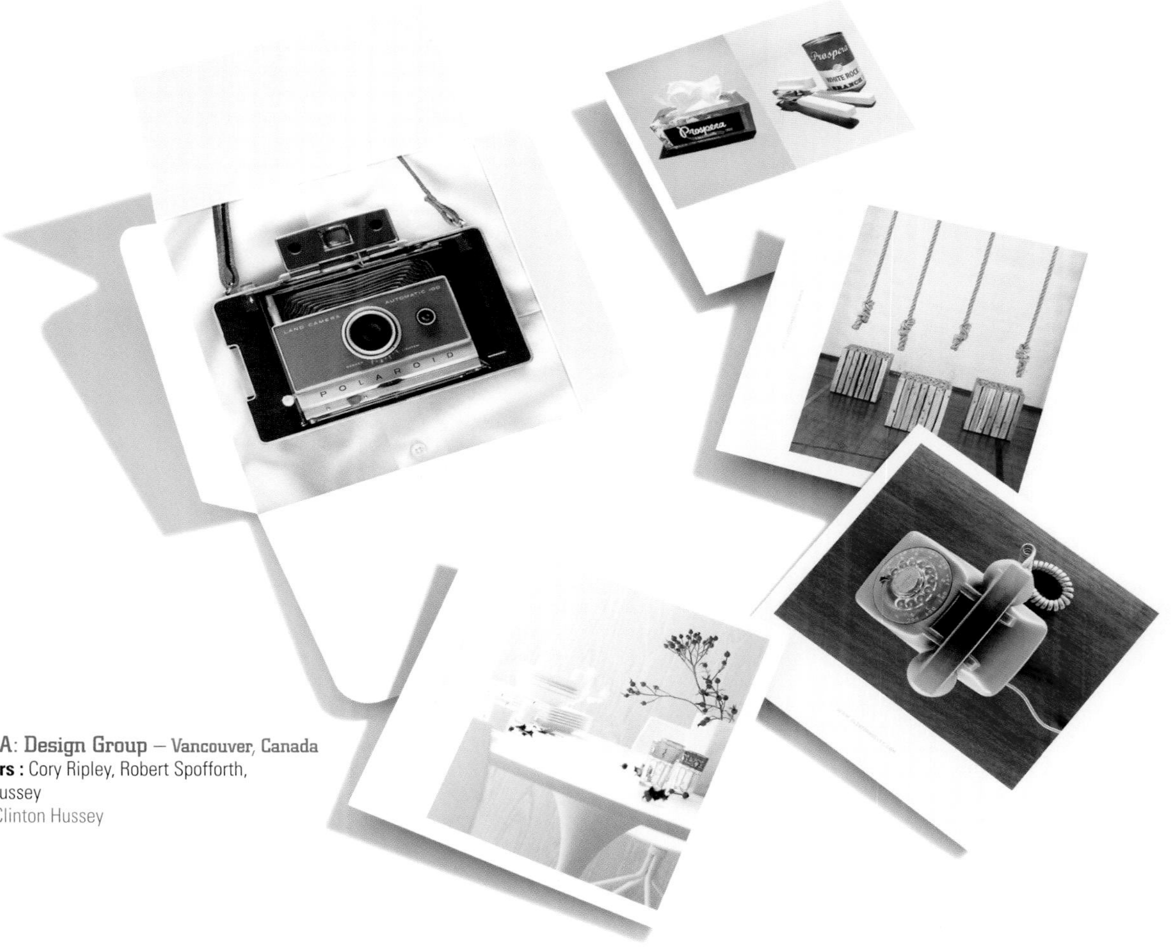

Exhibit A: Design Group – Vancouver, Canada
Designers : Cory Ripley, Robert Spofforth, Clinton Hussey
Client : Clinton Hussey

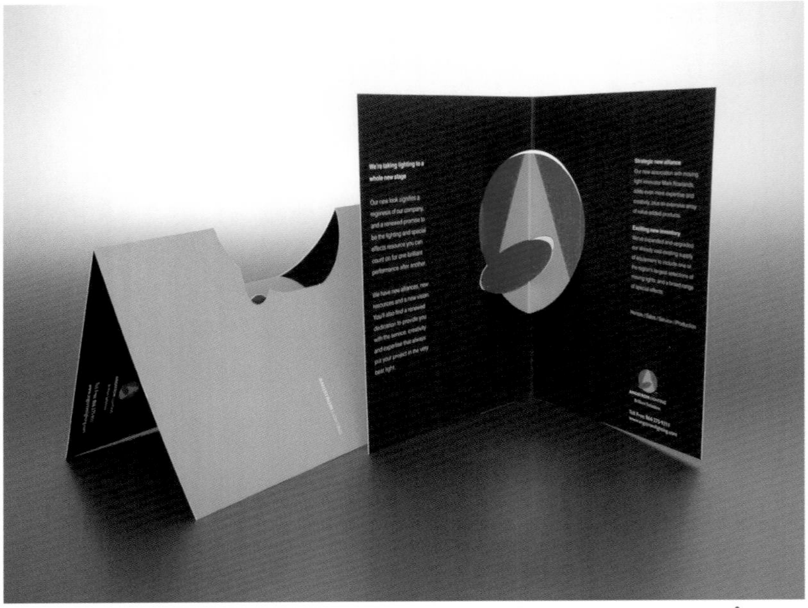

Shimokochi-Reeves – Los Angeles, California
Designers : Mamoru Shimokochi, Anne Reeves
Client : Angstrom Lighting

A pop-up design will draw more attention than a similar flat piece. Putting your logo in 3-D suggests dimension in your business and spotlights your identity.

Delphine Keim-Campbell – Moscow, Idaho
Designers : Delphine Keim-Campbell, Daniel Mullin
Client : DK Mullin Architects

Knowlton Multimedia – Highlands Ranch, Colorado
Designer : Ron Knowlton
Client : Attention Software, Inc.

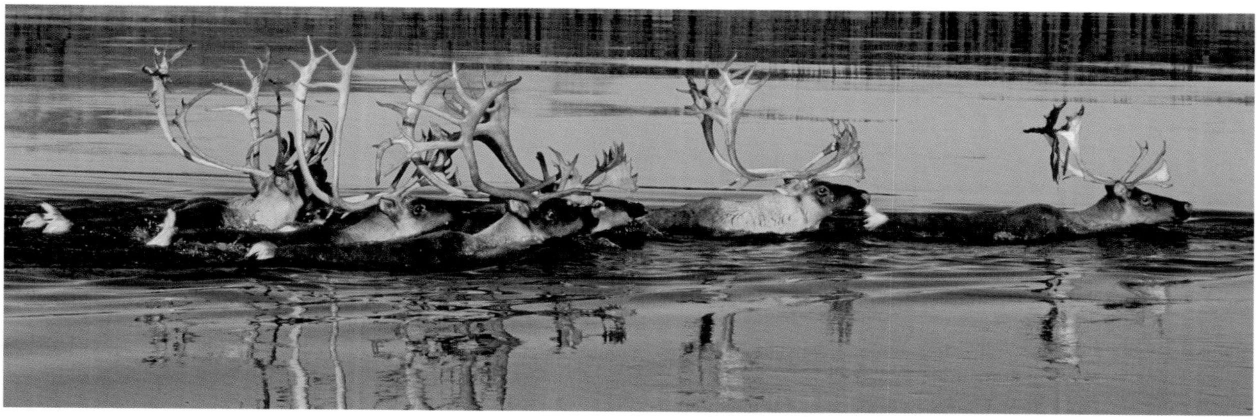

Summer days in Alaska are so loud and bright, it's no wonder they burn out quickly. Autumn days, on the other hand, sneak in quietly and linger for months. As red and gold creep down our mountains, most Alaskans relax a bit. But not Alaska Stock. With hundreds of new summer shots to add, blazing fall colors to capture, and a season of snow right around the corner, we're busier than ever. But we don't mind. You don't get this far north of normal without working for it.
Alaska Stock
IMAGES

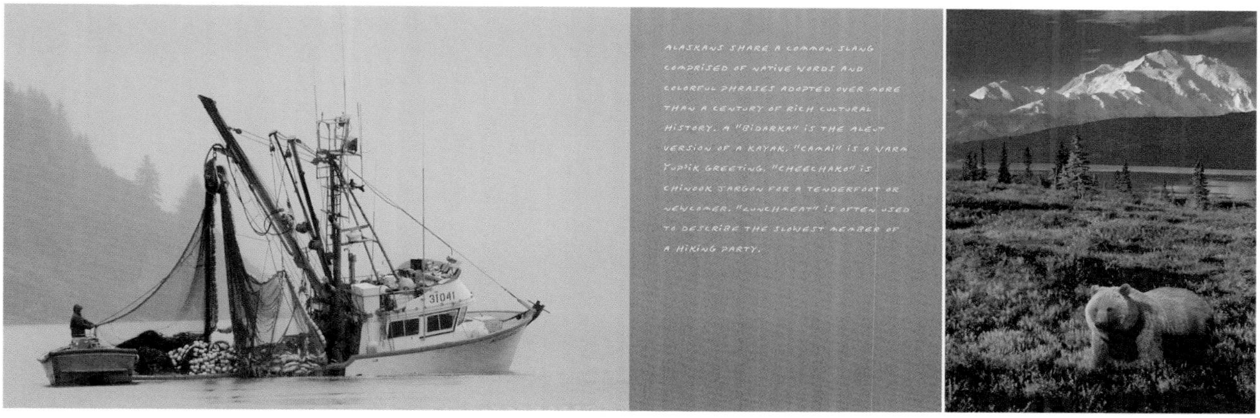
Alaskans share a common slang comprised of native words and colorful phrases adopted over more than a century of rich cultural history. A "Bidarka" is the Aleut version of a kayak. "Camai" is a Yupik greeting. "Cheechako" is Chinook jargon for a tenderfoot or newcomer. "Lunchmeat" is often used to describe the slowest member of a hiking party.
31041

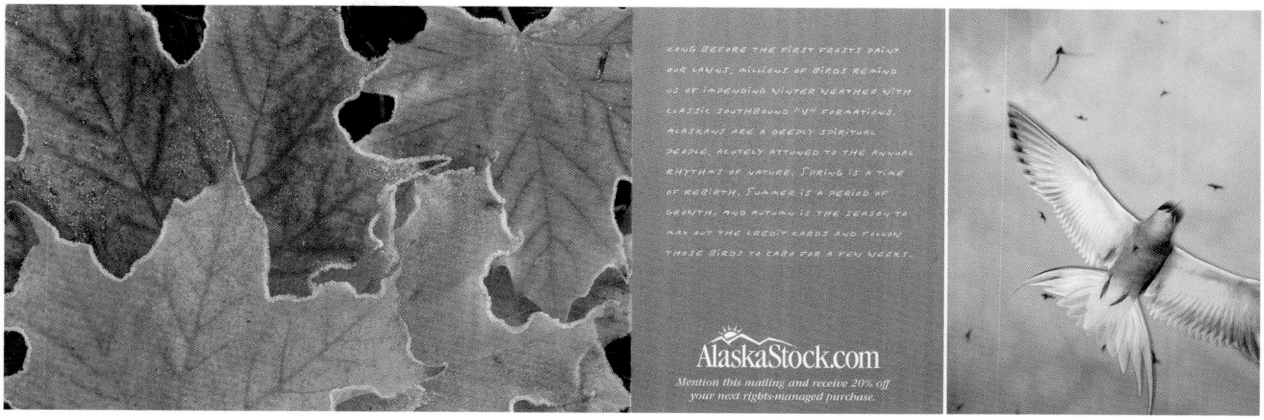
Long before the first frosts paint our lawns, millions of birds remind us of impending winter weather with classic southbound "V" formations. Alaskans are a deeply spiritual people, acutely attuned to the annual rhythms of nature. Spring is a time of rebirth, Summer is a period of growth, and Autumn is the season to max out the credit cards and follow those birds to Cabo for a few weeks.
AlaskaStock.com
Mention this mailing and receive 20% off your next rights-managed purchase.

Mad Dog Graphx – Anchorage, Alaska
Designer : Michael Ardaiz
Client : Alaska Stock Images

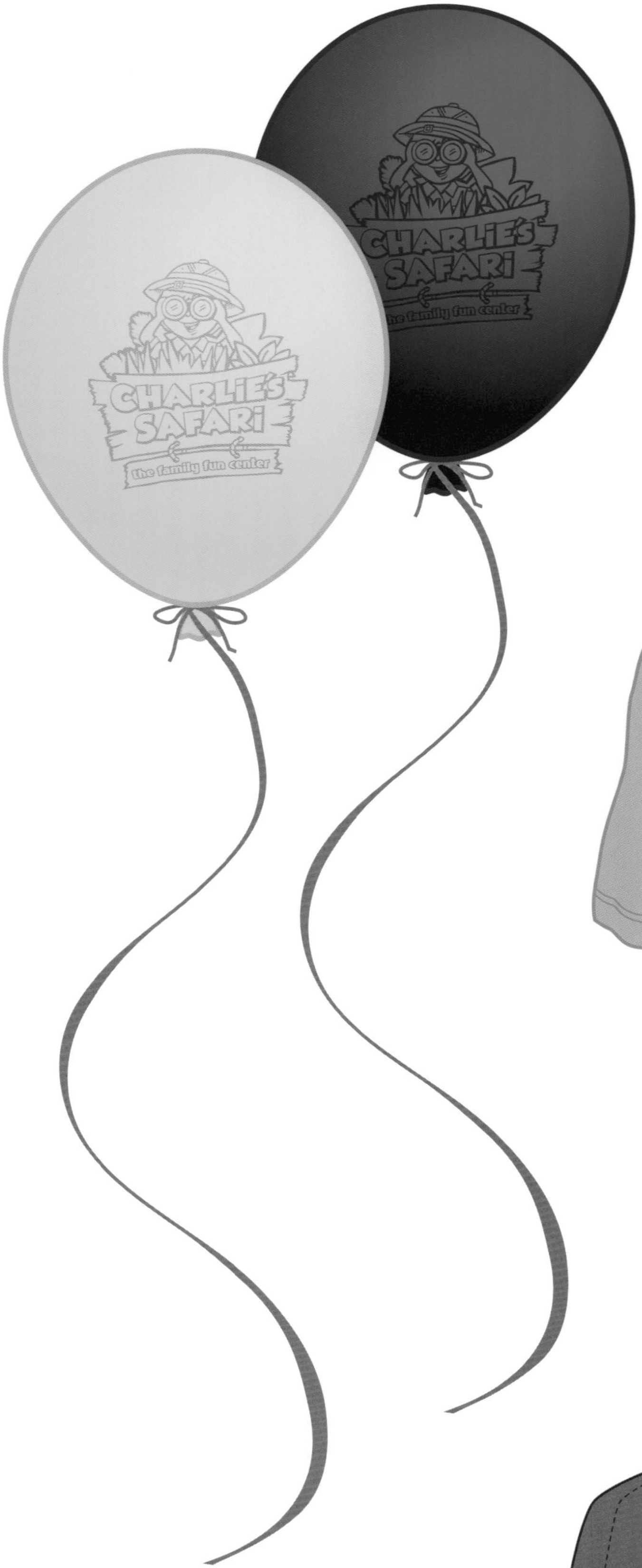

Sungrafx – Silverdale, Washington
Designer : Laura Zander
Client : Charlie's Safari

Roycroft Design – Boston, Massachusetts
Designer : Jennifer Roycroft
Client : AQUENT

James Marsh Design – Hythe, England
Client : Guinness

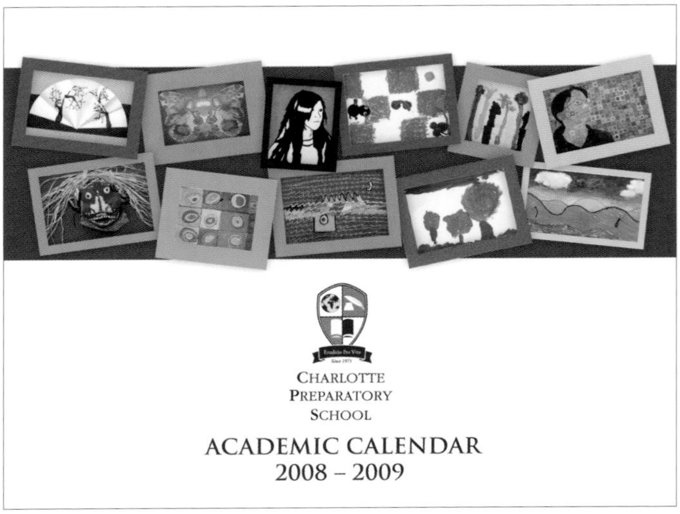

Artwork by: Kerchuan, Eighth Grade

JUNE 2009

SUNDAY	MONDAY	TUESDAY	WEDNESDAY	THURSDAY	FRIDAY	SATURDAY
	1 Academic Awards Ceremony (4th - 8th)	2 Graduation	3 MS Field Day	4 Last Day of School for Lower and Middle School Early Dismissal for LS & MS ASC Available	5	6
7	8 LS Summer Session Begins	9	10	11 Final Report Cards Sent Home (K - 8)	12	13
14	15 Summer Camp Begins	16	17	18	19	20
21	22	23	24	25	26	27
28	29	30				

Early Dismissal Times: Early School and Kindergarten - 11 am, 1st through 4th Grade - 11:15 am, 5th through 8th Grade - 11:45 am

Moonlight Creative Group – Charlotte, North Carolina
Designers : Dawn Newsome, Jenni Miehle
Client : Charlotte Preparatory School

Sutton Watkins Advertising – Las Vegas, Nevada
Designers : Alicia Braach, Stacie Daigle, Jennifer Green
Client : MCDM Landscape

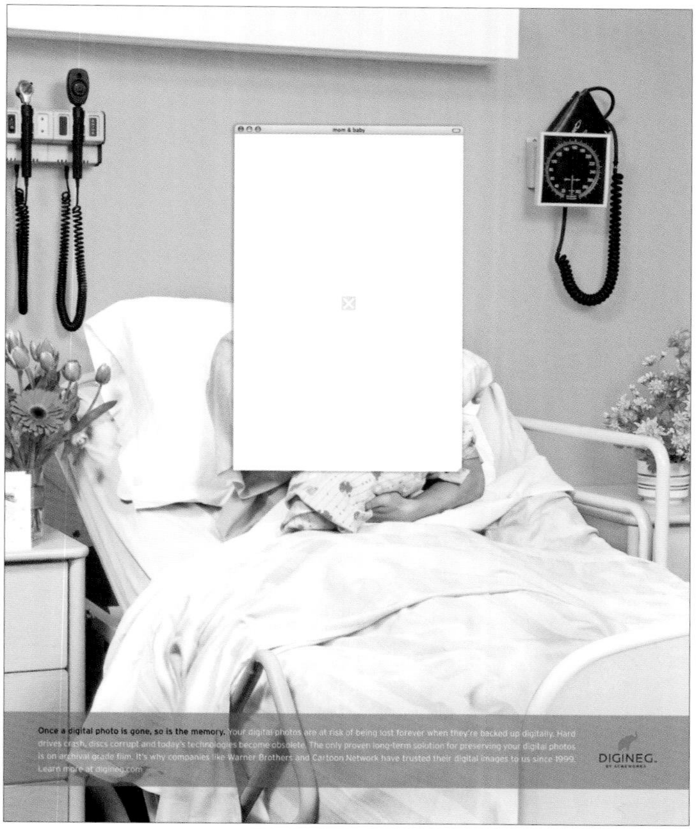
Once a digital photo is gone, so is the memory. Your digital photos are at risk of being lost forever when they're backed up digitally. Hard drives crash, discs corrupt and today's technologies become obsolete. The only proven long-term solution for preserving your digital photos is on archival grade film. It's why companies like Warner Brothers and Cartoon Network have trusted their digital images to us since 1999. Learn more at digineg.com
DIGINEG.

Once a digital photo is gone, so is the memory. Your digital photos are at risk of being lost forever when they're backed up digitally. Hard drives crash, discs corrupt and today's technologies become obsolete. The only proven long-term solution for preserving your digital photos is on archival grade film. It's why companies like Warner Brothers and Cartoon Network have trusted their digital images to us since 1999. Learn more at digineg.com
DIGINEG.

WAX – Calgary, Canada
Designers : Joe Hospodarec, Jonathan Jungwirth, Nick Asik, Jean Perron
Client : DIGINEG

Sponsored by
Sue and Steve Bralove,
John and Linda Derrick,
Wendy and Frank Raines,
Mark and Merril Shugoll &
Dick and Katie Snowdon
The 2006/07 season is sponsored by
Joan and David Maxwell
Illustration by Olaf Hajek
Dear Friend
she loves me
delightful musical comedy
Anna Karenina
book by Joe Masteroff
lyrics by Sheldon Harnick
music by Jerry Bock
based on a play by Miklos Laszlo
directed by Kyle Donnelly
November 17 through December 31, 2006
in the Fichandler
arena stage
Molly Smith, Artistic Director 2006/07 Season www.arenastage.org

MiresBall – San Diego, California
Designers : Scott Mires, Leslie Quinn, Olaf Hajek
Client : Arena Stage

d-10.net – Dundee, Scotland
Designer : Douglas Mullen
Client : Cicada Magazine

Studio QED, Inc.
– San Mateo, California
Designer : Steven Wright
Client : Square Soft

Sayles Graphic Design – Des Moines, Iowa
Designer : John Sayles
Client : International Carwash Association

Artwork inspired by mid-century graphics perfectly complements this campaign reminiscent of gas station games and giveaways.

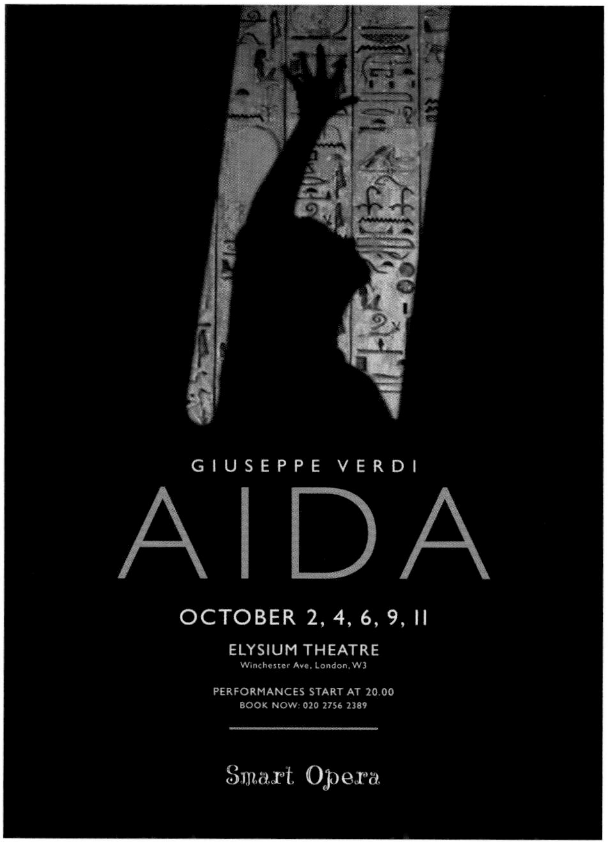
GIUSEPPE VERDI
AIDA
OCTOBER 2, 4, 6, 9, 11
ELYSIUM THEATRE
Winchester Ave, London, W3
PERFORMANCES START AT 20.00
BOOK NOW: 020 2756 2389
Smart Opera

Elixirion – Thessaloniki, Greece
Designers : Michael Sachpazis, Konstantinos Petridis
Client : Opera of Thessaloniki

An In-Depth Look at: DULCE PHOTOGRAPHY/VISIONARI

Hawaii is a popular destination for couples looking to get married, but capturing the memory in photos can be a less-than-enchanting expense. That's why high-end Honolulu photography company Visionari established a midrange sub-brand to appeal to brides and grooms on a budget—and hired John Wingard of John Wingard Design to get the word out. "Instead of referring the customers to a photographer outside the company, Visionari started Dulce," he says.

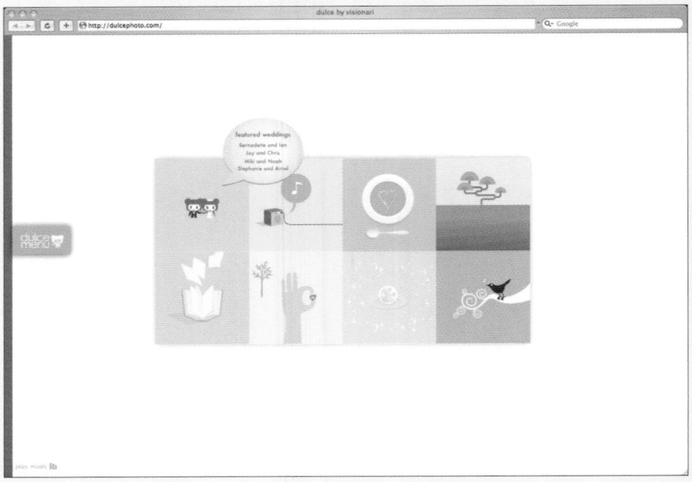

The Web site isn't your typical wedding vendor site. "Usually wedding photographers' Web sites have a certain look. You know it—black, with the white scrolling letters," Wingard says. "We said, 'We're going to do something different.'" Wingard opted for a pastel palette with funky, Japanese-inspired iconography featuring a cartoon character of indeterminate species. "He's just cute," Wingard says of the original, yet instantly familiar, creature. "Hawaii has this East-meets-West kind of feel." To appeal to twentysomethings from the islands and beyond, Wingard designed the entire site with that demographic in mind. "They tend to be more savvy with the Internet," he says, "and we really wanted to take chances with every interaction a client has with the brand." The site features elegant photography, but Wingard's whimsical vision serves both as a contrast and a showcase for Dulce's art. "There's a balance between the unique navigation system and full-screen images, letting the product be featured. It completely paid off."

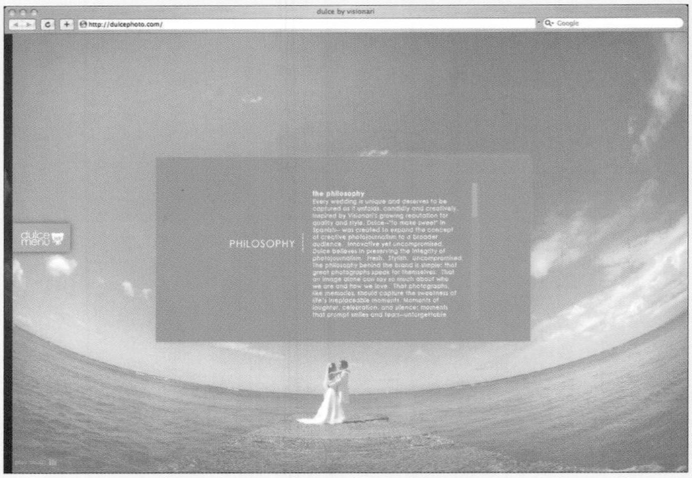

With graphics, not photographs, at the main level, selling the site to Dulce proved to be a surprisingly compatible creative endeavor. "Visionari told us, 'These guys have excellent taste. We're looking for something fresh.' I said, 'Let's take a chance on this.' When we presented our illustration boards, they were sophisticated enough to say, 'This isn't what we've seen before.' They had input that was always excellent." After Wingard presented about a dozen concepts for the brand, Dulce found exactly what it was looking for—as well as an unexpected symbiosis. "We worked with the client to come up with a concept we all felt was strongest," he says, "and one thing that makes our job as designers easy is great source photography."

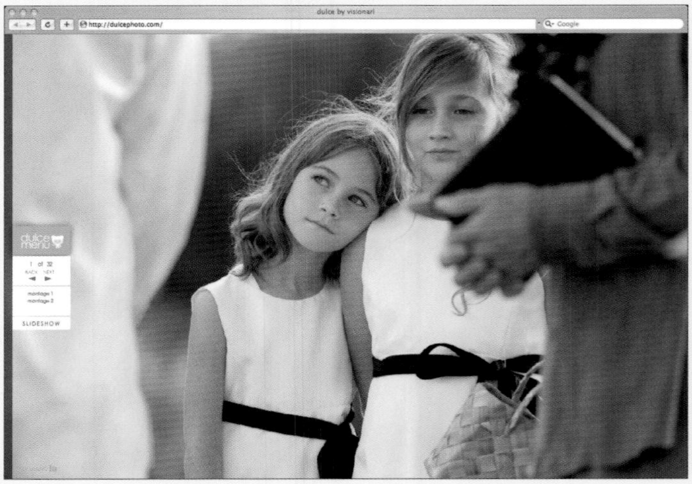

But a brand isn't built on a Web site alone, which is why Dulce had Wingard develop a complete promotional presentation as part of its branding, starting with a high-profile booth at a wedding expo. The booth featured signage and candy jars with the Dulce logo and character in blue, pink, and brown. "We gave away tote bags, and

John Wingard Design/Hibiscus Interactive – Honolulu, Hawaii
Designer: John Wingard
Client: dulce photography/Visionari

people walked around with an ad for Dulce on it," Wingard says. "The pink ones were gone fast. It created a lot of buzz." Wingard continues to see mobile advertisements for Dulce as young women use the bags as purses around town—and beyond. "This was a full, complete brand package," he says. "Name, expo booth, Web site, marketing concepts, national advertising."

As Dulce eyes expansion to other Hawaiian islands, Wingard is pleased with the reaction to his branding campaign—and to the photographers' services themselves. "The response has been phenomenal," he says. "We're trying to connect with customers on an emotional level, and it's working. They're booked solid week after week." Wingard is enthusiastic about Dulce and the image he helped create, describing it as "cute, clean, contemporary, slick, and feminine with an underlying sophistication—a certain kind of finished depth. It's super fun."

Los Alamos National Laboratory Creative Arts and Services – Los Alamos, New Mexico
Designer : Allen Hopkins
Client : Environment, Safety, Health, and Quality Directorate

Symbiotic Solutions – East Lansing, Michigan
Designer : Chris Corneal
Client : Alarm Will Sound

Joven Orozco Design – Newport Beach, California
Designers : Joven Orozco, Kenneth Lim
Client : RFQ

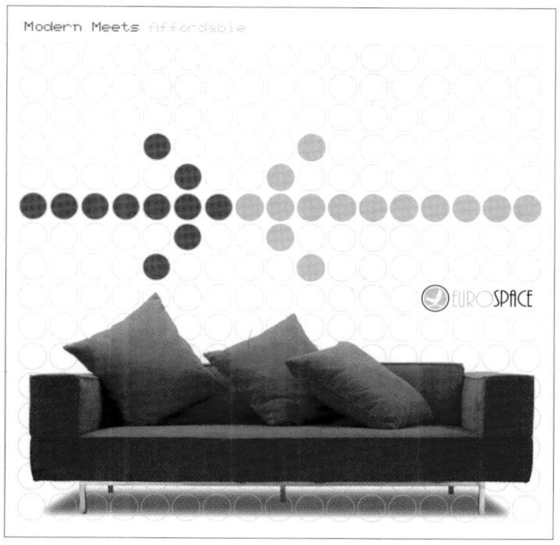

2nd Floor Design
— Portsmouth, Virginia
Designer : Mary Hester
Client : Eurospace

Levine & Associates, Inc.
— Washington, D.C.
Designer : Maggie Soldano
Client : Verizon Center

sms poruka iz prirode

sms

ekstra
djevičansko
maslinovo
ulje
sms

212
Product of Croatia
džem od
suhe
marelice
sms
minimalno 85% voća
212
Product of Croatia
džem od
suhe šljive
sms
minimalno 87% voća

Studio International – Zagreb, Croatia
Designers : Boris Ljubicic, Igor Ljubicic
Client : SMS Food Factory

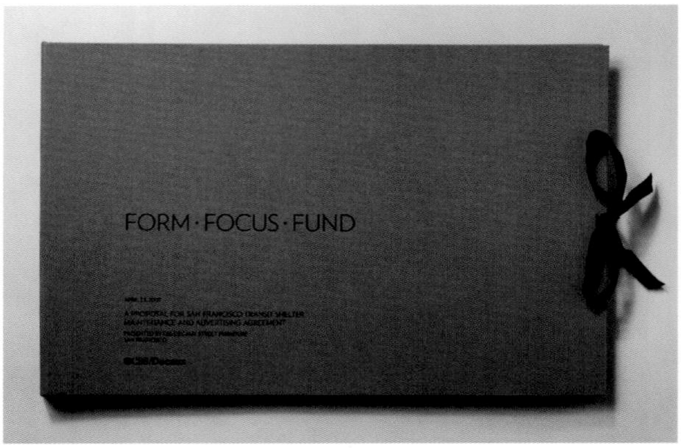
FORM · FOCUS · FUND

FOCUS
FUND

49 COUNTRIES
3,500
CITIES and TOWNS
716,000 ADVERTISING PANELS
80,400
BUS SHELTERS
and over
3,000
AUTOMATED PUBLIC TOILETS

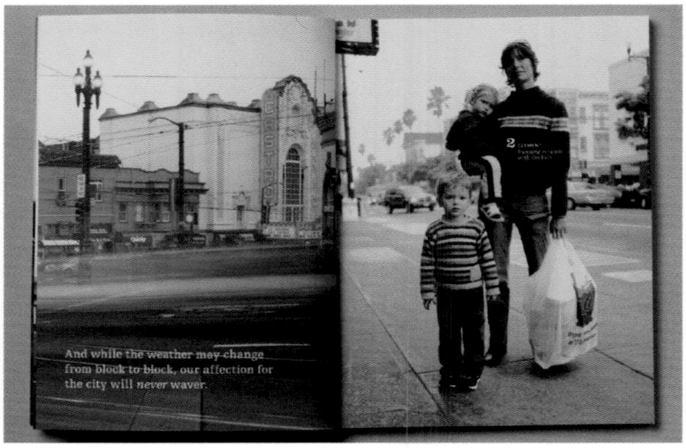
And while the weather may change from block to block, our affection for the city will never waver.

In our years working here in San Francisco, we've learned that everything about the city is world class—from architecture, arts and culture to gourmet dining.

Factor Design – San Francisco, California
Designers : Tim Guy, Katie Heit, Uwe Melichar, Lena Vollmert
Client : JCDecaux

Tread Creative – Los Gatos, California
Designers : Phil Mowery, Russ Birtola
Client : Positio Public Relations

POSITIO PR
Now Presenting
NEWSMAKERS 2006
SAN FRANVEGAS BABY!
SEMICON WEST
2006 Semicon West NewsMakers Reception
POSITIO
PUBLIC RELATIONS
SAN FRANVEGAS BABY!
Where the industry's leading CEOs, editors & analysts hook-up for lasting relationships.

EMBEDDED IN LIFE
Unless you're into really painful experiences...
Use Zatara™ and take the agony out of the fast growing world of secure transactions. We've been the vendor of choice for secure transactions for more than 20 years. We're the first to recognize that in today's highly connected world where theft, fraud and attacks by hackers occurs every second, the need for a trusted, high security, high performance, and highly integrated solution is enormous.
Our new Zatara™ 32-bit ARM-based ASSP protects your point-of-sales (POS) transactions like no other. The Zatara™ single-chip solution is PCI PED & EMV compliant. Its robust data security with an integrated security sub-system, embedded card reading with smartcard and magnetic stripe capabilities and flexible communications interfaces makes it the obvious choice for your next-generation POS systems.
Check out Zatara™ at Booth 4M 141, Hall 4 and enter a chance to win a new Apple IPOD Touch.
For more information on Zilog and Zatara, visit www.zilog.com.
zatara
zilog

Tread Creative – Los Gatos, California
Designers : Phil Mowery, Stew Chalmers
Client : Zilog

MiresBall – San Diego, California
Designers : Scott Mires, Leslie Quinn, Olaf Hajek
Client : Arena Stage

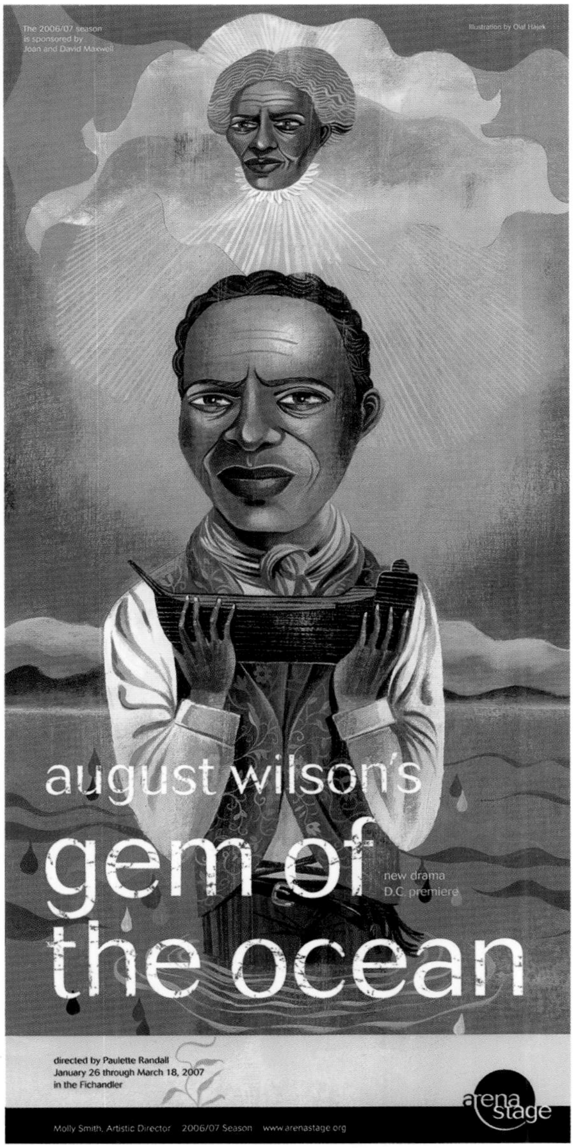

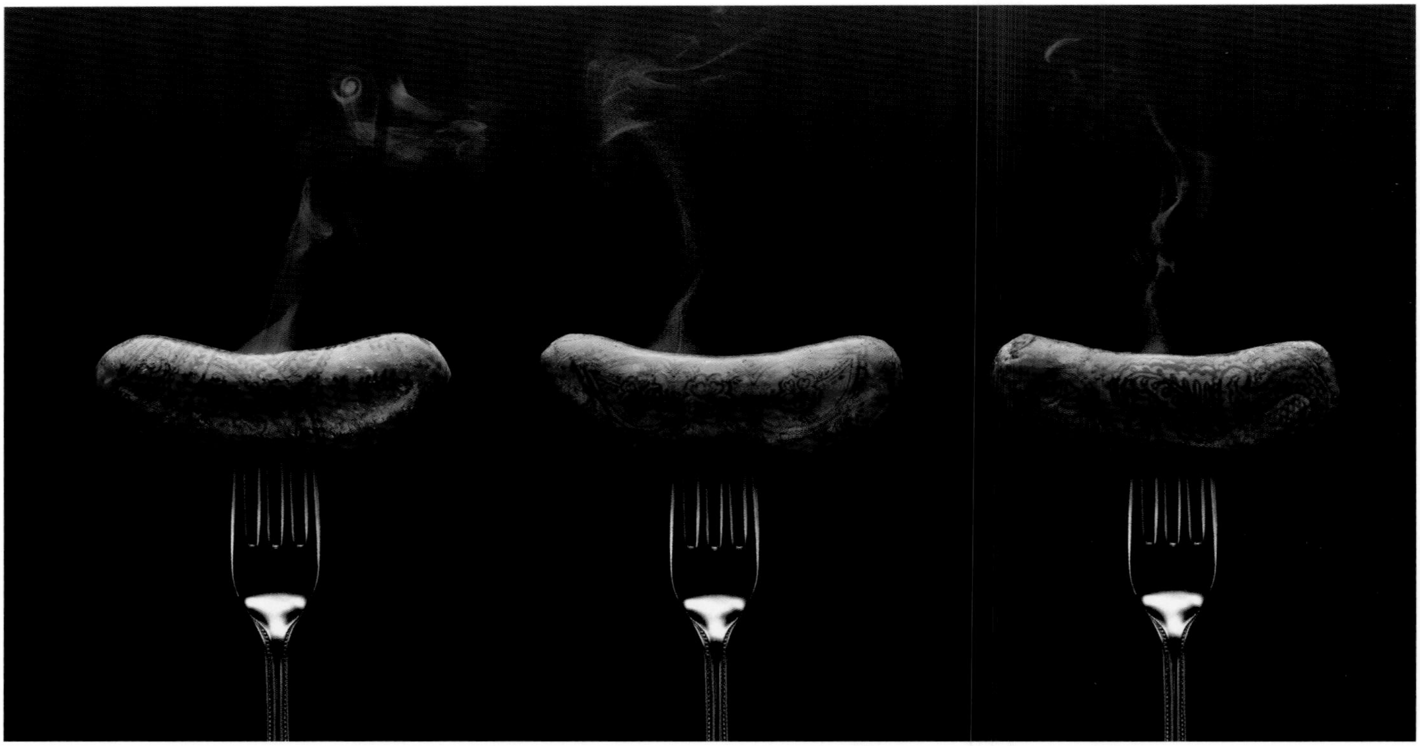

The Partners – London, England
Designers : Miranda Bolter, Paul Currah, Nick Eagleton, Alex John
Client : Mr. Singh's Bangras

Elixirion – Thessaloniki, Greece
Designers : Michael Sachpazis, Konstantinos Petridis
Client : Opera of Thessaloniki

Each of these posters is specifically designed to represent a season of the year. Each one is hugely successful in communicating its theme. At the same time, there is no question that each one is a part of a series. Visual consistency—font usage, layout, color values, single photographic image, geometric graphics—binds them in a way that words never could.

Los Alamos National Laboratory Creative Arts and Services
– Los Alamos, New Mexico
Designer: Allen Hopkins
Client: Environmental Protection Division

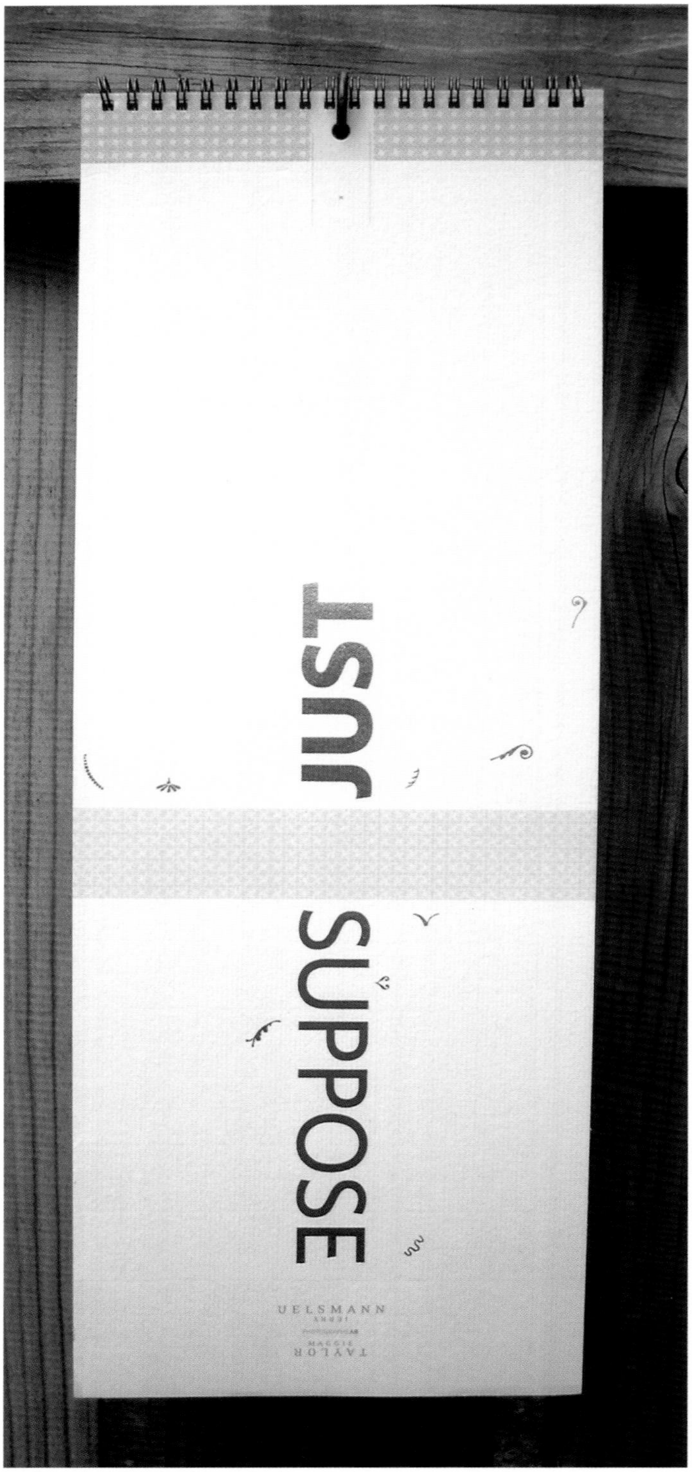

Connie Hwang Design – San Francisco, California
Designer : Connie Hwang
Client : University Galleries

Silver foil-stamping coordinates nicely with teal accents on the cover of this spiral-bound brochure. Inside, the works of two artists are repeatedly juxtaposed on a single sheet, silently inviting the viewer to contrast and compare.

CONTRARY TO REASON
WAKEFUL RABBIT

It's All About . . .

The Event

Holiday or Seasonal Promotions

Open Creative Group – Birmingham, Alabama
Designers : April Mraz
Client : Heather Monahan Photography

Bleu Sky Creative – Burlington, Vermont
Designers : Michelle Hobbs, Jennifer Adrian
Client : Bleu Sky Creative

DON'T CHILL OUT, DON'T TAKE A BREATH, DON'T COUNT TO TEN, DON'T PICTURE YOUR SPECIAL HAPPY PLACE. THIS IS THE ONE DAY OF THE YEAR WHEN YOU CAN
TOTALLY LOSE IT,
TAKE A CLOSER LOOK AT
CRAPPER DAY!
THE 27TH DAY OF JANUARY
STUDIOS
is pleased to welcome you to
UNCANNY
AND COMPLIMENTARY
MONTH
CLUB!
PY HOLIDAYS
DEED!
STYLISH, AND REALLY QUITE BULLY
GOODWILL!
THE CRAP

CDI Studios – Las Vegas, Nevada
Designers : Victoria Hart, Brian Felgar, Aaron Moses, Dan McElhattan III, Tracy Brockhouse
Client : CDI Studios

You are Invited to the Tom Fowler, Inc.
SUMMER PATIO PARTY
BE THERE OR BE SQUARE!
Cut out along the outer edge and then fold along the perforated lines to make a Tom Fowler, Inc. party cube for your desk.
RAIN OR
SHINE
SUMMER PATIO PARTY 2007
Tom Fowler Inc.
Please join us on Wednesday, July 11 at 5pm for casual cocktails and hors'douvres at Tom Fowler, Inc. 111 Westport Ave. Norwalk, CT 06851
RSVP by Monday, July 9th 203.845.0700
SUMMER PATIO PARTY 2007
BE THERE OR BE SQUARE

The collateral for this summer patio party all played on the theme of "Be there or be square." Brightly-colored invitations arrived with easy-to-follow instructions that allowed the recipient to transform the flat sheet into a three-dimensional cube/decoration. Much larger versions were stacked onsite as eye-catching announcements and directional aids.

TFI Envision, Inc. – Norwalk, Connecticut
Designers : Elizabeth P. Ball, Mary Ellen Butkus
Client : Tom Fowler, Inc.

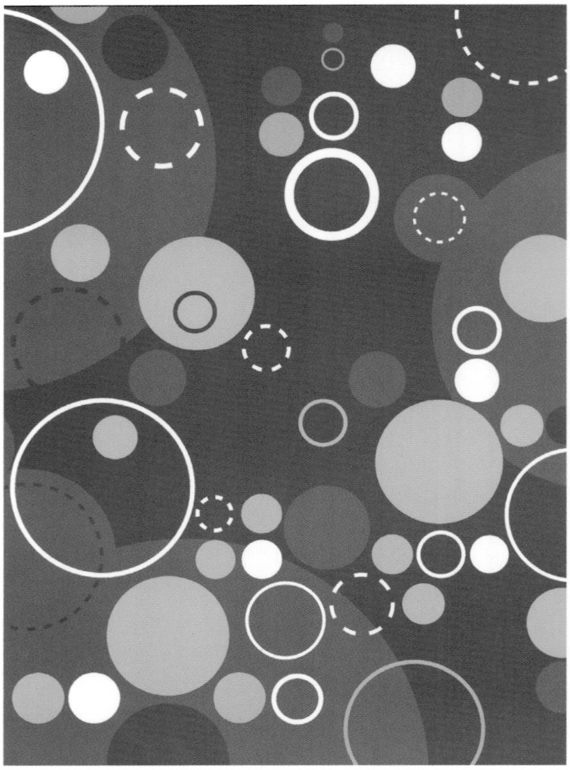

Wishing you
a season of
inspiration
from your friends at BBMG
BBMG

BBMG – Des Moines, Iowa
Designers : Molly Conley, Scott Ketchum
Client : BBMG

Shimokochi-Reeves – Los Angeles, California
Designers : Mamoru Shimokochi, Coco Klinkenberg
Client : Angstrom Lighting

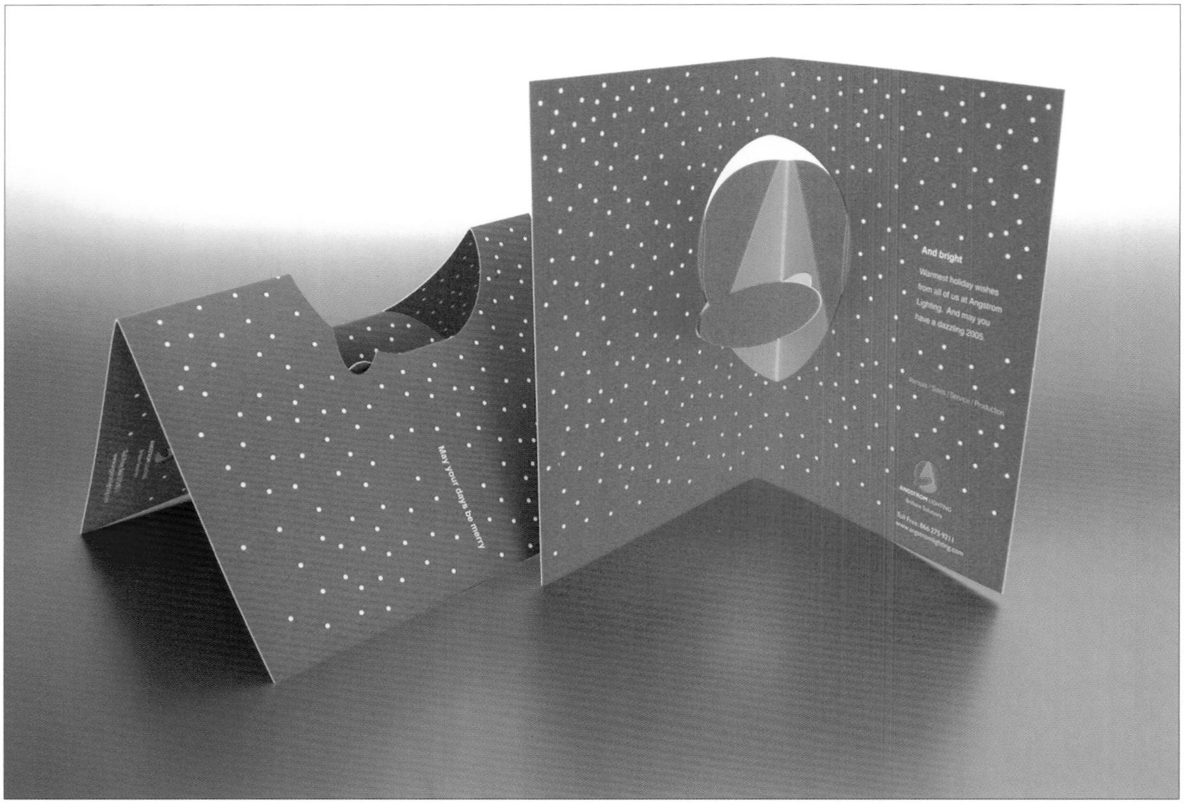
May your days be merry
And bright
Warmest holiday wishes from all of us at Angstrom Lighting. And may you have a dazzling 2005.

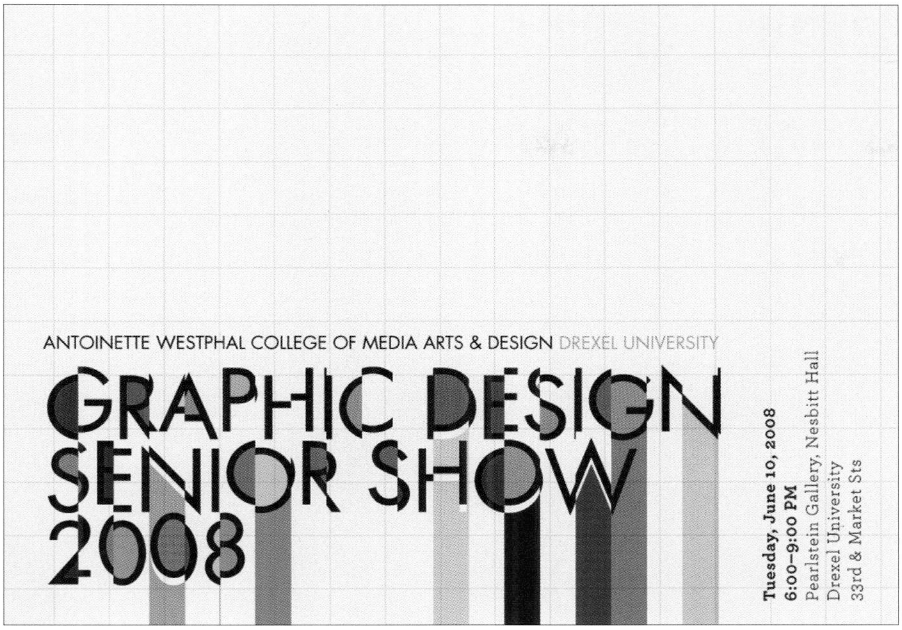
ANTOINETTE WESTPHAL COLLEGE OF MEDIA ARTS & DESIGN DREXEL UNIVERSITY
GRAPHIC DESIGN SENIOR SHOW 2008
Tuesday, June 10, 2008
6:00–9:00 PM
Pearlstein Gallery, Nesbitt Hall
Drexel University
33rd & Market Sts

Putting themselves in a PMS swatch book suggests each of these graduating seniors is a tool no design firm could do without.

Drexel University, Antoinette Westphal College of Media Arts & Design, Graphic Design Program – Philadelphia, Pennsylvania
Designers : Kyle Cook, Jody Graff
Client : Drexel University, Antoinette Westphal College of Media Arts & Design, Graphic Design Program

HAPPY HALLOWEEN FROM SHIMOKOCHI-REEVES

Shimokochi-Reeves – Los Angeles, California
Designers : Mamoru Shimokochi
Client : Shimokochi-Reeves

Wishing You Great Presents of Mime
this Season and in the Coming Year.
Ventress Design Group
In accordance with your beliefs and practices, we wish you a: Merry Christmas • Happy Hanukah • Super Solstice • Jolly Festivus • Kickin' Kwanzaa • Happy New Year

Ventress Design Group – Franklin, Tennessee
Designers : Tom Ventress, Eric Ventress, Dan Loftin
Client : Ventress Design Group

Curiosity Group — **Portland, Oregon**
Designers : Yvonne Perez Emerson, Alberto Cerriteño
Client : Curiosity Group

An In-Depth Look at: BÜRO NORTH

The environmentally-unfriendly practice of chopping living trees and the attendant danger of fire have caused fresh Christmas trees to fall out of favor in recent years. So you may be surprised to learn that when Melbourne design company Büro North sent their clients wooden trees in 2007, "things really went wild"—in the best way imaginable.

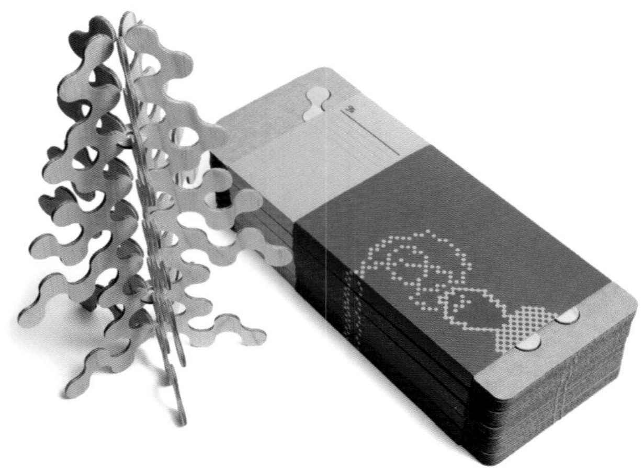

According to creative director Soren Luckins, the "plywood alternative" trees—a collapsible combination of plywood, CNC routing and natural linseed oil—were developed "to solve a problem and address an unsustainable social habit." Shipped in a flat, modular package, the trees grew from a small giveaway to clients, potential clients, and friends to a worldwide sensation. "There were about fifty at first, but after we paid a thousand dollars to set up the production run it cost significantly less to do some more," he says. Media interest took root after the trees appeared at a design market in Melbourne. "It was blogged about on some Web sites, written up in a couple of Melbourne and Sydney newspapers, magazines, and *Monocle* magazine," Luckins says. "Then things really went wild. We got orders from Europe, the U.K., the U.S., Japan."

While Luckins believes that Büro North's holiday promotion was the first of its kind, the deeper meaning is there for the recipients to discover—if they choose. "Part of the corporate gift is to go through the process of a life cycle analysis and show our clients how it's going to be in the future," he says. "The inside of the package has information about us and how to assemble (the tree) and information about the life cycle analysis, packaged like a little Christmas bauble."

While the trees helped reinforce Büro North's place on the Australian design map, they also served to accommodate a demographic traditionally underserved by the traditional Christmas decoration market. "People of my generation are less religious and more interested in embracing the celebration of it," says Luckins. "They may not buy a tree every year but when they do they want something small and high quality." He adds that due to restrictions on new residential construction, the trees were especially popular among apartment dwellers; while the 2007 version came in three sizes ranging from 400 to 2,300 millimeters (1.31 to 7.55 feet), future editions will feature a new size based on customers' suggestions. And while lifelike artificial trees continue to be perennial favorites, Luckins sees a definite place for the plywood alternative trees: they're eighty percent more "green" than traditional Christmas trees and even more environmentally responsible than the fake tree you may recycle by taking it out of the basement year after year. "These are more sustainable than plastic trees, which have oils and [more industrial chemical] manufacture involved," he says.

In the meantime, Büro North works on what it does best, looking ahead to the next year's design while avoiding unnecessary trips to the post office. "It'll be a little different," Luckins says. "We have to work out distribution and logistical issues. We're a design firm."

Büro North – **Melbourne, Australia**
Designers: Soren Luckins, Sarah Napier, Skye Luckins, Tom Allnutt, David Williamson
Client: Büro North

We don't often think of Abraham Lincoln and Thanksgiving in synonymous terms, but in October 1863, three months after the battle of Gettysburg, the 16th president proclaimed the last Thursday in November to be Thanksgiving Day. Lincoln established the holiday thanks in part to a persistent letter-writing campaign by a woman named Sarah Hale, in which she encouraged him to proclaim a national day of thanksgiving. In her correspondence to Lincoln, Hale included an editorial she wrote for her *Lady's Book* magazine and explained that a "national feeling of Thanksgiving" would benefit the country in the midst of the Civil War. Happy holIDays.

ThanksforThanksgiving.

the**ID**entity®

HAPPY

HOLIDAYS

the**ID**entity

MEMORIAL DAY WAS ORIGINALLY KNOWN AS DECORATION DAY BECAUSE IT WAS A TIME SET ASIDE TO HONOR THE NATION'S CIVIL WAR DEAD BY DECORATING THEIR GRAVES. IT WAS FIRST WIDELY OBSERVED ON MAY 30, 1868, BY PROCLAMATION OF GENERAL JOHN A. LOGAN OF THE GRAND ARMY OF THE REPUBLIC, AN ORGANIZATION OF FORMER SAILORS AND SOLDIERS.

ReMemberorial Day.

MEMORIAL DAY IS MUCH MORE THAN A THREE-DAY WEEKEND THAT MARKS THE BEGINNING OF SUMMER. TO MANY PEOPLE, ESPECIALLY THE NATION'S THOUSANDS OF COMBAT VETERANS, THIS DAY, WHICH HAS A HISTORY STRETCHING BACK ALL THE WAY TO THE CIVIL WAR, IS AN IMPORTANT REMINDER OF THOSE WHO DIED IN THE SERVICE OF THEIR COUNTRY. **HAPPY HOLIDAYS.**

the**ID**entity®

THOMAS NAST FIRST DREW SANTA CLAUS FOR THE 1862 Christmas season *Harper's Weekly* cover to memorialize the family sacrifices of the Union during the early and, for the north, darkest days of the Civil War. When Nast created his image of Santa Claus he was drawing on his native German tradition of Saint Nicholas, a fourth century bishop known for his kindness and generosity. Nast combined this tradition

WISHING YOU A HOLIDAY OF HISTORIC PROPORTIONS

of Saint Nicholas with other German folk traditions of elves to draw his Santa. The modern American celebration of Christmas, with its commercialized gift exchanges, developed after 1880. The jolly old fellow at right was titled, "Merry Old Santa Claus", from the January 1, 1881 issue of *Harper's Weekly* magazine. Happy holIDays.

the**ID**entity®

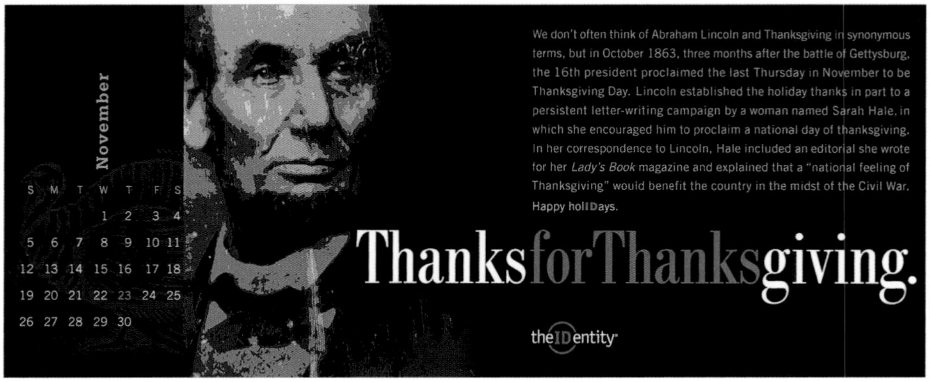

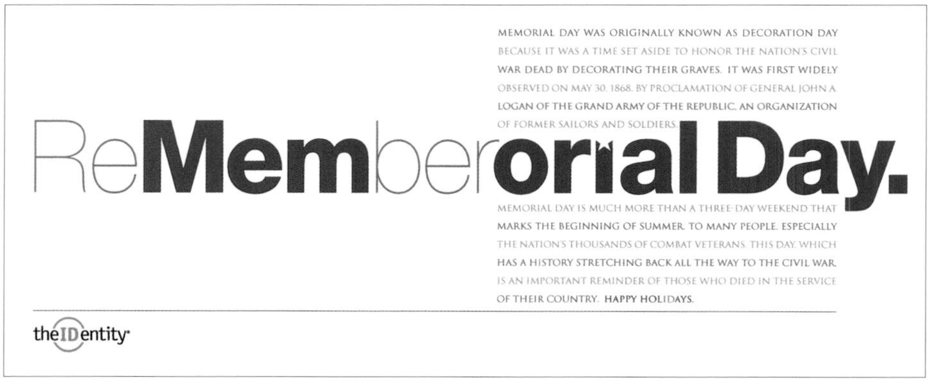

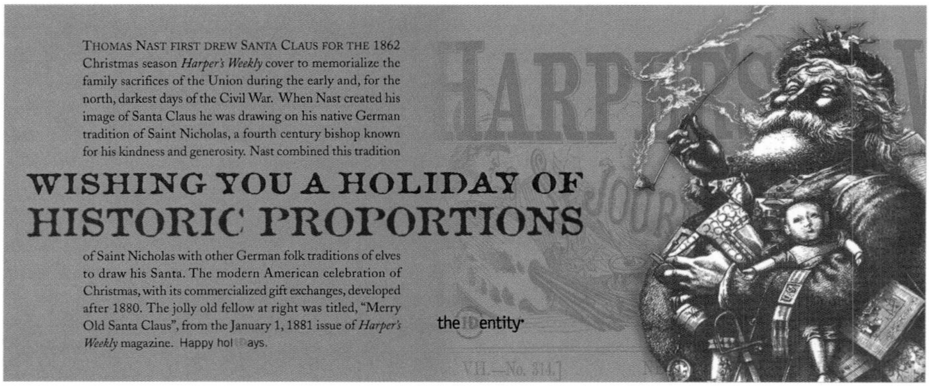

The Id Entity – Fredericksburg, Virginia
Designers : Jackson Foster
Client : The Id Entity

Typically, a holiday thank-you is sent around Christmas, but who says you have to wait until the end of the year or limit your promotional contact to a solitary annual event? This series of cards, sent as the calendar marked other special days, was a regular reminder of The ID Entity's presence. After relocating to a new city, the firm began working with historic-related organizations and used historic motifs on the cards to punctuate that capability.

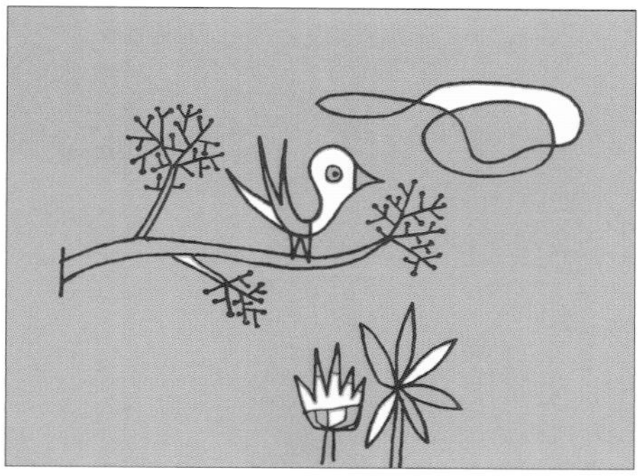

SPRING HAS SPRUNG!
Wishing you ...
ALWAYS REMEMBER YOUR UMBRELLA WHEN APRIL SHOWERS
sweet spring breezes
A DANDELION-FREE LAWN
a big tax refund
a glorious mayday bouquet
and a fresh, new look for your
corporate identity or company literature!
Your friends at
Sayles Graphic Design

Sayles Graphic Design – Des Moines, Iowa
Designers : John Sayles, Bridget Drendel
Client : Sayles Graphic Design

3rd Edge Communications – Jersey City, New Jersey
Designers : Frankie Gonzalez, Melissa Mackin, Michelle Wang
Client : 3rd Edge Communications

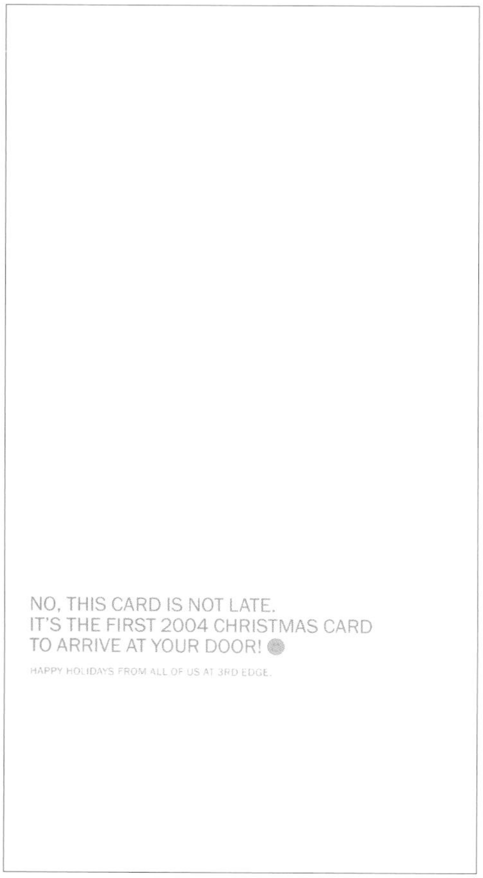
NO, THIS CARD IS NOT LATE.
IT'S THE FIRST 2004 CHRISTMAS CARD
TO ARRIVE AT YOUR DOOR!
HAPPY HOLIDAYS FROM ALL OF US AT 3RD EDGE.

12 04*
happy holidays

JINGLE BELLS!
JINGLE BELLS!
JINGLE ALL THE
WAAAAAAY!!
3rd Edge Wishes You a Boisterous Christmas and a Happy New Year

Happy Holidays

Leibold Associates, Inc. – Neenah, Wisconsin
Designers : Chad Fulwiler, Jane Oliver, Ryan Wienandt,
Nick Maggio, Therese Joanis, Jason Harttert, Jake Weiss, Greg Madson
Client : Leibold Associates, Inc.

Reminiscent of the "from our house to yours" Christmas sentiment, this selection of treats comes in a box cleverly designed to model Leibold Associates' office.

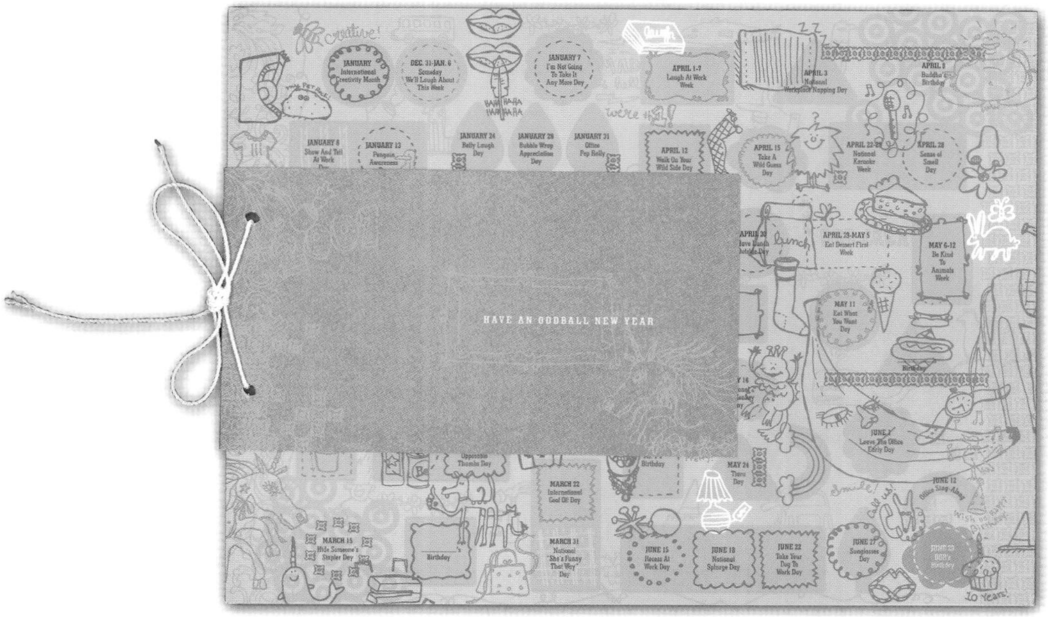

BBR Creative – Lafayette, Louisiana
Designer : Denise Gallagher
Client : BBR Creative

CDI Studios – Las Vegas, Nevada
Designers : Victoria Hart, Brian Felgar, Tracy Brockhouse, Eddie Roberts, Dan McElhattan II
Client : CDI Studios

IE Design + Communications – **Hermosa Beach, California**
Designers : Marcie Carson, Jane Lee, Nicole Bednarz,
Christine Kenney, Kenny Goldstein, Lisa Arnett, Jonathan Lackey
Client : IE Design + Communications

Happy Holidays
Snowflake Sugar Cookies
A simple sugar cookie recipe with a tender, flaky texture and a buttery taste. Yum! Makes about 24
YOU WILL NEED:
1 cup butter, softened
1 cup granulated sugar
1 large egg
Beat together butter and sugar until light and fluffy. Add egg and vanilla, mix until just combined. Add flour and baking powder in intervals. Dough will seem as if doesn't have enough moisture but continue to mix with mixer until combined (it will come together when chilled). Divide the dough into four equal parts, shape into four disks, wrap with plastic wrap and refrigerate about an hour or until firm. Preheat oven to 375 F.
Roll out dough between 2 sheets of waxed paper, about 1/4 inch thick for crispier cookies and 1/3 inch thick for softer cookies. Cut out shapes with cookie cutters and place on prepared baking sheets. Bake for 7-8 minutes or until edges just start to turn a golden color. For softer cookies, do not allow the cookies to take on color. Remove from oven, let cool for one minute and then transfer to wire rack. Allow cookie sheet to cool thoroughly before placing uncooked dough on it. Decorate cookies with Royal Icing or Buttercream Frosting and sprinkles.
Happy Holidays

Octavo Designs – **Frederick, Maryland**
Designers : Sue Hough, Mark Burrier
Client : Octavo Designs

Paragon Marketing Communications – **Salmiya, Kuwait**
Designers : Louai Alasfahani, Konstantin Assenov, Huzaifa Kakumama
Client : National Financial

Sabingrafik, Inc. – Carlsbad, California
Designers : Tracy Sabin, Bridget Sabin
Client : Sabingrafik, Inc.

I'm not kidding—these are exactly the same kind of cards I gave and received at St. Valentine's Day when I was in grade school (and still have in my childhood scrapbook). Sayles Graphic Design refashioned them for a lighthearted and nostalgic promo that gives the recipient "the thrill of being the kid in school who got the most Valentines!"

VALENTINE, NUTS
BEE OUR VALENTINE
AND WE'LL CREATE BUZZ FOR YOU!
A-ROUND!
SUCCESS BAG VALENTINE!
VALENTINE, YOU PUT THE WIND IN OUR SAYLES
VALENTINE HOOKED
EXPLORE VALENTINE
OKAY,
YOU'RE OUR CANDIDATE
WE'RE TUNED IN TO YOU VALENTINE!
ROSES ARE RED VIOLETS ARE BLUE HERE ARE SOME SPECIAL VALENTINE WISHES FOR YOU!
APE TO WORK FOR YOU
VALENTINE
WISHING YOU... RED ROSES FROM YOUR SWEETHEART
A SATIN BOX OF CHOCOLATES WITH A BIG VELVET BOW
A RED CONSTRUCTION PAPER AND WHITE DOILY MASTERPIECE MADE WITH LOVE BY A CHILD
YOUR FILL OF CANDY CONVERSATION HEARTS AND HERSHEY KISSES
CUPID'S ARROW RIGHT ON TARGET
AND MOST OF ALL...
THE SPECIAL THRILL OF BEING THE ... IN SCHOOL WHO GOT ...

Sayles Graphic Design – Des Moines, Iowa
Designer : John Sayles
Client : Sayles Graphic Design

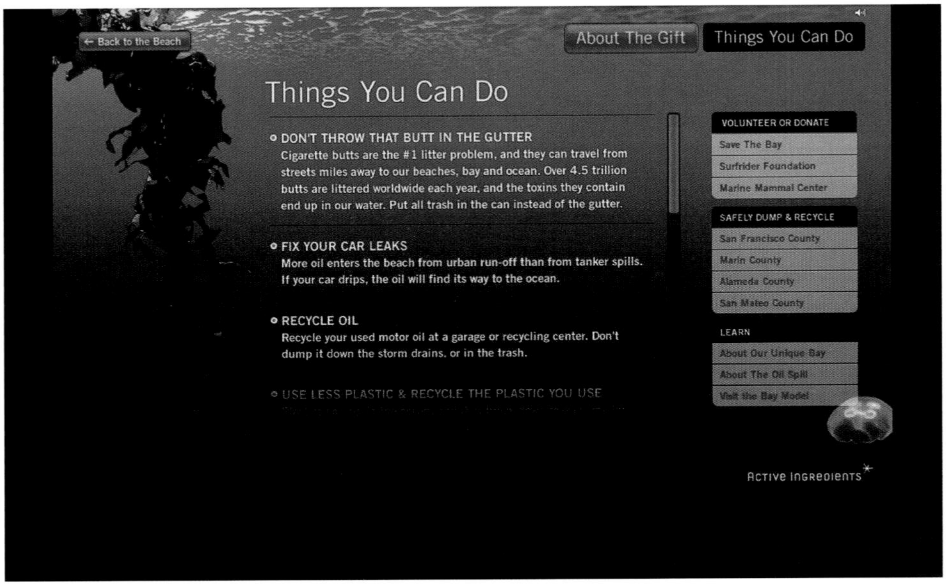
← Back to the Beach
About The Gift
Things You Can Do
Things You Can Do
DON'T THROW THAT BUTT IN THE GUTTER
Cigarette butts are the #1 litter problem, and they can travel from streets miles away to our beaches, bay and ocean. Over 4.5 trillion butts are littered worldwide each year, and the toxins they contain end up in our water. Put all trash in the can instead of the gutter.
FIX YOUR CAR LEAKS
More oil enters the beach from urban run-off than from tanker spills. If your car drips, the oil will find its way to the ocean.
RECYCLE OIL
Recycle your used motor oil at a garage or recycling center. Don't dump it down the storm drains, or in the trash.
USE LESS PLASTIC & RECYCLE THE PLASTIC YOU USE
VOLUNTEER OR DONATE
Save The Bay
Surfrider Foundation
Marine Mammal Center
SAFELY DUMP & RECYCLE
San Francisco County
Marin County
Alameda County
San Mateo County
LEARN
About Our Unique Bay
About The Oil Spill
Visit the Bay Model
Active Ingredients

To the bay, with love
XOX Active Ingredients
About The Gift
Things You Can Do
Active Ingredients

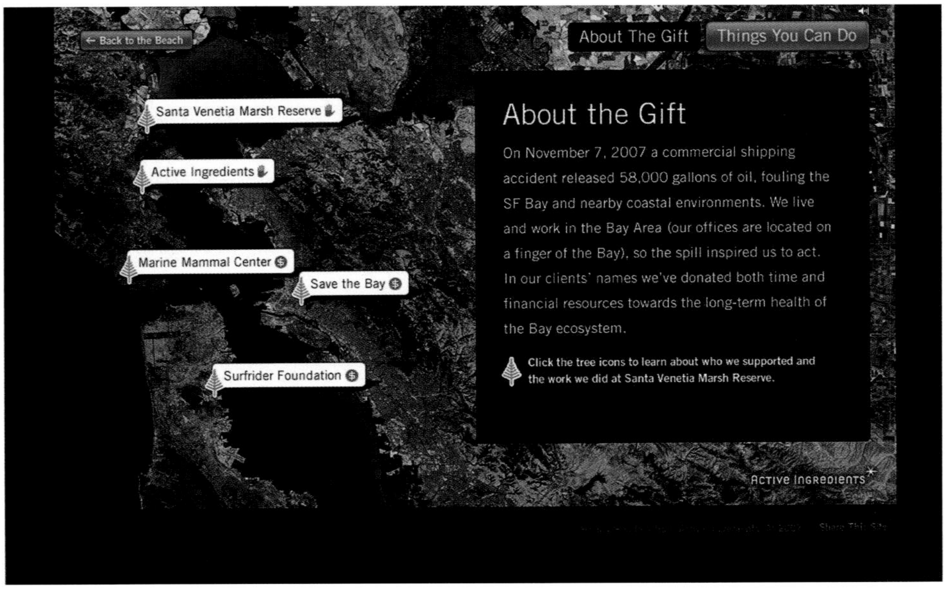
← Back to the Beach
About The Gift
Things You Can Do
Santa Venetia Marsh Reserve
Active Ingredients
Marine Mammal Center
Save the Bay
Surfrider Foundation
About the Gift
On November 7, 2007 a commercial shipping accident released 58,000 gallons of oil, fouling the SF Bay and nearby coastal environments. We live and work in the Bay Area (our offices are located on a finger of the Bay), so the spill inspired us to act. In our clients' names we've donated both time and financial resources towards the long-term health of the Bay ecosystem.
Click the tree icons to learn about who we supported and the work we did at Santa Venetia Marsh Reserve.
Active Ingredients

Active Ingredients, Inc.
– Larkspur, California
Designers : Amanda Dowd, Brian West, Matthew Hazard
Client : Active Ingredients, Inc.

Arvids Baranovs – Riga, Latvia
Designer : Arvids Baranovs
Client : www.aleluja.lv/2008

52 Ellen Street, Winnipeg, MB, Canada R3A 0Z7
ph: 204.475.0614 www.velocitydesignworks.com
VELOCITYDESIGNWORKS
VELOCITYDESIGNWORKS

Velocity Design Works – Winnipeg, Canada
Designer : Velocity Design Works
Client : Velocity Design Works

Paragon Marketing Communications – Salmiya, Kuwait
Designers : Louai Alasfahani, Konstantin Assenov, Huzaifa Kakumama
Client : Paragon Marketing Communications

There's no idea too big for us.
We hunt 'em all down, with
faultless accuracy and
bloodthirsty passion
PARAGON
MARKETING COMMUNICATIONS

RAZZLE DAZZLE
SNOWFLAKE
SOIREE
BELFOR
THE LOOT IS ON US AT THE
BOOTLEG CASINO
HOT TUNES
JOIN US IF YOU'RE
HIP TO THE JIVE!

BBR Creative – Lafayette, Louisiana
Designer : Denise Gallagher
Client : BELFOR

Rickabaugh Graphics – Gahanna, Ohio
Designers : Eric Rickabaugh, Dave Cap, Chris Franklin, Nathan Orensten, Jason Jourdan, Dean DeShetler
Client : Rickabaugh Graphics

2creativo – Barcelona, Spain
Designers : 2creativo Team
Client : 2creativo

TrueBlue – **Chattanooga, Tennessee**
Designers : Ria Fisher, James Lawton
Client : TrueBlue

Originally developed as a Thanksgiving gift, this notecard set translates easily into a promotion for any patriotic holiday. Gold foil stamping, blind embossing, textured cover stock, and a color photo glued to the exterior all contribute to the tactile presence of the presentation folder.

Hacia el papel va un dibujo RIN RIN,
yo te diseñaba, yo te diseñé,
yo te hice un diseño, yo te lo entregué ...
RECOGEMOS INQUIETUDES,
PRESENTAMOS SOLUCIONES.
Diseño Profesional, diseño que funciona.
FISIOGIM
MUY CREATIVO
MUY ÚTIL
MUY EFICAZ
LLEGAMOS
A NUESTROS OBJETIVOS
COMUNICACIÓN
QUE DESTACA

2creativo – Barcelona, Spain
Designers : 2creativo Team
Client : 2creativo

Sayles Graphic Design – Des Moines, Iowa
Designers : John Sayles, Bridget Drendel
Client : Iowa Wine Festival

IOWA
WINE
2008
IOWA WINE
FESTIVAL
Saturday
8/23/08
ADMIT ONE
IOWA
WINE
FEST

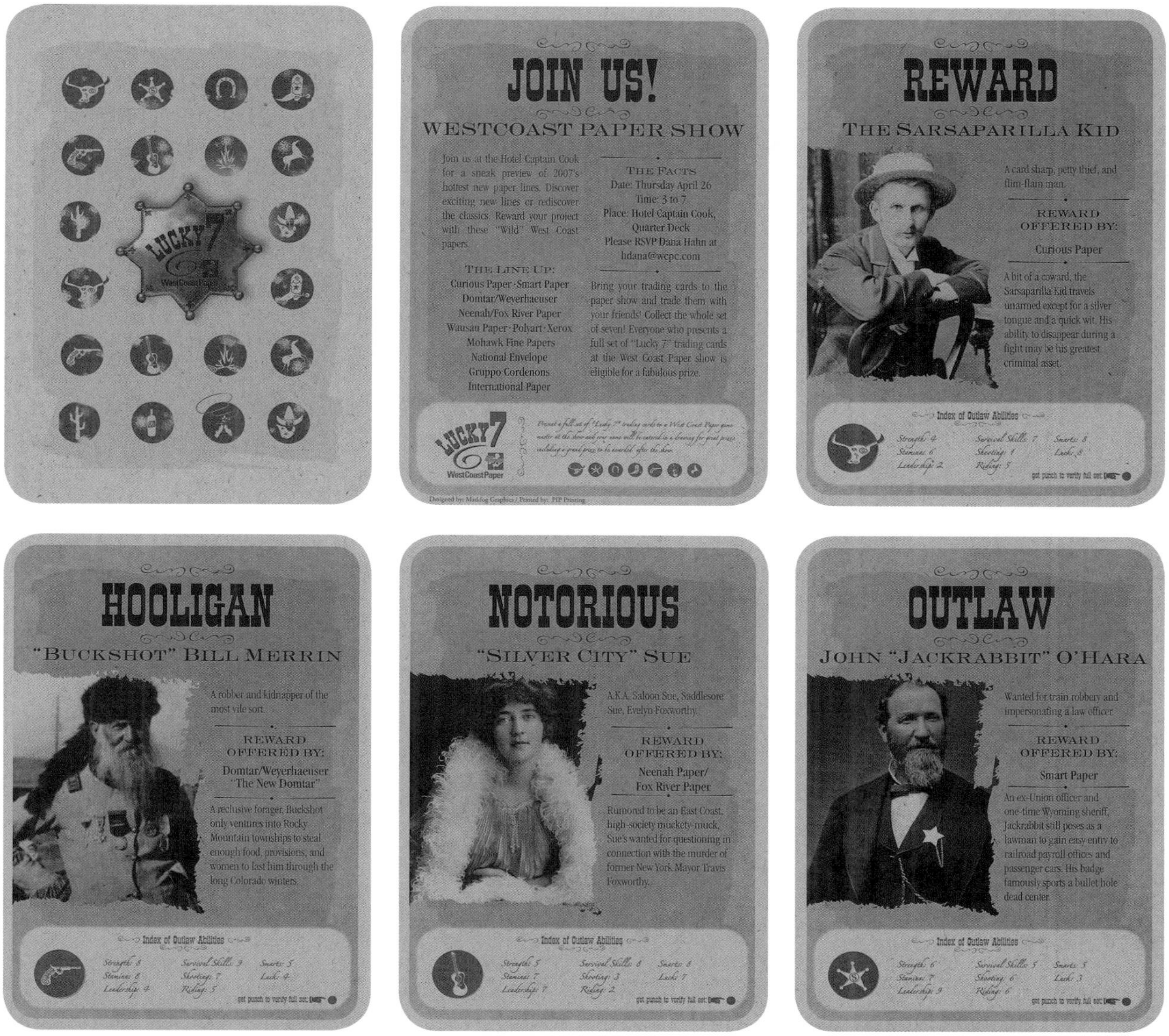
LUCKY 7
WestCoastPaper
JOIN US!
WESTCOAST PAPER SHOW
Join us at the Hotel Captain Cook for a sneak preview of 2007's hottest new paper lines. Discover exciting new lines or rediscover the classics. Reward your project with these "Wild" West Coast papers.
THE LINE UP:
Curious Paper · Smart Paper
Domtar/Weyerhaeuser
Neenah/Fox River Paper
Wausau Paper · Polyart · Xerox
Mohawk Fine Papers
National Envelope
Gruppo Cordenons
International Paper
THE FACTS
Date: Thursday April 26
Time: 5 to 7
Place: Hotel Captain Cook, Quarter Deck
Please RSVP Dana Hahn at hdana@wcpc.com
Bring your trading cards to the paper show and trade them with your friends! Collect the whole set of seven! Everyone who presents a full set of "Lucky 7" trading cards at the West Coast Paper show is eligible for a fabulous prize.
LUCKY 7
WestCoastPaper
Designed by: Maddog Graphics / Printed by: PIP Printing
REWARD
THE SARSAPARILLA KID
A card sharp, petty thief, and flim-flam man.
REWARD OFFERED BY:
Curious Paper
A bit of a coward, the Sarsaparilla Kid travels unarmed except for a silver tongue and a quick wit. His ability to disappear during a fight may be his greatest criminal asset.
Index of Outlaw Abilities
Strength: 4
Stamina: 6
Leadership: 2
Survival Skills: 7
Shooting: 1
Riding: 5
Smarts: 8
Luck: 8
get punch to verify full set:
HOOLIGAN
"BUCKSHOT" BILL MERRIN
A robber and kidnapper of the most vile sort.
REWARD OFFERED BY:
Domtar/Weyerhaeuser "The New Domtar"
A reclusive forager, Buckshot only ventures into Rocky Mountain townships to steal enough food, provisions, and women to last him through the long Colorado winters.
Index of Outlaw Abilities
Strength: 8
Stamina: 8
Leadership: 4
Survival Skills: 9
Shooting: 7
Riding: 5
Smarts: 5
Luck: 4
get punch to verify full set:
NOTORIOUS
"SILVER CITY" SUE
A.K.A. Saloon Sue, Saddlesore Sue, Evelyn Foxworthy.
REWARD OFFERED BY:
Neenah Paper/ Fox River Paper
Rumored to be an East Coast, high-society muckety-muck, Sue's wanted for questioning in connection with the murder of former New York Mayor Travis Foxworthy.
Index of Outlaw Abilities
Strength: 5
Stamina: 7
Leadership: 7
Survival Skills: 6
Shooting: 3
Riding: 2
Smarts: 8
Luck: 7
get punch to verify full set:
OUTLAW
JOHN "JACKRABBIT" O'HARA
Wanted for train robbery and impersonating a law officer.
REWARD OFFERED BY:
Smart Paper
An ex-Union officer and one-time Wyoming sheriff, Jackrabbit still poses as a lawman to gain easy entry to railroad payroll offices and passenger cars. His badge famously sports a bullet hole dead center.
Index of Outlaw Abilities
Strength: 6
Stamina: 7
Leadership: 9
Survival Skills: 5
Shooting: 6
Riding: 6
Smarts: 5
Luck: 3
get punch to verify full set:

Mad Dog Graphx – Anchorage, Alaska
Designers : Kris Ryan-Clarke
Client : West Coast Paper

Factor Design – San Francisco, California
Designers : Tim Guy, Jeff Zwerner, Lily Lin
Client : Factor Design

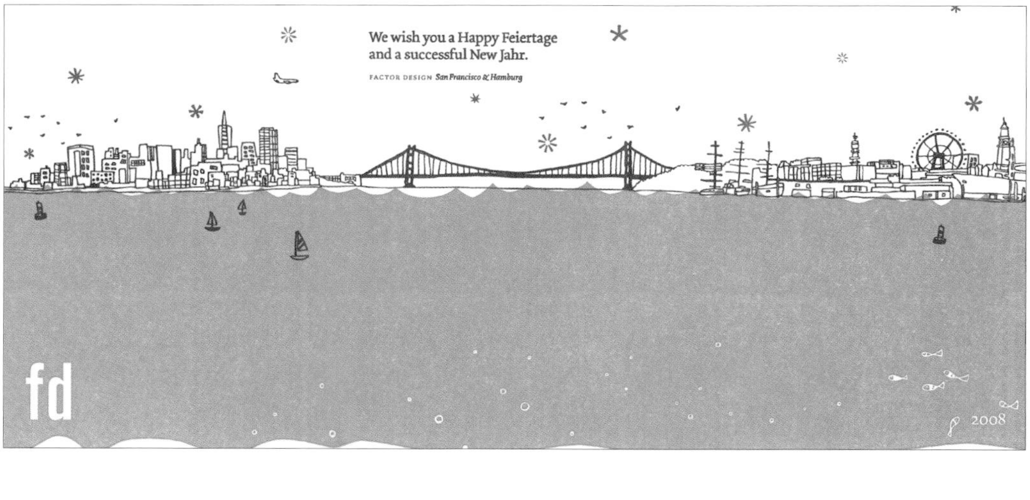
We wish you a Happy Feiertage
and a successful New Jahr.
FACTOR DESIGN San Francisco & Hamburg
fd
2008

IE Design + Communications – Hermosa Beach, California
Designers : Marcie Carson, Jane Lee,
Nicole Bednarz, Kenny Goldstein, Mike Kramer
Client : IE Design + Communications

Cheers
Sterling Cross Creative
Cheers
Sterling Cross Creative

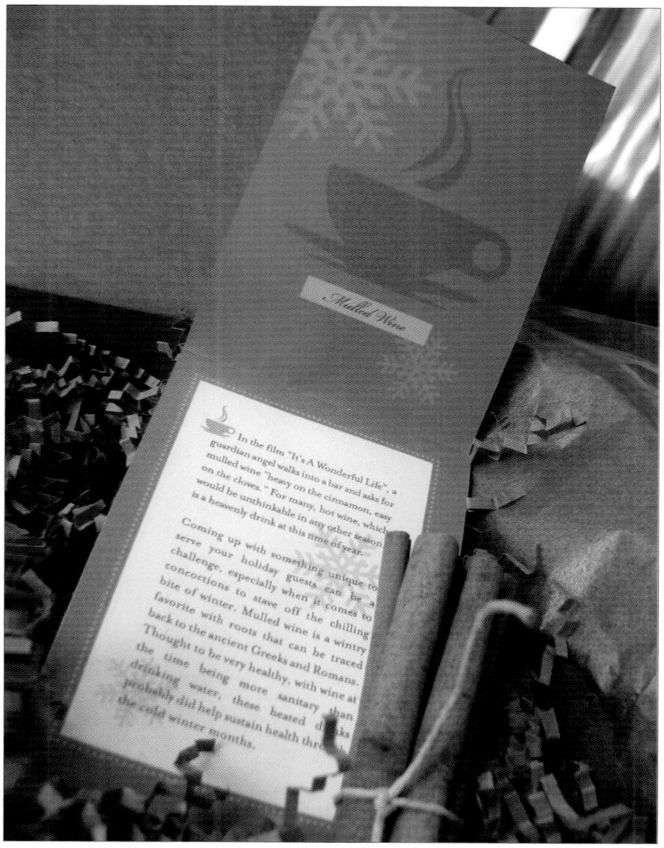
Mulled Wine
In the film "It's A Wonderful Life", a guardian angel walks into a bar and asks for mulled wine "heavy on the cinnamon, easy on the cloves." For many, hot wine, which would be unthinkable in any other season, is a heavenly drink at this time of year.

Providing the additive ingredients for mulled wine touches on holiday tradition while allowing the receiver to share the cheer.

Sterling Cross Creative – Sonoma, California
Designer : Peggy Cross
Client : Sterling Cross Creative

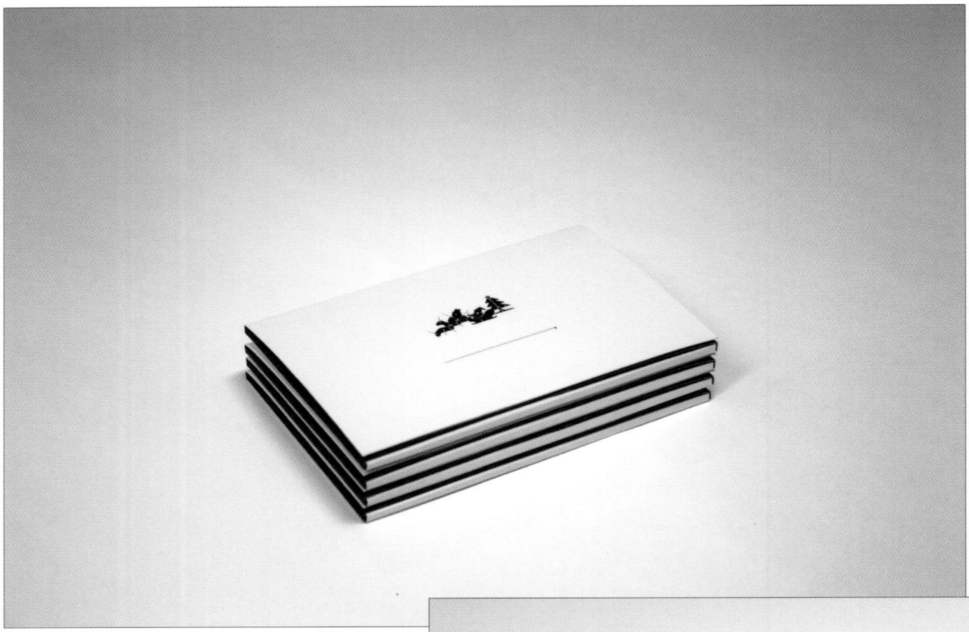

Jonathan Yuen – Singapore
Designers : Jonathan Yuen, B.G. Tan
Client : Jonathan Yuen, B.G. Tan

Merry X'mas! Isn't it
wonderful? Can't wait
for our get together!
Miss your cooking!
Happy Holidays. James.

A beautiful
X'mas is what
you make of it.

A beautiful
X'mas is what
you make of it.

A beautiful
X'mas is what
you make of it.

'tis the season…

…for the
Sugar
Plumb
Fairy.
We wish
you a joyous
holiday season.
Ventress Design Group
IN ACCORDANCE WITH YOUR BELIEFS AND PRACTICES, WE WISH YOU A: MERRY CHRISTMAS • HAPPY HANUKAH • SUPER SOLSTICE • JOLLY FESTIVUS • KICKIN' KWANZAA • HAPPY NEW YEAR

Ventress Design Group – Franklin, Tennessee
Designers : Tom Ventress
Client : Ventress Design Group

Paragon Marketing Communications – Salmiya, Kuwait
Designers : Louai Alasfahani, Konstantin Assenov, Huzaifa Kakumama
Client : Salhiya Complex

مبارك عليكم الشهر
مجمع الصالحية
SALHIA COMPLEX
www.salhiacomplex.com

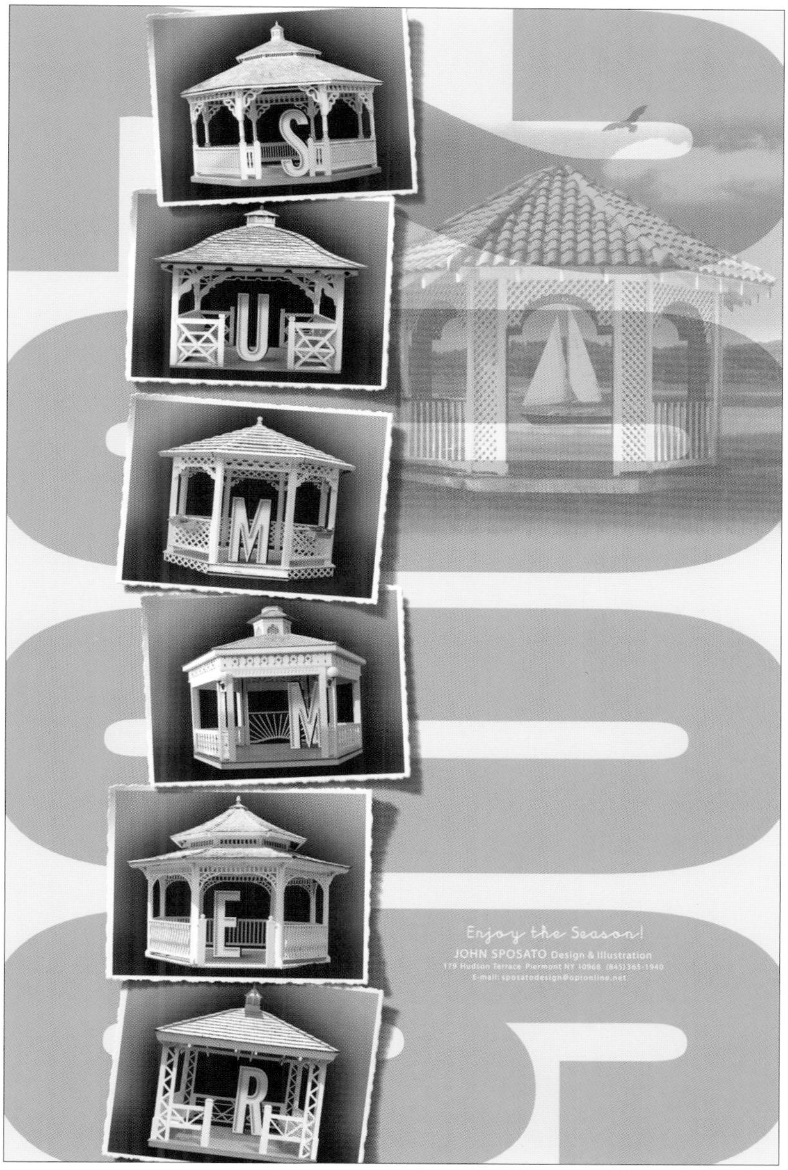

John Sposato Design + Illustration – Piermont, New York
Designer : John Sposato
Client : John Sposato Design + Illustration

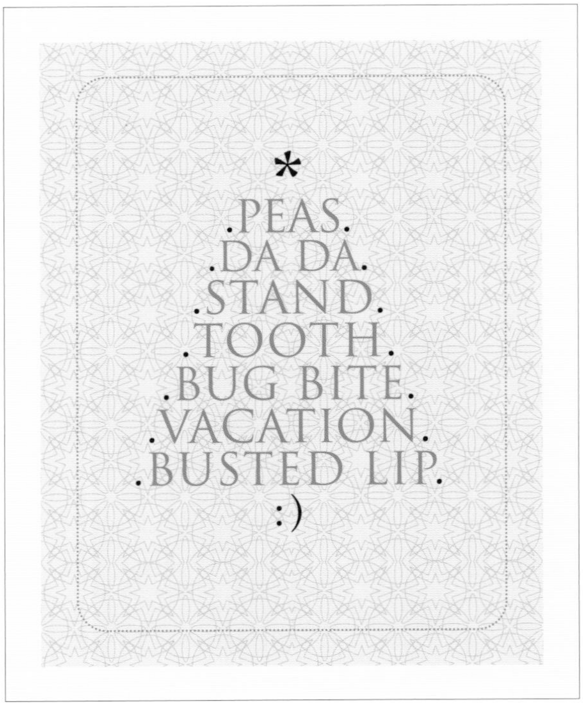
*
.PEAS.
.DA DA.
.STAND.
.TOOTH.
.BUG BITE.
.VACATION.
.BUSTED LIP.
:)

WITH ALL THE FIRSTS
WE'VE ENJOYED THIS YEAR,
HOW COULD THIS CHRISTMAS
BE ANYTHING BUT MERRY?
Michael, April & Martin
Hope your holidays
are just as special.

Open Creative – Birmingham, Alabama
Designers : April Mraz, Alan Whitley
Client : Martin Vizzina

Pensaré Design Group – Washington, D.C.
Designers : Mary Ellen Vehlow, Lauren Emeritz
Client : National Cherry Blossom Festival

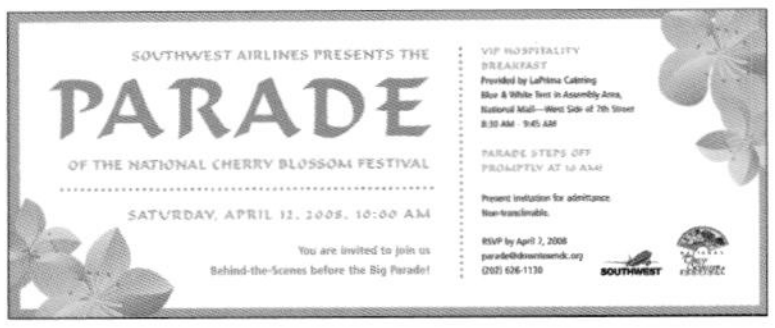

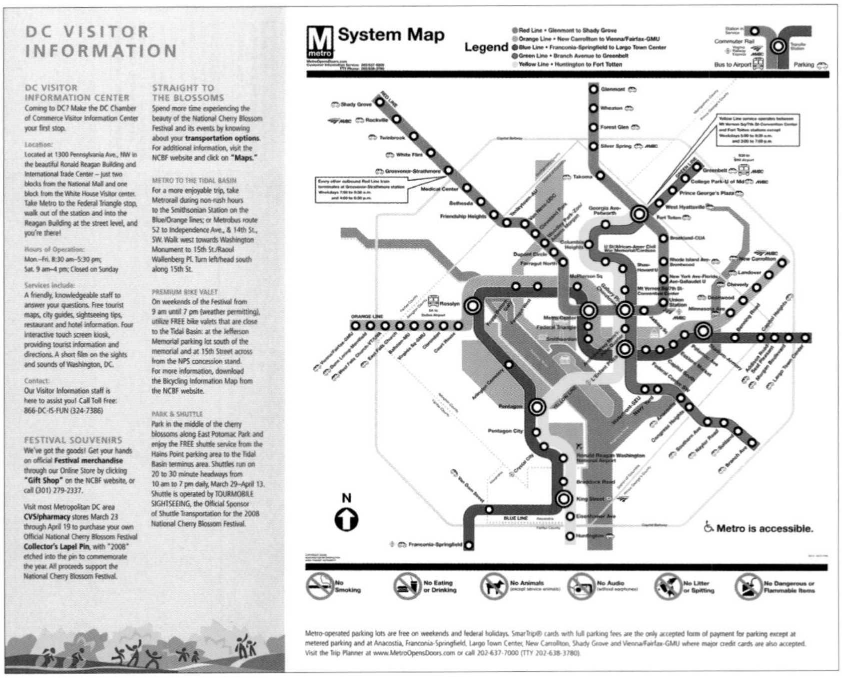

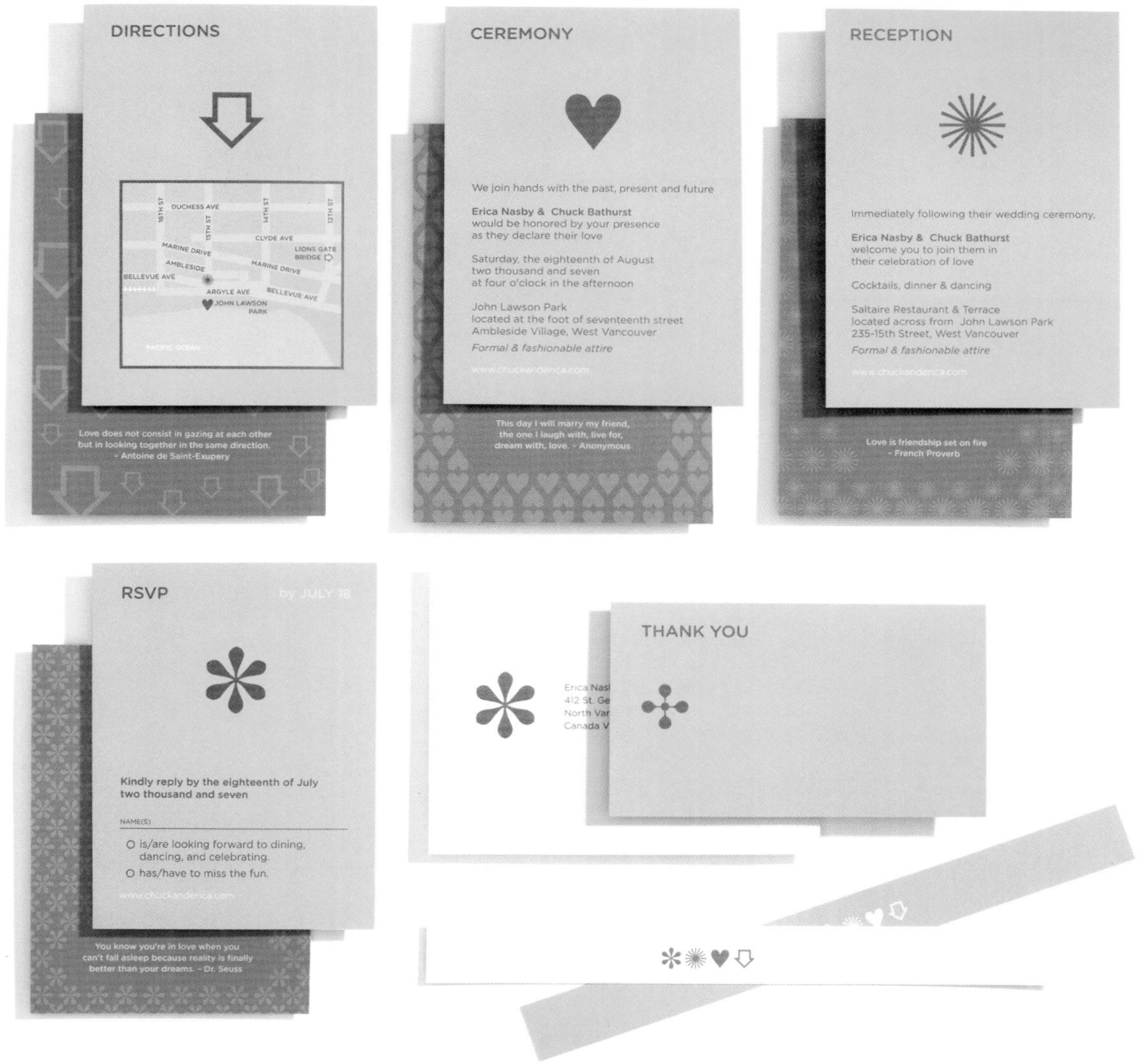
DIRECTIONS
DUCHESS AVE
16TH ST
15TH ST
14TH ST
13TH ST
CLYDE AVE
MARINE DRIVE
LIONS GATE BRIDGE
AMBLESIDE
MARINE DRIVE
BELLEVUE AVE
ARGYLE AVE
BELLEVUE AVE
JOHN LAWSON PARK
PACIFIC OCEAN
Love does not consist in gazing at each other but in looking together in the same direction. - Antoine de Saint-Exupery
CEREMONY
We join hands with the past, present and future
Erica Nasby & Chuck Bathurst
would be honored by your presence
as they declare their love
Saturday, the eighteenth of August
two thousand and seven
at four o'clock in the afternoon
John Lawson Park
located at the foot of seventeenth street
Ambleside Village, West Vancouver
Formal & fashionable attire
www.chuckanderica.com
This day I will marry my friend, the one I laugh with, live for, dream with, love. - Anonymous
RECEPTION
Immediately following their wedding ceremony,
Erica Nasby & Chuck Bathurst
welcome you to join them in
their celebration of love
Cocktails, dinner & dancing
Saltaire Restaurant & Terrace
located across from John Lawson Park
235-15th Street, West Vancouver
Formal & fashionable attire
www.chuckanderica.com
Love is friendship set on fire - French Proverb
RSVP
by JULY 18
Kindly reply by the eighteenth of July
two thousand and seven
NAME(S)
is/are looking forward to dining, dancing, and celebrating.
has/have to miss the fun.
www.chuckanderica.com
You know you're in love when you can't fall asleep because reality is finally better than your dreams. - Dr. Seuss
THANK YOU

Exhibit A: Design Group – Vancouver, Canada
Designer : Cory Ripley
Client : Erica and Chuck Bathurst

Melvin Ng – **Singapore**
Designer : Melvin Ng
Client : Singapore Post

Poul Lange Design – New York, New York
Designer : Poul Hans Lange
Client : Poul Hans Lange

Neill Fox took a very important piece of advice from his British-born father when opening a design firm in Phoenix. "Back in England, it's a common word—a common thing to say, 'Use your noggin.' Use your head. My last name's Fox, and we try to be very thoughtful in our creative solutions." From that very thought process came Foxnoggin—and from there, a memorable holiday promotion for the Arizona company.

NuTmeg
CiNnAmoN
FiLL YouR NoggiN
with good stuff

"The [promotions] always turn into something completely different, but we try to play off our name," Fox says. The "Eggnoggin" box did just that, as Fox and his crew sent approximately seventy-five eggnog kits to clients, potential clients, friends, and family. Nestled in a warm brown box, the kits, each comprised of two custom-designed mugs, whole nutmeg and cinnamon, ground tinned spices, and a drink recipe, also feature a card depicting a caricature of Neill and wife Kathy "pouring peace and love and hope and joy out of the cups and into our heads." In other words, Fox says, echoing the legend inscribed on the mugs, "Fill your noggin with good stuff."

eggnoggin
by foxnoggin
ingredients
1 quart milk
2 cinnamon sticks
1 vanilla bean, split
5 cloves
10 blades of mace
12 egg yolks
1-1/2 cups sugar
1-1/2 cups dark rum
1-1/2 cups brandy
1 tablespoon vanilla
1 quart of half & half
3 more cups milk
freshly grated nutmeg & cinnamon to taste
yields 12 servings
to lower the alcohol content, use lower proof rum/brandy or substitute 1 cup of milk for every cup of alcohol removed.
directions
1. combine milk and spices, including vanilla bean in a heavy saucepan and let them infuse over lowest possible heat for 5 minutes. meanwhile, combine yolks and sugar in a large bowl and whisk until mixed.
2. bring milk to a boil and gradually whisk it into the yolk mixture. return the mixture to the saucepan. cook over medium heat, stirring steadily with a wooden spoon, for 2 to 3 minutes, or until foam subsides and mixture thickens to consistency of heavy cream. (mixture should thickly coat the back of the wooden spoon.) do not boil, or mixture will curdle.
3. strain mixture into a large bowl and let cool to room temperature. slowly stir in rum, brandy, half & half and vanilla.
4. refrigerate eggnog for at least 2 hours, preferably overnight. just before serving, dust top of eggnog with additional cinnamon and nutmeg.
FiLL YouR NoggiN
with good stuff!

Spreading "good stuff" and goodwill turned out to be a hit, leading to the warm glow of new business. "We've had people notice," Fox says. "They'd say, 'Wow, I need a unique direct mail piece.' It helps a lot; it's better than just sending out the typical greeting card. I'm not a big believer in cheesy corporate promos. This is...the whole atmosphere that we try to package."

While Fox hasn't yet exploited the "fox" part of his company name, he does acknowledge the natural relationship of his dad's pet aphorism to the perennially favorite cordial. "*Noggin* is such a unique word," he says. "Foxnoggin...noggin...eggnog...that's the seed that grew the idea. 'How do we make that?' 'Now we need something to put it in.'"

And how does one make an Eggnoggin eggnog? "We had to hunt around for [the recipe]," Fox says. "We made one batch—we figured we'd better before we sent it out." And although he admits to not being a big eggnog fan himself, the packaging makes it attractive even to those who would otherwise wish to abstain: "It's appealing enough that you'd almost want to try it!"

happy holidays
from foxnoggin
Fill Your Noggin
Cinnamon
Nutmeg
eggnoggin
ingredients
directions
1 quart milk
2 cinnamon sticks
10 blades of mace
12 egg yolks
1-1/2 cups sugar
1-1/2 cups dark rum
1-1/2 cups brandy
1 tablespoon vanilla
1 quart of half & half
3 more cups milk
freshly grated nutmeg
& cinnamon to taste
yields 12 servings
to lower the alcohol content, use lower proof rum/brandy or substitute 1 cup of milk for every cup of alcohol removed.

foxnoggin-thinking design – Phoenix, Arizona
Designers : Neill Fox, Curtis Parker
Client : foxnoggin-thinking design

THIS WEEKEND AT COOKS OF CROCUS HILL
Sample HAND-PICKED HERITAGE TURKEYS
DEMONSTRATIONS • TURKEY TALK • TIPS & TECHNIQUES
WORD
ON THE BIRD

Rotor – Minneapolis, Minnesota
Designers : Andy Weaverling, Matt Travaille, Kevin Hayes
Client : Cooks of Crocus Hill

Ramadan Kareem
Happy Eid
Season's Greetings
Season's Greetings

Paragon Marketing Communications – Salmiya, Kuwait
Designers : Louai Alasfahani, Konstantin Assenov, Huzaifa Kakumama
Client : Kuwait Projects Co.

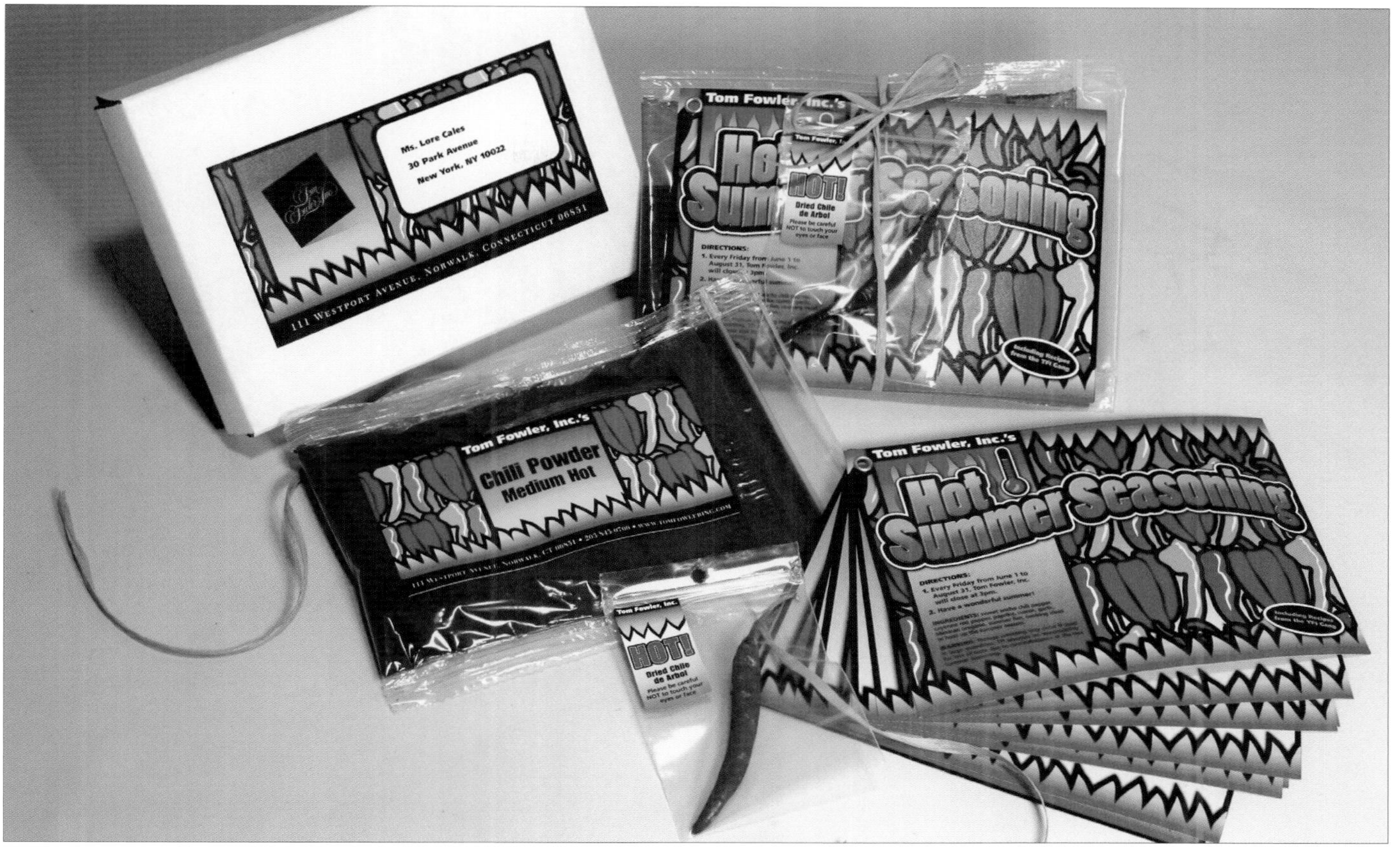

TFI Envision, Inc. – Norwalk, Connecticut
Designer : Elizabeth P. Ball
Client : Tom Fowler, Inc.

Belyea – Seattle, Washington
Designers : Ron Hansen, Aaron Clifford, Patricia Belyea, Nicholas Johnson
Client : Belyea

To Celebrate the Holidays
with Tom Fowler, Inc.
Dec 9 6-9pm
9 Webbs Hill Road
Stamford, CT
RSVP by Dec 5 203-845-0700
It's that time . . .

TFI Envision, Inc. – Norwalk, Connecticut
Designer : Elizabeth P. Ball
Client : Tom Fowler, Inc.

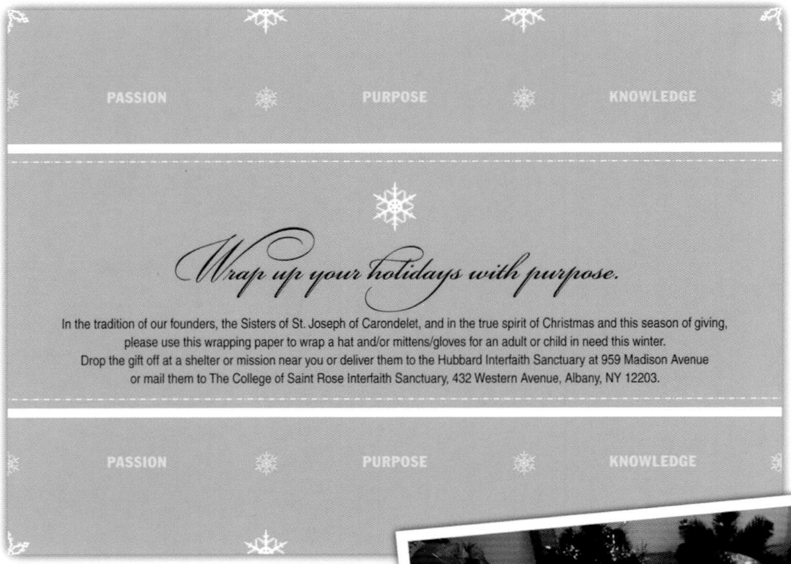
PASSION PURPOSE KNOWLEDGE
Wrap up your holidays with purpose.
In the tradition of our founders, the Sisters of St. Joseph of Carondelet, and in the true spirit of Christmas and this season of giving, please use this wrapping paper to wrap a hat and/or mittens/gloves for an adult or child in need this winter.
Drop the gift off at a shelter or mission near you or deliver them to the Hubbard Interfaith Sanctuary at 959 Madison Avenue or mail them to The College of Saint Rose Interfaith Sanctuary, 432 Western Avenue, Albany, NY 12203.
PASSION PURPOSE KNOWLEDGE

Meaningful

The College of Saint Rose, Office of Publc Relations & Marketing – Albany, New York
Designers : Mark Hamilton, Lisa Haley Thomson, Kathleen Sullivan
Client : The College of Saint Rose

Hatch Design – San Francisco, California
Designers : Katie Jain, Joel Templin, Nancy Hsieh, Lisa Pemrick
Client : Hatch Design

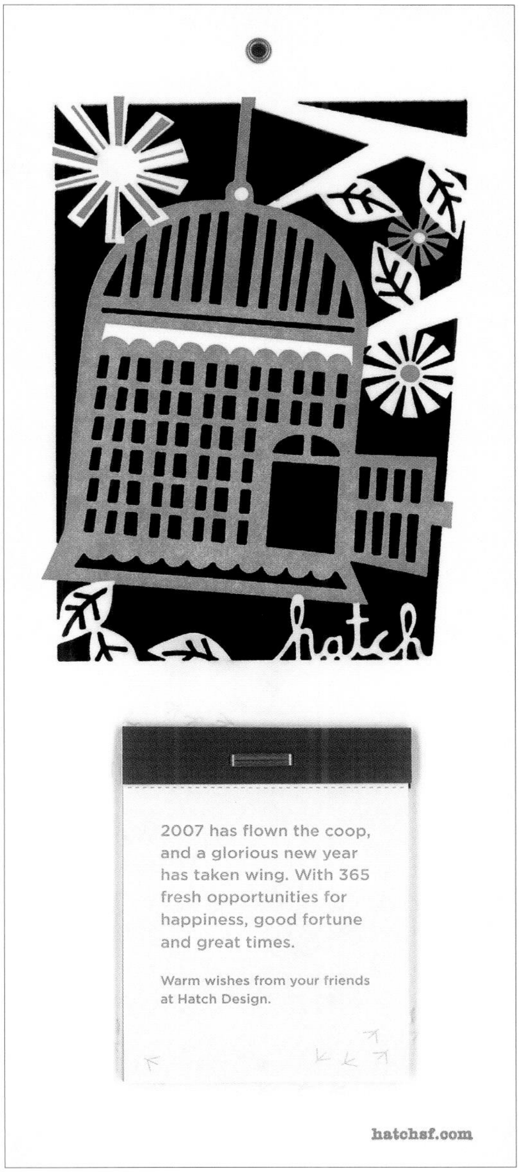
hatch
2007 has flown the coop, and a glorious new year has taken wing. With 365 fresh opportunities for happiness, good fortune and great times.
Warm wishes from your friends at Hatch Design.
hatchsf.com

These "beach-infused coasters" not only serve as a holiday freebie, but reiterates the firm's recent move to the Pacific Coast Highway in Hermosa Beach, California.

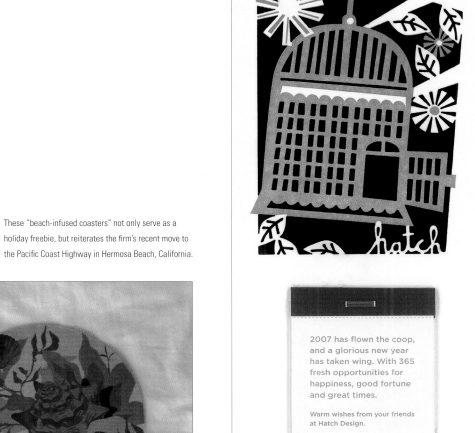

IE Design + Communications – Hermosa Beach, California
Designers : Marcie Carson, Jane Lee, Cya Nelson, Amy Klas, Nicole Bednarz
Client : IE Design + Communications

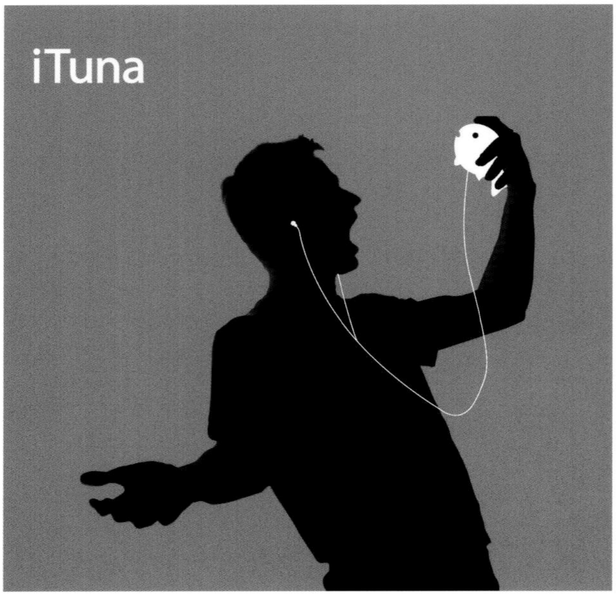

Wallace Church, Inc. – New York, New York
Designers : Stan Church, Maritess Manaluz
Client : Wallace Church, Inc.

Each year Wallace Church throws a Tuna Party where they grill fresh tuna for clients and friends. This year's invitation was found inside a tin housing accompanying a brightly-colored card to be used as a raffle ticket to win an iPod Shuffle the night of the party.

WALLACE CHURCH
Cocktails, food, fun, grill, patio, and of course, tuna.

Wallace Church, Inc. – New York, New York
Designers : Stan Church, Chung-Tao Tu
Client : Wallace Church, Inc.

This origami fish is printed as a small poster, black on black, then folded. It's tucked into a clear plastic pillow envelope and the recipient tugs at the designated fin to unfold the fish and reveal the invitation.

"Tattuna" features an actual tuna can. The can label includes party details printed as ingredient and nutritional facts. Inside the can are five fun tattoos for guests to apply before, during, or after the event.

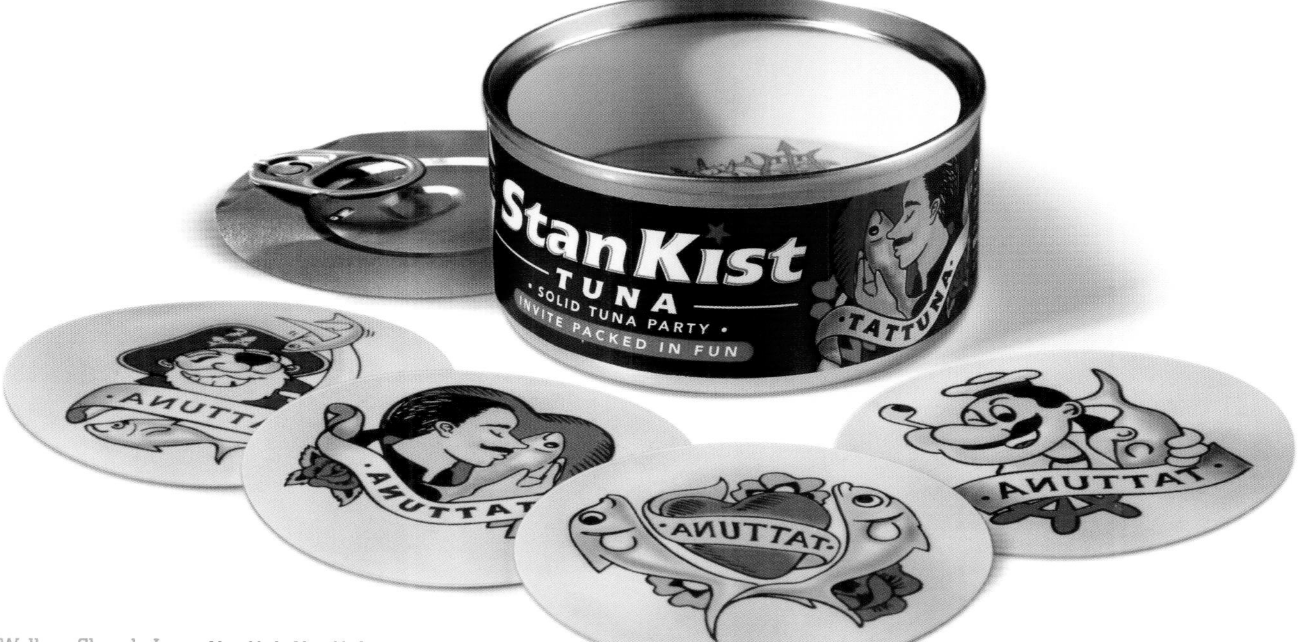

Wallace Church, Inc. – New York, New York
Designers : Stan Church, Bird Tubkam
Client : Wallace Church, Inc.

SUMMER
08
Enoy the Season!
JOHN SPOSATO Design & Illustration
179 Hudson Terrace Piermont NY 10968 (845) 365-1940
E-mail: sposatodesign@optonline.net

John Sposato Design + Illustration – Piermont, New York
Designer : John Sposato
Client : John Sposato Design + Illustration

SMART
CELEBRATING 10 YEARS
Downtown BID
INVITING
CELEBRATING 10 YEARS
Downtown BID
VIBRANT
CELEBRATING 10 YEARS
Downtown BID

Pensaré Design Group – Washington, D.C.
Designers : Mary Ellen Vehlow, Amy E. Billingham
Client : Downtown DC Business Improvement District

Skidmore – Royal Oak, Michigan
Designers : Mae Skidmore, Bob Nixon, Mark Arminski

Sayles Graphic Design – Des Moines, Iowa
Designer : John Sayles
Client : Sayles Graphic Design

James Marsh Design – Kent, England
Client : James Marsh Design

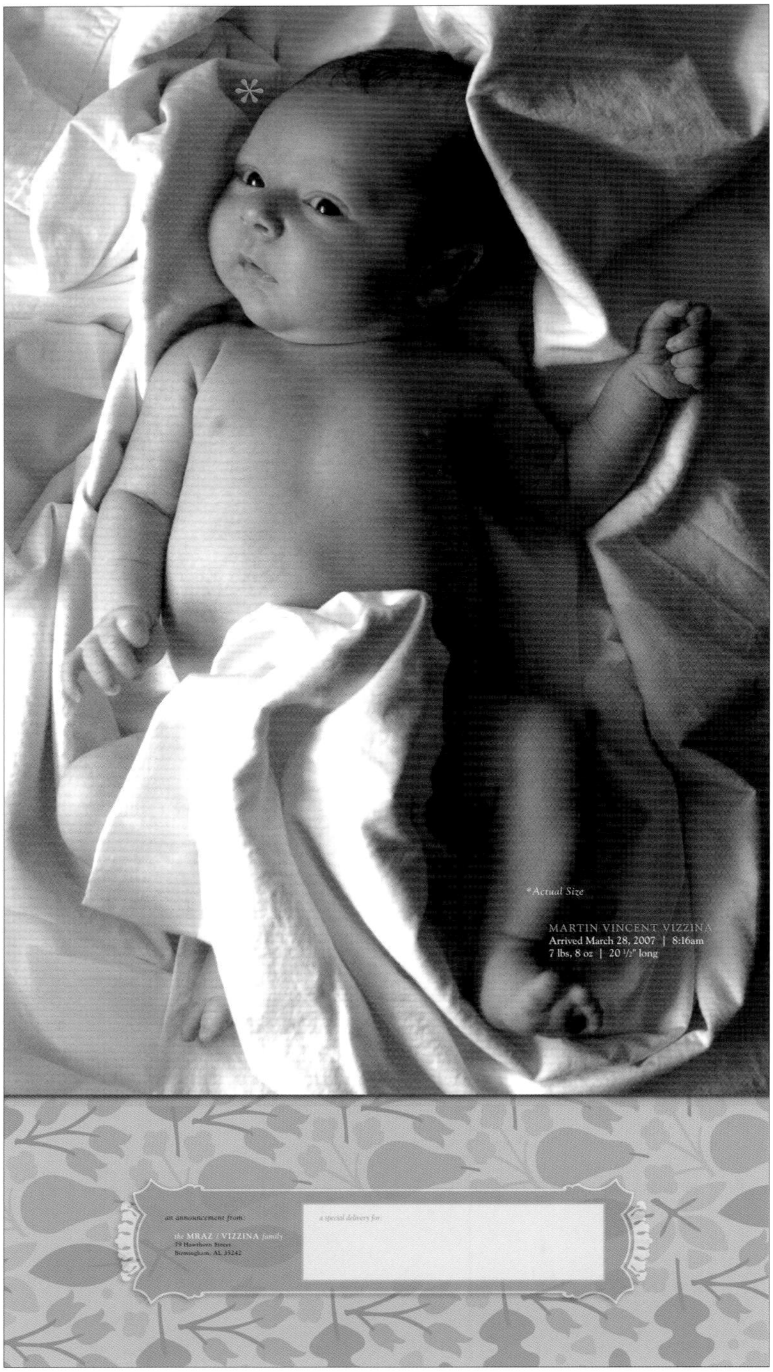

Open Creative Group – Birmingham, Alabama
Designers : April Mraz, Alan Whitley
Client : Mraz/Vizzina Family

20

Dotzero Design – **Portland, Oregon**
Designers : Karen Wippich, Jon Wippich
Client : West Coast Paper

Gough Graphics
– **Bradford, Massachusetts**
Designer : Rob Gough
Client : The Amica Insurance Breakers Marathon

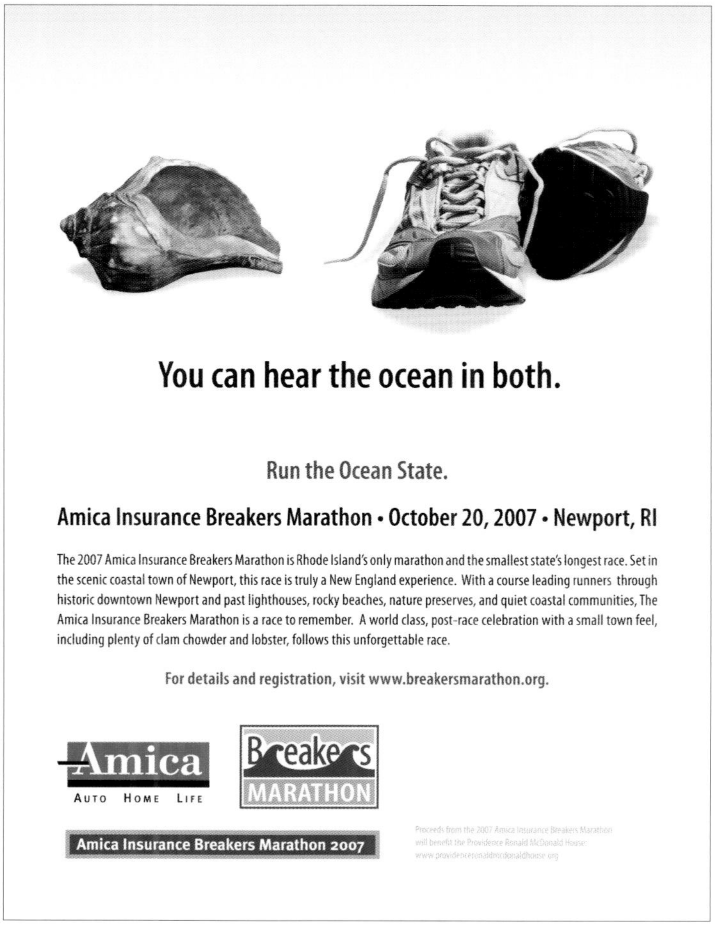
You can hear the ocean in both.
Run the Ocean State.
Amica Insurance Breakers Marathon • October 20, 2007 • Newport, RI
The 2007 Amica Insurance Breakers Marathon is Rhode Island's only marathon and the smallest state's longest race. Set in the scenic coastal town of Newport, this race is truly a New England experience. With a course leading runners through historic downtown Newport and past lighthouses, rocky beaches, nature preserves, and quiet coastal communities, The Amica Insurance Breakers Marathon is a race to remember. A world class, post-race celebration with a small town feel, including plenty of clam chowder and lobster, follows this unforgettable race.
For details and registration, visit www.breakersmarathon.org.
Amica
Auto Home Life
Breakers
MARATHON
Amica Insurance Breakers Marathon 2007
Proceeds from the 2007 Amica Insurance Breakers Marathon
will benefit the Providence Ronald McDonald House:
www.providenceronaldmcdonaldhouse.org

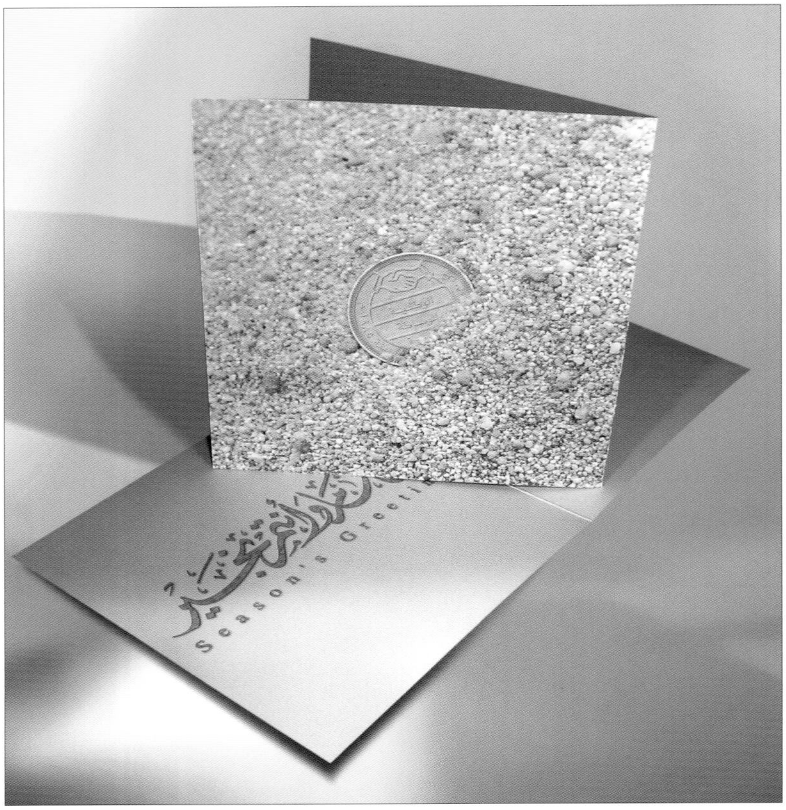

Paragon Marketing Communications – Salmiya, Kuwait
Designers : Louai Alasfahani, Konstantin Assenov, Huzaifa Kakumama
Client : Al Wasata Financing

John Sposato Design + Illustration – Piermont, New York
Designer : John Sposato
Client : John Sposato Design + Illustration

Frangipanni Communications – Singapore
Designers : Joan Low, Emily Tan
Client : Frangipanni Communications

Sabingrafik, Inc. – Carlsbad, California
Designers : Tracy Sabin, Bridget Sabin
Client : Sabingrafik, Inc.

Sabingrafik offered this homemade candy bar as a holiday promotion. The lighthearted illustration appeals to dog lovers while displaying a sample of Tracy Sabin's art.

TFI Envision, Inc. – Norwalk, Connecticut
Designer : Elizabeth P. Ball
Client : Tom Fowler, Inc.

A three-dimensional asterisk makes the perfect Christmas ornament and gift for a design firm wanting to focus on its typographic strengths.

So often the lowly asterisk is only a simple indicator of additional information.
*While the asterisk is typically encumbered with countless caveats... this holiday greeting celebrates the quirky typographic symbol and comes with no legal implications or consequences** and simply represents a warm and shiny thank you for your business and friendship during the past year.***
***From all your friends at foxnoggin, we truly wish you a "fantasteriskic" holiday season!

foxnoggin - thinking design – Phoenix, Arizona
Designers : Neill Fox, Cathy Fox, Lesley Kitts
Client : foxnoggin - thinking design

Paragon Marketing Communications – Salmiya, Kuwait
Designers : Louai Alasfahani, Konstantin Assenov, Huzaifa Kakumama
Client : Wafra Real Estate Co.

Bronson Ma Creative – San Antonio, Texas
Designer : Bronson Ma
Client : The MG Herring Group

PARAGON
MARKETING COMMUNICATIONS
In the advertising jungle we are at the top of the food chain
Ramming furiously through different medias we are the creative leaders and the protectors of our herd of clients
We are the restless observer fully devoted to search for new, out of the box creative concepts and destroy every conventional idea that get's in the way
In the market, sticking around that long means that you're tough - thus we have proved that we are here to stay!

Paragon Marketing Communications – Salmiya, Kuwait
Designers : Louai Alasfahani, Konstantin Assenov, Huzaifa Kakumama
Client : Paragon Marketing Communications

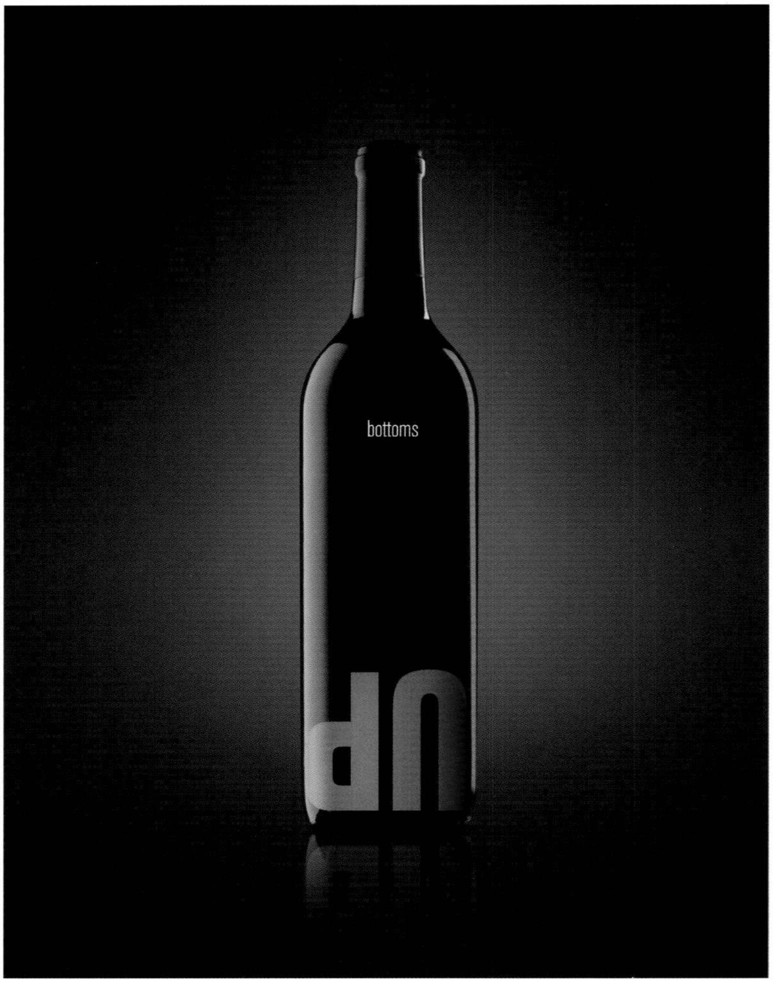
bottoms
UP

Wallace Church, Inc. – New York, New York
Designers : Stan Church
Client : Wallace Church, Inc.

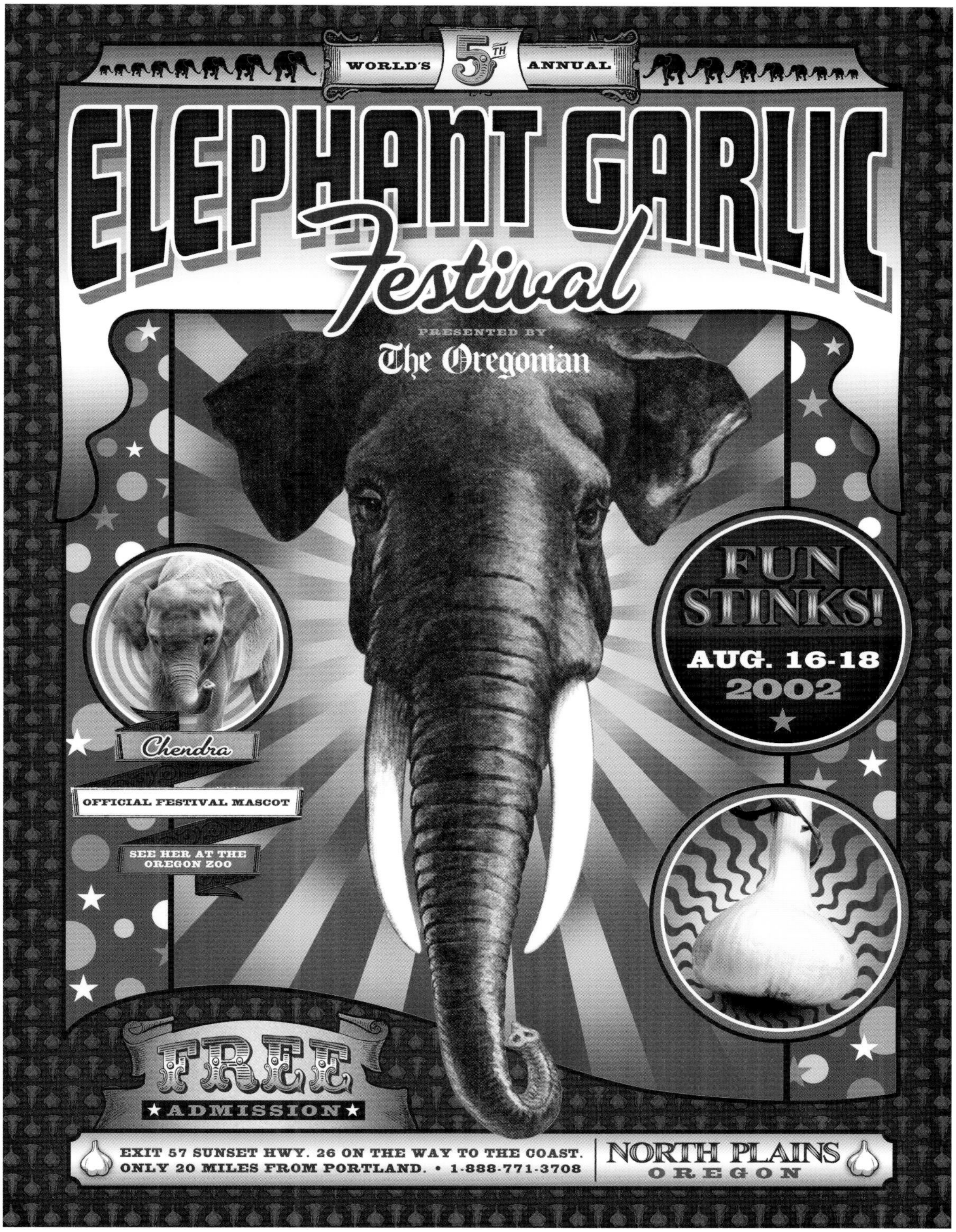

Dotzero Design – Portland, Oregon
Designers : Karen Wippich, Jon Wippich
Client : Elephant Garlic Festival

Presented by the Frederick Arts Council
dancefest
08
Sunday
May 4 2:00 pm
Weinberg Center for the Arts
$12 adults; $6 students/seniors
for tickets call 301.600.2828
Sponsored by Footlights Dance & Theatre Boutique
featuring:
24/7 Dance Studio, Bernetta R. Brown Y.G.B. Dance Troupe, Bettie Jane's Center of Dance Art, Dance Etc., Dance Unlimited, Davidson School of Scottish Dancing, Dee Buchanan Studio of Dance, Elite Feet Dance Studio, Elower-Sicilia Productions Performing Co., Hood College Dance Ensemble, Mid-Maryland Performing Arts Center, Middletown High School Dance Team, Urbana Dance Studio, & the FAC dance scholarship recipients

Kalico Design – Frederick, Maryland
Designer : Kimberly Dow
Client : Frederick Arts Council

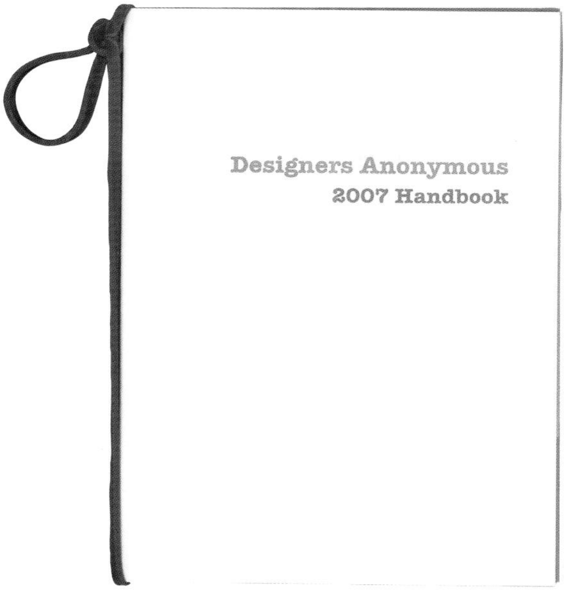
Designers Anonymous
2007 Handbook

3 Dogz Creative, Inc. – Toronto, Canada
Designers : Dave Gouveia, Chris Elkerton, Ryan Broadbent, Kathleen Scott
Client : 3 Dogz Creative, Inc.

Step 5
Get out
of your
creative
rut.
Step 6
Social responsibility,
pro-bono, and you.

"Type isn't measured in inches."
TYPE ISN'T MEASURED IN INCHES · TYPE ISN'T MEASURED IN INCHES ·
HELLO
my name is
Instructions: Peel. Stick.

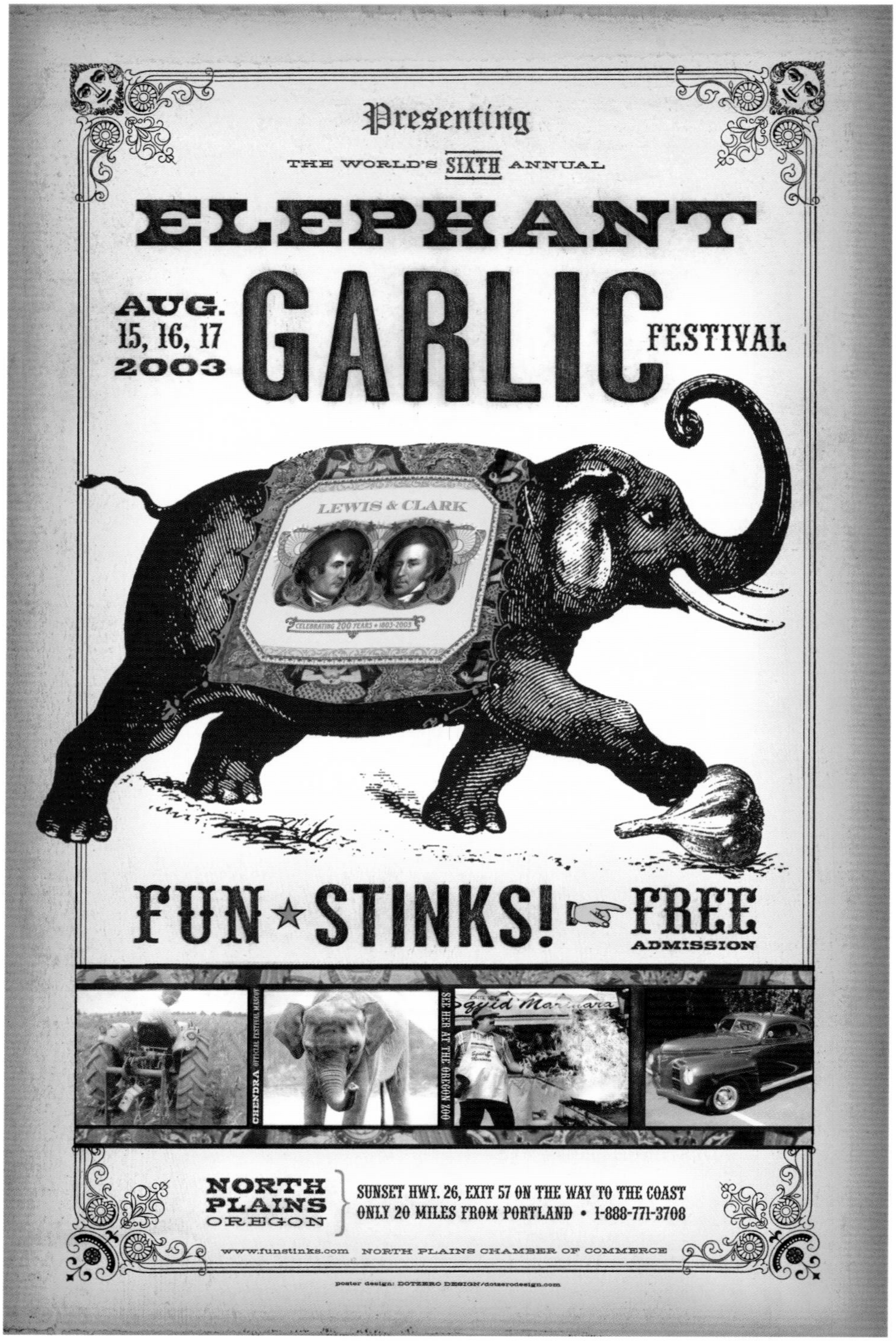

Dotzero Design – Portland, Oregon
Designers : Karen Wippich, Jon Wippich
Client : Elephant Garlic Festival

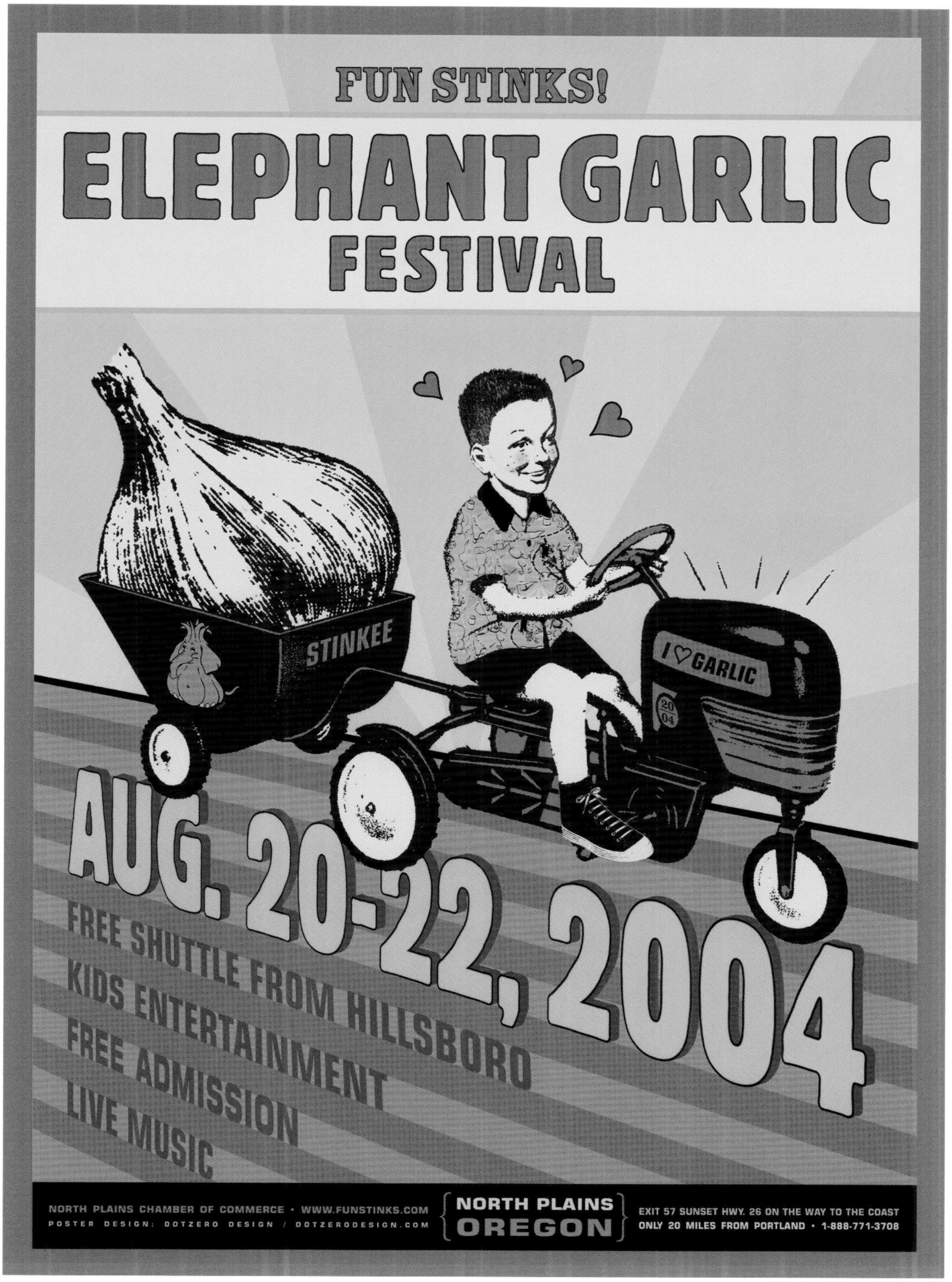

Don't make the mistake of taking yourself too seriously. When not executed too harshly, self-deprecating humor can be a very effective technique in letting the consumer know your client is offering a fun-filled day of events.

TNESIHASEA
PULL HERE
SUDDENLY, ANESTHESIA MAKES SENSE.
The business side of Anesthesia can be terribly confusing and difficult to manage. The problems are many, and the stakeholders are often at odds. But what if there was a way to bring harmony and order to all of the chaos?
There is.
And VitalMed can deliver it.
PULL HERE
ANESTHESIA

Open Creative Group – Birmingham, Alabama
Designers : April Mraz, Alan Whitley
Client : Vitalmed

Sliding out the informational card moves the letters in the die-cut windows so the word *anesthesia* appears. This is a nice visual aid reiterating that making sense of the process of anesthesia can be easily accomplished.

Paragon Marketing Communications – Salmiya, Kuwait
Designers : Louai Alasfahani, Konstantin Assenov, Huzaifa Kakumama
Client : Iris Group

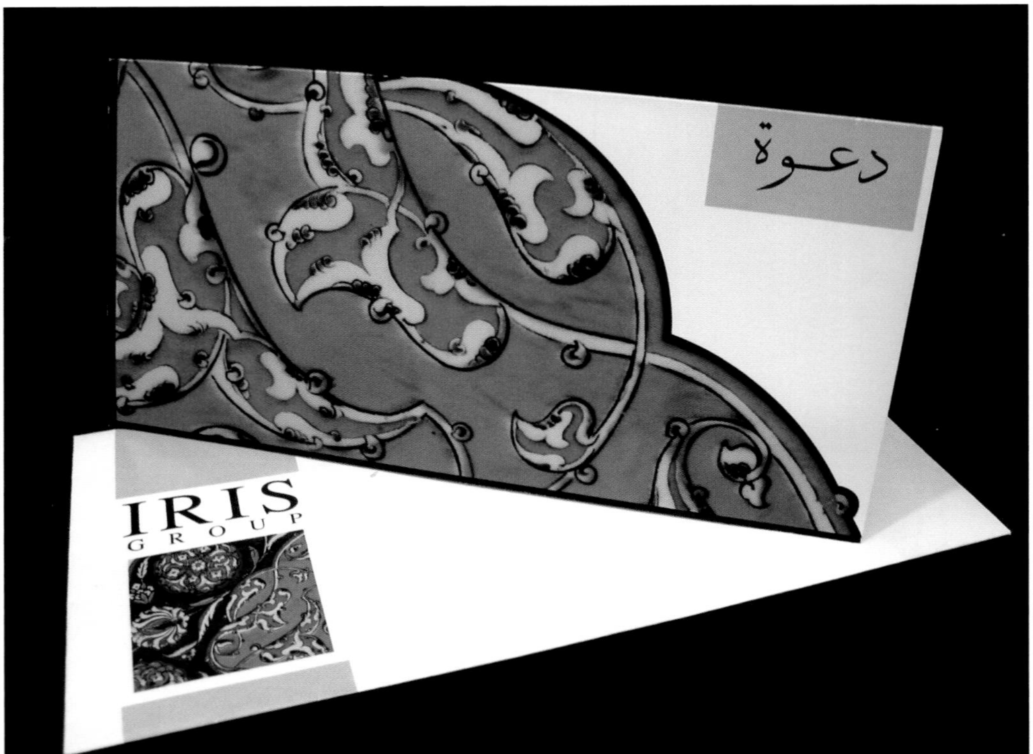
دعوة
IRIS
GROUP

Ana recieved an unwanted Christmas gift.
Now she has to go to www.sretanbizic.com
to exchange it

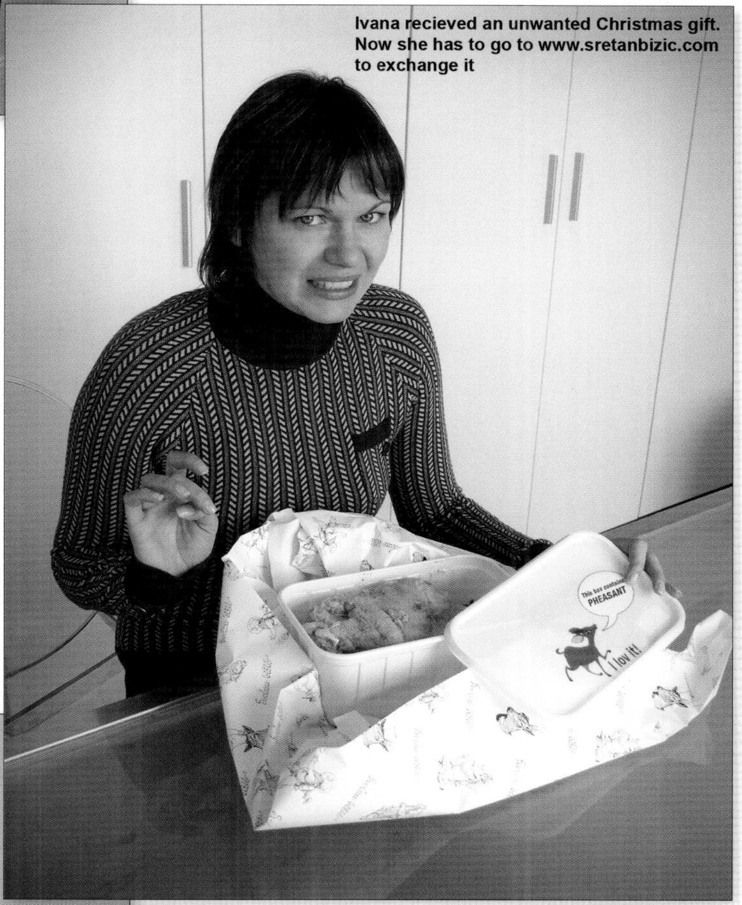
Ivana recieved an unwanted Christmas gift.
Now she has to go to www.sretanbizic.com
to exchange it
PHEASANT
I lov it!

Thomas recieved an unwanted Christmas gift.
Now he has to go to www.sretanbizic.com
to exchange it
USSELL
ATHLETIC

Bruketa & Zinic Om – Zagreb, Croatia
Designers : Ana Belic, Moe Minkara, Daniel Vukovic, Ana Sutic
Client : Bruketa & Zinic Om

WISHING
YOU...
TO:VIVAPRODUCTIONS

RUSSELL CROWE
GLADIATOR
WIDESCREEN
THE INCREDIBLES
2-DISC COLLECTOR'S EDITION
A CHRISTMAS STORY
Peace, Harmony, Comfort and Joy... Maybe Next Year.
AN EPIC, ANIMATED, HOLIDAY!
From typeEdesign,
We'll be your leader in the creative arena, be more reliable than the homing device on a super-suit, and always deliver everything you're hoping for and more...
YOU...
TO:VIVAP

Type E Design – Alexandria, Virginia
Designers : Tipy Taylor, Tina Taylor, Sonia Ourmanova
Client : Type E Design

Paragon Marketing Communications – Salmiya, Kuwait
Designers : Louai Alasfahani, Konstantin Assenov, Huzaifa Kakumama
Client : Grass Exhibition

Belyea – Seattle, Washington
Designers : Ron Hansen, Aaron Clifford, Patricia Belyea
Client : ColorGraphics

English
中文版

Happy Holidays! This year, instead of our usual animated holiday card, we thought we'd test your holiday knowledge.
We hope you'll play along – we think you'll have fun, and we bet you may even learn a thing or two.
Happy Holidays!
Let's get started
No thanks

1. How long should a menorah burn each night during Chanukah?
A Until dawn
B Until Tony Orlando and Dawn
C Until the appearance of 3 medium sized stars

2. 非洲Kwanzaa节日是那日庆祝?
A 十二月滿月至年終
B 感恩节至12月24日
C 12月26日至正月1日

Andigo New Media – New York, New York
Designers : Andrew Schulkind, Go Lertworachon, Kian-Lam Kho
Client : Andigo New Media

Available on their Web site, this animated holiday card is a cleverly-conceived—and all-inclusive—quiz. Note the spiritually sensitive snowman who dresses appropriately for each special day.

OrangeSeed Design – Minneapolis, Minnesota
Designers : Damien Wolf, Kevin Hayes, Tonja Larson, Kelly Munson, Renea Thull, Jenny Weisensel, John Wieland
Client : OrangeSeed Design

ORANGESEED
Baby it's cold outside! But what better way to share the warmth of the season than with a cup of hot tea. Our special blend of apple pieces, hibiscus flowers and orange peel (of course!) is guaranteed to tempt your taste buds and bring a sweet smile to your day.
WARM WISHES

1st Annual
Shoreline Wine Festival
Join Us for the 1st Annual Shoreline Wine Festival.
Sample and drink wine from Connecticut Wineries. Eat food from local restaurants. Visit local Businesses sampling their goods and services. Listen and dance to live music and entertainment. Entertainment for Kids (Face Painting, Moon Bounce and more). Food and Wine Seminars from Local Experts. And Much, Much More!!
Whether a Wine conissuer or a Beginner, you are bound to have a good time!!
Shoreline Wine Festival
2007
Saturday, August 18
Sunday, August 19
11:00am - 6:00pm
Bishop's Orchards Winery
1355 Boston Post Road
Guilford, CT 06437
Ticket Prices
Adult:
$20.00
Children:
$5.00
Designated Driver:
$10.00
Two Day Festival Pass:
$30.00
Info
(203)458-pick (7425)
shorelinewinefestival.com
www.shorelinewinefestival.com

2nd Floor Design — Portsmouth, Virginia
Designer : Mary Hester
Client : Shoreline Wine Festival

Sabingrafik, Inc. – Carlsbad, California
Designers : Tracy Sabin, Bridget Sabin
Client : Sabingrafik, Inc.

The Seafarer Baking Company products are home-baked goods produced as a holiday gift/promotion/design sample for clients and potential clients of Sabingrafik, Inc. A new baked treat, with custom package design, is sent out each year during the month of December.

Turkish Delight
Happy Holidays 2005
A product of Seafarer Baking Co.

Biscotti
al cioccolato
Buon Natale
2005

panettone
Seafarer Baking Company

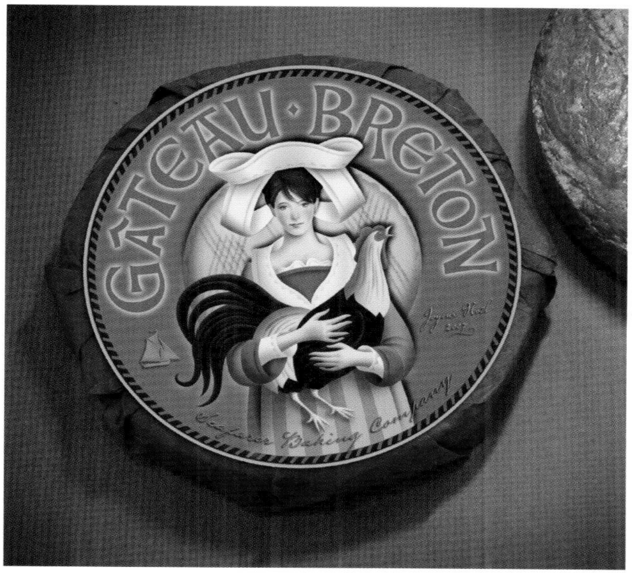
GÂTEAU·BRETON
Seafarer Baking Company

Springerle
Seafarer Baking Company
CARLSBAD, CALIFORNIA

Bounty from the Sea
From the Ovens of the Seafarer Baking Co.

BE MINE!
HAPPY VALENTINES DAY!
LOVE,
©TIM GOLDMAN

Seasons Greetings!
from
©TIM GOLDMAN

ERIN GO BRAUGH
Happy St. Patrick's Day!
from
©TIM GOLDMAN

Happy Easter!
& Happy Passover!
from
©TIM GOLDMAN

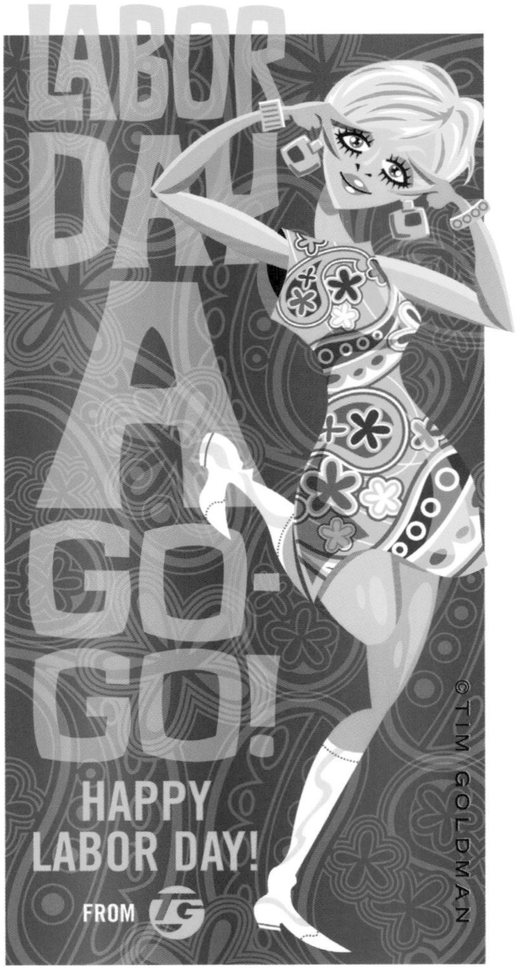
LABOR DAY A GO-GO!
HAPPY LABOR DAY!
FROM
©TIM GOLDMAN

HAVE A HAPPY HALLOWEEN!
FROM
TG
©TIM GOLDMAN

Tim Goldman Illustration Design – Jackson Heights, New York
Designer : Tim Goldman
Client : Tim Goldman Illustration Design

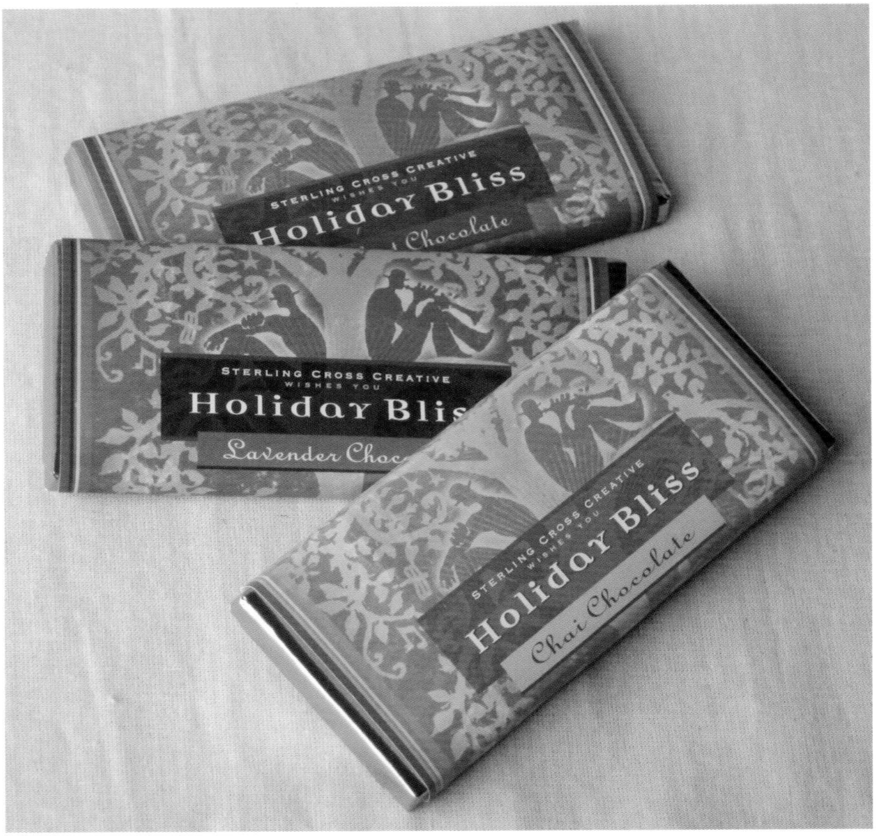

Sterling Cross Creative – Sonoma, California
Designers : Peggy Cross
Client : Sterling Cross Creative

Sabä Dö Graphix – White Rock, New Mexico
Designer : Allen Hopkins

WAX – Calgary, Canada
Designers : Monique Gamache, Jonathan Herman, Jonathan Jungworth, Suro Ghazarian, Christoph Wieman
Client : WAX

Instead of sending a greeting card with best wishes, this firm sent a greeting card kit so the *client* could send best wishes. Filled with solid color envelopes and cards, illustration and word stickers are also included so each sentiment can be a completely individualized one.

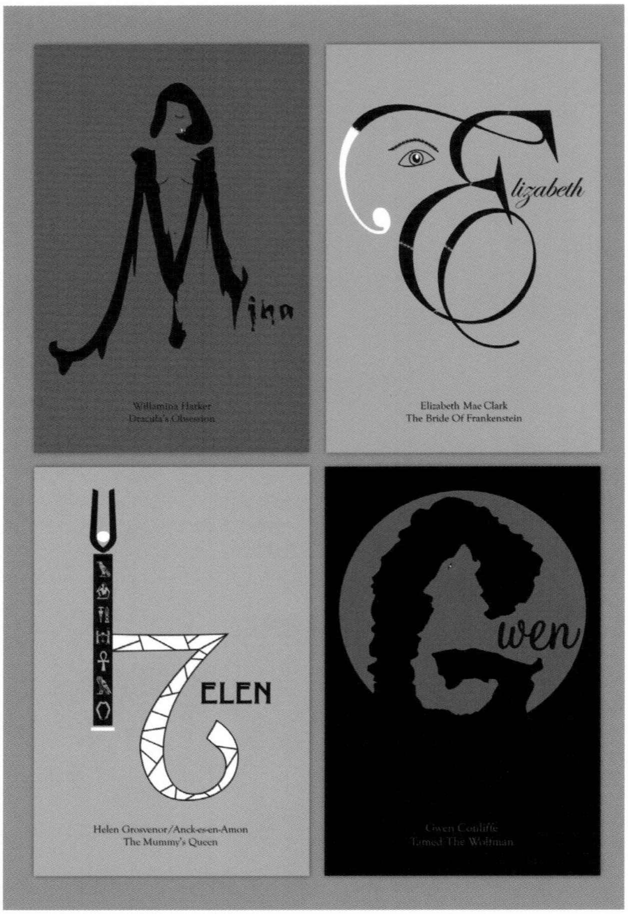

Zc Creative – Wyncote, Pennsylvania
Designer : Scott Laserow
Client : Zc Creative

MSLK Graphic Design – Long Island, New York
Designers : Marc S. Levitt, Sheri S. Koetting, Ellen K. Johnston
Client : MSLK

This specially-designed Thanksgiving wine bottle displays a whimsical turkey created from a classic fork, together suggesting a turkey feast with a good wine.

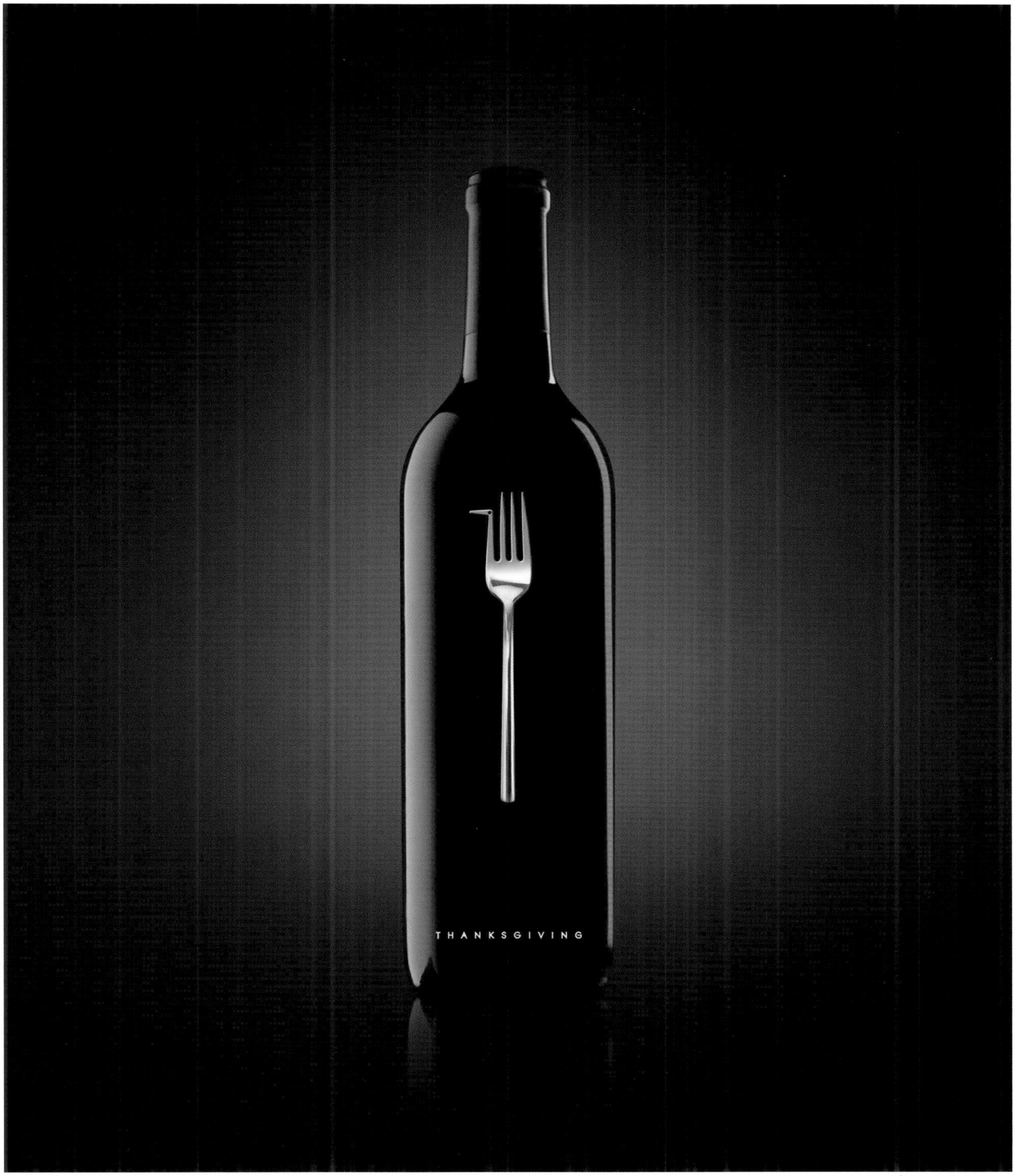

Wallace Church, Inc. – New York, New York
Designers : Stan Church, Bird Tubkam, Chung-Tao Tu
Client : Wallace Church, Inc.

Paragon Marketing Communications – Salmiya, Kuwait
Designers : Louai Alasfahani, Konstantin Assenov, Huzaifa Kakumama
Client : iCity

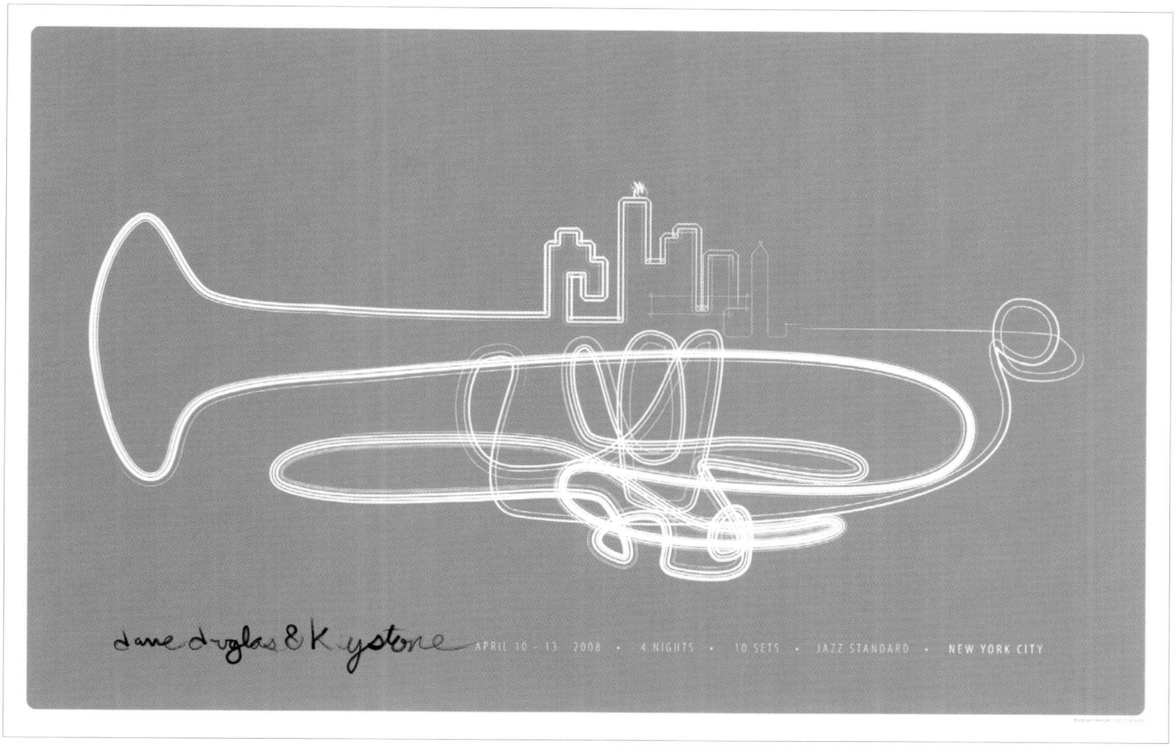

Get A Clue Design – Hickory, North Carolina
Designers : Matt Pfahlert
Client : Tony Margherita Management

Studio QED, Inc. – San Mateo, California
Designer : Steven Wright
Client : Studio QED, Inc.

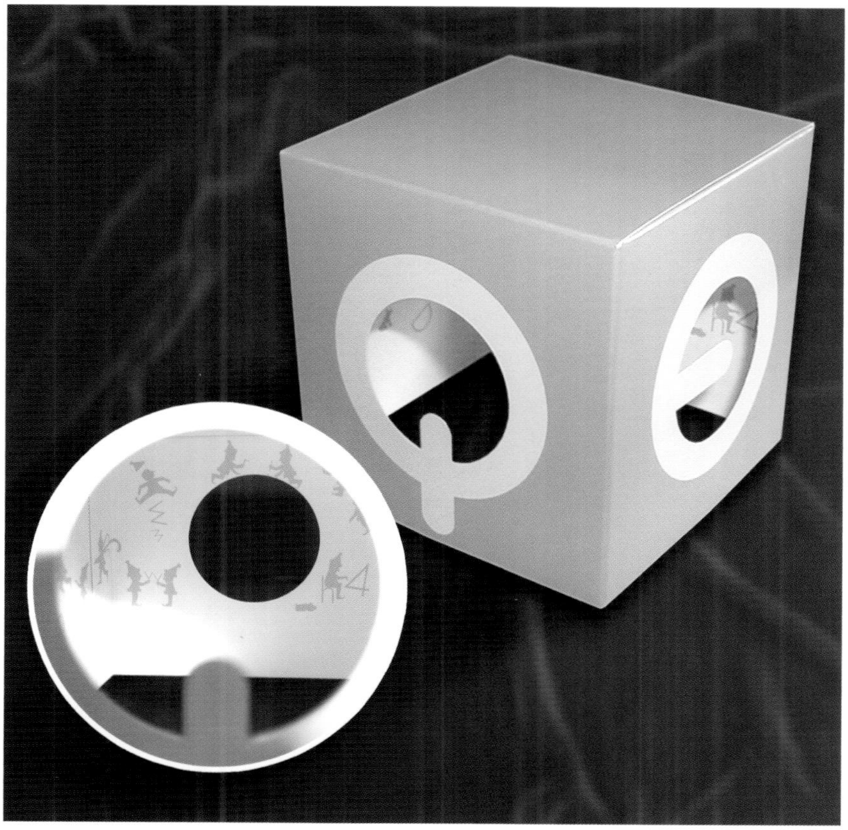

Stylized letters taken from the company's name are die cut from the sides of this cube to offer a peek inside at exactly what keeps Santa's elves so busy.

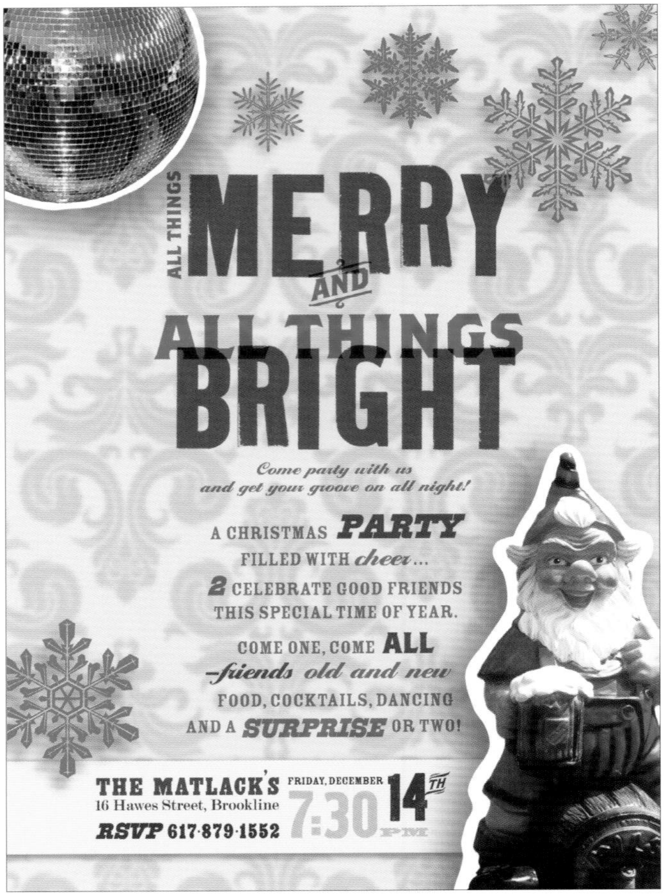
ALL THINGS
MERRY
AND
ALL THINGS
BRIGHT
Come party with us
and get your groove on all night!
A CHRISTMAS PARTY
FILLED WITH cheer...
2 CELEBRATE GOOD FRIENDS
THIS SPECIAL TIME OF YEAR.
COME ONE, COME ALL
–friends old and new
FOOD, COCKTAILS, DANCING
AND A SURPRISE OR TWO!
THE MATLACK'S
16 Hawes Street, Brookline
RSVP 617·879·1552
FRIDAY, DECEMBER
14TH
7:30 PM

Fresh Oil – Pawtucket, Rhode Island
Designer : Dan Stebbings
Client : Rafanelli Events

Alexander Isley, Inc. – Redding, Connecticut
Designers : Alexander Isley, Aline Hilford
Client : Alexander Isley, Inc.

Underscoring the concept of classic design, Alexander Isley chose to send this high-quality stapler as a gift. Now *that*'s something they'll keep on their desk all year 'round.

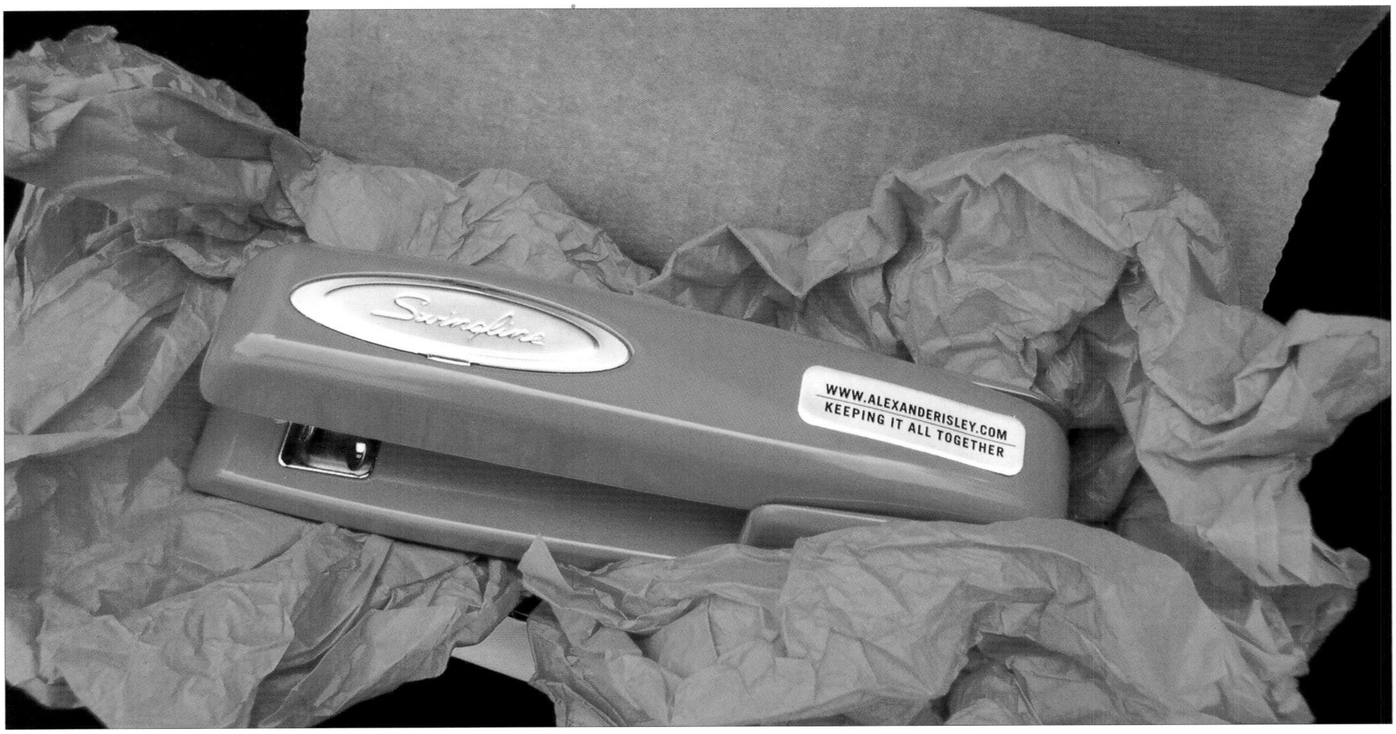
Swingline
WWW.ALEXANDERISLEY.COM
KEEPING IT ALL TOGETHER

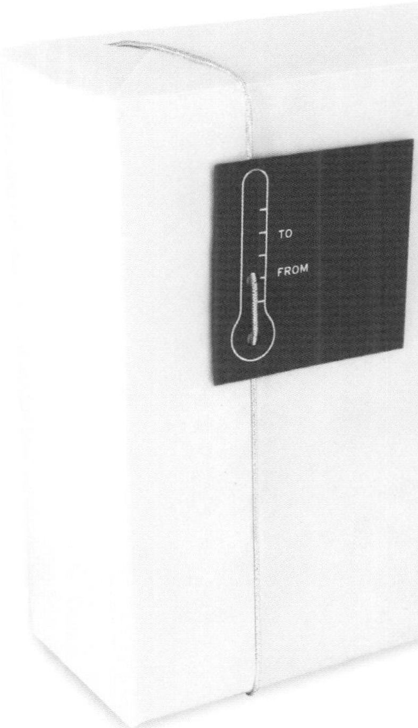
TO
FROM

MSLK Graphic Design – Long Island, New York
Designers : Marc S. Levitt, Sheri L. Koetting, Luise Sitte-Zöllner
Client : MSLK

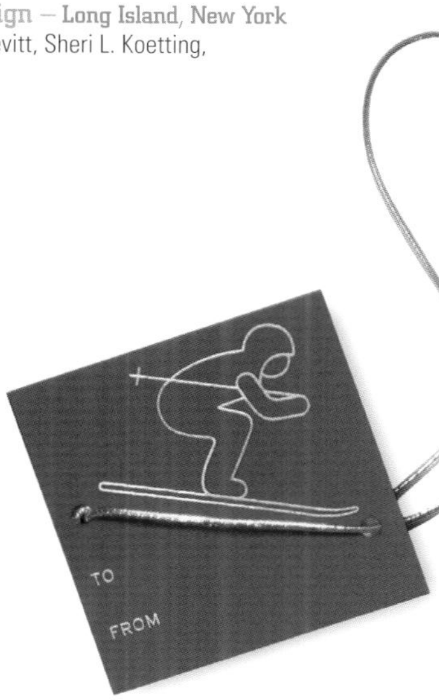
TO
FROM

WRAP. ATTACH. GIVE. ENJOY.
TO
FROM
HAPPY HOLIDAYS. MSLK

Gray
Christopher
May 5, 2007

of your company
at the marriage of
on Saturday, the fifth of May
Two thousand and seven
at half past six in the evening
The Creek Club at I'On
44 Saturday Road
Charleston, South Carolina
Gray Christopher

The Celebration and Blessing of a Marriage

GHL Design
– **Raleigh, North Carolina**
Designer : Gray Heffner
Client : Herndon Destination Wedding

Special tea promotion associates a variety of flavors with specific quali•teas the firm would like to share with the client.

Sterling Cross Creative – Sonoma, California
Designers : Peggy Cross, Jerome Maureze, Rico Pengs, Awan Sri
Client : Sterling Cross Creative

hatchsf.com/easter
1st Annual
EASTER EGG COLORING CONTEST
ENTER YOUR EGG ONLINE!
hatch
hatch design
1st Annual
EASTER EGG COLORING KIT
YOU'D BE A DIP NOT TO TRY IT!
THIS COLORING KIT INCLUDES:
Everything you need to create Easter Eggs to dye for...
6 magic color tablets, 1 wire egg dipper, 4 egg stands, 50 decorative stickers and 1 drying tray, 1 white crayon.
Happy Easter

Hatch Design – San Francisco, California
Designers : Katie Jain, Joel Templin, Eszter T. Clark, Lisa Pemrick
Client : Hatch Design

wishing ewe
a merry holiday
fleece navidad

Jill Lynn Design – Atlanta, Georgia
Designer : Jill Anderson
Client : Jill Lynn Design

A ceramic ornament accompanies a coordinating card, making a whimsical holiday giveaway.

Goodform Design – Brooklyn, New York
Client : Goodform Design

Warmest greetings have been sent your way.
So take a moment, have fun and play.
Fold up Santa's village.
Stand each piece up in line.
And enjoy some Christmas art with heart
from your friends at Sayles Graphic Design.
APPY HOLIDAYS
ME
YOU
FROM

Sayles Graphic Design – Des Moines, Iowa
Designer : John Sayles
Client : Sayles Graphic Design

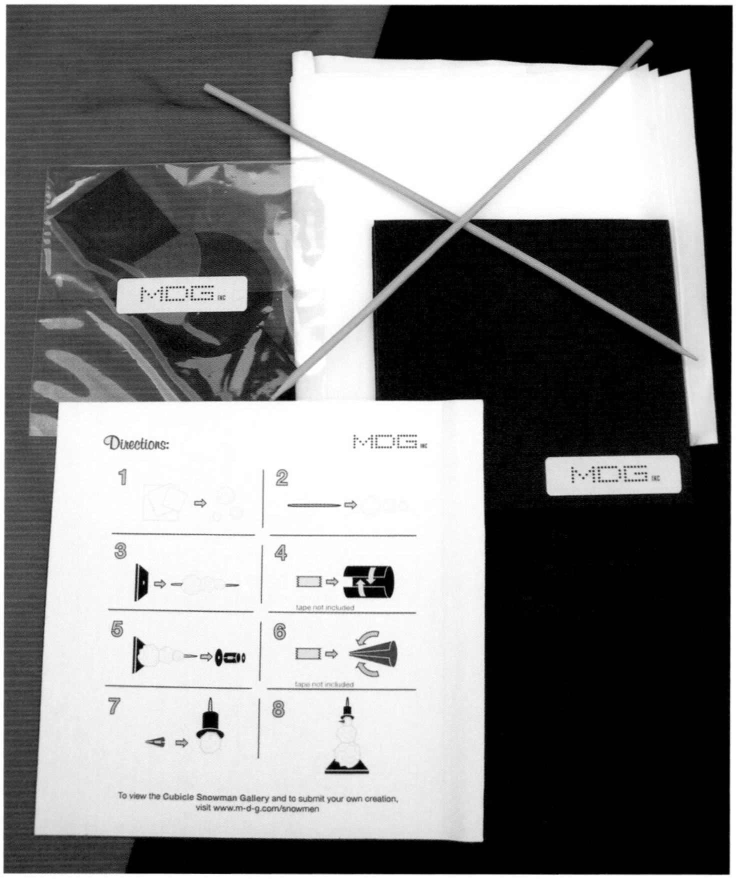
MDG
Directions:
MDG
tape not included
tape not included
To view the Cubicle Snowman Gallery and to submit your own creation,
visit www.m-d-g.com/snowmen
MDG

You don't need to wait for snow to utilize this snowman kit including white paper for the body. Then, submit your creation online at MDG's Cubicle Snowman Gallery to see how yours stacks up against the others!

MDG Strategic Branding – Holliston, Massachusetts
Designers : Kris Greene, Tim Merry, Mike Eaton
Client : MDG Strategic Branding

happyholidays
an assortment of festive
gift tags -- designed
to adorn your
holiday packages!
enjoy the season!
cheers!
an assortment of festive
gift tags -- designed
with you in mind!
happy holidays
and best wishes for
wonderful new year from
angryporcupine_design!
enjoy the season!
happy new year!
season's greetings!

angryporcupine*design — Park City, Utah
Designer : Cheryl Roder-Quill
Client : angryporcupine*design

Levine & Associates, Inc. – Washington, D.C.
Designer : Greg Sitzmann
Client : Verizon Center

GHL Design – Raleigh, North Carolina
Designer : Gray Heffner
Client : GHL Design

GHL Design punctuates metallic paper with a three-dimensional blossom made of matte paper petals and corduroy-covered button.

Molly Pengra & Brian Walsh
invite you to join them
in joyfully celebrating their marriage
on Saturday, the tenth of May,
two thousand & eight

Drive Thru Tree Park
Leggett, California

For full details on the weekend's activities,
destination, accommodations and to RSVP,
please visit www.mollyandbrian.us

Your response is requested
by April 10, 2008

There will also be a BBQ on
Friday night at
Dean Creek Resort.
Please visit the website for full details.
mollyandbrian.us

DK Design – Oakland, California
Designers : Darilyn Kotzenberg, Matt Jervis (Kulturehero.com)
Client : Molly Pengra & Brian Walsh

It's All About . . .

The Toys

Wearables, Games, and Miscellanous Items

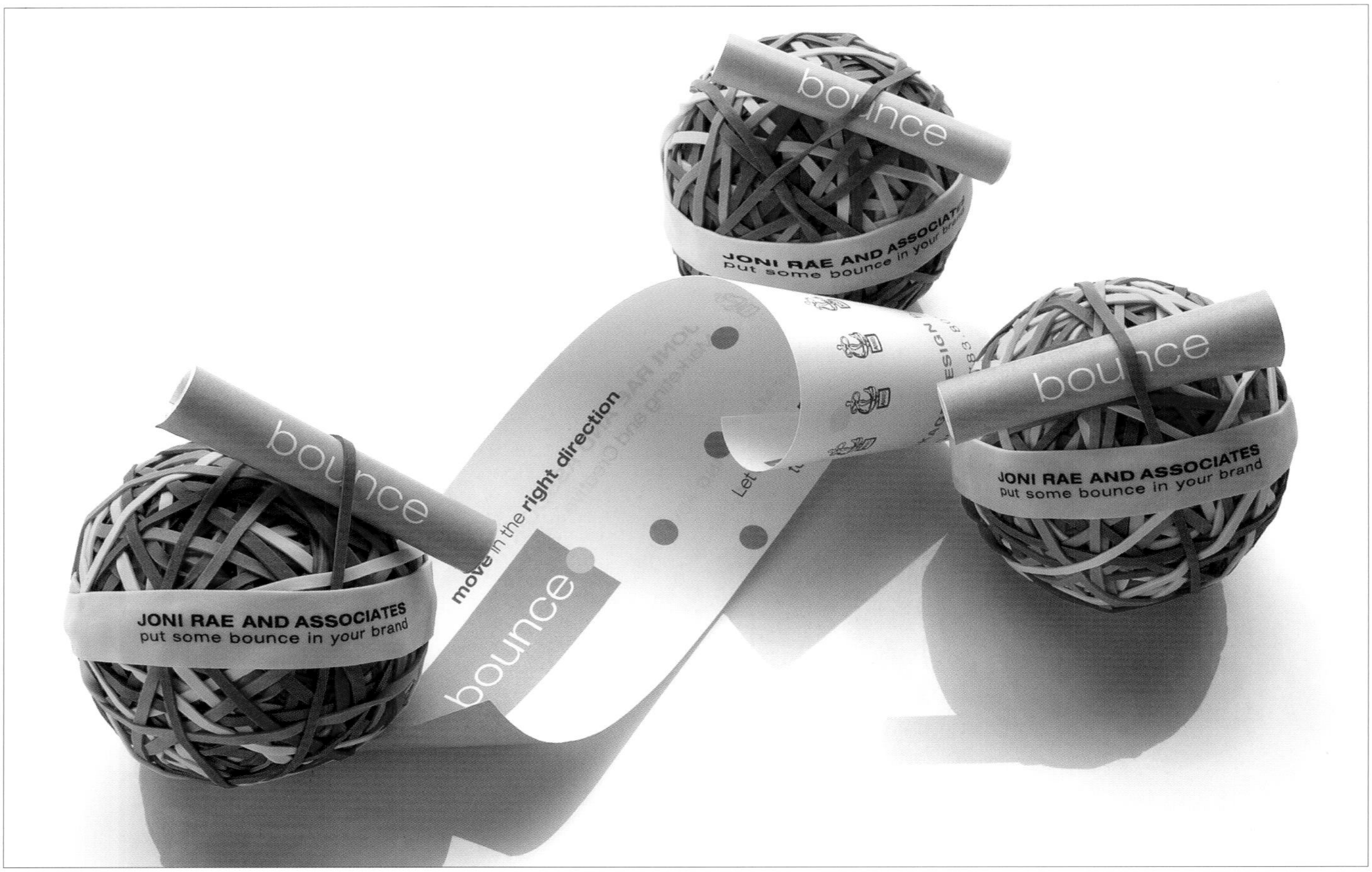

Joni Rae and Associates – Encino, California
Designers : Joni Rae Russell, Beverly Trengrove
Client : Joni Rae and Associates

BBR Creative – Lafayette, Louisianna
Designers : Cathi Pavy, Maria Lambert
Client : BBR Creative

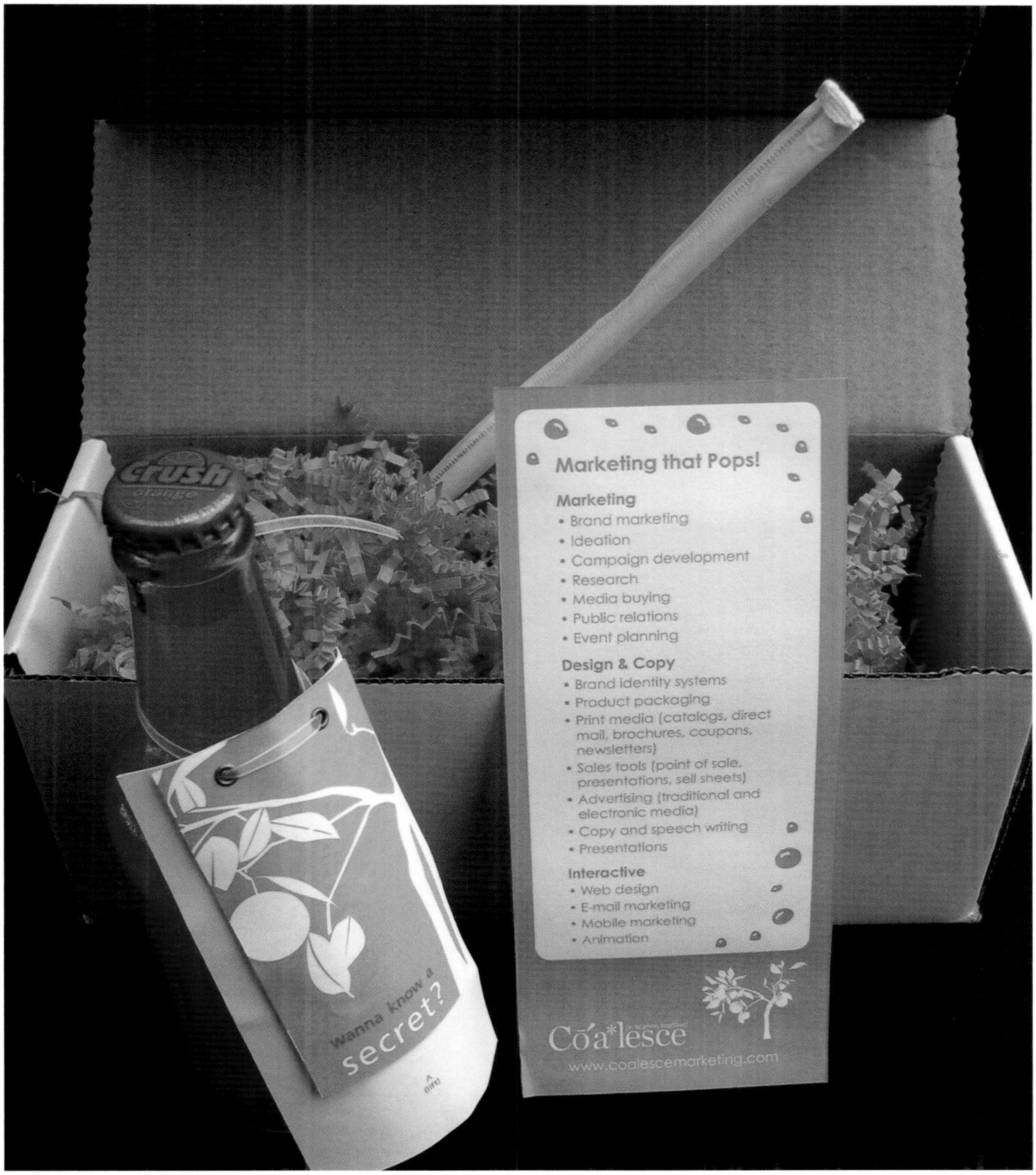
Crush
orange
Marketing that Pops!
Marketing
• Brand marketing
• Ideation
• Campaign development
• Research
• Media buying
• Public relations
• Event planning
Design & Copy
• Brand identity systems
• Product packaging
• Print media (catalogs, direct mail, brochures, coupons, newsletters)
• Sales tools (point of sale, presentations, sell sheets)
• Advertising (traditional and electronic media)
• Copy and speech writing
• Presentations
Interactive
• Web design
• E-mail marketing
• Mobile marketing
• Animation
Co'a*lesce
www.coalescemarketing.com
wanna know a
secret?

Coalesce Marketing & Design, Inc. – Appleton, Wisconsin
Designers : Lisa Piikkila, Michael Gehrman, Michelle Richard
Client : Coalesce Marketing & Design, Inc.

Factor Design – San Francisco, California
Designers : Tim Guy, Jeff Zwerner, Lily Lin
Client : MSFriends

IE Design + Communications – Hermosa Beach, California
Designer : Marcie Carson
Client : IE Design + Communications

DK Design – **Oakland, California**
Designers : Darilyn Kotzenberg, Nick Myerhoff
Client : DK Design

This urban chic ball cap drives home the idea of several hat analogies indicated in the accompanying literature. Each cap is spray-painted individually for a unique gift every time!

T.A.G. ...
Not just another pretty face!

Created to wear on field trips so students may easily recognize their group in a larger crowd, this bright shirt included a tongue-in-cheek rebuttal to the notion that one may be gifted either intellectually or physically, but not both.

Designs on You! – **Ashland, Kentucky**
Designers : Suzanna MW Stephens, Anthony B. Stephens
Client : Amber Hockman, Cedar Bluff Middle School Talented and Gifted Group

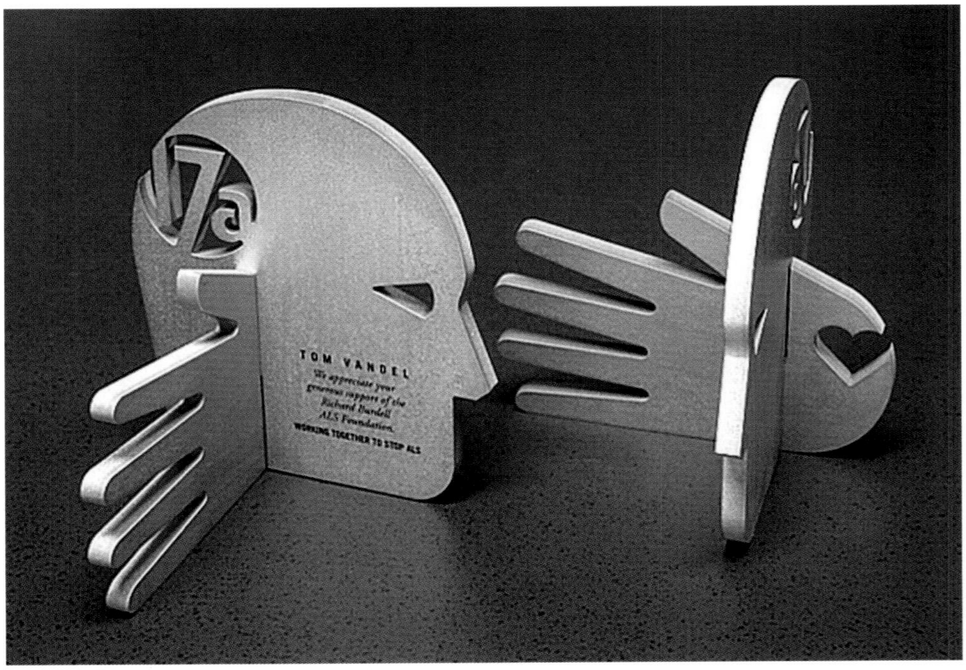
TOM VANDEL
WORKING TOGETHER TO STOP ALS

Dotzero Design – **Portland, Oregon**
Designers : Jon Wippich, Karen Wippich
Client : ALS Association

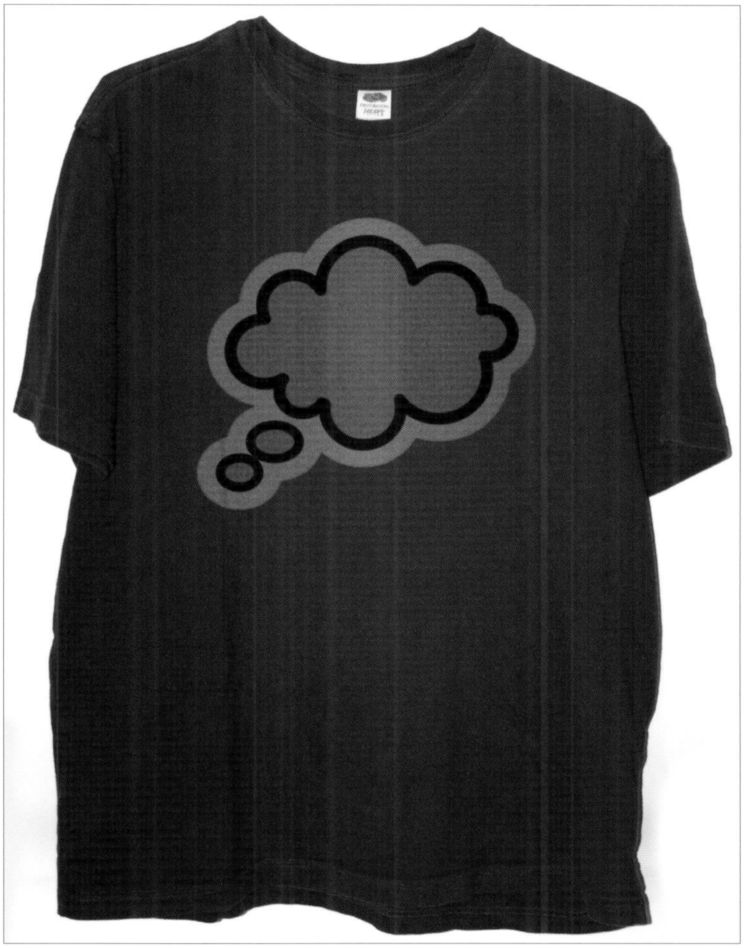

Open Studio Design – New York, New York
Designer : Shelly Fukushima
Client : Open Studio Design

Zc Creative – Wyncote, Pennsylvania
Designer : Scott Laserow
Client : Zc Creative

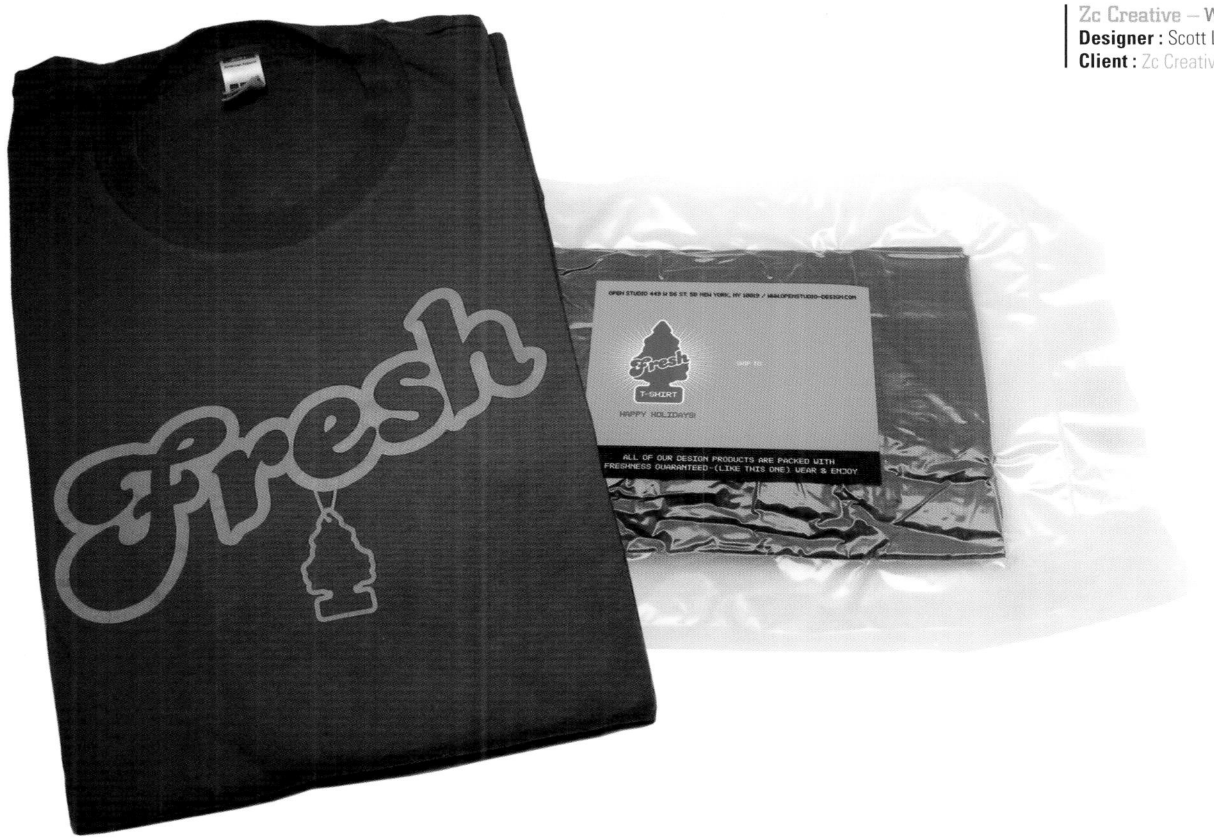
Fresh
Fresh
T-SHIRT
HAPPY HOLIDAYS!
ALL OF OUR DESIGN PRODUCTS ARE PACKED WITH
FRESHNESS GUARANTEED-(LIKE THIS ONE) WEAR & ENJOY

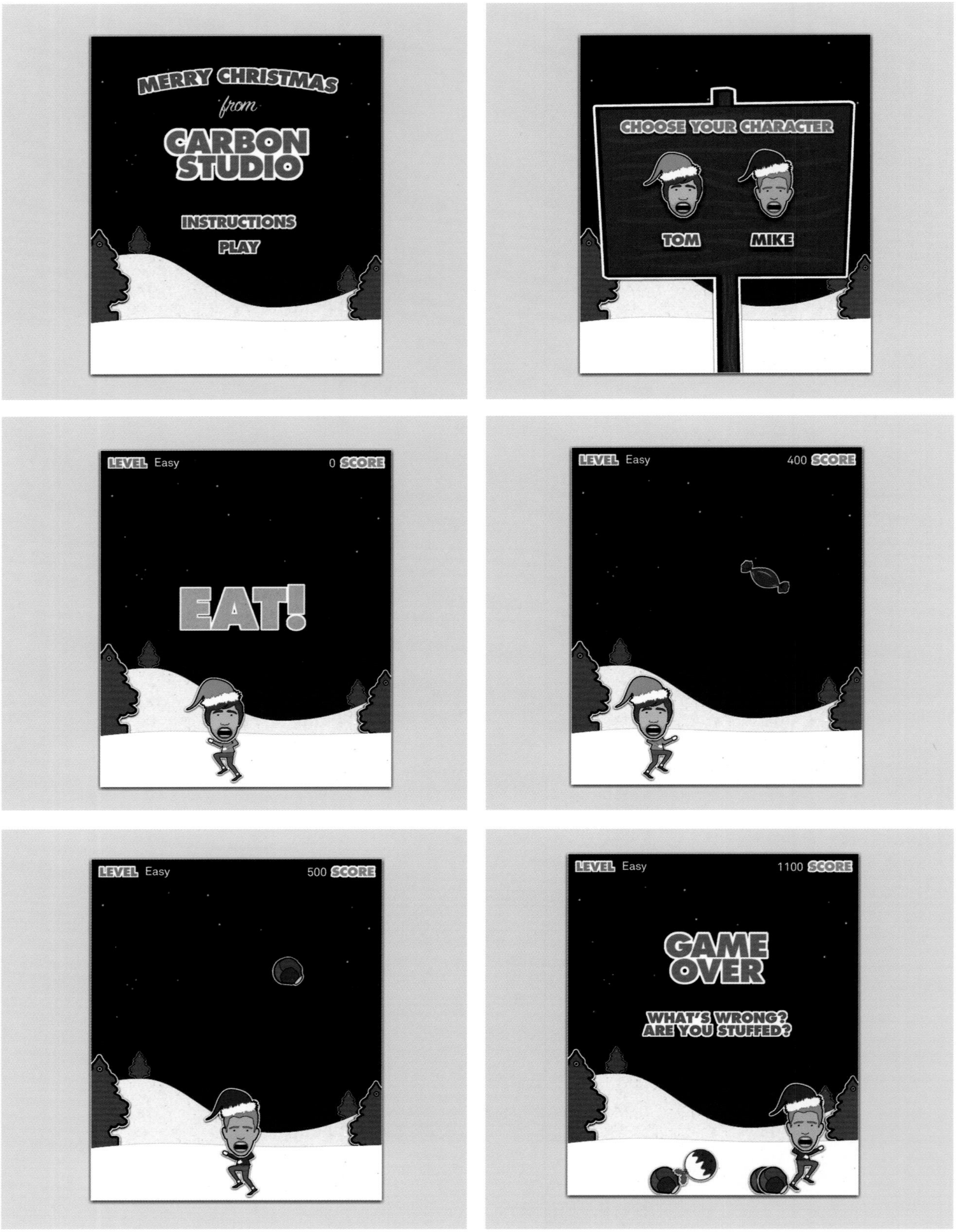

Carbon Studio – Cardiff, England
Designers : Mike Clague, Tom Tribe
Client : Carbon Studio

In this video game you can appropriate the personalities of the game's creators and eat all the Christmas candy you can hold.

FOCUS
Crankin out news you can use since 1978
Concept and Design by Get A Clue Design Studio • Promotional Printing: Premier Screen Printing PremierPromos.info

Get A Clue – Hickory, North Carolina
Designer : Matt Pfahlert
Client : Get A Clue Design/Focus Newspaper

Urban Geko, Inc. – Newport Beach, California
Designer : Monique Lefrancois
Client : Advantage Sales and Marketing

The Partners – London, England
Designers : Jack Renwick, Hannah Ferguson, Tim Brown
Client : Wolf Theiss

*FESTIVE MEAL DISCLAIMER

*FESTIVE MEAL DISCLAIMER
In no event shall the wearer of this apron ("apron-holder") be liable for any direct, indirect, punitive, incidental, special, consequential damage, or any damage whatsoever arising out of or in connection with the consumption of any festive meal prepared by the apron-holder. The wearer of this apron hereby disclaims any liability for material losses resulting from delays, non-deliveries or service interruptions caused by the apron-holder, any third-party acts or the oven not working properly.

NOTE TO CONSUMER: No reindeer were harmed in the harvesting of this fine product. This product has not been proven to be fine. It may possibly kill you. We don't know. This product has not been tested by the FDA or even the PTA for that matter. Do not eat this product (it's snot...that's just gross). Please do not use this product if you are pregnant with a reindeer's child. Please do not do anything that would cause you to get pregnant with a reindeer's child. If you must...PLEASE do not tell us!

Pi Design – Camarillo, California
Designers : Sharene Lewis, Shannon Parsons
Client : Pi Design

Dotzero Design – Portland, Oregon
Designers : Karen Wippich, Jon Wippich
Client : Dotzero Design

Hull Creative Group – **Brookline, Massachusetts**
Designers : Caryl H. Hull, Carol Thistle, Chris Klein, Sherman Morss, Pat King Powers, Nicole L. Vecchiotti
Client : Boston Harbor Island Alliance

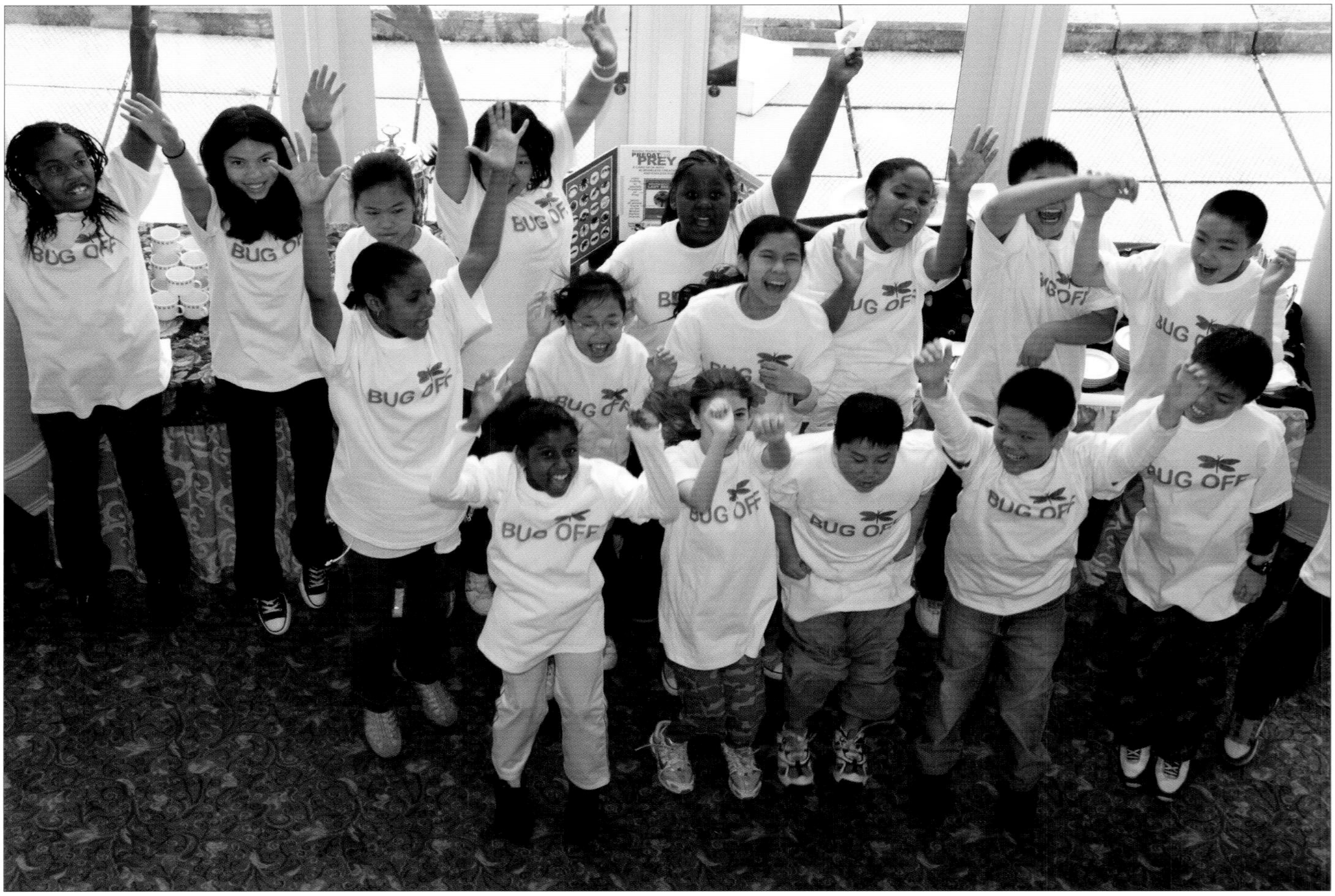

Ambient Creative Arts studio – Vista, California
Designer : Scott Mosher
Client : Monuments of Chaos

Get A Clue Design – Hickory, North Carolina
Designer : Matt Pfahlert
Client : Get A Clue Design

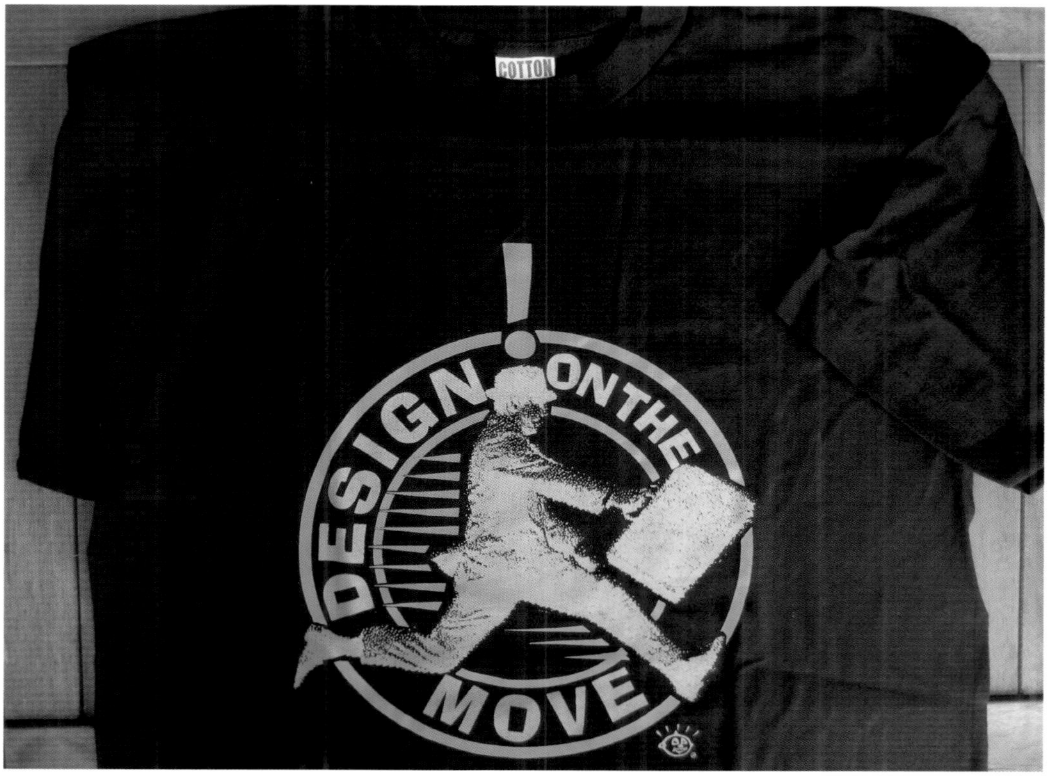

An In-Depth Look at: TRUEBLUE

Creative director Ria Fisher didn't grow up in Tennessee, but she's passionate about showing her adopted hometown to the world—and in the most complimentary light possible. So when her graphic design/photography/printing firm, TrueBlue, wanted to produce its annual year-end promotion for 2007, she envisioned a desk planner unlike any other. The resulting piece, "Reflections of Chattanooga," is the fruit of this inspiration.

"My goal was to find a person in Chattanooga that had a different perspective, one from the view of a visitor," Fisher says of her search for a photographic collaborator with a truly fresh set of eyes. After meeting Virginia Webb by chance at a local bookstore, she knew that she'd found her creative match—and muse. "Virginia is an artist whose medium is photography, and she shoots from the emotions of what hits her." The title, too, evokes a particular emotional state: "'Reflections' refers to the reflections of the river but also reflections of her as a person and how it affects her. She's a lady who has a great story to tell."

The planner, which, Fisher says, can also double as a coffee table book of the city, takes the reader through a year in Chattanooga against a backdrop of the Tennessee River and its bridges. While Fisher plans to recast her "Reflections" theme, the current version "reflects what a person's experience could be if they're on the waterfront. Next time, we'll focus on the historical buildings of Chattanooga." Subdivided into four sections—one for each season—stunning images of the area unfold in panoramic spreads, and many photos in the book find new life as removable notecards for readers to frame or send. And even though 2007 is in the past, that doesn't mean that people who pick up the planners will find it, well, dated. "It's a usable, viable product for our clients to enjoy... [so] we're developing it into a retail product and making it non-date-specific," she says. "Eventually every person who comes to Chattanooga is going to want to buy one of these planners. The locals are going to want one!"

TrueBlue has developed different self-promotions throughout the years, including a cookbook and a portfolio of patriotic notecards, but the planner is something that Fisher feels has lasting appeal for people who answer the call to visit Tennessee's fourth-largest city. "We got such a good reaction," she says. "So many [souvenirs] are cheesy, but this is a great thing for visitors; they can bring it back home with them." And those who already call Chattanooga home? "We wanted to raise the bar and create a quality piece. It's by Chattanoogans and for Chattanoogans and it inspires people."

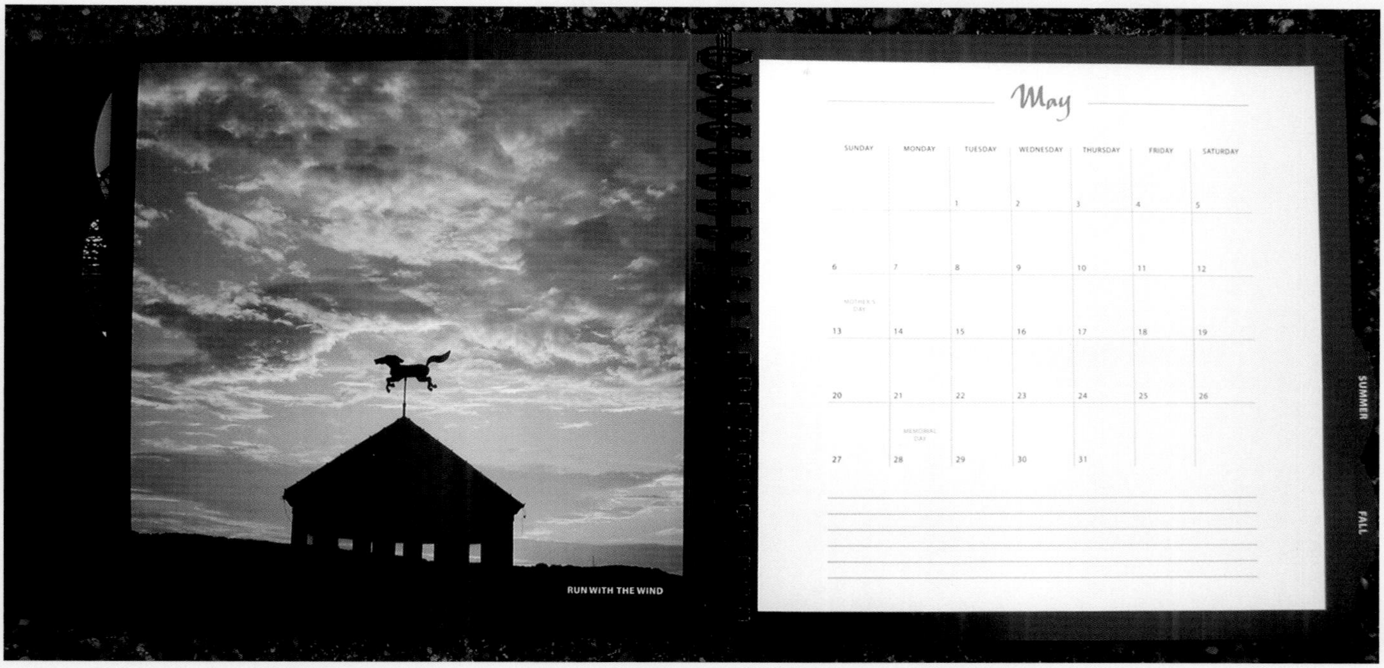

TrueBlue – Chattanooga, Tennessee
Designers : Ria Fisher, Zach Hobbs
Client : TrueBlue

Dotzero Design – Portland, Oregon
Designers : Karen Wippich, Jon Wippich
Client : Dotzero Design

Get A Clue Design – Hickory, North Carolina
Designer : Matt Pfahlert
Client : Get A Clue Design

NALINDESIGNô – Neuenrade, Germany
Designer : Andre Weier
Client : NALINDESIGNô

Ambigrams are created from stylized, calligraphic designs. They are identical when read as is and when rotated 180º.

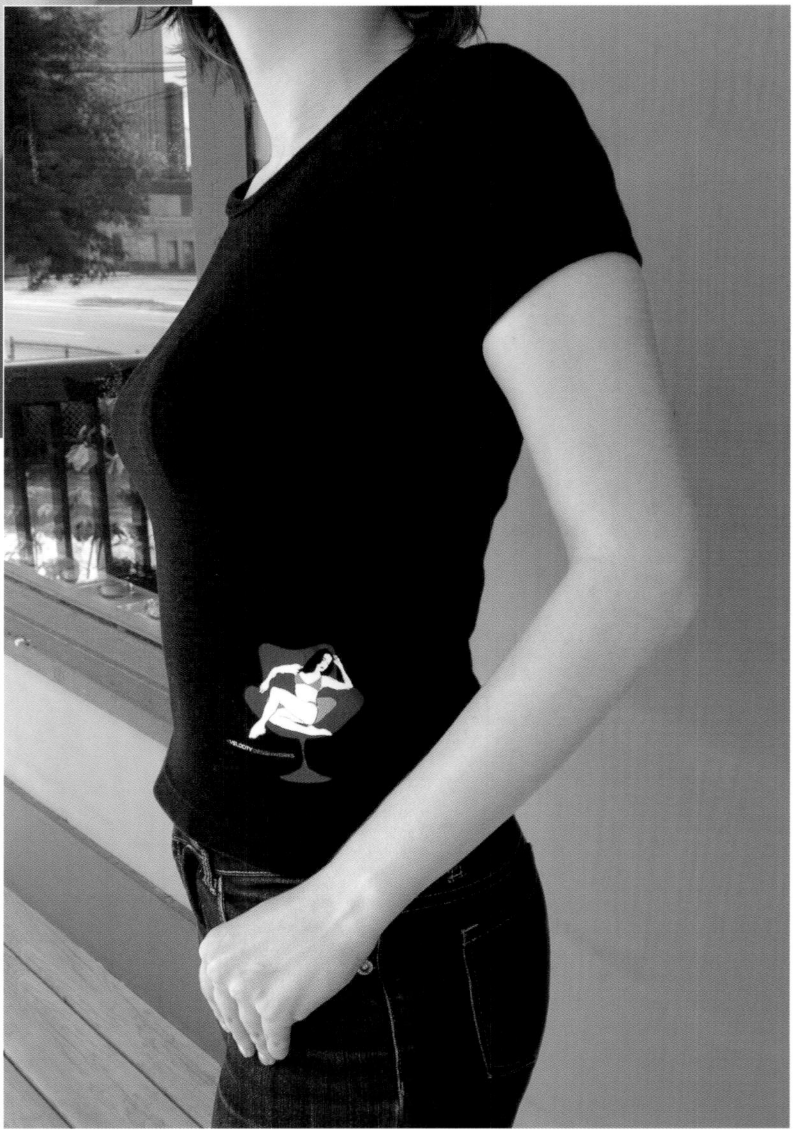

Velocity Design Works – Winnipeg, Canada
Designers : Velocity Design Works
Client : Velocity Design Works

Q – **Wiesbaden, Germany**
Designer : Marcel Kummerer
Client : Q

Zc Creative – **Wyncote, Pennsylvania**
Designer : Scott Laserow
Client : Tyler School of Art, Temple University

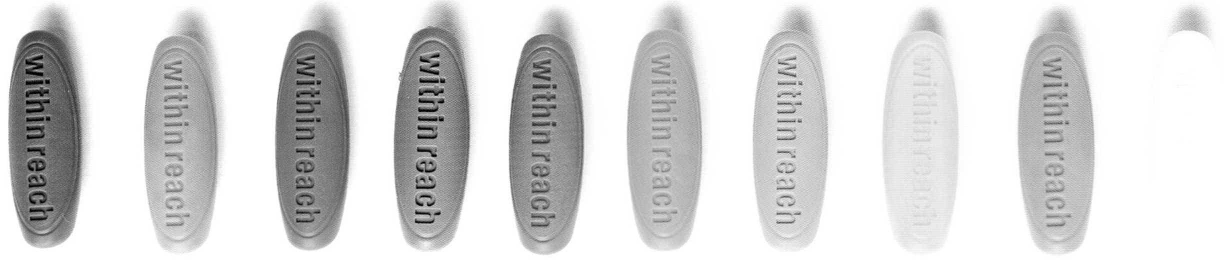

Minds on Marketing – Lewis Center, Ohio
Designers : Tom Augustine, Poormehr Honarmand, Doug Stitt, Randy James
Client : Juvenile Diabetes

Feel great about yourself and what you're doing every time you say "no" to both paper and plastic and use this convenient, flat-folding canvas bag.

Earth Day!
THANK YOU
THANK YOU
THANK YOU
THANK YOU
THANK YOU
THANK YOU
THANK YOU
HAVE A NICER TOMORROW
WARNING: TO AVOID DANGER OF SUFFOCATION, PLEASE KEEP PLASTIC BAGS OFF THE PLANET. DO NOT USE THEM FOR SHOPPING, TAKE-OUT OR GROCERIES.
Reuse this bag
Design with a purpose. ©2008 Open Studio Design

Open Studio Design – New York, New York
Designer : Shelly Fukushima
Client : Open Studio Design

BBR Creative – Lafayette, Louisiana
Designer : Denise Gallagher
Client : Fred's Lounge

COURIR DE MARDI GRAS
MAMOU, LA 70554
TANTE SUE
Laissez Les Bon Temps Rouler!
2007
KVPI RADIO AM1050
FRED'S LOUNGE
No Kissing!
Please DO Not stand on the Tables, Chairs Cigarette Machine, Booths, and Juke-Box! Thank You. Fred
HOT DAMN

Dotzero Design – Portland, Oregon
Designer : Karen Wippich, Jon Wippich
Client : Dotzero Design

2creativo – Barcelona, Spain
Designers : 2creativo Team
Client : Shopping Mall Maremagnum

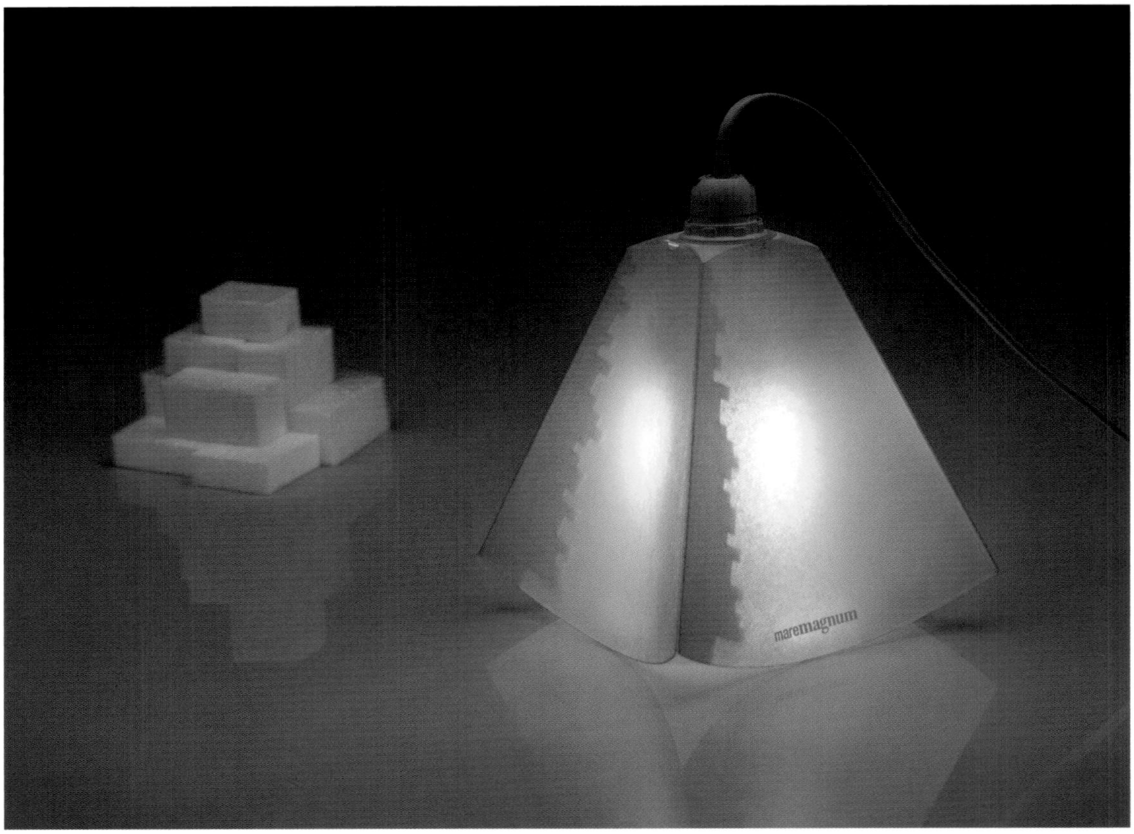

hELLO.
hELLO. YO VISIT
CULVER CITY
IT'S AWESOME!

Hello Design – Culver City, California
Designers : David Lai, Ron Thompson
Client : Hello Design

It's your shirt. What do you want it to say? Create an LED-like display by filling in white squares with a permanent marker—and wear your message.

DIG IN!
TASTY DESIGN INSIDE!

Get A Clue – Hickory, North Carolina
Designer : Matt Pfahlert
Client : Get A Clue Design

An In-Depth Look at: TOP DESIGN

Peleg Top loves self-promotion—and makes sure his clients always get something out of it, too. "Self-promotion is all about giving," the founder of Los Angeles' Top Design says. "Ultimately [a promotion is] a useful piece."

Top's calendars turned out to be his longest-running promotion in a number of ways. Produced from 1993 to 2007, the calendars weren't just quick, year-end promos tucked in with a mass-produced holiday card, but a work of art that arrived every thirty or so days. For the first eight years, Top designed the calendars himself, taking time monthly to create something fun and extraordinary. "It was a great creative outlet for me, to sit down once a month and design something for myself and share it with clients." Collaborations followed, as Top brought in other illustrators and photographers to design different looks for each new year's theme, be it a delicate tapestry, a bold, hand-drawn seasonal image series or twelve solid blocks describing the etymology of the twelve months. "It opened up a whole new world of possibilities," he says; Top Design got an ever-changing, fresh perspective on their self-promotional pieces and the collaborators got a bright and timely showpiece for their own advertising efforts. The economy of digital printing, too, made the continuing mailings easy and affordable. "That's the beauty of it," says Top. "This was our way of keeping in touch on a regular basis."

Top's choice of size and shape—eight-by-eight squares—was a "natural," given the firm's previous experience designing record covers. "I love anything square," he says. And he built them to last. "The first time we'd send one out, the client would get a 'calendar pack' with a custom-designed, clear acrylic desk stand to slide [the month's calendar] into." With that durable setup, it wasn't unusual for Top to come across his designs in the wild. "I can't describe how many times I saw my calendars in people's offices," he says. "Often it'd be the only piece of art in the office. It looked really cool."

Producing an attractive piece, although enjoyable, wasn't the only benefit for Top Design. "We really, carefully cultivated [our lists],"

Top Design – Los Angeles, California
Designers: Peleg Top, Shachar Laui, Audra Keefe, Rebekah Albrecht
Client: Top Design
(continued on following spread)

Top says of the three-hundred-odd monthly recipients. "Someone interested in our work, a qualified prospect or someone who might know someone who might be. We know the power of referrals; we wanted to make sure we were using this promotion effectively." Not only did Top harness the power of referrals, he also knows how to wield the power of persistence and consistency. "For a first-time prospect, we'd send them the calendars for a year, then touch base and follow up. It was a reason to call them." Even two or three years after that first contact, Top says, "people would hire us, because they were really impressed with the consistency, getting something from us every month. And because [each month's calendar] was time sensitive, it forced us to get it done."

While Top Design no longer produces calendars, Top still focuses his efforts on getting out the good word. "The beauty of self-promotion is consistency…Always [give] something someone can use," he advises. "Hit people from different directions with different promotions. The key thing is that this stuff works."

An In-Depth Look at: TOP DESIGN

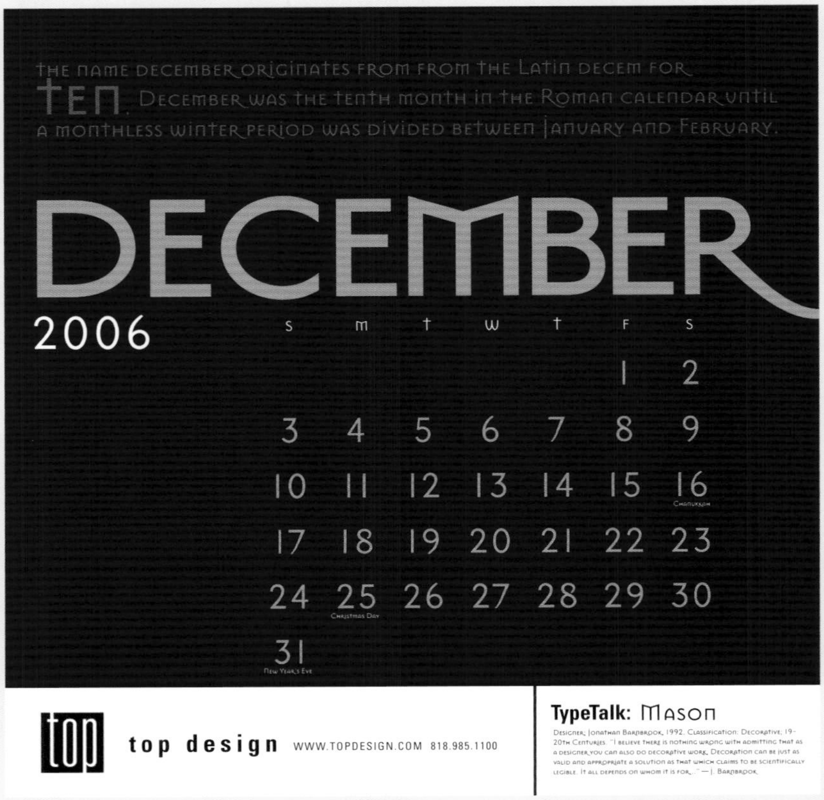

01|07
S M T W T F S
orange
top design

03|07
S M T W T F S
green
top design

04|07
S M T W T F S
1 2 3 4 5 6 7
PASSOVER
8 9 10 11 12 13 14
EASTER
15 16 17 18 19 20 21
22 23 24 25 26 27 28
29 30
If purple is your favorite color, you are a visionary. Your life essence is one of spiritual consciousness and awareness. You believe yourself to be a strong and independent person, while others perceive you as sensitive and observant. You find it natural to express yourself aesthetically and artistically.
purple
top design
WWW.TOPDESIGN.COM | 818-985-1100

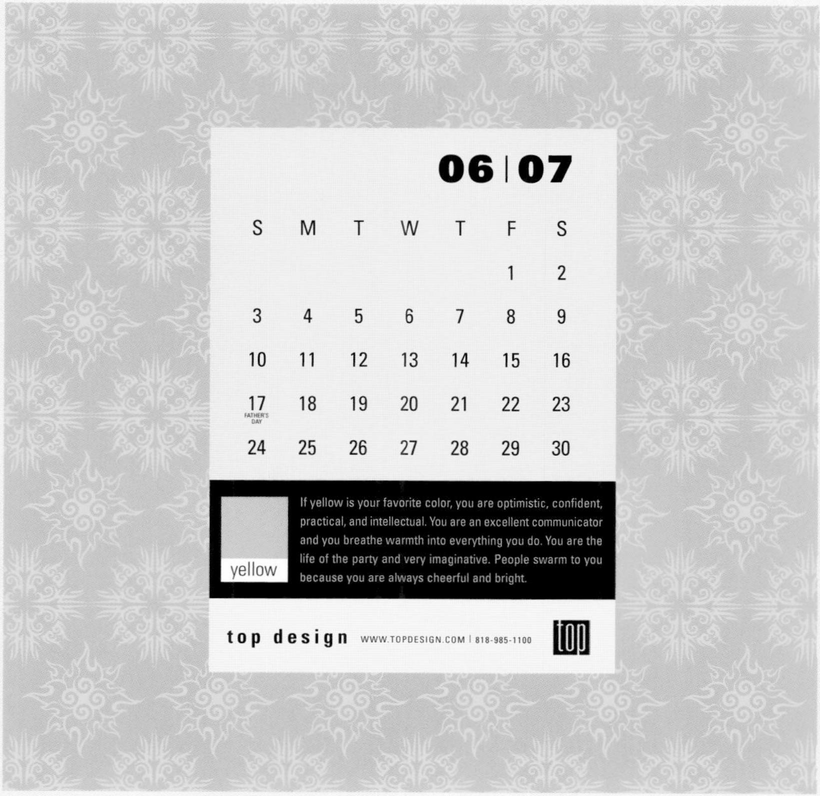
06|07
S M T W T F S
1 2
3 4 5 6 7 8 9
10 11 12 13 14 15 16
17 18 19 20 21 22 23
FATHER'S DAY
24 25 26 27 28 29 30
If yellow is your favorite color, you are optimistic, confident, practical, and intellectual. You are an excellent communicator and you breathe warmth into everything you do. You are the life of the party and very imaginative. People swarm to you because you are always cheerful and bright.
yellow
top design
WWW.TOPDESIGN.COM | 818-985-1100

07|07
S M T W T F S
blue
top design

11|07
S M T W T F S
brown
top design

Dotzero Design – Portland, Oregon
Designers : Karen Wippich, Jon Wippich
Client : Dotzero Design

Bohnsack Design – Vail, Arizona
Designer : Chris Bohnsack
Client : Bohnsack Design

I ♥ STANLEY
STANLEY'S
CITY SLICKERS
Cystic Fibrosis Great Strides Walk // Battery Park City, NYC // 5.19.2007

Open Studio Design – New York, New York
Designer : Shelly Fukushima

Calagraphic Design – Elkins Park, Pennsylvania
Designers : Ronald J. Cala II, Joe Scorsone

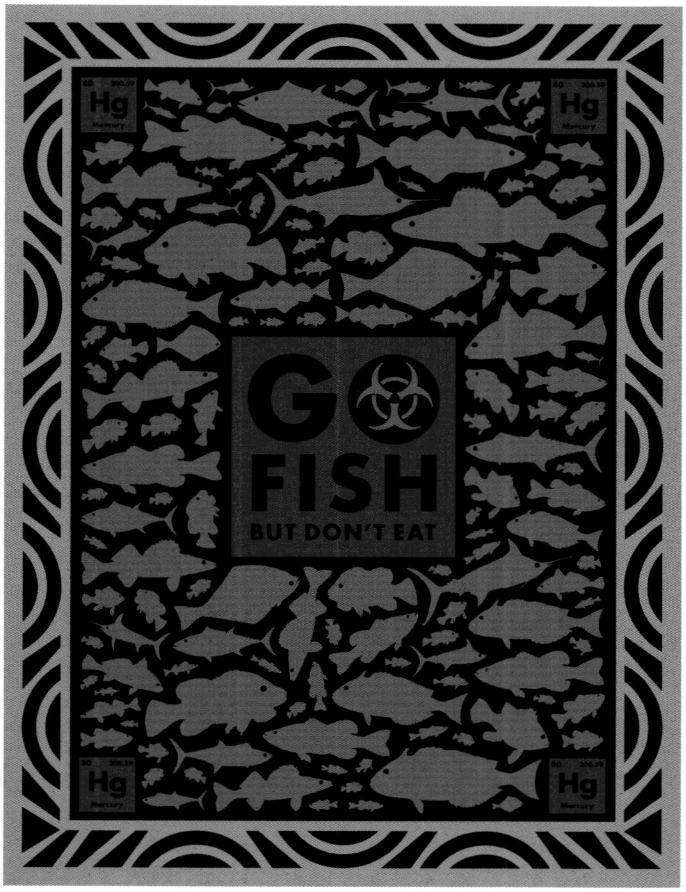
Hg
Mercury
GO
FISH
BUT DON'T EAT

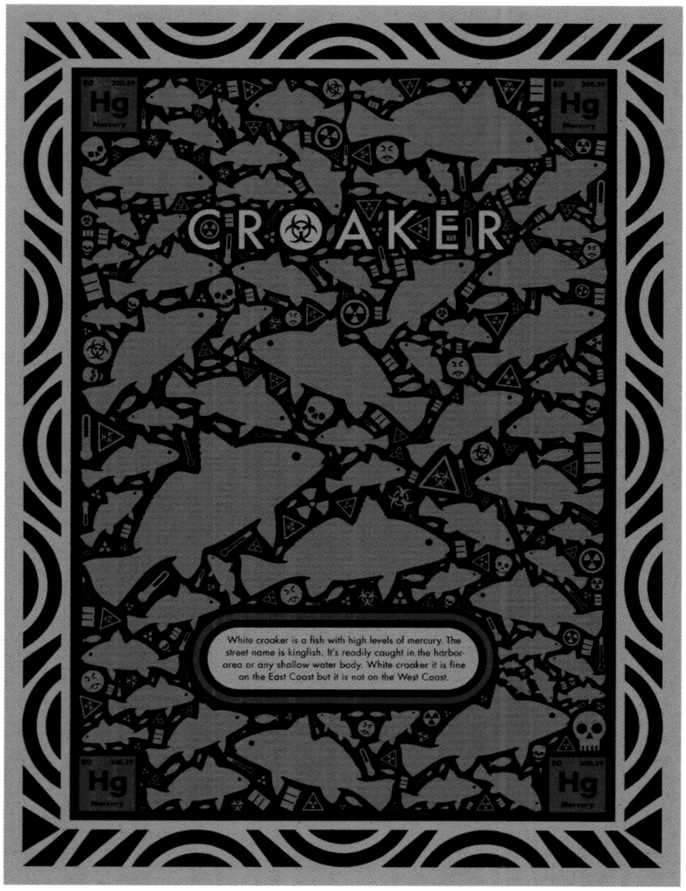
Hg
Mercury
CROAKER
White croaker is a fish with high levels of mercury. The street name is kingfish. It's readily caught in the harbor-area or any shallow water body. White croaker it is fine on the East Coast but it is not on the West Coast.

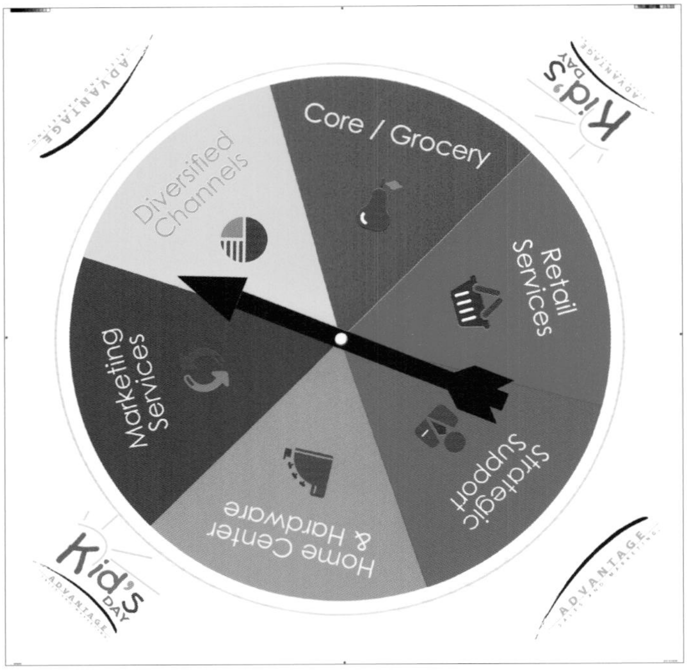

Urban Gecko Inc. – Newport Beach, California
Designer : Monique Lefrancois
Client : Advantage Sales and Marketing

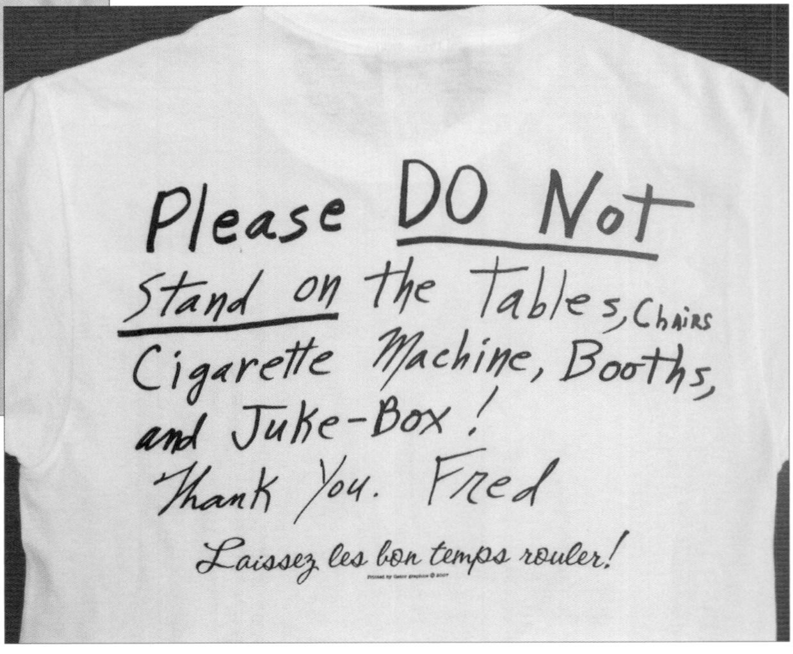

BBR Creative – Lafayette, Louisiana
Designer : Maria Lambert
Client : Fred's Lounge

Hello Design – Culver City, California
Designers : David Lai, Ron Thompson
Client : Hello Design

Designs on You! – Ashland, Kentucky
Designers : Suzanna MW Stephens, Anthony B. Stephens
Client : Dayspring Family Care

THE GIRL WHO REACHED FOR THE STAR
Written by Wendy Awkerman Lyons
Illustrated by John Sayles
THE GIRL WHO REACHED FOR THE STAR

Sayles Graphic Design – Des Moines, Iowa
Designers : John Sayles, Bridget Drendel, Wendy Awkerman Lyons
Client : P.E.O. Sisterhood

Factor Design – San Francisco, California
Designers : Tim Guy, Jeff Zwerner, Lily Lin
Client : MSFriends

Rock for MS

When t-shirts are created for a specific event, like this fundraiser for research for a cure for multiple sclerosis, they can carry a message and increase awareness long after the event has ended—IF they are designed well and people choose to continue wearing them.

Dotzero Design – Portland, Oregon
Designer : Karen Wippich, Jon Wippich
Client : Dotzero Design

Gough Graphics – Bradford, Massachusetts
Designer : Rob Gough
Client : The Amica Insurance Breakers Marathon

The College of Saint Rose,
Office of Public Relations & Marketing – Albany, New York
Designers : Mark Hamilton, Chris Parody
Client : The College of Saint Rose

Studio QED, Inc. – San Mateo, California
Designer : Steven Wright
Client : Square Emix

NALINDESIGNô – Neuenrade, Germany
Designer : Andre Weier
Client : NALINDESIGNô

Sabä Dö Graphix – White Rock, New Mexico
Designer : Allen Hopkins
Client : Sabä Dö Graphix

It's All About . . .

The Greater GOOD

Promotions for Nonprofit Organizations

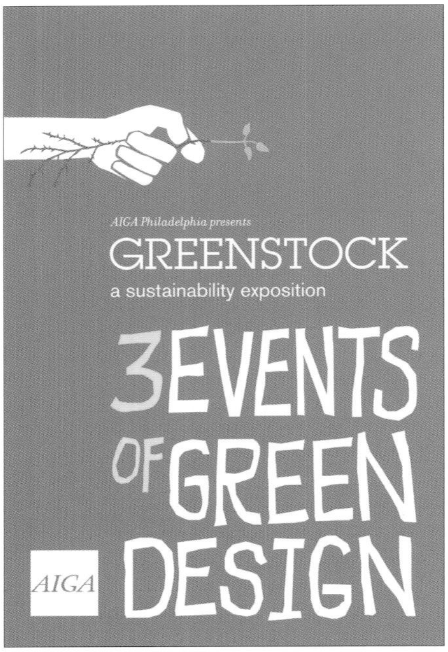
AIGA Philadelphia presents
GREENSTOCK
a sustainability exposition
3EVENTS OF GREEN DESIGN
AIGA

AIGA Philadelphia presents
GREENSTOCK
a sustainability exposition
3EVENTS OF GREEN DESIGN
AIGA

AIGA Philadelphia presents
GREENSTOCK
a sustainability exposition
3EVENTS OF GREEN DESIGN
AIGA

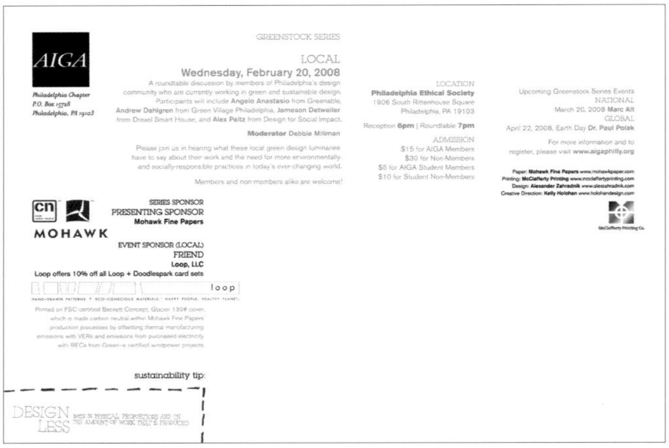
AIGA
Philadelphia Chapter
P.O. Box 15718
Philadelphia, PA 19103
GREENSTOCK SERIES
LOCAL
Wednesday, February 20, 2008
A roundtable discussion by members of Philadelphia's design community who are currently working in green and sustainable design. Participants will include Angelo Anastasio from Greenable, Andrew Dahlgren from Green Village Philadelphia, Jameson Detweiler from Drexel Smart House, and Alex Peltz from Design for Social Impact.
Moderator Debbie Millman
Please join us in hearing what these local green design luminaries have to say about their work and the need for more environmentally- and socially-responsible practices in today's ever-changing world.
Members and non-members alike are welcome!
LOCATION
Philadelphia Ethical Society
1906 South Rittenhouse Square
Philadelphia, PA 19103
Reception 6pm | Roundtable 7pm
ADMISSION
$15 for AIGA Members
$30 for Non-Members
$5 for AIGA Student Members
$10 for Student Non-Members
Upcoming Greenstock Series Events
NATIONAL
March 20, 2008 Marc Alt
GLOBAL
April 22, 2008, Earth Day Dr. Paul Polak
For more information and to register, please visit www.aigaphilly.org
SERIES SPONSOR
PRESENTING SPONSOR
Mohawk Fine Papers
MOHAWK
EVENT SPONSOR (LOCAL)
FRIEND
Loop, LLC
Loop offers 10% off all Loop + Doodlespark card sets
loop
sustainability tip:
DESIGN LESS

Holohan Design – Philadelphia, Pennsylvania
Designers : Kelly Holohan, Alexander Zahradnik
Client : AIGA Philadelphia

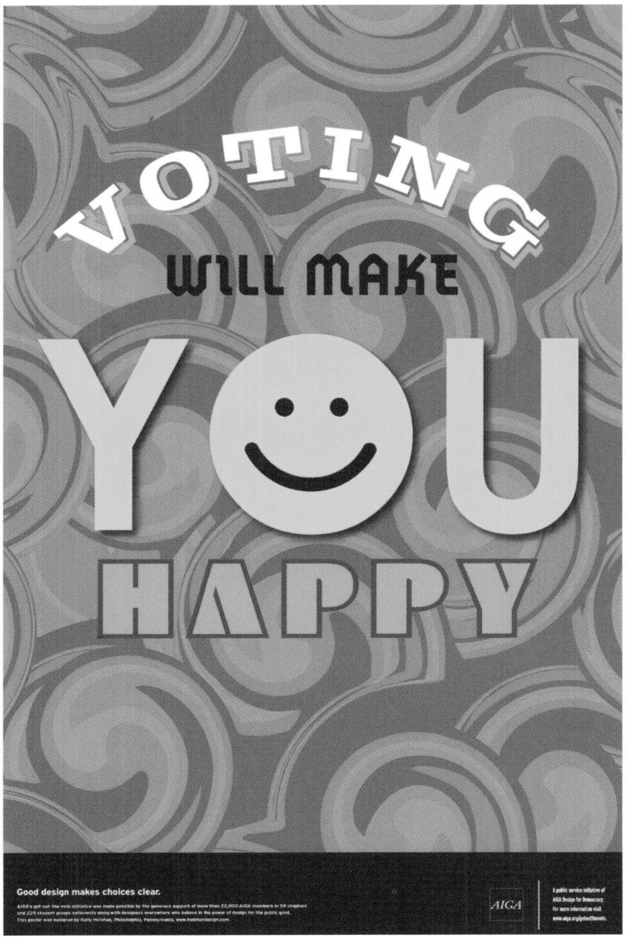
VOTING
WILL MAKE
YOU
HAPPY
Good design makes choices clear.
AIGA

Holohan Design – Philadelphia, Pennsylvania
Designer : Kelly Holohan
Client : AIGA

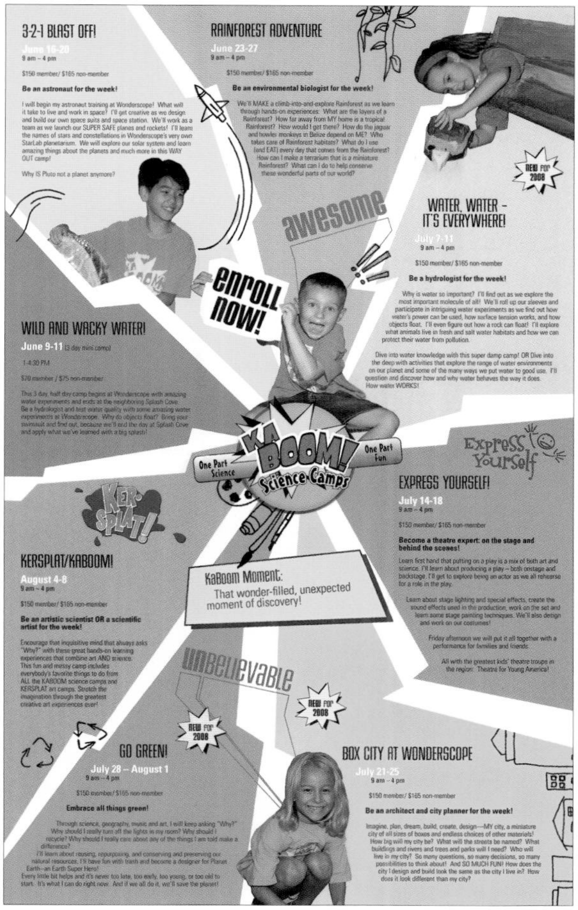

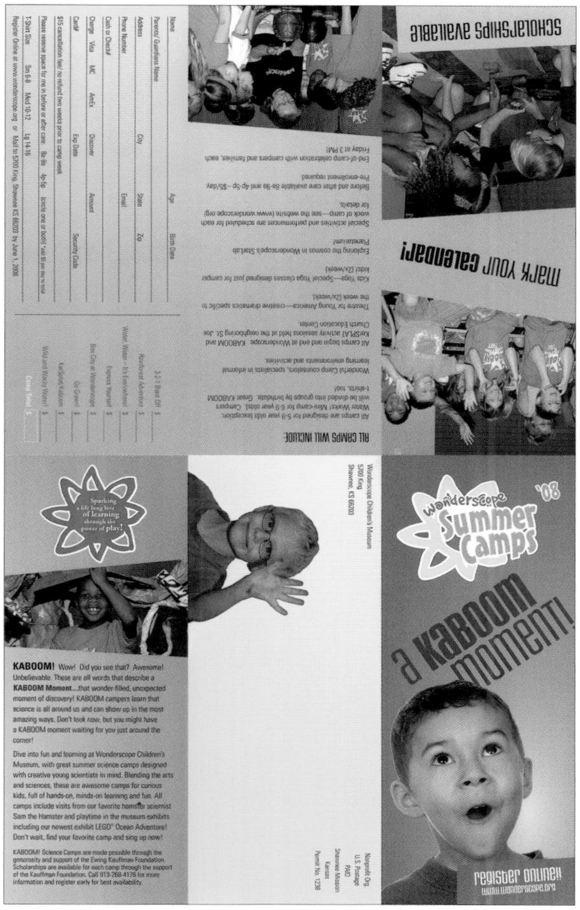

REACTOR — Kansas City, Missouri
Designers : Clifton Alexander, Chase Wilson
Client : Wonderscope

BBMG — New York, New York
Designers : Molly Conley, Scott Ketchum
Client : Social Venture Network

who we are

The leading network **connecting** business, community and spirit **for the common good.**

Social Venture Network is the leading organization of CEOs, investors, and social entrepreneurs dedicated to building and growing socially responsible enterprises.

From organics to fair trade to clean energy, Social Venture Network is transforming the way the world does business.

We leverage our collective strengths of vision, knowledge and innovation to create a more just economy and sustainable planet.

"When I joined SVN, my life and work as a social entrepreneur were changed forever. This is clearly one of the most inspiring and important communities in the world today."

ZAK ZAIDMAN
KOPALI ORGANICS

"SVN has had a strong influence on our company's socially responsible business practices, and I deeply value the connections I've made through the network."

EILEEN FISHER
EILEEN FISHER INC

Get involved.

Join the leading network of socially responsible business leaders and social entrepreneurs. Attend an event, apply for membership, or visit us online at www.svn.org.

Social Venture Network
P.O. Box 29221
San Francisco, CA 94129-0221
415.561.6501

our impact

Bringing **big ideas** to life

Sustainability

From inventing renewable energy technologies to going carbon neutral to striving for zero waste, we are creating far-reaching strategies to tread lightly on the Earth and protect the planet for future generations.

Economic Justice

By championing fair trade, investing in local communities and supporting employee ownership and profit-sharing, we're working together to create a more just and sustainable economy.

Socially Responsible Business

We support companies that commit to the triple bottom line – people, planet and profits. Our members are pioneering new social ventures that offer innovative solutions to environmental and social challenges. And they're supporting and inspiring the next generation of socially responsible business leaders.

"SVN is an incredible resource for learning how to align your business practices with your values, and a great place to meet like-minded people. My life wouldn't be the same without it!"

CHIP CONLEY
JOIE DE VIVRE

"SVN has been an incredible community in which I've grown as a socially responsible businessperson, which has given me the strength and the knowledge to inspire my own communities of employees and Warm Spirit consultants. SVN is a community where business leaders can grow and be affirmed in their pursuit to have a values based business."

NADINE THOMPSON
CO FOUNDER AND CEO
WARM SPIRIT

"We ask companies the questions that no one else is asking, putting important issues on the table for discussion. We believe that business and building a better world aren't opposing forces. Why? Because we're dreamers, realists, and bridge-builders."

AMY DOMINI
DOMINI SOCIAL INVESTMENTS

"I have been called to serve my people. It's a privilege leading a company that invests in people and community. I wouldn't have it any other way, and wouldn't be where I am today without the support and dedication that is SVN."

JULIUS WALLS, JR
GREYSTON BAKERY

what we do

Inspiring, connecting and supporting social entrepreneurs.

Through transformative events and practical resources, Social Venture Network offers ideas and insights to enhance your business and expand your impact.

Networking

From inspiring conferences to Social Venture Institutes to SVN's Member Connection Service, we forge deep relationships while creating and sharing ideas to improve the triple bottom line.

Tools and Resources

Our tools and best practices, Carbon Neutral Initiative, online resources and member-authored SVN books provide practical information on how to build and sustain a socially responsible business.

Partnerships

Our Social Impact Leadership Coalition is setting the bar for organizations to operate in socially responsible ways.

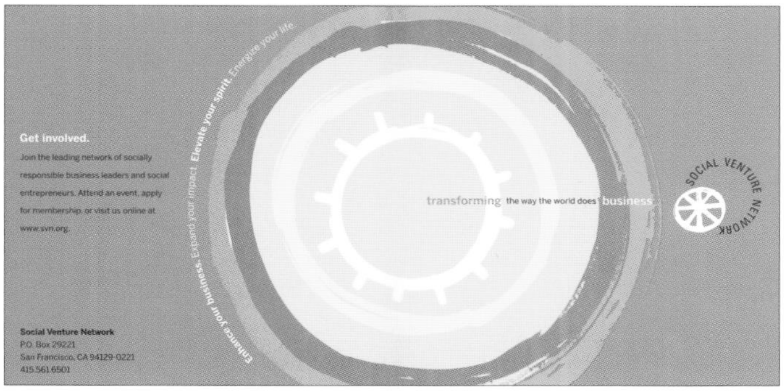

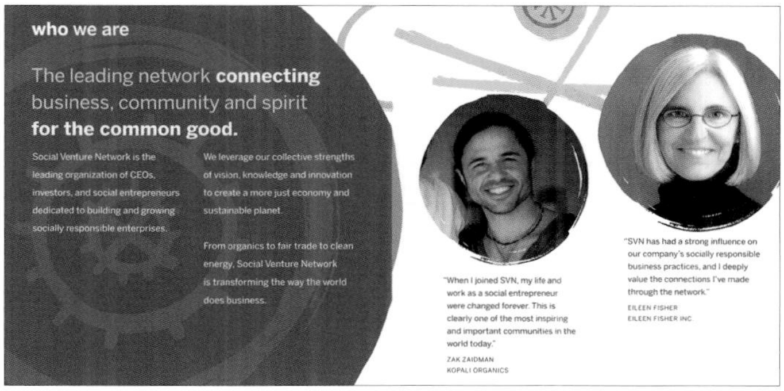

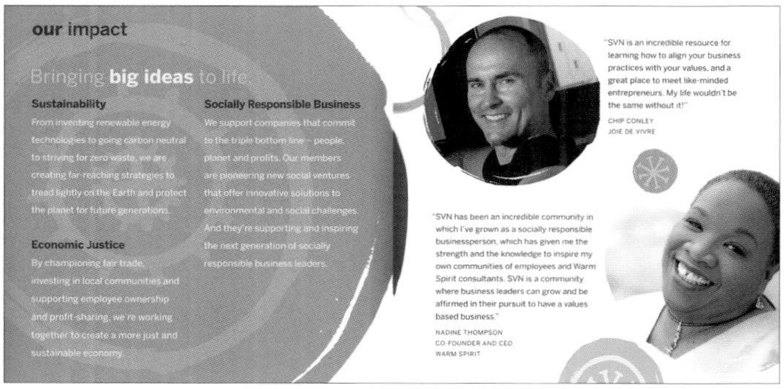

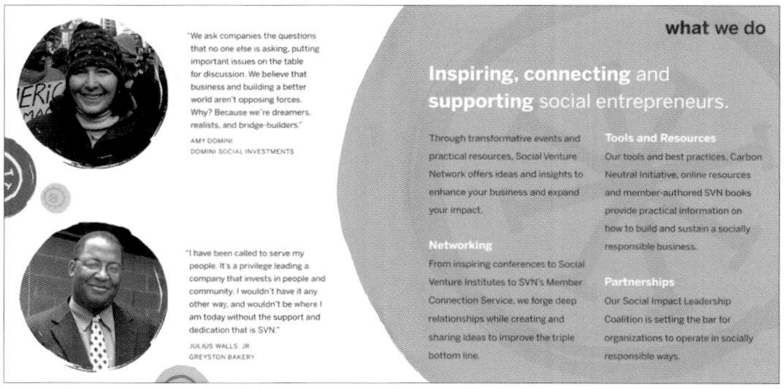

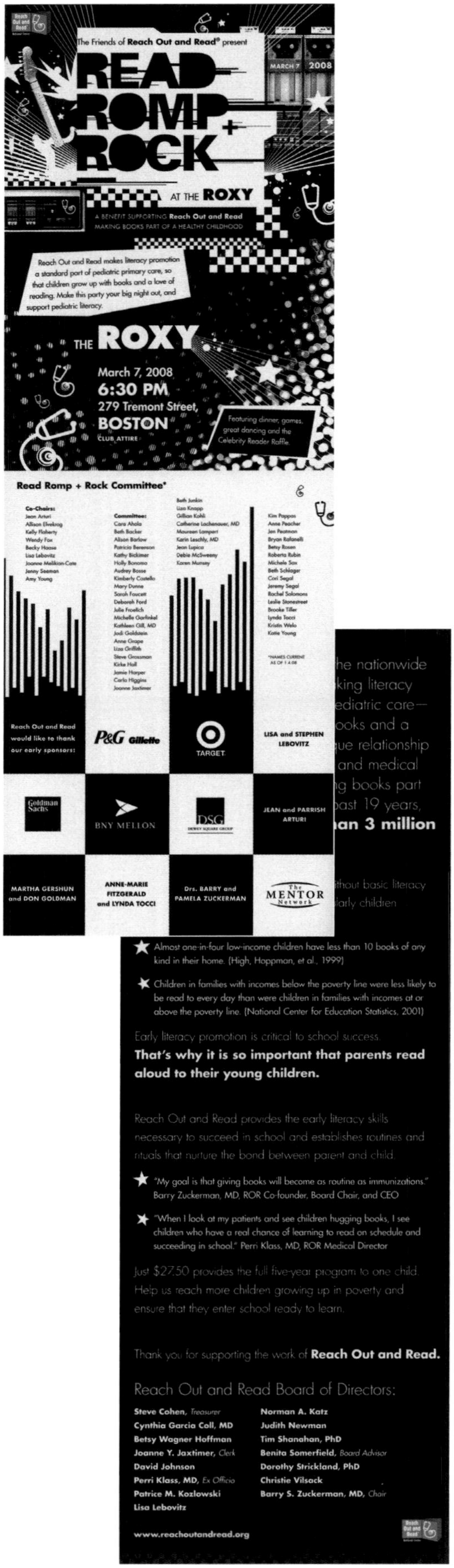
The Friends of Reach Out and Read® present
READ ROMP + ROCK
MARCH 7 2008
AT THE ROXY
A BENEFIT SUPPORTING Reach Out and Read
MAKING BOOKS PART OF A HEALTHY CHILDHOOD
Reach Out and Read makes literacy promotion a standard part of pediatric primary care, so that children grow up with books and a love of reading. Make this party your big night out, and support pediatric literacy.
THE ROXY
March 7, 2008
6:30 PM
279 Tremont Street,
BOSTON
CLUB ATTIRE
Featuring dinner, games, great dancing and the Celebrity Reader Raffle
Read Romp + Rock Committee*
Reach Out and Read would like to thank our early sponsors:
P&G Gillette
TARGET
LISA and STEPHEN LEBOVITZ
Goldman Sachs
BNY MELLON
DSG
JEAN and PARRISH ARTURI
MARTHA GERSHUN and DON GOLDMAN
ANNE-MARIE FITZGERALD and LYNDA TOCCI
Drs. BARRY and PAMELA ZUCKERMAN
The MENTOR Network
Almost one-in-four low-income children have less than 10 books of any kind in their home. (High, Hoppman, et al., 1999)
Children in families with incomes below the poverty line were less likely to be read to every day than were children in families with incomes at or above the poverty line. (National Center for Education Statistics, 2001)
Early literacy promotion is critical to school success.
That's why it is so important that parents read aloud to their young children.
Reach Out and Read provides the early literacy skills necessary to succeed in school and establishes routines and rituals that nurture the bond between parent and child.
"My goal is that giving books will become as routine as immunizations." Barry Zuckerman, MD, ROR Co-founder, Board Chair, and CEO
"When I look at my patients and see children hugging books, I see children who have a real chance of learning to read on schedule and succeeding in school." Perri Klass, MD, ROR Medical Director
Just $27.50 provides the full five-year program to one child. Help us reach more children growing up in poverty and ensure that they enter school ready to learn.
Thank you for supporting the work of Reach Out and Read.
Reach Out and Read Board of Directors:
Steve Cohen, Treasurer
Cynthia Garcia Coll, MD
Betsy Wagner Hoffman
Joanne Y. Jaxtimer, Clerk
David Johnson
Perri Klass, MD, Ex Officio
Patrice M. Kozlowski
Lisa Lebovitz
Norman A. Katz
Judith Newman
Tim Shanahan, PhD
Benita Somerfield, Board Advisor
Dorothy Strickland, PhD
Christie Vilsack
Barry S. Zuckerman, MD, Chair
www.reachoutandread.org

Somerset
Jazz
Consortium
www.somersetjazz.com
Jim Jasion 732 238 7564 · 732 325 7464 cell
JAM SESSIONS
PJ's Coffee, 315 Raritan Ave, Highland Park, Sundays 1PM to 5PM
Rhythms/JP's Steakhouse, 729 South Main St, Manville, Wednesdays 7PM to 10PM

RDormann Design – Milltown, New Jersey
Designer: Roger Dormann
Client: Jim Jasion, Somerset Jazz Consortium

Fresh Oil – Pawtucket, Rhode Island
Designers: Dan Stebbings, Nelson Couto
Client: Reach Out and Read

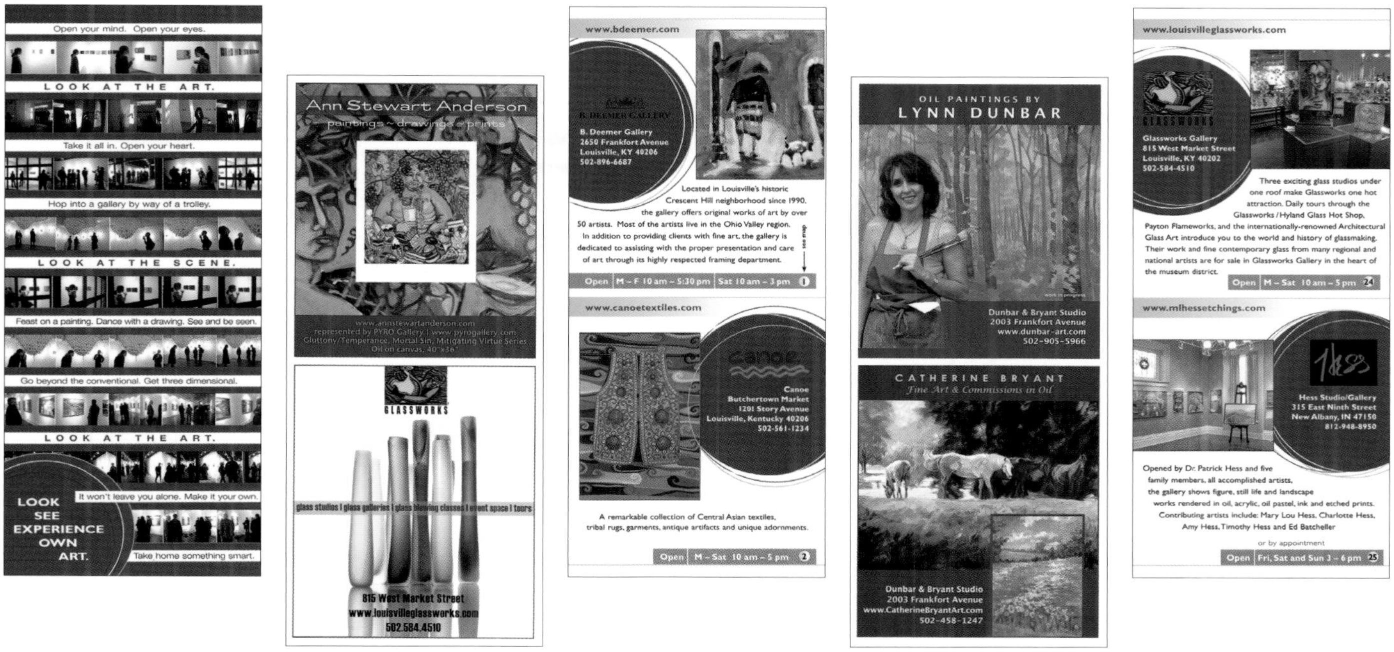
Open your mind. Open your eyes.
LOOK AT THE ART.
Take it all in. Open your heart.
Hop into a gallery by way of a trolley.
LOOK AT THE SCENE.
Feast on a painting. Dance with a drawing. See and be seen.
Go beyond the conventional. Get three dimensional.
LOOK AT THE ART.
It won't leave you alone. Make it your own.
Take home something smart.
LOOK
SEE
EXPERIENCE
OWN
ART.
Ann Stewart Anderson
paintings ~ drawings ~ prints
GLASSWORKS
815 West Market Street
www.louisvilleglassworks.com
502.584.4510
www.bdeemer.com
B. Deemer Gallery
2650 Frankfort Avenue
Louisville, KY 40206
502-896-6687
Located in Louisville's historic Crescent Hill neighborhood since 1990, the gallery offers original works of art by over 50 artists. Most of the artists live in the Ohio Valley region. In addition to providing clients with fine art, the gallery is dedicated to assisting with the proper presentation and care of art through its highly respected framing department.
Open M – F 10 am – 5:30 pm Sat 10 am – 3 pm
www.canoetextiles.com
canoe
Canoe
Butchertown Market
1201 Story Avenue
Louisville, Kentucky 40206
502-561-1234
A remarkable collection of Central Asian textiles, tribal rugs, garments, antique artifacts and unique adornments.
Open M – Sat 10 am – 5 pm
OIL PAINTINGS BY
LYNN DUNBAR
Dunbar & Bryant Studio
2003 Frankfort Avenue
www.dunbar-art.com
502-905-5966
CATHERINE BRYANT
Fine Art & Commissions in Oil
Dunbar & Bryant Studio
2003 Frankfort Avenue
www.CatherineBryantArt.com
502-458-1247
www.louisvilleglassworks.com
Glassworks Gallery
815 West Market Street
Louisville, KY 40202
502-584-4510
Three exciting glass studios under one roof make Glassworks one hot attraction. Daily tours through the Glassworks / Hyland Glass Hot Shop, Payton Flameworks, and the internationally-renowned Architectural Glass Art introduce you to the world and history of glassmaking. Their work and fine contemporary glass from many regional and national artists are for sale in Glassworks Gallery in the heart of the museum district.
Open M – Sat 10 am – 5 pm
www.mlhessetchings.com
Hess Studio/Gallery
315 East Ninth Street
New Albany, IN 47150
812-948-8950
Opened by Dr. Patrick Hess and five family members, all accomplished artists, the gallery shows figure, still life and landscape works rendered in oil, acrylic, oil pastel, ink and etched prints. Contributing artists include: Mary Lou Hess, Charlotte Hess, Amy Hess, Timothy Hess and Ed Batcheller
or by appointment
Open Fri, Sat and Sun 3 – 6 pm

21 Skye Design – Prospect, Kentucky
Designer : Elizabeth Perry Spalding
Client : LOOK

Wildlife & Whimsy – Missoula, Montana
Designer : Haley Newberg
Client : American Association of Zoo Keepers

www.wildlifeandwhimsy.com
EYE MOVEMENT
The American Association of Zoo Keepers, Inc.

Arriving in a square envelope, this invitation unfolds to reveal pertinent information across three panels, front and back. A sponsorship reply card is included.

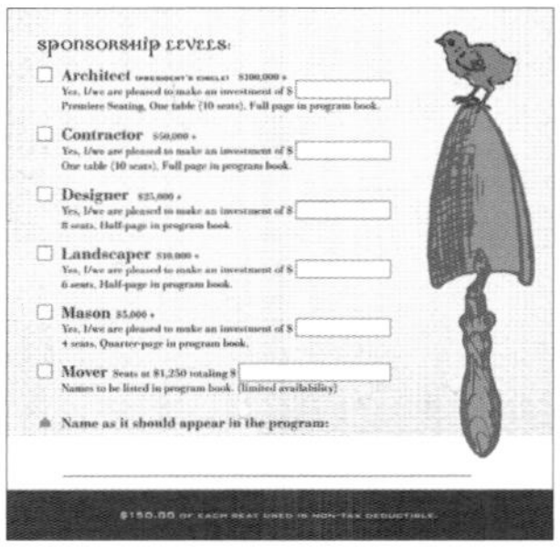

Fresh Oil – Pawtucket, Rhode Island
Designer : Dan Stebbings
Client : Boys & Girls Clubs of Boston

BBMG – New York, New York
Designers : Raphael Bemporad, Scott Ketchum
Client : Robert Wood Johnson Health Policy Fellowships

THE
ROBERT
WOOD
JOHNSON
HEALTH
POLICY
FELLOWSHIPS
PROGRAM

KINCAID PARK
CELEBRATING TWENTY YEARS 1986-2006
NORDIC SKIING ASSOCIATION OF ANCHORAGE

Mad Dog Graphx
– Anchorage, Alaska
Designer : Kris Ryan-Clarke
Client : Nordic Skiing Association of Anchorage

cornbeefwindstorm designs – Nashville, Tennessee
Designer : Shannon O'Kelley
Client : Kids on the Block

CHAIR-ISH 2008
ART YOU HAVE TO TAKE SITTING DOWN!
Cocktail Supper & Art Auction
April 11, 2008
7:00 pm
Cheekwood Botanical Garden & Museum
TWELFTH ANNUAL
"CHAIR-ISH THE KIDS"
benefitting
KIDS ON THE BLOCK
HONORARY CHAIR:
Alva Duke,
founder of Nashville's Kids on the Block
CHAIRS:
Nancy Bunting & Daphne Butler
HOST COMMITTEE:
Louisa Altman
Jen Bottorff
Bridgette Butler
Laura Chadwick
Liz Daly
Mary Denson
Phyllis Fridrich
Liza Graves
Meredith Griffith
Sarah Higgins
Diane Lance
Hannah Lavey
Kelli Myers
Page Parker
Susan Quasdvlieg
Tracy Rankin
Lina Rowland
Annie Schaefer
Tonya Stevens
Parian Strang
Jennifer Taylor
Elizabeth Trabue
Kimberly White
Birgitta Williamson
Kerry Wilson
Mary Wilson
The mission of Kids on the Block is to educate children, as well as the broader community, about health and social concerns that affect their lives. Using puppets and other teaching tools, Kids on the Block promotes understanding and acceptance of all children and adults, regardless of their differences.
Vanderbilt Medical Center
HCA
Gibson
ups
invitation design by Shannon O'Kelley
www.myOWNvitations.com
RSVP

A NATIONAL PARK AREA
BOSTON HARBOR ISLANDS
minutes away.
worlds apart.
breathe
"The Boston Harbor Islands are one of the hidden jewels of Boston." Mayor Thomas M. Menino
bostonharborislands.org
Brought to you by Boston Harbor Island Alliance

A NATIONAL PARK AREA
BOSTON HARBOR ISLANDS
minutes away.
worlds apart.
relive history
"The Boston Harbor Islands are one of the hidden jewels of Boston." Mayor Thomas M. Menino
bostonharborislands.org
Brought to you by Boston Harbor Island Alliance

A NATIONAL PARK AREA
BOSTON HARBOR ISLANDS
minutes away.
worlds apart.
adventure awaits
"The Boston Harbor Islands are one of the hidden jewels of Boston." Mayor Thomas M. Menino
bostonharborislands.org
Brought to you by Boston Harbor Island Alliance

A NATIONAL PARK AREA
BOSTON HARBOR ISLANDS
minutes away.
worlds apart.
discover
"The Boston Harbor Islands are one of the hidden jewels of Boston." Mayor Thomas M. Menino
bostonharborislands.org
Brought to you by Boston Harbor Island Alliance

A NATIONAL PARK AREA
BOSTON HARBOR ISLANDS
minutes away.
worlds apart.
escape
"The Boston Harbor Islands are one of the hidden jewels of Boston." Mayor Thomas M. Menino
bostonharborislands.org
Brought to you by Boston Harbor Island Alliance

A NATIONAL PARK AREA
BOSTON HARBOR ISLANDS
minutes away.
worlds apart.
splash
"The Boston Harbor Islands are one of the hidden jewels of Boston." Mayor Thomas M. Menino
bostonharborislands.org
Brought to you by Boston Harbor Island Alliance

A NATIONAL PARK AREA
BOSTON HARBOR ISLANDS
sail
minutes away.
worlds apart.
"The Boston Harbor Islands are one of the hidden jewels of Boston." Mayor Thomas M. Menino
bostonharborislands.org
Brought to you by Boston Harbor Island Alliance

Hull Creative Group – Brookline, Massachusetts
Designers : Caryl H. Hull, Carol Thistle, Chris Klein, Sherman Morss, Pat King Powers, Nicole L. Vecchiotti
Client : Boston Harbor Island Alliance

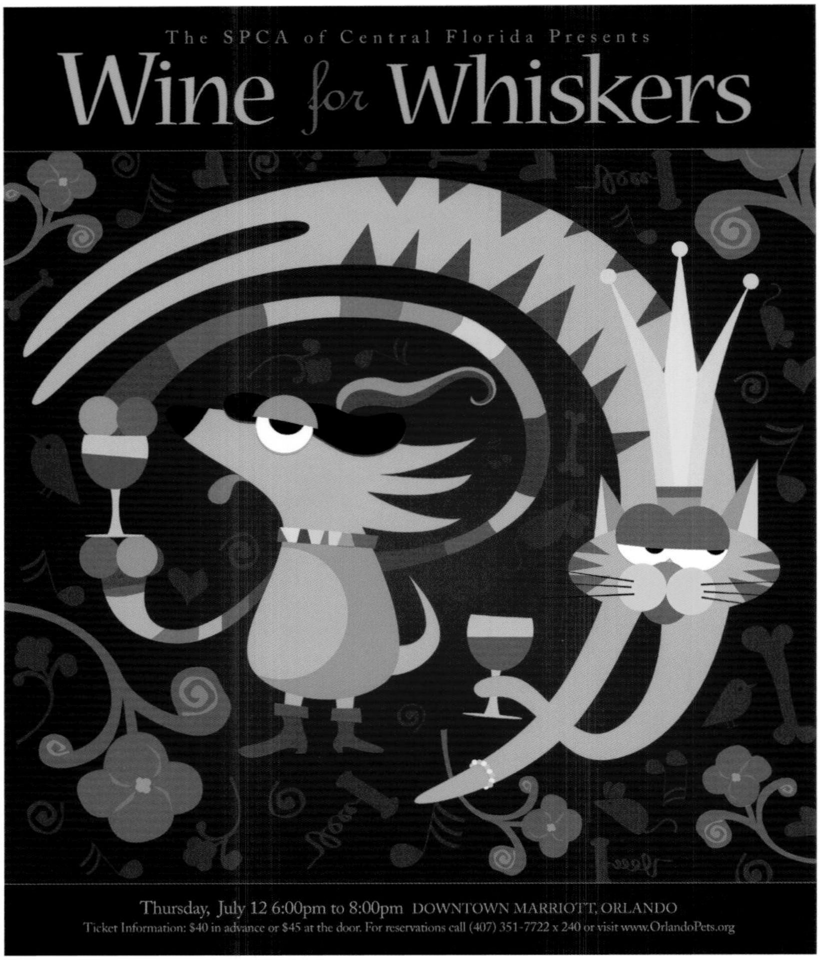
The SPCA of Central Florida Presents
Wine for Whiskers
Thursday, July 12 6:00pm to 8:00pm DOWNTOWN MARRIOTT, ORLANDO
Ticket Information: $40 in advance or $45 at the door. For reservations call (407) 351-7722 x 240 or visit www.OrlandoPets.org

Cosmic – St. Petersburg, Florida
Designer: David Scott
Client: SPCA of Central Florida

Holohan Design – Philadelphia, Pennsylvania
Designer: Kelly Holohan

PLACE YOUR BETS
HIV+
HIV–

With the current popularity of gambling in the U.S., this is a timely concept in the communication of a decades-old problem.

[California poppy]
[WATER IS LIFE]
From poppies to people, our lives depend on it.
Save it while we've got it.
WE SEE WATER
Santa Clara Valley Water District

Tread Creative – Los Gatos, California
Designers : Phil Mowery, Achille Bigliardi, Doug Stamm, Glenn McCrea, Stock Photography
Client : Santa Clara Valley Water District (SCVWD)

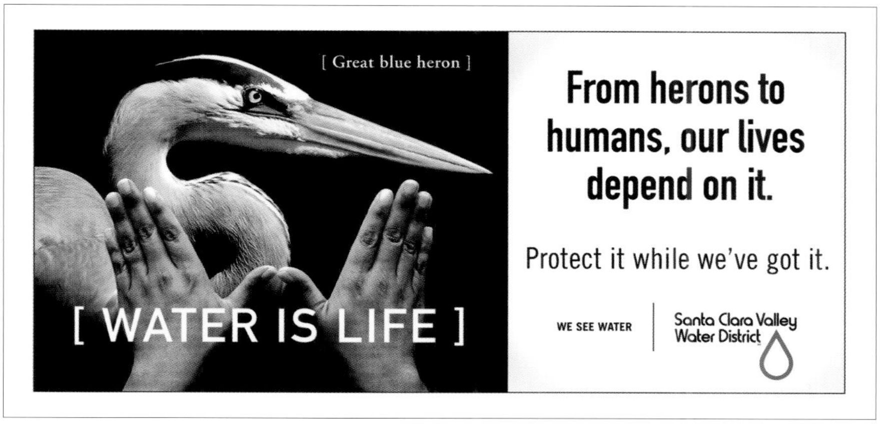
[Great blue heron]
[WATER IS LIFE]
From herons to humans, our lives depend on it.
Protect it while we've got it.
WE SEE WATER
Santa Clara Valley Water District

[Steelhead trout]
[WATER IS LIFE]
From trout to tots, our lives depend on it.
Protect it while we've got it.
WE SEE WATER
Santa Clara Valley Water District

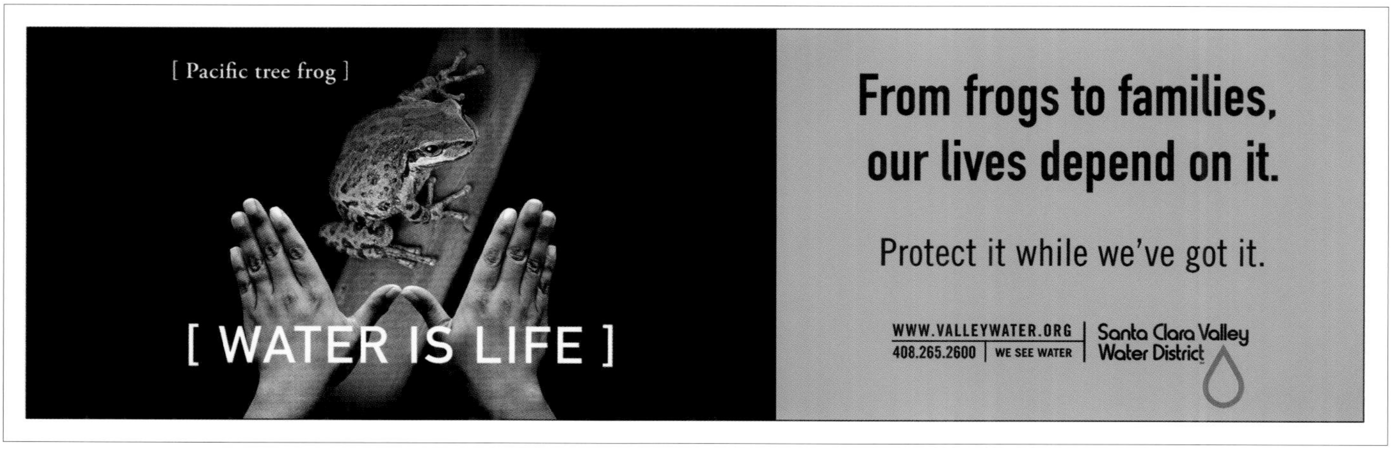
[Pacific tree frog]
[WATER IS LIFE]
From frogs to families, our lives depend on it.
Protect it while we've got it.
WWW.VALLEYWATER.ORG
408.265.2600 | WE SEE WATER
Santa Clara Valley Water District

photography
painting
animation

Department of Art,
Sam Houston State University – Huntsville, Texas
Designers : Taehee Kim, Ivan Leung
Client : Department of Art, Sam Houston State University

Besides the actual Braille card on the cover, the vellum pages contribute to the varied textures of this brochure.

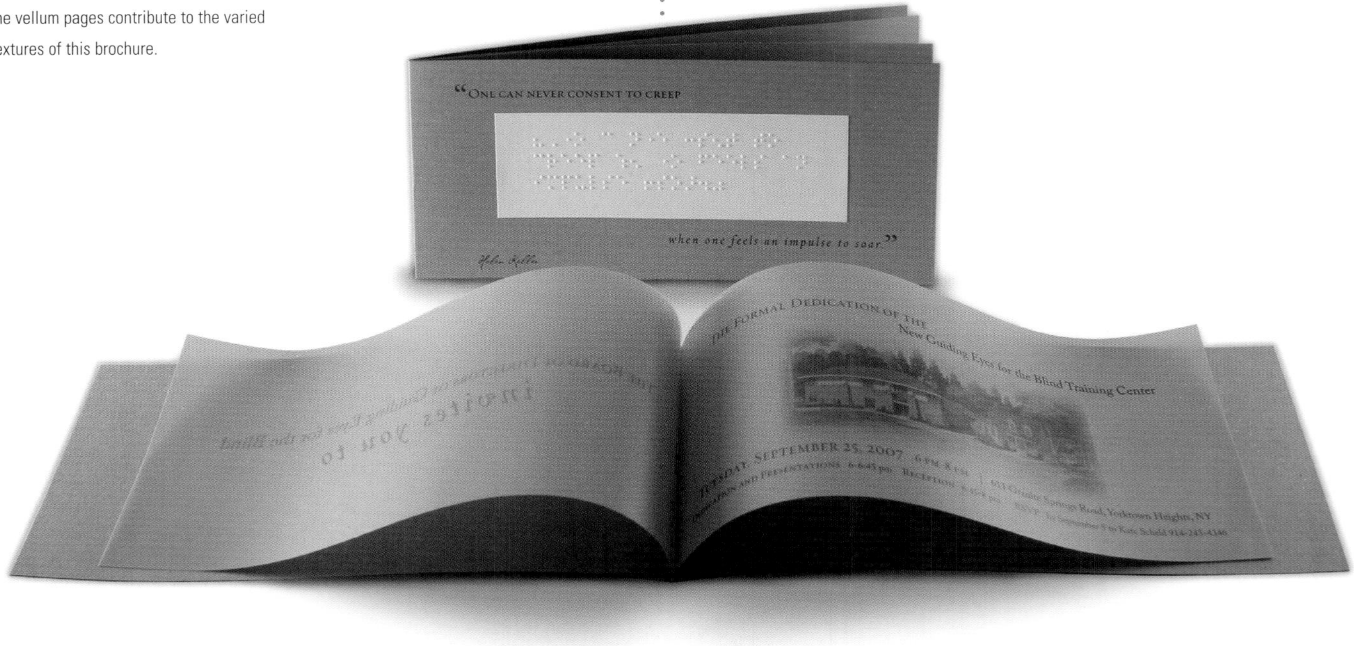
“One can never consent to creep
when one feels an impulse to soar.”
The Formal Dedication of the
New Guiding Eyes for the Blind Training Center
invites you to
Tuesday, September 25, 2007

TFI Envision, Inc. – Norwalk, Connecticut
Designers : Elizabeth P. Ball, Mary Ellen Butkus, Brien O'Reilly
Client : Guiding Eyes for the Blind

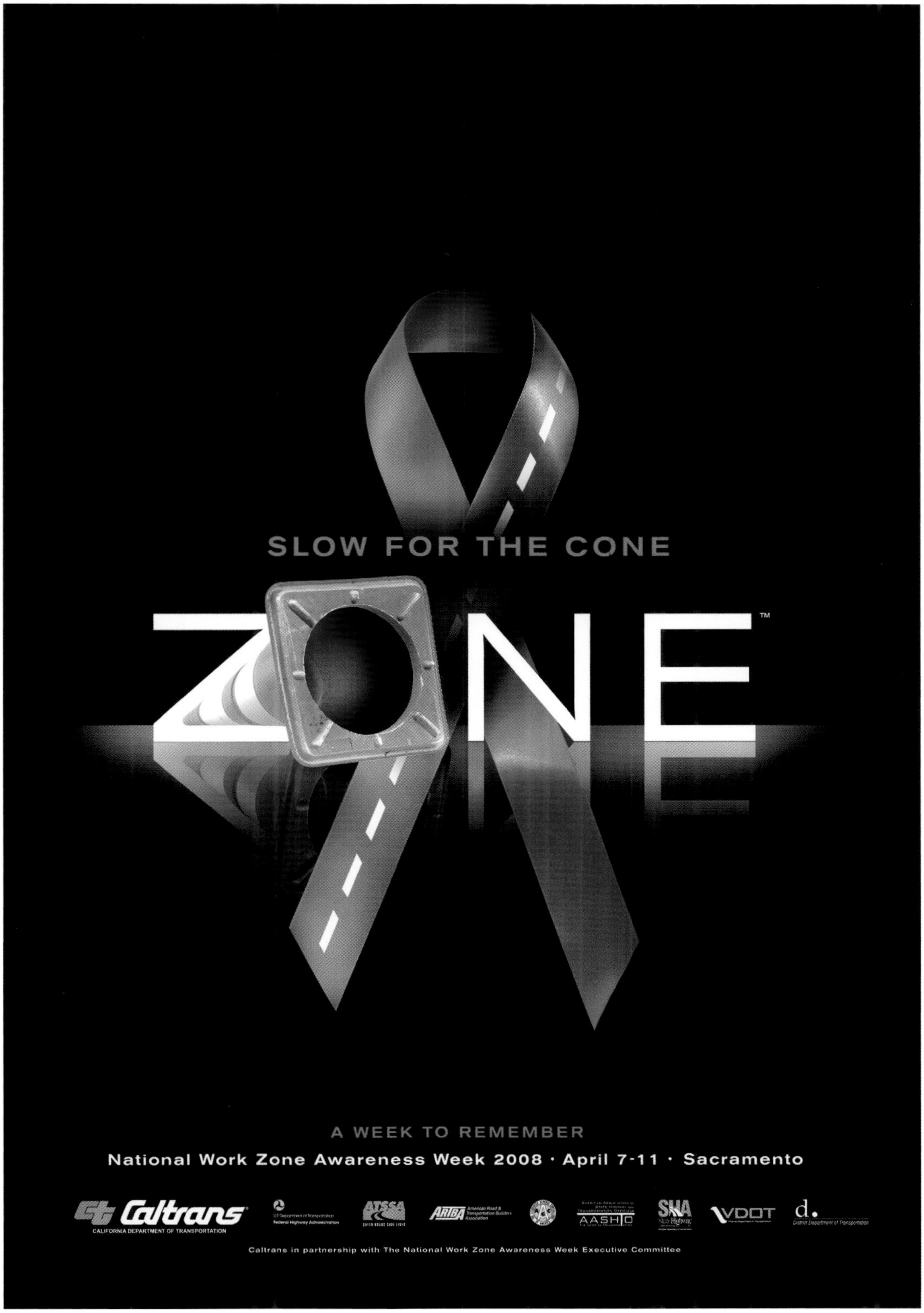

Sol Design Group – Sacramento, California
Designers : Kelly Cooper Kwoka
Client : California Department of Transportation

Virginia Wimberly Theatre at the Calderwood Pavilion
Boston Center for the Arts • 527 Tremont Street • Boston, Massachusetts 02116
For Tickets www.bostontheatrescene.com 617.933.8600 and at www.worldmusic.org 617.876.4275
Snappy
Dance Theater
CELEBRATING 10 YEARS
30 MAY – 10 JUNE 2007
STRING BEINGS WORLD PREMIERE

Snappy far surpassed our expectations. The audience was enthralled, impressed and marveled about the performance for weeks after... Even people who came in with the attitude that this was going to be another boring dance performance were completely transformed into fans.

Christopher Booras, Programming Director, Ohlone College, CA 2004

-20-

2006

1999

On The Road / Off Stage

-25-

I can't say enough about this infectiously creative company and the impact they had on our students and staff.

Rick Ash, Camden Regional Highschool, Maine 2006

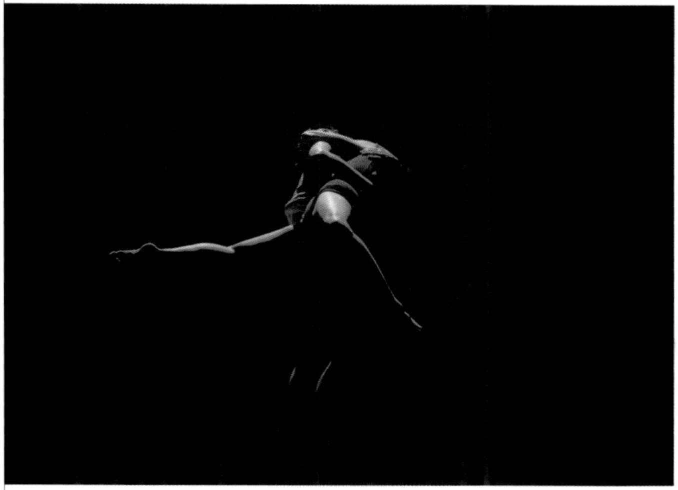

Aliens could learn a lot about humanity watching this company perform; people can too.

Albany Times Union 2006

Nassar Design – Brookline, Massachusetts
Designers : Nelida Nassar, Philippe Naulot
Client : Snappy Dance Theater

-21-

SOMEONE
in our community
IS ALL ALONE
what matters is that you can help.
United Way
United Way of Central Alabama, Inc.

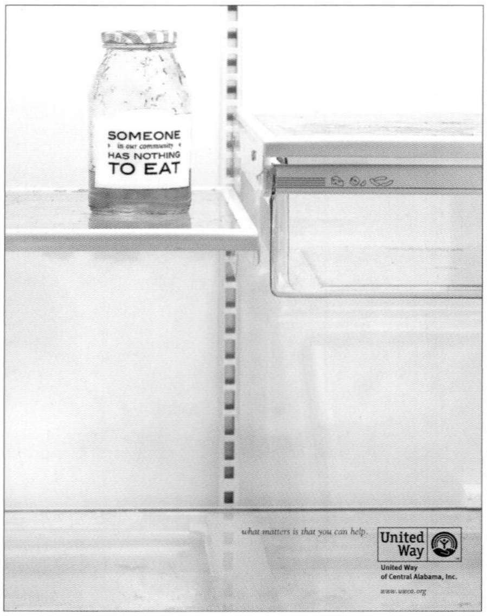
SOMEONE
in our community
HAS NOTHING
TO EAT
what matters is that you can help.
United Way
United Way of Central Alabama, Inc.

SOMEONE
in our community
HAS LOST
EVERYTHING
what matters is that you can help.
United Way
United Way of Central Alabama, Inc.

Open Creative Group – Birmingham, Alabama
Designers : April Mraz, Alan Whitley
Client : United Way of Central Alabama

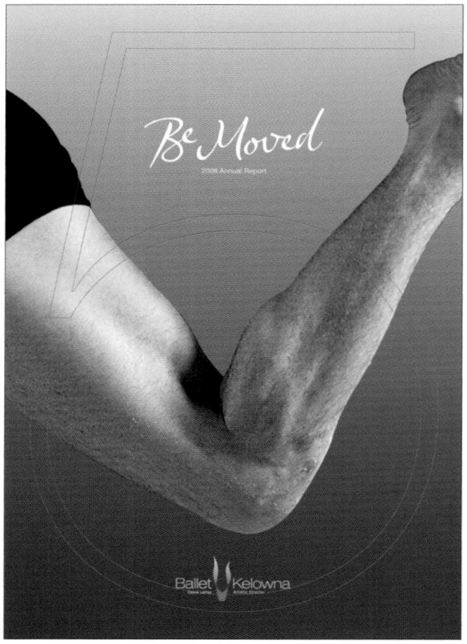
Be Moved
2008 Annual Report
Ballet Kelowna

One- or two-color printing doesn't need to mean a boring piece. Interesting typography and powerful images are very often accented by the vivid contrast between black and white.

Splash:Design – Kelowna, Canada
Designer : Phred Martin
Client : Ballet Kelowna

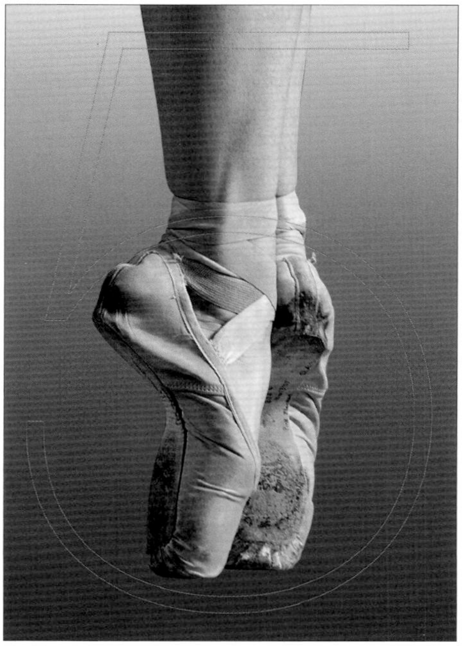

Message from the Board President
It has been a privilege to have served 3 terms as President for the Kelowna Ballet Society during these initial years of exciting growth and development.

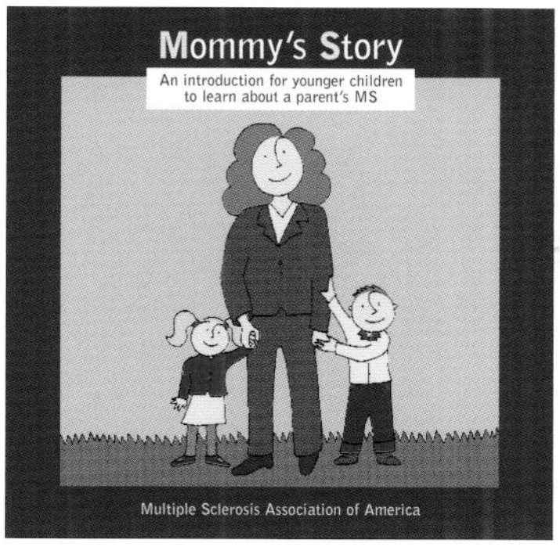
Mommy's Story
An introduction for younger children to learn about a parent's MS
Multiple Sclerosis Association of America

Your mommy is very special. She loves you more than anything else in the whole world.
2
3

Your mommy takes good care of you.
She helps you get dressed.
She plays with you.
She gives you good things to eat.
She kisses you goodnight.
4
5

Speedy Motorcycle Studio – Medford, New Jersey
Designers: E. June Roberts-Lunn, Susan Wells Courtney, Andrea Borkowski
Client: Multiple Sclerosis Association of America

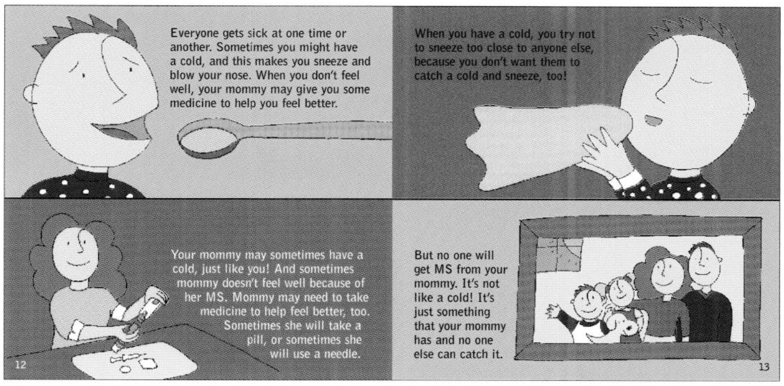
Everyone gets sick at one time or another. Sometimes you might have a cold, and this makes you sneeze and blow your nose. When you don't feel well, your mommy may give you some medicine to help you feel better.
When you have a cold, you try not to sneeze too close to anyone else, because you don't want them to catch a cold and sneeze, too!
Your mommy may sometimes have a cold, just like you! And sometimes mommy doesn't feel well because of her MS. Mommy may need to take medicine to help feel better, too. Sometimes she will take a pill, or sometimes she will use a needle.
But no one will get MS from your mommy. It's not like a cold! It's just something that your mommy has and no one else can catch it.
12
13

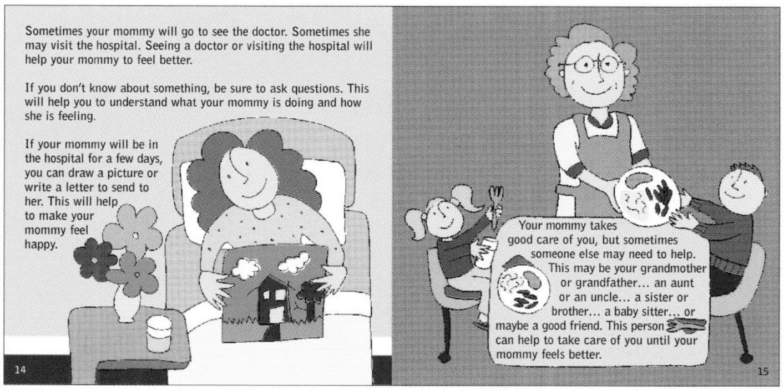
Sometimes your mommy will go to see the doctor. Sometimes she may visit the hospital. Seeing a doctor or visiting the hospital will help your mommy to feel better.
If you don't know about something, be sure to ask questions. This will help you to understand what your mommy is doing and how she is feeling.
If your mommy will be in the hospital for a few days, you can draw a picture or write a letter to send to her. This will help to make your mommy feel happy.
Your mommy takes good care of you, but sometimes someone else may need to help. This may be your grandmother or grandfather... an aunt or an uncle... a sister or brother... a baby sitter... or maybe a good friend. This person can help to take care of you until your mommy feels better.
14
15

Does your mommy have MS? She may sometimes feel tired or walk more slowly, but that's okay. Your mommy takes good care of you, and you can help her, too – by doing things like bringing a pillow... playing quietly... holding hands... opening a door... giving hugs... and saying, "I love you!"
Your mommy is very special. She loves you more than anything else in the whole world.
And that's Mommy's Story.
16

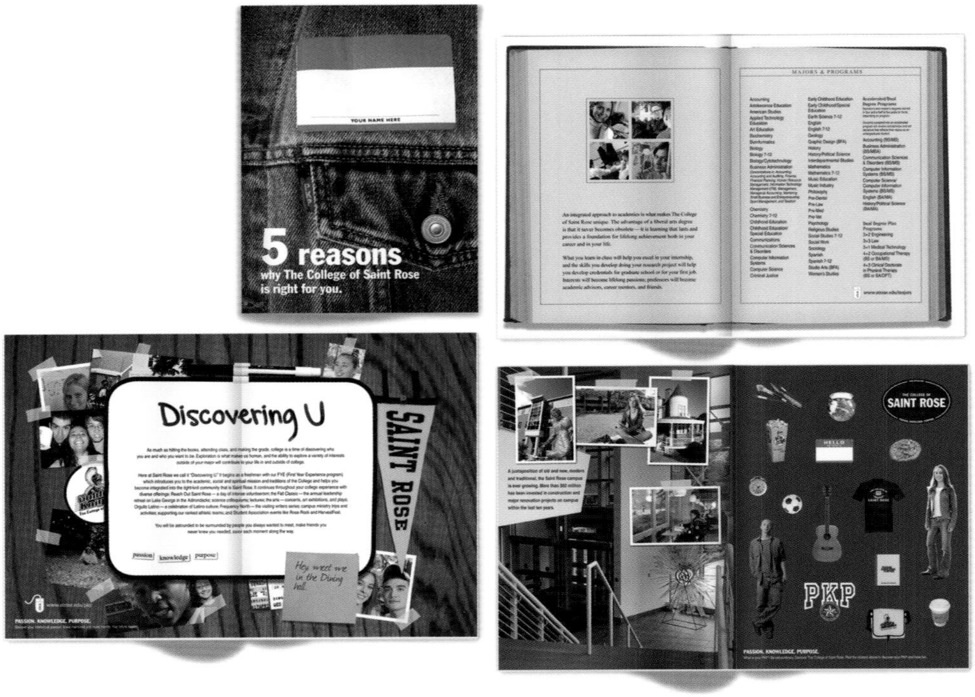
YOUR NAME HERE
5 reasons
why The College of Saint Rose is right for you.
MAJORS & PROGRAMS
Discovering U
SAINT ROSE
passion knowledge purpose
Hey, meet me in the Dining hall.
PASSION. KNOWLEDGE. PURPOSE.
THE COLLEGE OF SAINT ROSE
PKP

The College of Saint Rose,
Office of Public Relations and Marketing – Albany, New York
Designers : Mark Hamilton, Chris Parody, Lisa Haley Thompson, Luigi Benincasa
Client : The College of Saint Rose

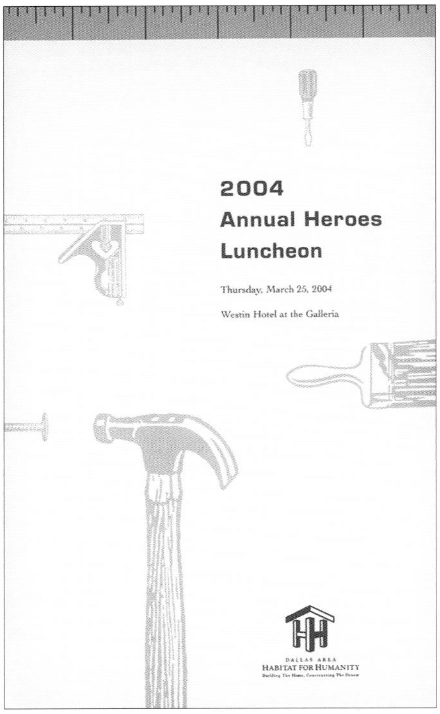
2004
Annual Heroes
Luncheon
Thursday, March 25, 2004
Westin Hotel at the Galleria
DALLAS AREA
HABITAT FOR HUMANITY

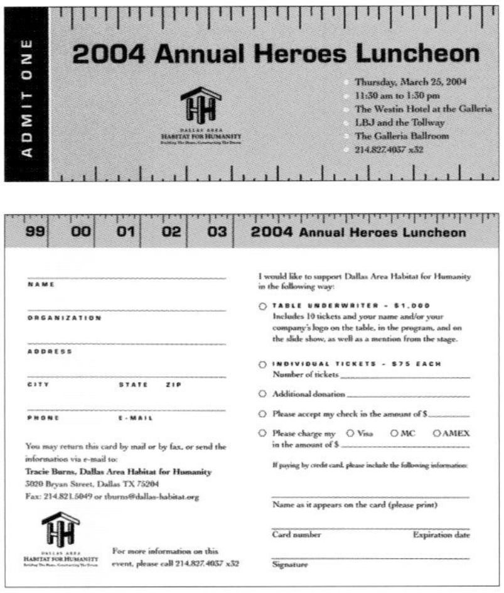
ADMIT ONE
2004 Annual Heroes Luncheon
Thursday, March 25, 2004
11:30 am to 1:30 pm
The Westin Hotel at the Galleria
LBJ and the Tollway
The Galleria Ballroom
214.827.4037 x32
99 00 01 02 03
2004 Annual Heroes Luncheon
NAME
ORGANIZATION
ADDRESS
CITY STATE ZIP
PHONE E-MAIL
You may return this card by mail or by fax, or send the information via e-mail to:
Tracie Burns, Dallas Area Habitat for Humanity
3020 Bryan Street, Dallas TX 75204
Fax: 214.821.5049 or tburns@dallas-habitat.org
For more information on this event, please call 214.827.4037 x32
I would like to support Dallas Area Habitat for Humanity in the following way:
TABLE UNDERWRITER - $1,000
Includes 10 tickets and your name and/or your company's logo on the table, in the program, and on the slide show, as well as a mention from the stage.
INDIVIDUAL TICKETS - $75 EACH
Number of tickets
Additional donation
Please accept my check in the amount of $
Please charge my Visa MC AMEX in the amount of $
Name as it appears on the card (please print)
Card number
Expiration date
Signature

Bronson Ma Creative – San Antonio, Texas
Designer : Bronson Ma
Client : Dallas Area Habitat for Humanity

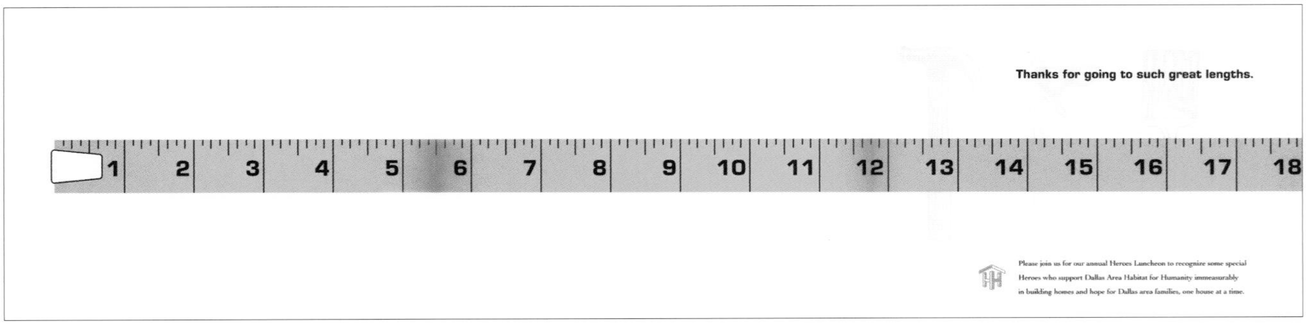
Thanks for going to such great lengths.
1 2 3 4 5 6 7 8 9 10 11 12 13 14 15 16 17 18
Please join us for our annual Heroes Luncheon to recognize some special Heroes who support Dallas Area Habitat for Humanity immeasurably in building homes and hope for Dallas area families, one house at a time.

CONNECTICUT GRAND OPERA & ORCHESTRA
Laurence Gilgore
Conductor
2006 - 2007
SEASON
The Connecticut Grand Opera & Orchestra is dedicated to presenting world-class operatic and orchestral performances featuring international talent and innovative productions to area residents and visitors. In addition, we strive to foster an appreciation and under-standing of opera and orchestral works through education and outreach programs for people of all ages and socio-economic backgrounds.
MORE TANGO & ZARZUELA
SATURDAY, MARCH 10, 2007
The Palace Theatre, Stamford, CT
The Connecticut Grand Opera & Orchestra, conducted by Maestro Laurence Gilgore, will present an electrifying and dazzling evening of Latin music and dance. It will feature the Latin-American vocal tradition, as it has evolved through the early part of the twentieth century, as well as its vast repertoire of tango and zarzuela.
A spectacular evening with Latin singers and dancers... come join the fun!
Josemaria Condemi
Director
Laurence Gilgore
Conductor
PUCCINI
MADAMA BUTTERFLY
SATURDAY, NOVEMBER 18, 2006
The Palace Theatre, Stamford, CT
et in early 20th century Japan, Madama
utterfly is the unfolding drama of a
autiful, young and naive Japanese woman
o abandons her family, faith and tradition
ollow a charming and cunning American
er. The marriage proves to be an endless
of deception that will lead the love-
en Butterfly to a heartbreaking escape.
na Butterfly, one of Puccini's most
ted operas, has a disarming sweet-
melodic sweep and a tragic depth
rresting and memorable.
ee for all opera lovers!
Sabina Kim
Soprano
Daniel Mobbs
Baritone
Laurence Gilgore
Conductor
David Pomeroy
Tenor
Robert Galbraith
Director
DONIZETTI LUCIA DI LAMMERMOOR
SATURDAY, MAY 5, 2007 The Palace Theatre, Stamford, CT
Set in 17th century Scotland, this late masterpiece of Bel Canto by composer Gaetano Donizetti is full of beauty, romance and drama. Lucia di Lammermoor is in love with Edgardo, a sworn enemy of her very powerful family. Her brother Enrico deceives her into believing that her lover has betrayed her. Then, taking advantage of her despair, he forces her into a politically and financially gainful union with Lord Arturo. The intrigue will lead to a riveting and tragic ending. This is a fully staged production of one of the most romantic operas ever written, featuring a cast of young superstars!
David Grabarkewitz
Director
Laurence Gilgore
Conductor
American Airlines The Official Airline of Connecticut Grand Opera & Orchestra
WITH OUR GRANDEST THANKS TO OUR GRANDEST PATRONS
Bank of America
XEROX
UBS
Iroquois
October Hill Foundation
tom fowler, inc

TFI Envision, Inc. – Norwalk, Connecticut
Designers : Elizabeth P. Ball, Phillip Doherty
Client : Connecticut Grand Opera & Orchestra

Cala/Krill Design – Claymont, Delaware
Designers : Ronald J. Cala II, Alyssa Krill

BLOW POP
BUBBLE GUM
CHERRY ARTIFICIAL
CLINTON VS BUSH

Wildlife & Whimsy – Missoula, Montana
Designer : Haley Newberg
Client : Chimfunshi Wildlife Orphanage

Pensaré Design Group – Washington, D.C.
Designers : Mary Ellen Vehlow, Lauren Emeritz
Client : Midtown Association

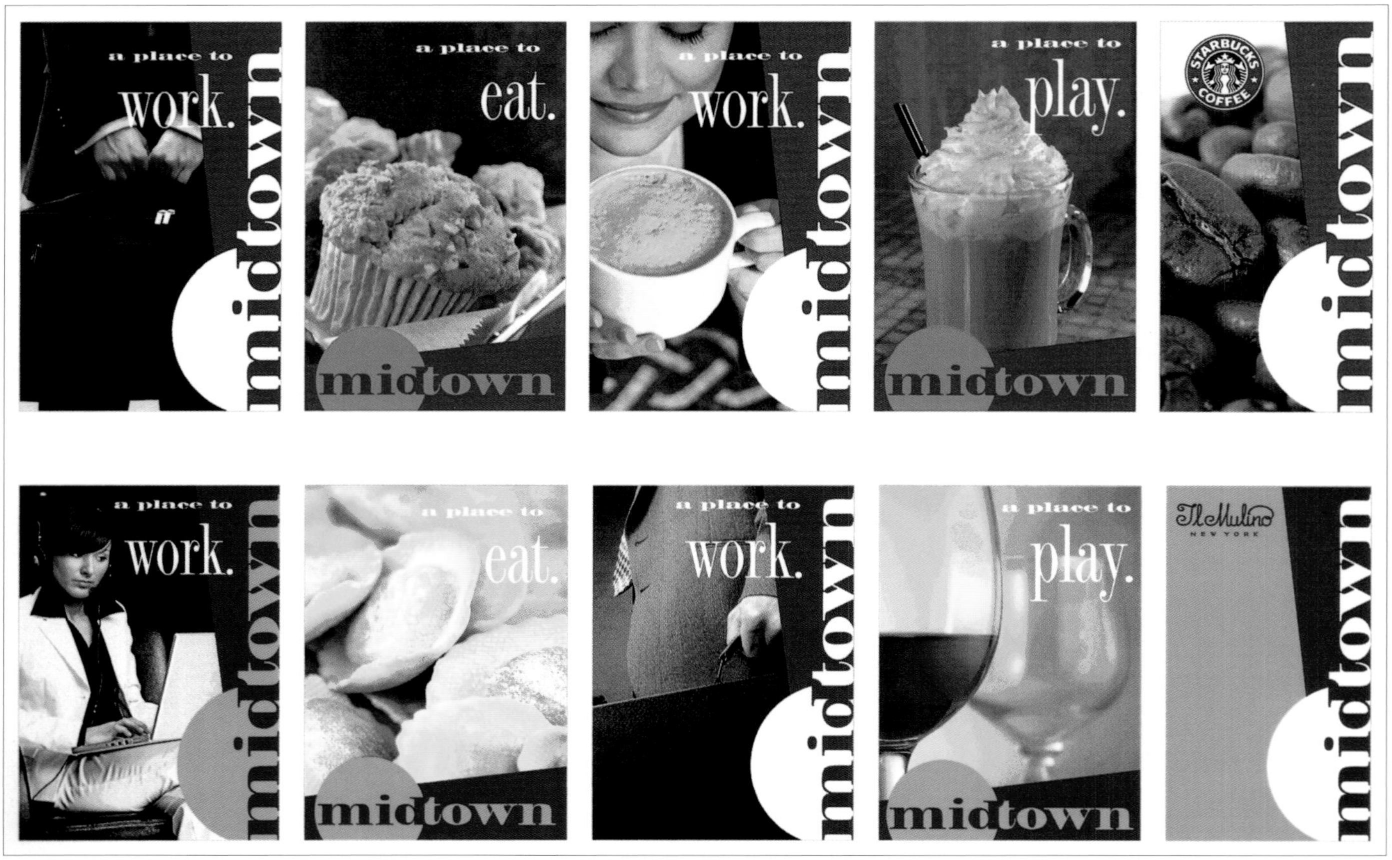

COMMUNITY BLOOD CENTER of the Carolinas
Every Drop Stays Here.
Saving Local Lives.
www.cbcc.us

COMMUNITY BLOOD CENTER of the Carolinas
(704) 972-4700
www.cbcc.us

COMMUNITY BLOOD CENTER of the Carolinas
Every Drop Stays Here.
Saving Local Lives.
www.cbcc.us

COMMUNITY BLOOD CENTER of the Carolinas
(704) 972-4700 | www.cbcc.us
Every Drop Stays Here. Saving Local Lives.

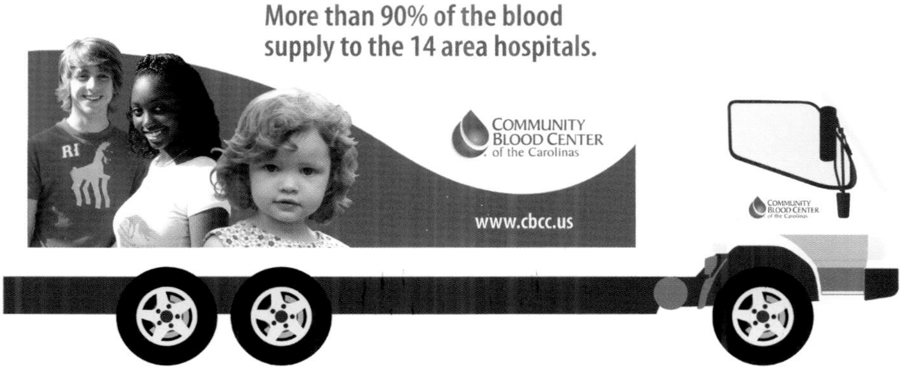
More than 90% of the blood
supply to the 14 area hospitals.
COMMUNITY BLOOD CENTER of the Carolinas
www.cbcc.us

COMMUNITY BLOOD CENTER of the Carolinas

Moonlight Creative Group – Charlotte, North Carolina
Designers : Dawn Newsome, Jenni Miehle
Client : Community Blood Center of the Carolinas

The word *lawyers* tends to bring to mind sharks or snakes, but the Animal Legal Defense Fund would prefer a softer image evocative of your very own docile pet—but with teeth at the ready. "We wanted something that reflected our legal expertise and [says] that we *are* an animal rights organization," says the ALDF's Lisa Franzetta. With a pair of slogans and a logo—a shield flanked by a cat and a chimpanzee and topped with the scales of justice—Franzetta approached Brian Niemann of Dallas-based Niemann Design to make the organization's message compelling for a new, broader audience. "We love the logo," she says of the shield, initially created by San Francisco's Vertebrae design firm. "And we've been using the slogans, 'Abuse an animal, go to jail' and 'We may be the only lawyers on earth whose clients are all innocent,' for many years. So we really wanted to create cohesive visual elements."

Niemann did a whole new rebranding campaign based on the ALDF's existing taglines and shield, creating a full-page ad, stickers, a coffee mug, and more. In order to appeal to a diverse audience, Niemann created bold designs centered around an earthy palette of black, brown, and olive and a mix of stock and ALDF-provided photos of domestic and wild animals, including dogs, horses, and cows. "It's very broad," he says. "The law profession, of course, but also it cuts across all ages, male, female, many demographics. [ALDF] wants to appeal to an array of supporters. You have young people, who may be zealous about animal rights, but also older, more established donors, as well as legal professionals. So we want to appeal to all those."

While continually working to preserve the integrity of the ALDF's traditions, Niemann says that "all of these pieces echo the branding." He calls them "good stewards of their brand overall... It's important to keep it consistent, and through the years we've maintained that consistency."

Animal Legal Defense Fund – Cotati, California
Designer : (Bizarro comic) Dan Piraro
Client : Animal Legal Defense Fund

WE MAY BE THE
ONLY
LAWYERS
ON EARTH
WHOSE CLIENTS ARE ALL
INNOCENT
Animal Legal
Defense Fund
WE MAY BE THE
ONLY
LAWYERS
ON EARTH
WHOSE CLIENTS ARE ALL
INNOCENT

MusicFest
360
Benefiting the ISDD
Hosted by
English Nick
from 99X
Band together for
360 minutes of
music and break the
cycle of disadvantage
and disability in Atlanta.
Featuring Brady
The Futurists
Ryan McDougall,
Siberia &
Nicholas from Y O U
Tickets $10 Available at
Smith's Olde Bar or etix.com
Sunday,
March 4, 2007
6 PM–12 AM
Smith's Olde Bar
www.smithsoldebar.com
isdd institute for the study of disadvantage and disability
www.isdd-home.org

Jill Lynn Design – Atlanta, Georgia
Designer : Jill Anderson
Client : Institute for the Study of Disadvantage and Disability

3rd Edge Communications – Jersey City, New Jersey
Designers : Frankie Gonzalez, Nick Schmitz
Client : Crossroads Tabernacle

CROSSROADS TABERNACLE IN ASSOCIATION
WITH THE BODEN CENTER PERFORMING ARTS
PRESENTS
FRI 03*16*07
BEYOND ALL TIME
A NIGHT OF FINE ART, FINE DINING AND WORLD CLASS DANCE
CELEBRATING THE MUSIC OF RALPH CARMICHAEL
ART EXPO & HORS D'OEUVRES 6:30PM
DINNER & DANCE PROGRAM 7:30PM
$50 PER PERSON
CROSSROADS TABERNACLE / 1320 CASTLE HILL AVENUE / BRONX, NEW YORK
CONTACT / 718 904 0202
CROSSROADS
WWW.CROSSROADSTABERNACLE.COM

A real feather is tucked into the cover of this brochure. Relative to the "Help Us Build a New Nest" theme, it blends beautifully with the off-white card stock.

DONATIONS MAKE A DIFFERENCE

LEVELS FOR INDIVIDUAL DONATIONS AND TRIBUTE GIFTS ARE AS FOLLOWS:

GOLD DONORS
$20,000 - $25,000

THE FAMILY TREE
2008 CAMPAIGN LEADERSHIP TEAM

BRAD FRIZZELL
ALISHA HIGGINS
SARAH HYDE
RED LERILLE
BRENDA MATURIN
GARY MAURIN
GENE POOL

BILL BOWERS
TONY ROBICHAUX
JAY ROSENZWEIG
LINDA WOODSON
ELISE COLOMB
MARIA G. REYES

BOARD OF DIRECTORS
SECRETARY:
ALISHA HIGGINS

TREASURER:
JENNIFER ZIEGLER

AT-LARGE:
JAY ROSENZWEIG

AT-LARGE:
KIRK TAYLOR

GASPARD
ANDRY
LEBLANC
MISTROT
THOMAS

ADVISORY COMMITTEE:
TRACEY CURTIS
GENE POOL
ERIC FREY
LIZ VIATOR

me a volunteer, please contact us at:
337 - 237 - 2160 · fmlytree@bellsouth.net

→ HELP US BUILD A NEW NEST ←

THE FAMILY TREE
CAPITAL CAMPAIGN 2008

353

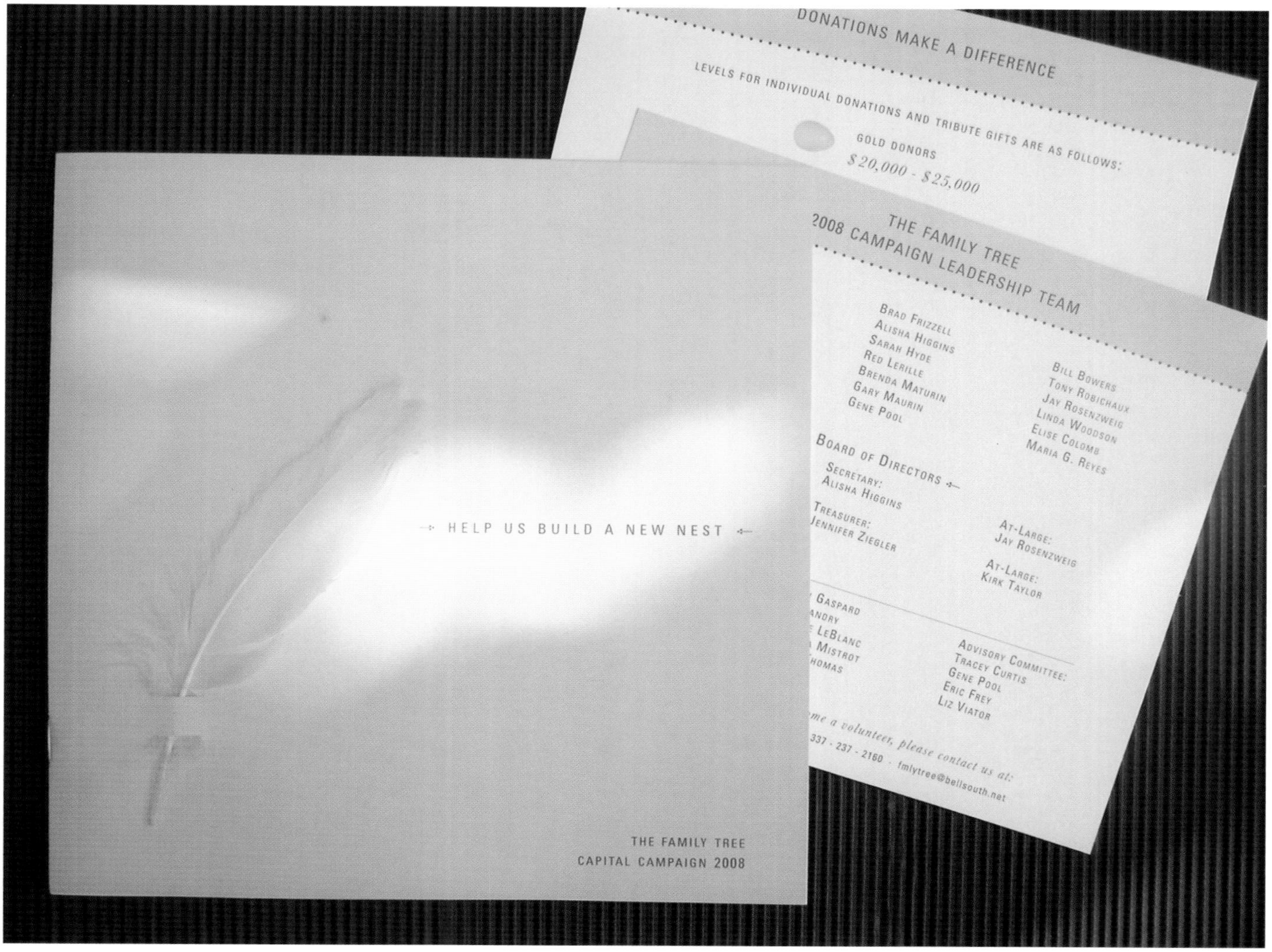

BBR Creative — Lafayette, Louisiana
Designers : Emily Williams, Cathi Pavy, Eddie Talbot
Client : The Family Tree

The College of Saint Rose,
Office of Public Relations and Marketing – Albany, New York
Designers : Mark Hamilton, Chris Parody, Daniel Nester
Client : The College of Saint Rose

BBMG – New York, New York
Designers : Mitch Baranowski, Terri Lahr
Client : Baruch College, School of Public Affairs

There are people beyond the numbers... Lives behind the vision.
Humanity
Uncover the Truth About Blindness
The patients profiled on the following pages represent the millions of children and adults who were fortunate to receive eye care services through ORBIS projects in 2006. Their stories are brought to life in the DVD included with this report. We invite you to read their compelling stories and to watch the DVD to learn more about the impact ORBIS has had on their lives.

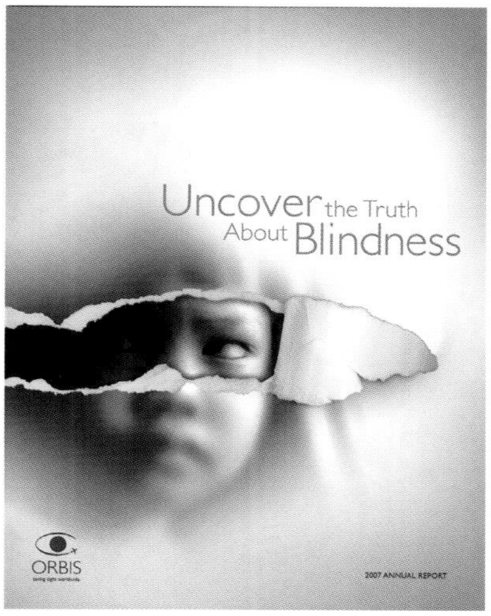
Uncover the Truth About Blindness
ORBIS
2007 ANNUAL REPORT

Vietnam
China

3rd Edge Communications – Jersey City, New Jersey
Designers : Frankie Gonzalez, Nick Schmitz
Client : Orbis International

Wildlife & Whimsy – Missoula, Montana
Designer : Haley Newberg
Client : Sequoia Park Zoo

www.SequoiaParkZoo.net
2nd Annual
Zootini
"Party in the Pampas Grass"
July 29, 2008
6-9pm
Oscar Larson & Associates
Ray Wolfe Construction
City Garbage Co.
Eureka Reporter
LOLETA
BLUE LAKE CASINO
BEAR RIVER CASINO
SEQUOIA PARK
ZOO
FOUNDATION

win$2K to ski better
show your mojo
mojo is big air. visualizing the run. reading the terrain. mojo is fresh powder. nailing a quad. hitting a clean air. mojo is waiting at the bottom of the hill for others. mojo is skiing faster, better, beyond your dreams. mojo is a breathless leap between the mountain and the wind. mojo is what you bring.
www. landosmojo.org
show your mojo.
LANDO'S MOJO
LANDON MORLEY SAWYER FOUNDATION

BBMG – New York, New York
Designers : Mitch Baranowski, Raphael Bemporad, Phil Sherer
Client : Landon Morley Sawyer Foundation

train harder fly higher be better
The Landon Morley Sawyer Foundation provides scholarships, training facilities and cross-cultural exchanges to help freestyle and aerial athletes achieve their dreams.
helping take FLIGHT
lando's mojo
our programs
get involved
Lando's Mojo Grants
Coach of the Year
World-Class Training Center
Ski Exchange Programs
win a grant. recognize a coach. join a cultural exchange. promote freestyle and aerial skiing for a new generation.
www. landosmojo.org
LANDO'S MOJO

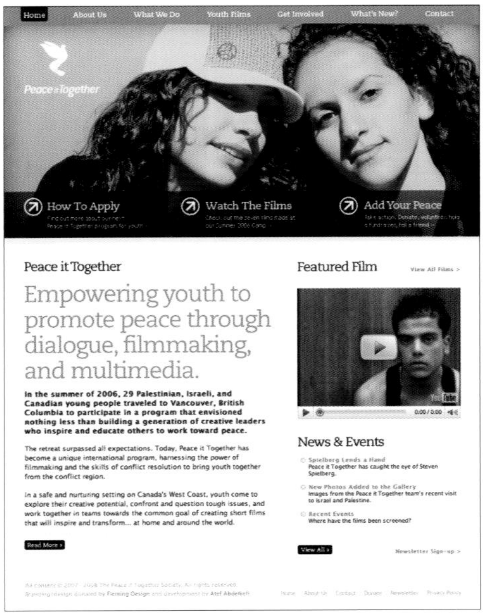
Home About Us What We Do Youth Films Get Involved What's New? Contact
Peace it Together
How To Apply
Watch The Films
Add Your Peace
Peace it Together
Featured Film
Empowering youth to promote peace through dialogue, filmmaking, and multimedia.
News & Events

Home About Us What We Do Youth Films Get Involved What's New? Contact
Peace it Together
2006 Films
Documentary
Drama
Animation
Add Your Peace
Be Part Of It

Fleming Design – Vancouver, Canada
Designers : Blair Pocock, Murray Falconer, Atef Abdelkefi, Felix Heinen, Mike Moraal
Client : Peace it Together

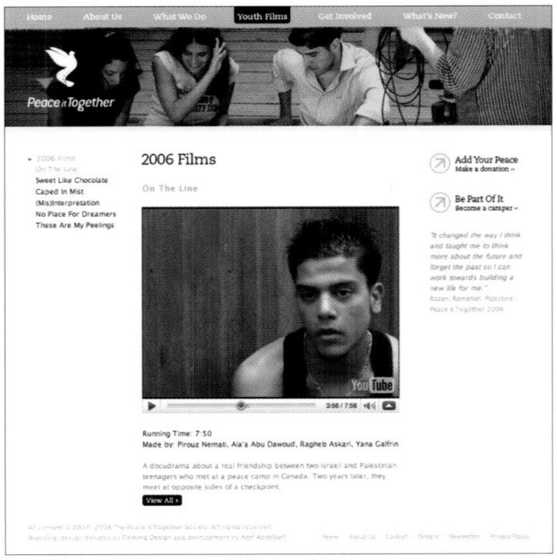
Home About Us What We Do Youth Films Get Involved What's New? Contact
Peace it Together
2006 Films
On The Line
Add Your Peace
Be Part Of It

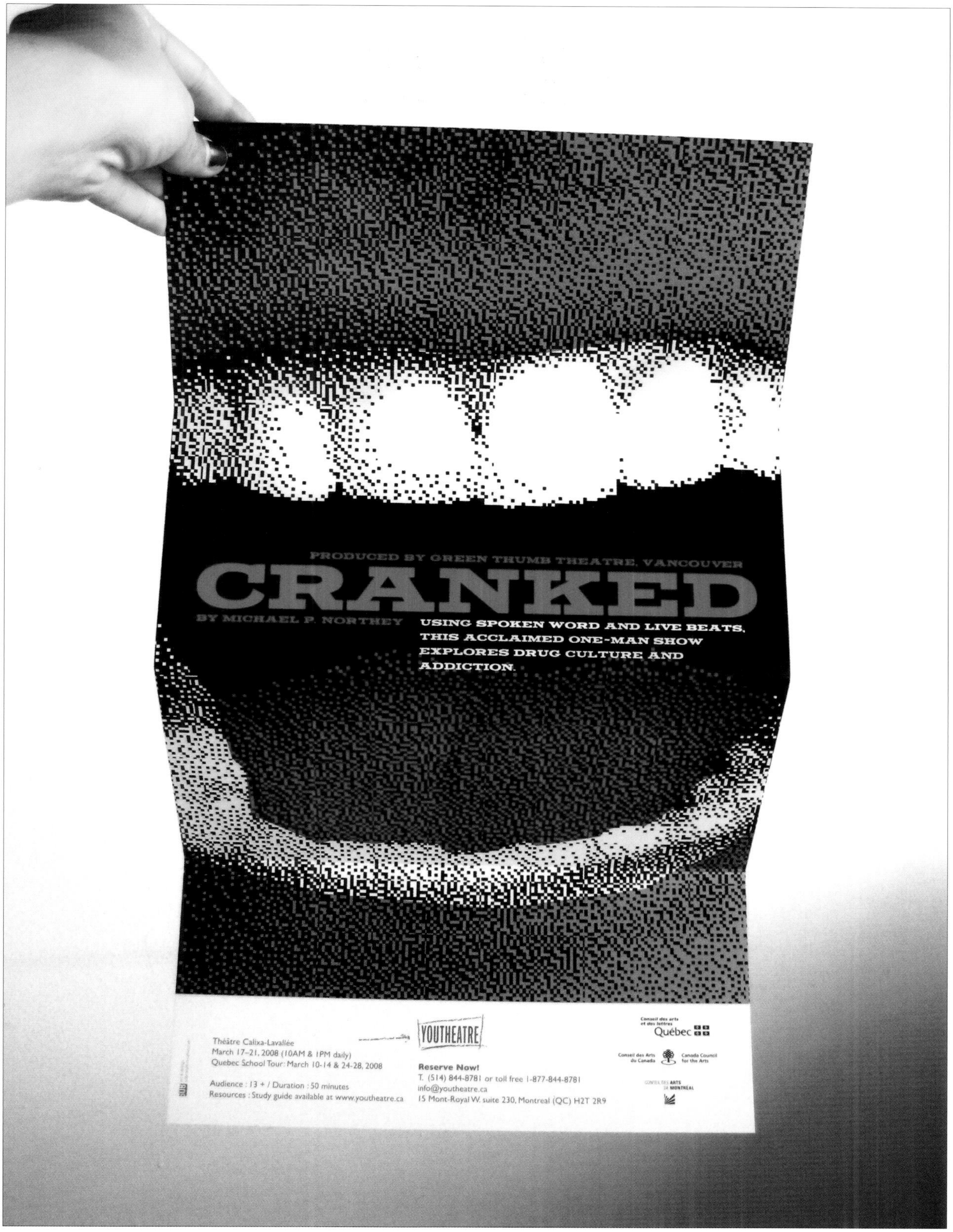

Subcommunication – Montréal, Canada
Designers : Sébastien Théraulaz
Client : Youtheatre

Bleeding an image off the boundaries of the paper can attribute a grandness that would otherwise be lost if held within a border.

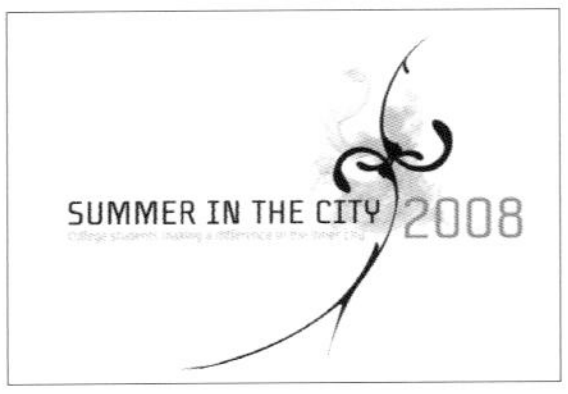

3rd Edge Communications – Jersey City, New Jersey
Designers : Frankie Gonzalez, Liesel Miksits
Client : Here's Life Inner City

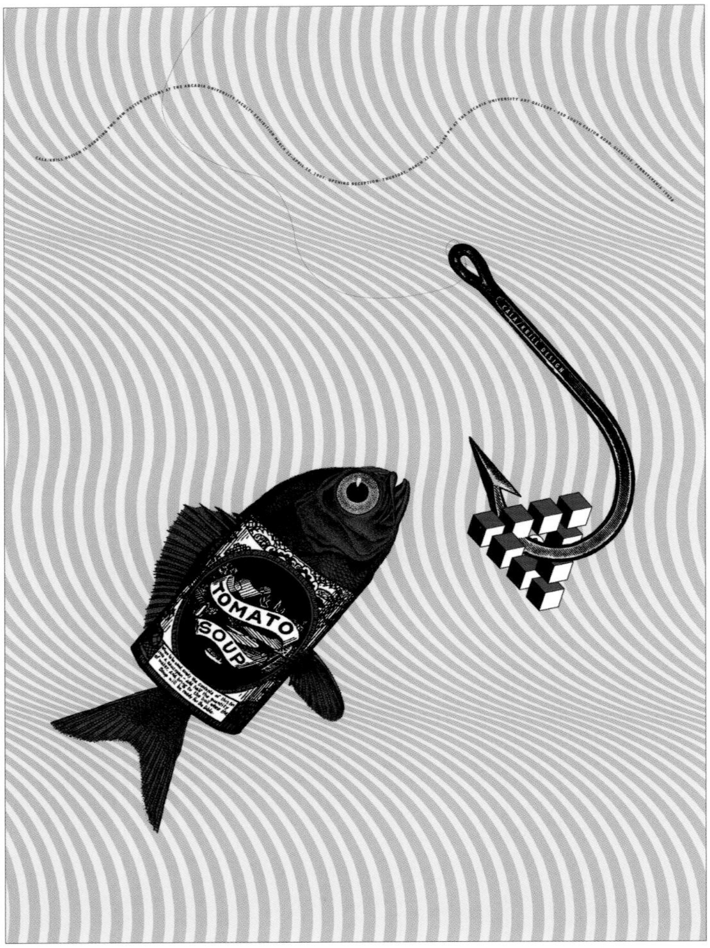

Cala/Krill Design – Claymont, Delaware
Designers : Ronald J. Cala II, Alyssa Krill

No one can appreciate
water as much as a fish
Only 1% of earth's water is drinkable
Every drop matters.. Save Water
PARAGON
MARKETING COMMUNICATIONS

Paragon Marketing Communications – Salmiya, Kuwait
Designers : Louai Alasfahani, Konstantin Assenov, Huzaifa Kakumama
Client : Paragon Marketing Communications

21 Skye Design – Prospect, Kentucky
Designer : Elizabeth Perry Spalding
Client : KY Museum of Art and Craft

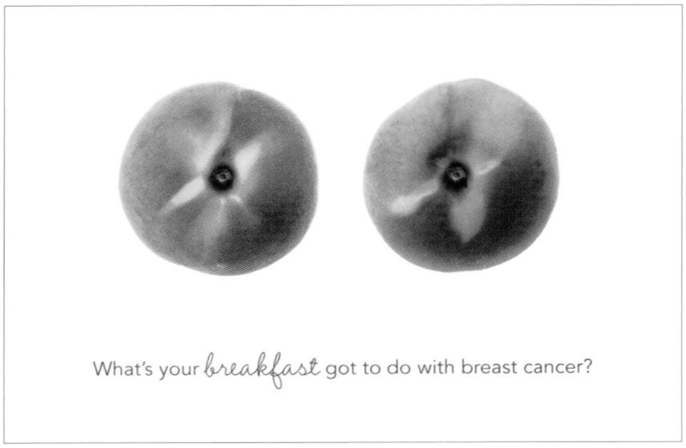

What's your breakfast got to do with breast cancer?

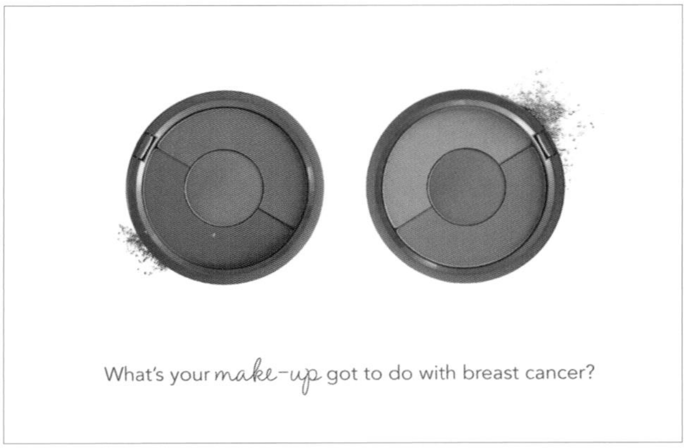

What's your make-up got to do with breast cancer?

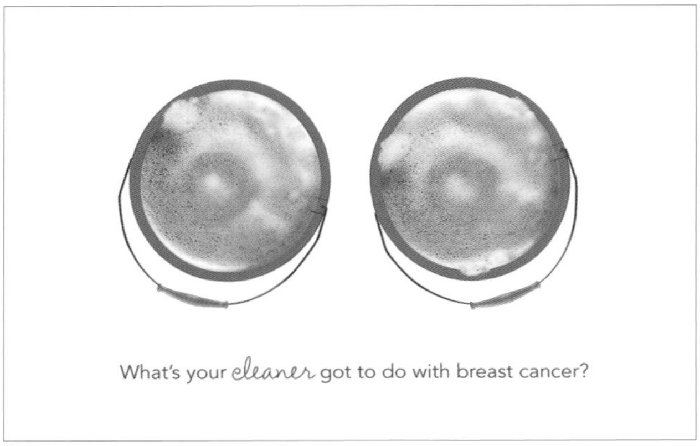

What's your cleaner got to do with breast cancer?

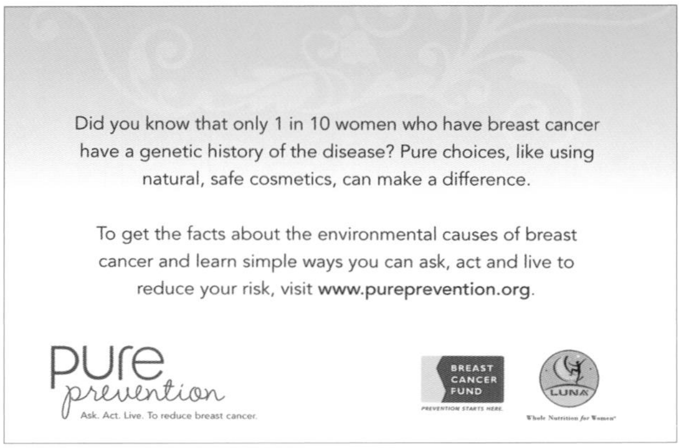

Did you know that only 1 in 10 women who have breast cancer have a genetic history of the disease? Pure choices, like using natural, safe cosmetics, can make a difference.
To get the facts about the environmental causes of breast cancer and learn simple ways you can ask, act and live to reduce your risk, visit www.pureprevention.org.
pure prevention

BBMG – New York, New York
Designers : Molly Conley, Scott Ketchum
Client : Breast Cancer Fund and LUNA

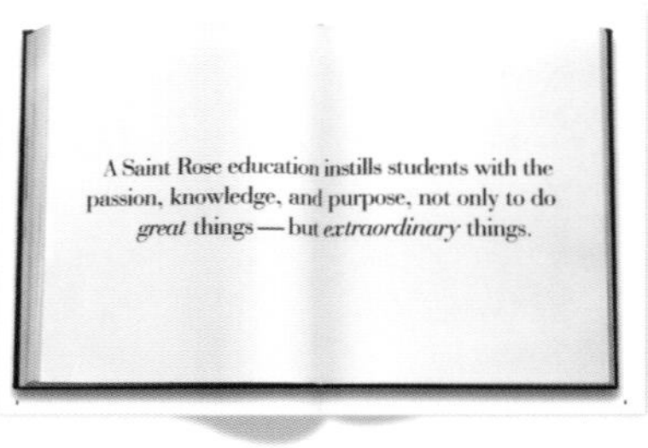

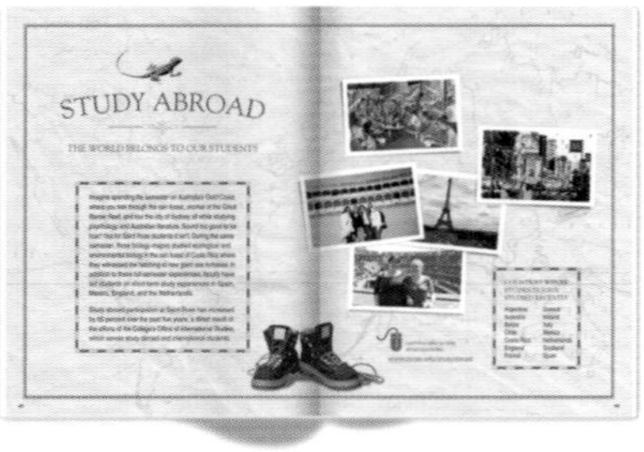

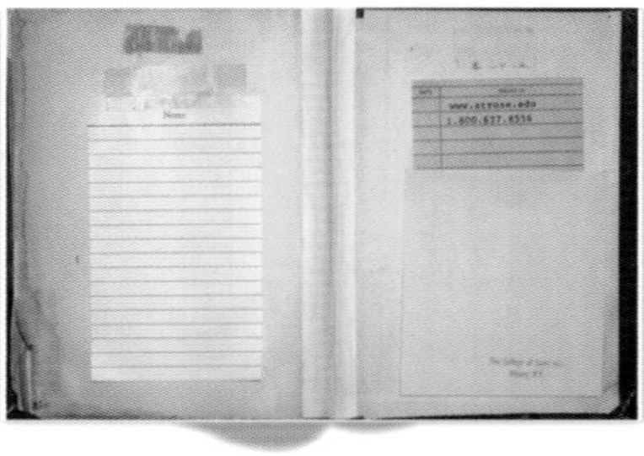

The College of Saint Rose, Office of Public Relations and Marketing – Albany, New York
Designers : Mark Hamilton, Chris Parody, Lisa Haley Thomson, John Backman
Client : The College of Saint Rose

"I WALKED WITH A ZOMBIE"
Chills! Thrills! And Startling Revelations
WE DARE YOU TO SEE IT!
LOST THEATRES of SOMERVILLE
FRANCES DEE
and the GOLDEN AGE
of HOLLYWOOD
Thursday, February 26, 7 PM
Frances Dee introduces her 1943
classic "I Walked With a Zombie"
at The Somerville Museum. Donation $5.
The Somerville Museum
One Westwood Road Somerville MA 02143
617-666-9810 www.lost theatres.org

IN PERSON
FRANCES
DEE
LOST
THEATRES
of
SOMERVILLE

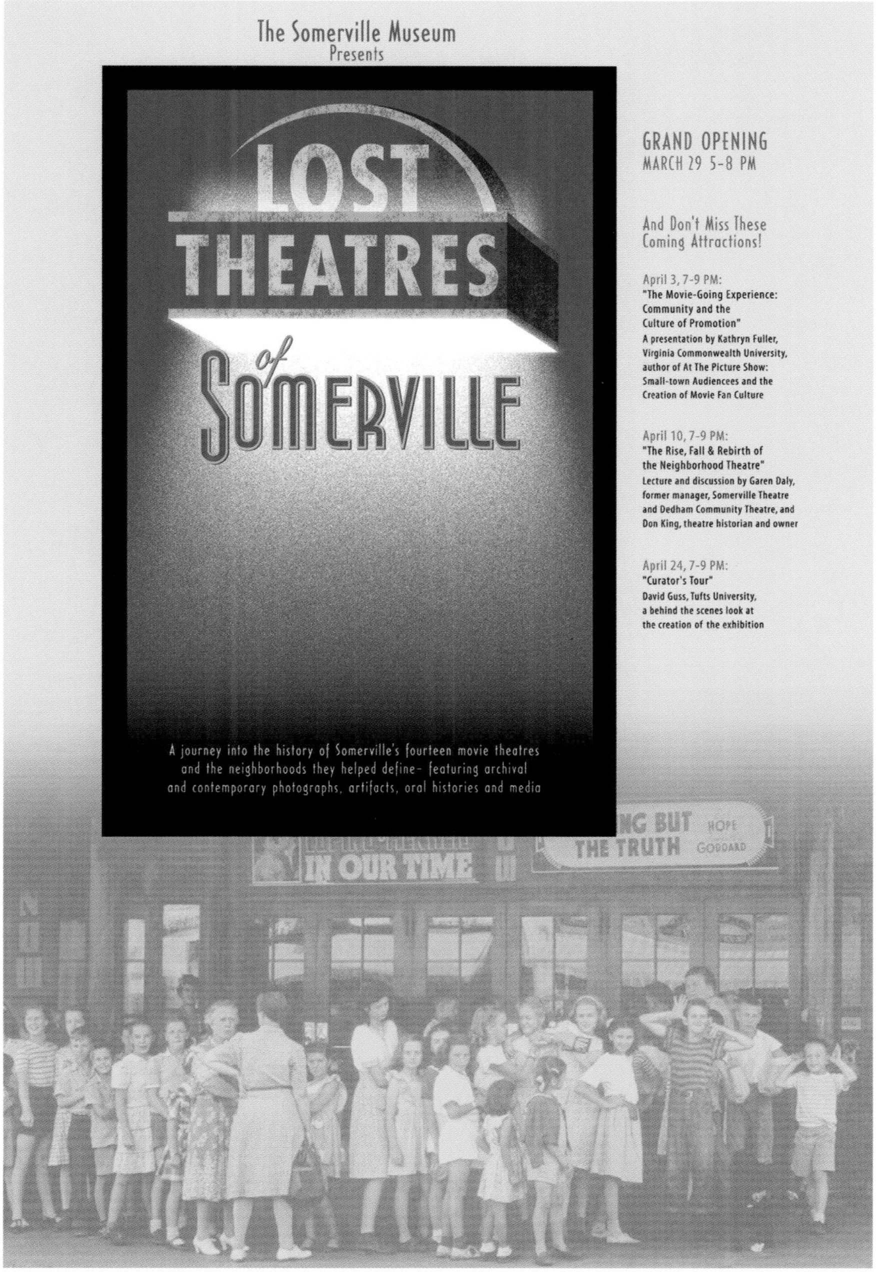
The Somerville Museum
Presents
LOST
THEATRES
of
SOMERVILLE
A journey into the history of Somerville's fourteen movie theatres
and the neighborhoods they helped define- featuring archival
and contemporary photographs, artifacts, oral histories and media
GRAND OPENING
MARCH 29 5-8 PM
And Don't Miss These
Coming Attractions!
April 3, 7-9 PM:
"The Movie-Going Experience:
Community and the
Culture of Promotion"
A presentation by Kathryn Fuller,
Virginia Commonwealth University,
author of At The Picture Show:
Small-town Audiencees and the
Creation of Movie Fan Culture
April 10, 7-9 PM:
"The Rise, Fall & Rebirth of
the Neighborhood Theatre"
Lecture and discussion by Garen Daly,
former manager, Somerville Theatre
and Dedham Community Theatre, and
Don King, theatre historian and owner
April 24, 7-9 PM:
"Curator's Tour"
David Guss, Tufts University,
a behind the scenes look at
the creation of the exhibition
IN OUR TIME
THE TRUTH

Interesting variety of techniques keeps the viewer's eye moving throughout the design. Distressed type, retro-style fonts, duotones, black and white photography, and dated photos all contribute to the prevailing nostalgic theme.

John Sposato Design & Illustration – Piermont, New York
Designer: John Sposato

Reactor – Kansas City, Missouri
Designers : Clifton Alexander, Chase Wilson
Client : Shawnee Chamber of Commerce

The College of Saint Rose,
Office of Public Relations and Marketing – Albany, New York
Designers : Mark Hamilton, Chris Parody
Client : The College of Saint Rose

44TH ANNUAL
A D C N J
AWARDS SHOW
MAY 4, 2007

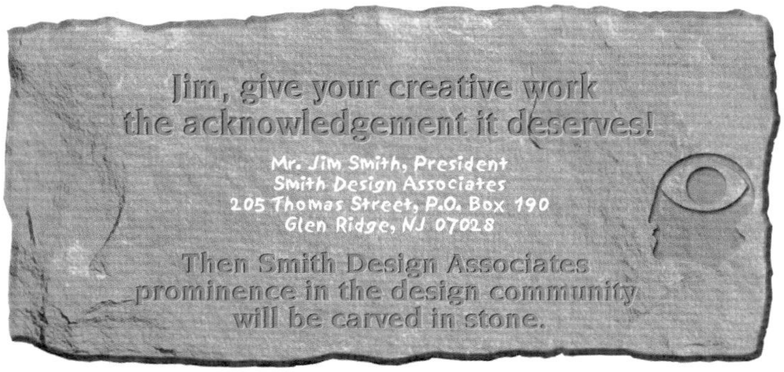
Jim, give your creative work
the acknowledgement it deserves!
Mr. Jim Smith, President
Smith Design Associates
205 Thomas Street, P.O. Box 190
Glen Ridge, NJ 07028
Then Smith Design Associates
prominence in the design community
will be carved in stone.

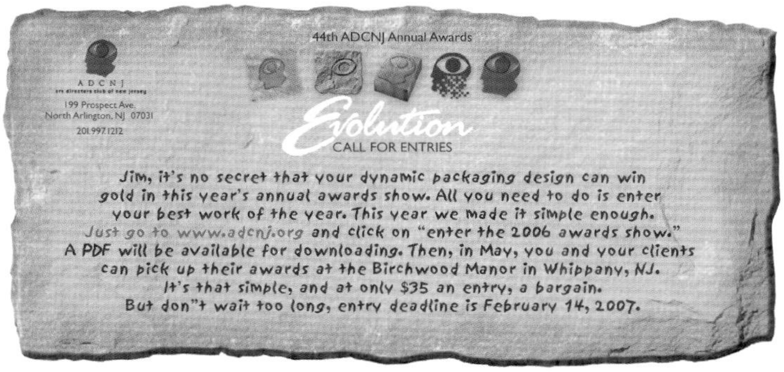
44th ADCNJ Annual Awards
ADCNJ
199 Prospect Ave.
North Arlington, NJ 07031
201.997.1212
Evolution
CALL FOR ENTRIES
Jim, it's no secret that your dynamic packaging design can win
gold in this year's annual awards show. All you need to do is enter
your best work of the year. This year we made it simple enough.
Just go to www.adcnj.org and click on "enter the 2006 awards show."
A PDF will be available for downloading. Then, in May, you and your clients
can pick up their awards at the Birchwood Manor in Whippany, NJ.
It's that simple, and at only $35 an entry, a bargain.
But don"t wait too long, entry deadline is February 14, 2007.

Digital Dimensions 3 – West Orange, New Jersey
Designers : Stephen Longo, Harvey Hirsch, Nikki Orzel
Client : The Art Directors Club of New Jersey

ADCNJ
Robert Braethwaithe
Art Director
Media Consultants
1123 North Hillside Ave.
Valley View, NJ 00000
Congratulations, Robert, your creativity has earned you
a seat at the Winner's Table. Your dinner reservation
and awards notification is enclosed.

44th ADCNJ Annual Awards
Evolution
Congratulations Robert
Robert,
your creative design work has been selected for
an ADCNJ award and will be presented to you
at this year's Annual Award Show, held again
at the Birchwood Manor in Whippany, NJ
on Friday, May 4, 2007. Our fabulous buffet
starts at 6pm with an open bar and music.
Please order your dinner reservations
on the enclosed card early and fax them
to our office as soon as possible.
Sincerely,
44th Annual Show Chairman
Harvey Hirsch
This year's show
was supported by:
THE CREATIVE GROUP
Rule Dies
P.S. Now's the time to get
all of your winning clients
to this event.
Reserve a table early.

Pat Harley
Executive Director
ART
DIRECTORS
CLUB OF
NEW JERSEY
V: 201.997.1212 • F: 201.998.7839
199 Prospect Ave., North Arlington, NJ 07031
www.info@adcnj.org

Evolution
Robert, during our awards presentation your
winning piece will be shown for everyone to see.
Please make sure all of your information is
correct. Fax back the hang tag as soon as possible.
Extra awards can be ordered until June 2007.

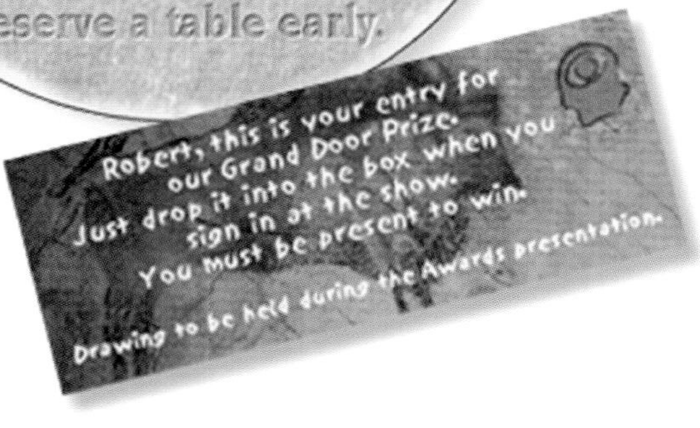
Robert, this is your entry for
our Grand Door Prize.
Just drop it into the box when you
sign in at the show.
You must be present to win.
Drawing to be held during the Awards presentation.

Nassar Design – Brookline, Massachusetts
Designers : Nelida Nassar, Missak Terzian
Client : 7th Beirut International Film Festival

BBMG – New York, New York
Designer : Molly Conley
Client : Appalachian Trail Conservancy

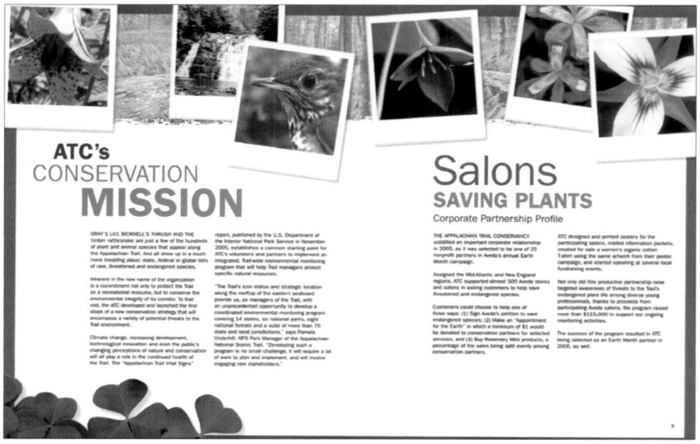

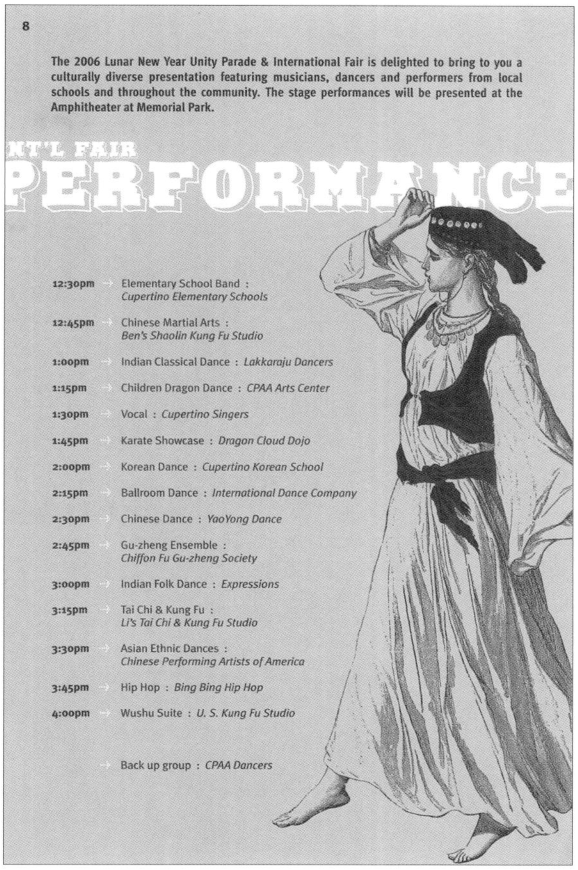
8
The 2006 Lunar New Year Unity Parade & International Fair is delighted to bring to you a culturally diverse presentation featuring musicians, dancers and performers from local schools and throughout the community. The stage performances will be presented at the Amphitheater at Memorial Park.
NT'L FAIR
PERFORMANCE
12:30pm Elementary School Band : Cupertino Elementary Schools
12:45pm Chinese Martial Arts : Ben's Shaolin Kung Fu Studio
1:00pm Indian Classical Dance : Lakkaraju Dancers
1:15pm Children Dragon Dance : CPAA Arts Center
1:30pm Vocal : Cupertino Singers
1:45pm Karate Showcase : Dragon Cloud Dojo
2:00pm Korean Dance : Cupertino Korean School
2:15pm Ballroom Dance : International Dance Company
2:30pm Chinese Dance : YaoYong Dance
2:45pm Gu-zheng Ensemble : Chiffon Fu Gu-zheng Society
3:00pm Indian Folk Dance : Expressions
3:15pm Tai Chi & Kung Fu : Li's Tai Chi & Kung Fu Studio
3:30pm Asian Ethnic Dances : Chinese Performing Artists of America
3:45pm Hip Hop : Bing Bing Hip Hop
4:00pm Wushu Suite : U. S. Kung Fu Studio
Back up group : CPAA Dancers

angryporcupine*design – Park City, Utah
Designer : Cheryl Roder-Quill
Client : Cupertino Lunar New Year Unity Parade

3rd Edge Communications – Jersey City, New Jersey
Designers : Frankie Gonzalez, Melissa Medina Mackin
Client : The Boden Center

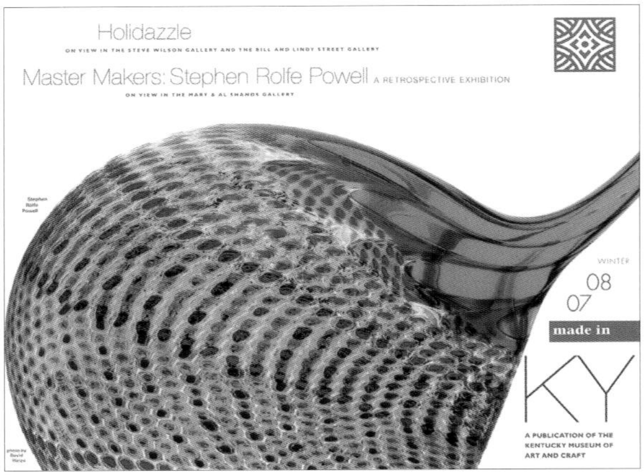

21 Skye Design – Prospect, Kentucky
Designers : Elizabeth Perry Spalding, Greg Stanfield
Client : KY Museum of Art and Design

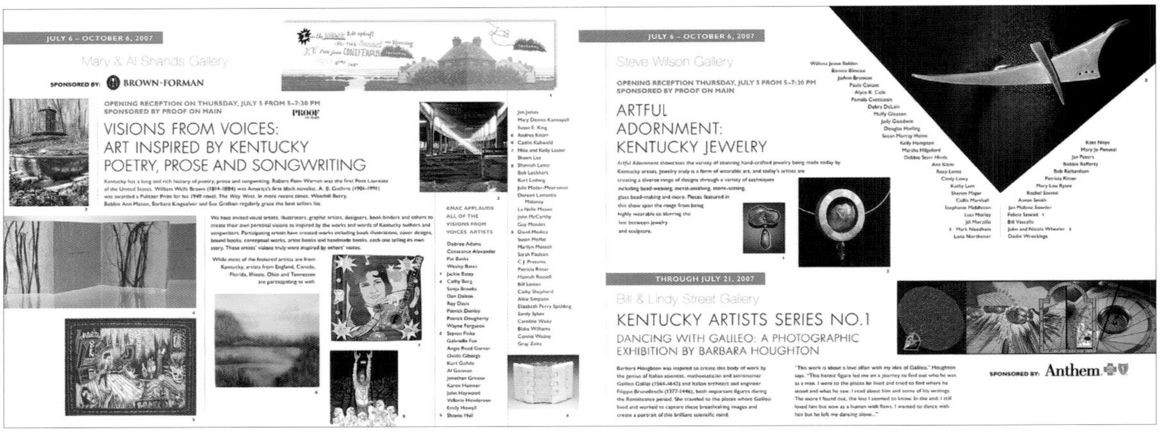

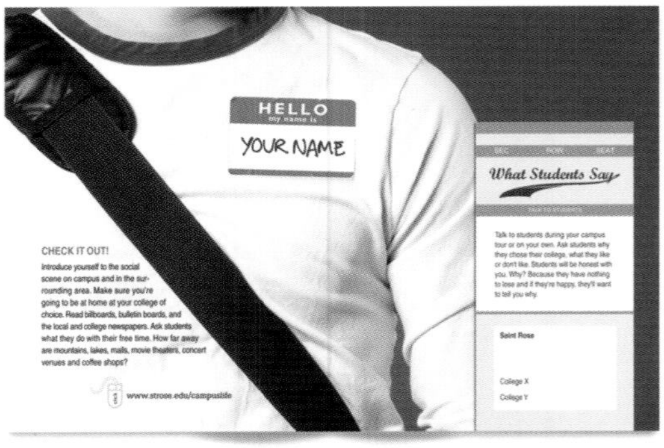

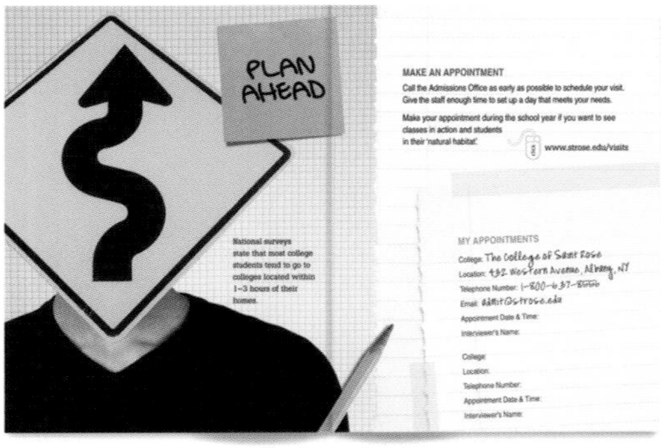

The College of Saint Rose,
Office of Public Relations and Marketing
– Albany, New York
Designers : Mark Hamilton, Chris Parody, Lisa Haley Thompson
Client : The College of Saint Rose

A monochromatic gold color scheme mirrors the title of the event "Tinsel and Treasures."

BBR Creative – Lafayette, Louisiana
Designer : Denise Gallagher
Client : Junior League of Lafayette

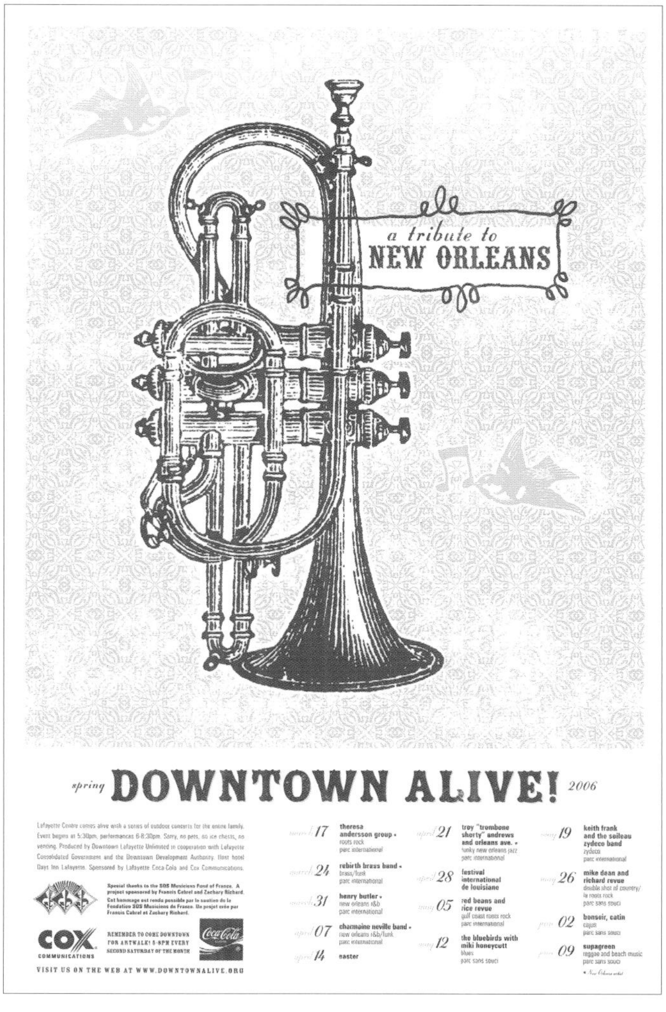

BBR Creative – Lafayette, Louisiana
Designer : Denise Gallagher
Client : Downtown Lafayette Unlimited

Meet Kate.

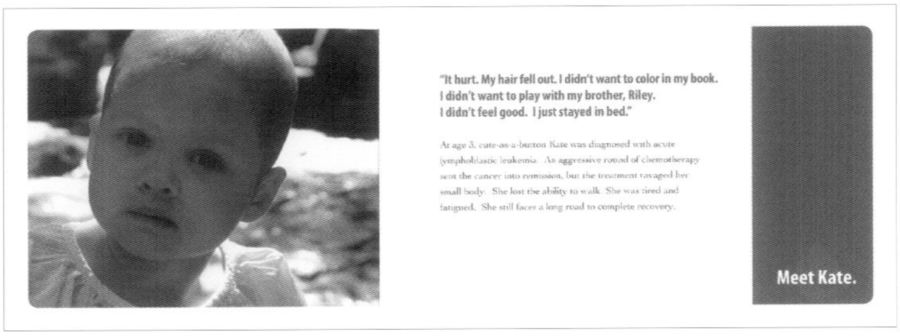
"It hurt. My hair fell out. I didn't want to color in my book.
I didn't want to play with my brother, Riley.
I didn't feel good. I just stayed in bed."
At age 3, cute-as-a-button Kate was diagnosed with acute lymphoblastic leukemia. An aggressive round of chemotherapy sent the cancer into remission, but the treatment ravaged her small body. She lost the ability to walk. She was tired and fatigued. She still faces a long road to complete recovery.
Meet Kate.

"Mommy and Daddy read to me, played games with me and tried to make me laugh. But I didn't feel like laughing. I just wanted to feel better."
Kate is undergoing a 130 week regimen - 2 ½ years - of chemotherapy. During her treatment she has needed a constant source of platelets, as many as eight doses every three days, to boost her blood's clotting ability. Kate also needed oxygen-carrying red blood cells to help her fight the fatigue caused by the chemotherapy.

Moonlight Creative Group – Charlotte, North Carolina
Designers : Dawn Newsome, Jesse Weser, Ken Akers
Client : Community Blood Center of the Carolinas

Kate, Kristin, Dylan, and Riley
Charlotte, NC
"I'm getting better every day. I run outside with Riley and love to paint and draw. Please help other people with cancer. Give blood. It's really easy and it helped save my life."
Often, when we think of the need for blood, we visualize emergencies and disasters. But, every day people of all ages suffering from cancer, heart disease and other major illnesses depend on an immediately available supply of blood to survive.
The Community Blood Center of the Carolinas is an independent, locally managed, non-profit steward of a priceless community resource: life-saving blood.
We provide more than 90% of the blood used by 14 area hospitals. Our goal is to make sure there's enough blood to allow kids like Kate to grow up.

BBR Creative – Lafayette, Louisiana
Designer : Denise Gallagher
Client : Lafayette Animal Aid

WELCOME
P.E.O. FOUNDATION
A GUIDE FOR
NEW MEMBERS
MEDIA KIT
A GUIDE FOR CHAPTERS
P.E.O. COUNSEL For Membership Booklet
PREACCEPTANCE COUNSELING
P.E.O. CUSTOMS
PEO

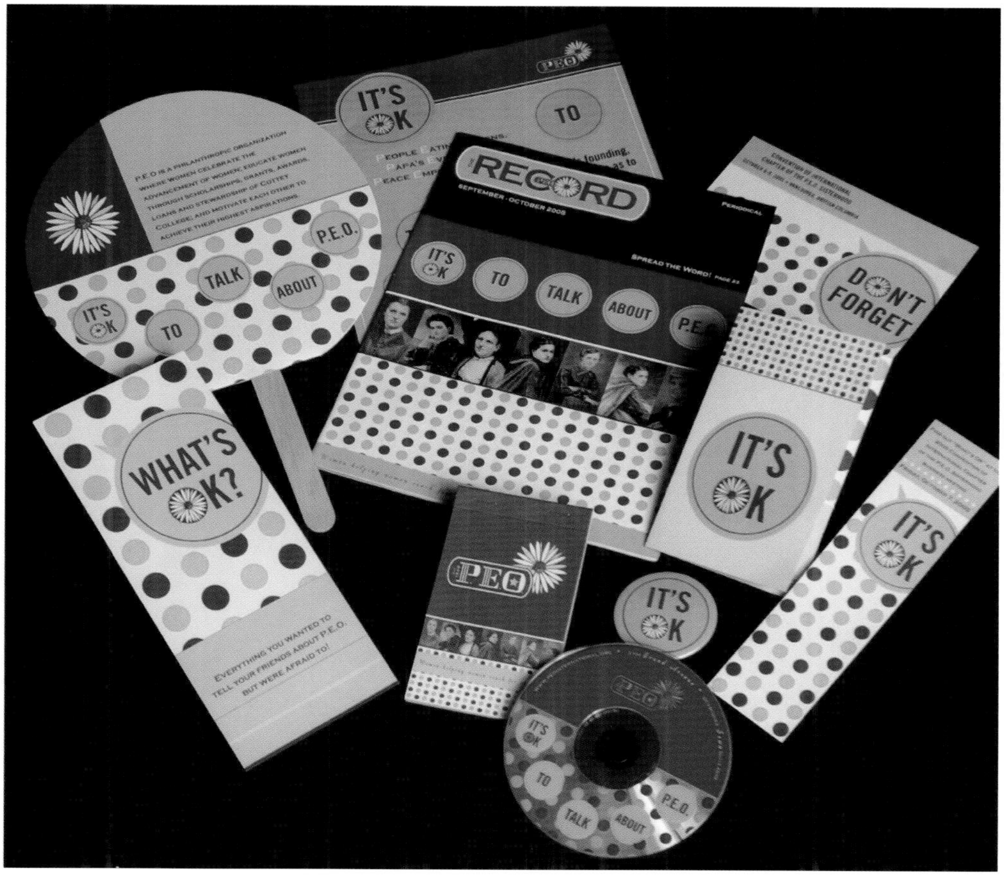
P.E.O. IS A PHILANTHROPIC ORGANIZATION WHERE WOMEN CELEBRATE THE ADVANCEMENT OF WOMEN; EDUCATE WOMEN THROUGH SCHOLARSHIPS, GRANTS, AWARDS, LOANS AND STEWARDSHIP OF COTTEY COLLEGE; AND MOTIVATE EACH OTHER TO ACHIEVE THEIR HIGHEST ASPIRATIONS.
IT'S OK
TO
TALK
ABOUT
P.E.O.
RECORD
SEPTEMBER · OCTOBER 2008
PERIODICAL
SPREAD THE WORD!
WHAT'S OK?
EVERYTHING YOU WANTED TO TELL YOUR FRIENDS ABOUT P.E.O. BUT WERE AFRAID TO!
DON'T FORGET
PEO

Sayles Graphic Design – Des Moines, Iowa
Designers : John Sayles, Sheree Clark
Client : P.E.O. Sisterhood

cdc
ONE CHILD, ONE FAMILY, ONE COMMUNITY:
OUR PRINCIPLES:
When a CHILD PLANTS A GARDEN,
When a FAMILY EMBRACES CHANGE,
they gain a sense of potential and purpose.
When a COMMUNITY NURTURES ITS CHILD
NURTURING A HEALTHY COMMUNITY
BY EMPOWERING YOUTH & FAMILIES

Rotor – Minneapolis, Minnesota
Designers : Matt Travaille, Andy Weaverling
Client : Community Design Center of Minnesota

BBMG – New York, New York
Designer : Molly Conley
Client : PENCIL

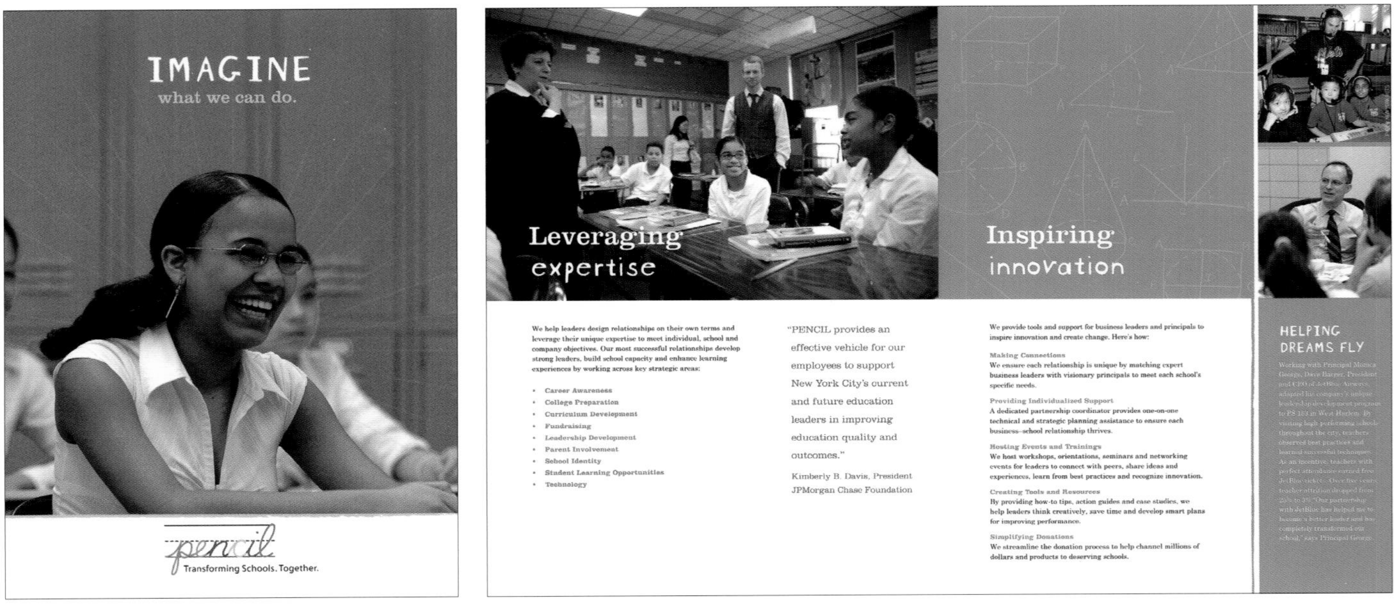
IMAGINE
what we can do.
pencil
Transforming Schools. Together.
Leveraging expertise
Inspiring innovation
HELPING DREAMS FLY
"PENCIL provides an effective vehicle for our employees to support New York City's current and future education leaders in improving education quality and outcomes."
Kimberly B. Davis, President
JPMorgan Chase Foundation

JUDY WICKS

10 LOCAL LIVING ECONOMIES

As a pioneer of the local living economy movement, Judy Wicks believes community self-reliance isn't just a utopian vision, but our very survival. "The corporate-controlled global economic system, based on the continual growth of large corporations and long distance shipping, is using up more natural resources than the earth can restore and contributing to global warming," Wicks says. "The solution is clear – we must decentralize business ownership, food production, and energy production into self-reliant local economies."

For Wicks, this vision grew from the business she founded in 1983, White Dog Café, and its mission to serve customers, community, employees and nature. Food is purchased from local farms where animals are raised on sustainably grown pasture and produce. Long distance purchasing is limited to what is not available locally. Operations are powered by electricity from wind power generated in Pennsylvania.

After achieving success with the café, Wicks had an epiphany. "It wasn't enough to have good business practices within one's own company," Wicks says. "We had to work cooperatively with other businesses to build a whole local economy based on these values." Taking what she learned to a higher level, Wicks started the White Dog Foundation, which uses 20% of the Café's profits to build a local living economy, including connecting local farmers with other restaurants.

David Korten, author of *When Corporations Rule the World*, came to SVN as a Visionary Advisor after meeting Wicks at a conference sponsored by *Yes!* magazine and the Positive Futures Network, which Korten co-founded to actively engage people in creating a just, sustainable and compassionate world.

At SVN, Wicks and Korten teamed up with Michael Shuman, author of *Going Local*, and Laury Hammel, owner of the Longfellow Clubs and a longtime activist in founding business organizations, such as BSR and its New England predecessor.

The solution is clear – we must decentralize business ownership, food production, and energy production into self-reliant local economies. JUDY WICKS

Wicks and Hammel co-founded the Business Alliance for Local Living Economies (BALLE) at the 2001 SVN Fall Conference, and currently serve as its co-chairs. Says Korten, who serves on the BALLE board along with Shuman, "with over 50 local networks and more than 15,000 members across North America, BALLE is starting to change the economic story that shapes business and consumer behavior, as well as government policy, by building awareness of the implications of each choice we make between a global corporation and a local business."

White Dog Café owner Judy Wicks

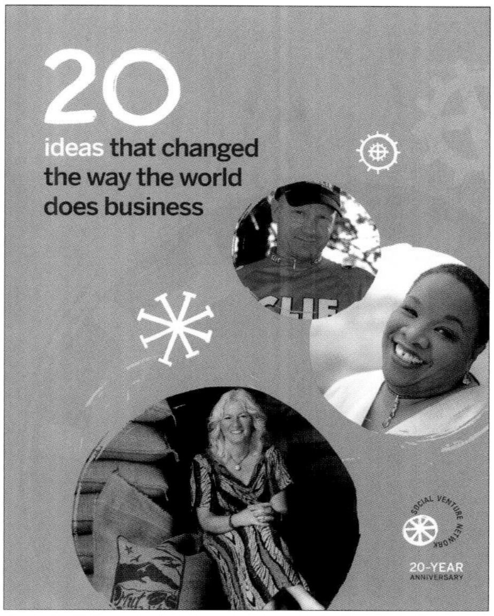
20
ideas that changed the way the world does business
SOCIAL VENTURE NETWORK
20-YEAR ANNIVERSARY

BBMG – New York, New York
Designers : Molly Conley, Scott Ketchum
Client : Social Venture Network

Holohan Design – Philadelphia, Pennsylvania
Designer : Kelly Holohan
Client : American Red Cross

Beauty From Adversity 8.29.05
Do something beautiful. Help with the hurricane relief effort.
www.thehurricaneposterproject.com

The higher goals of effective design are to encourage, inspire, educate, and bring about positive change. You can be your favorite superhero when you use your powers for good.

msFriends
presents
Rock
for ms
September 27th, 2007 at 6pm
Roe Restaurant
651 Howard Street, San Francisco
To purchase tickets and preview live auction photographs go to msFriends.org

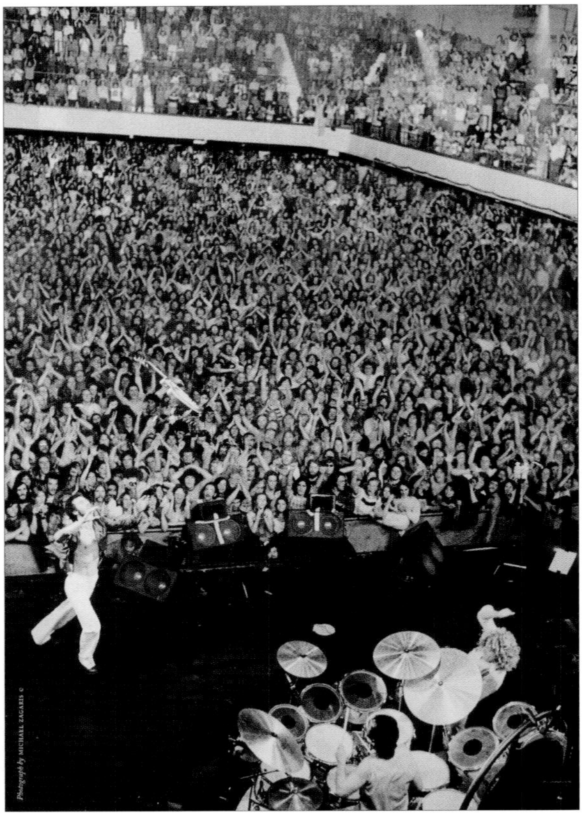

Factor Design – San Francisco, California
Designers : Tim Guy, Jeff Zwerner, Lily Lin
Client : MSFriends

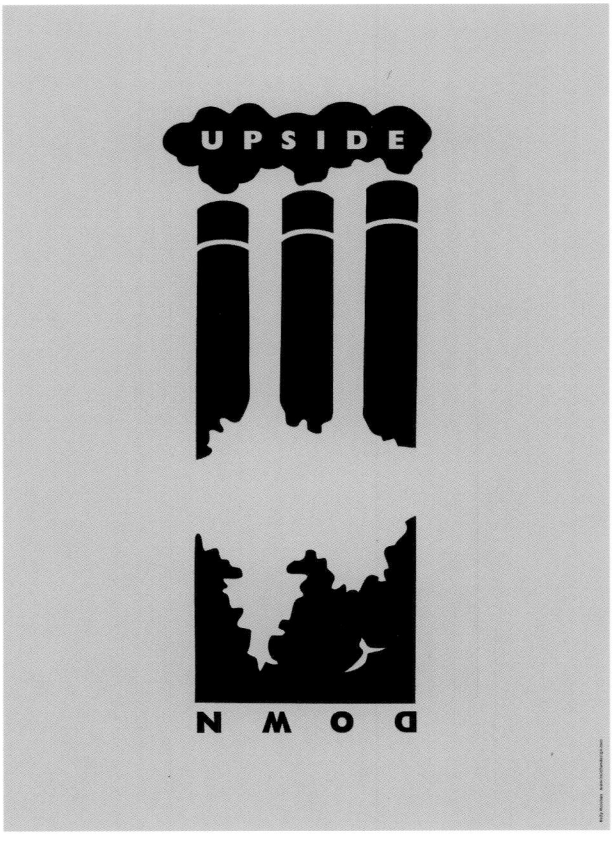
UPSIDE
DOWN

Holohan Design – Philadelphia, Pennsylvania
Designers : Kelly Holohan, Scott Laserow

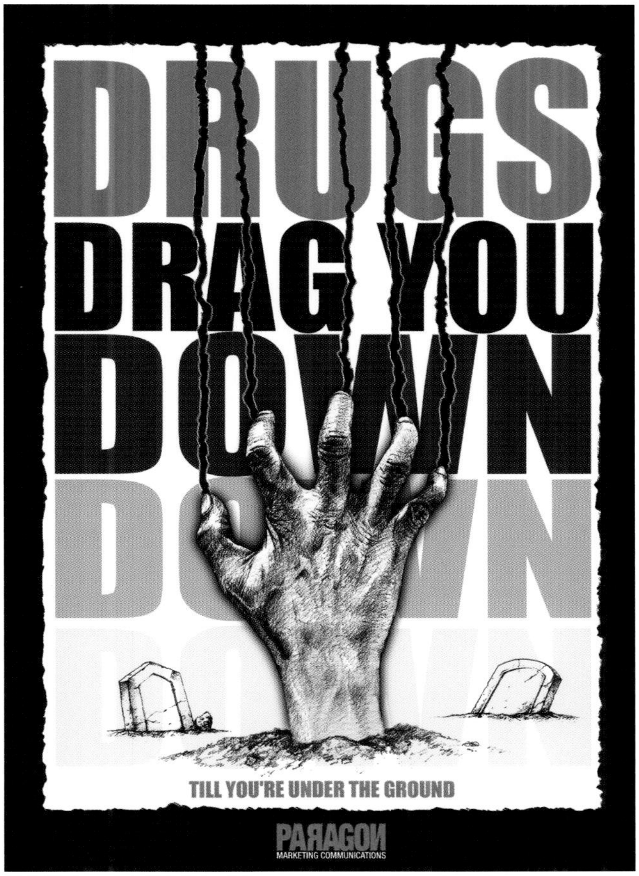

Paragon Marketing Communications
– Salmiya, Kuwait
Designers : Louai Alasfahani,
Konstantin Assenov, Huzaifa Kakumama
Client : Paragon Marketing Communications

Animal Legal Defense Fund – Cotati, California
Client : Animal Legal Defense Fund

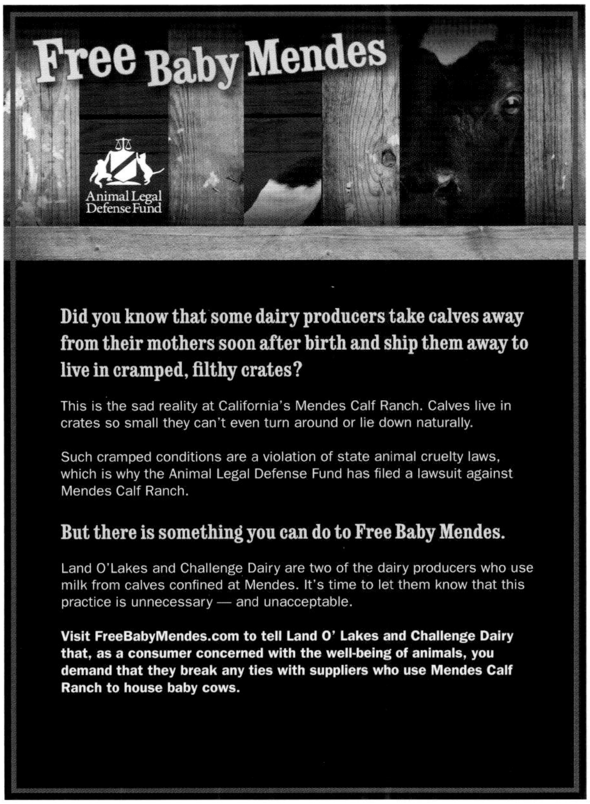
Free Baby Mendes
Animal Legal Defense Fund
Did you know that some dairy producers take calves away from their mothers soon after birth and ship them away to live in cramped, filthy crates?
This is the sad reality at California's Mendes Calf Ranch. Calves live in crates so small they can't even turn around or lie down naturally.
Such cramped conditions are a violation of state animal cruelty laws, which is why the Animal Legal Defense Fund has filed a lawsuit against Mendes Calf Ranch.
But there is something you can do to Free Baby Mendes.
Land O'Lakes and Challenge Dairy are two of the dairy producers who use milk from calves confined at Mendes. It's time to let them know that this practice is unnecessary — and unacceptable.
Visit FreeBabyMendes.com to tell Land O' Lakes and Challenge Dairy that, as a consumer concerned with the well-being of animals, you demand that they break any ties with suppliers who use Mendes Calf Ranch to house baby cows.

Mendes Calf Ranch is located in Tipton, California. The facility raises approximately 12,000 dairy calves at a time, from up to 80 different ranches, for the first several months of their lives.
The babies are taken from their mothers soon after birth and shipped away to live for extended periods in cramped, filthy crates — often without enough room to turn around or lie down naturally. Crates are often covered in feces, and calves struggle to reach out through breaks in the walls to have any sort of physical contact — a strong natural instinct — with calves next door.
Their confinement is intended to prepare them for the harsh demands of a future as a dairy cow on a factory farm. Then they are usually shipped back to the farms for a life of non-stop milk production, just like their mothers.
On June 19, 2006, the Animal Legal Defense Fund filed a complaint in Tulare County Superior Court against Mendes Calf Ranch for violating state anti-cruelty laws, which require that animals be provided with adequate exercise area.
Free Baby Mendes!
• Sign our letter to Land O'Lakes and Challenge Dairy at FreeBabyMendes.com
• Share this leaflet with friends
• Choose alternatives to dairy products
• Buy from small, local farms when possible
• If you're a student, ask your campus' food services to voice their concerns to Land O'Lakes and Challenge Dairy — or to stop carrying their products
• Find more ideas on how you can help stop the abuse of baby cows at FreeBabyMendes.com
Animal Legal Defense Fund
About The Animal Legal Defense Fund
The Animal Legal Defense Fund is a national non-profit organization dedicated to protecting the lives and advancing the interests of animals through the legal system. Student (SALDF) chapters are found on campuses of more than one hundred law schools throughout the country. For information on becoming an ALDF supporter, student member or attorney member, visit www.aldf.org.
ALDF • 170 East Cotati Avenue • Cotati, CA 94931 • 707-795-2533

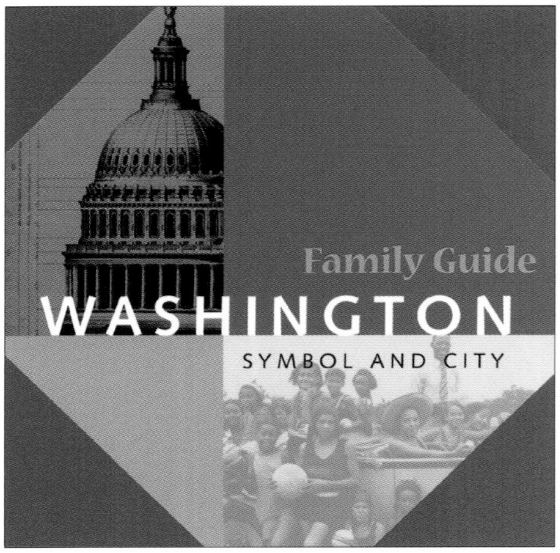
Family Guide
WASHINGTON
SYMBOL AND CITY

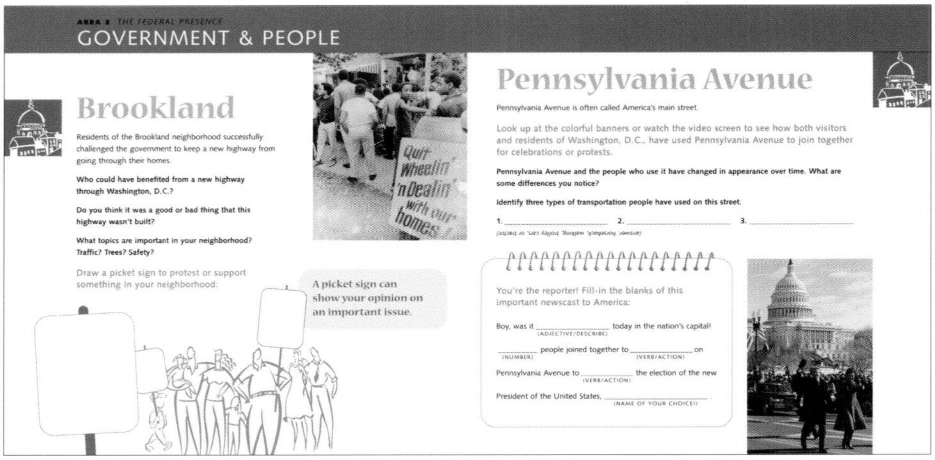
AREA 3 THE FEDERAL PRESENCE
GOVERNMENT & PEOPLE
Brookland
Residents of the Brookland neighborhood successfully challenged the government to keep a new highway from going through their homes.
Who could have benefited from a new highway through Washington, D.C.?
Do you think it was a good or bad thing that this highway wasn't built?
What topics are important in your neighborhood? Traffic? Trees? Safety?
Draw a picket sign to protest or support something in your neighborhood:
Quit Wheelin' 'n Dealin' with our homes
A picket sign can show your opinion on an important issue.
Pennsylvania Avenue
Pennsylvania Avenue is often called America's main street.
Look up at the colorful banners or watch the video screen to see how both visitors and residents of Washington, D.C., have used Pennsylvania Avenue to join together for celebrations or protests.
Pennsylvania Avenue and the people who use it have changed in appearance over time. What are some differences you notice?
Identify three types of transportation people have used on this street.
1. 2. 3.
You're the reporter! Fill-in the blanks of this important newscast to America:
Boy, was it (ADJECTIVE/DESCRIBE) today in the nation's capital!
(NUMBER) people joined together to (VERB/ACTION) on
Pennsylvania Avenue to (VERB/ACTION) the election of the new
President of the United States, (NAME OF YOUR CHOICE!).

Pensaré Design Group – Washington, D.C.
Designers : Mary Ellen Vehlow, Amy E. Billingham
Client : National Building Museum

More than just a city guide with a list of facts, this brochure involves hands-on learning with quizzes, fill-in-the-blanks, sketching, and more.

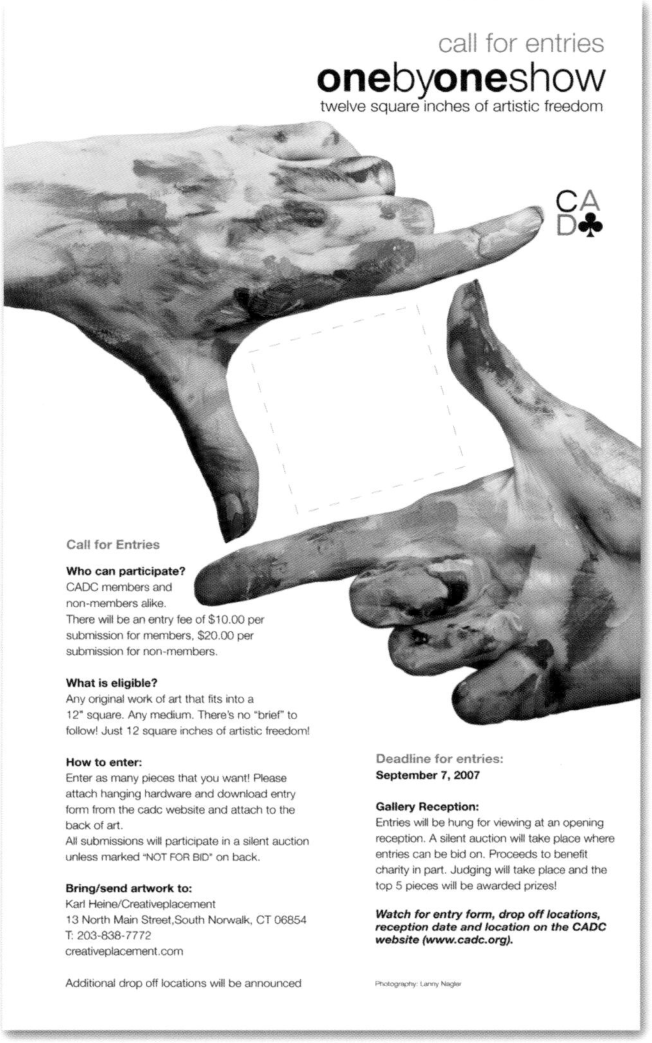
call for entries
onebyoneshow
twelve square inches of artistic freedom
CA
D
Call for Entries
Who can participate?
CADC members and non-members alike.
There will be an entry fee of $10.00 per submission for members, $20.00 per submission for non-members.
What is eligible?
Any original work of art that fits into a 12" square. Any medium. There's no "brief" to follow! Just 12 square inches of artistic freedom!
How to enter:
Enter as many pieces that you want! Please attach hanging hardware and download entry form from the cadc website and attach to the back of art.
All submissions will participate in a silent auction unless marked "NOT FOR BID" on back.
Bring/send artwork to:
Karl Heine/Creativeplacement
13 North Main Street,South Norwalk, CT 06854
T: 203-838-7772
creativeplacement.com
Additional drop off locations will be announced
Deadline for entries:
September 7, 2007
Gallery Reception:
Entries will be hung for viewing at an opening reception. A silent auction will take place where entries can be bid on. Proceeds to benefit charity in part. Judging will take place and the top 5 pieces will be awarded prizes!
Watch for entry form, drop off locations, reception date and location on the CADC website (www.cadc.org).
Photography: Lanny Nagler

TFI Envision, Inc. – Norwalk, Connecticut
Designers : Elizabeth P. Ball, Mary Ellen Butkus
Client : Connecticut Art Directors Club

What's missing in this picture?

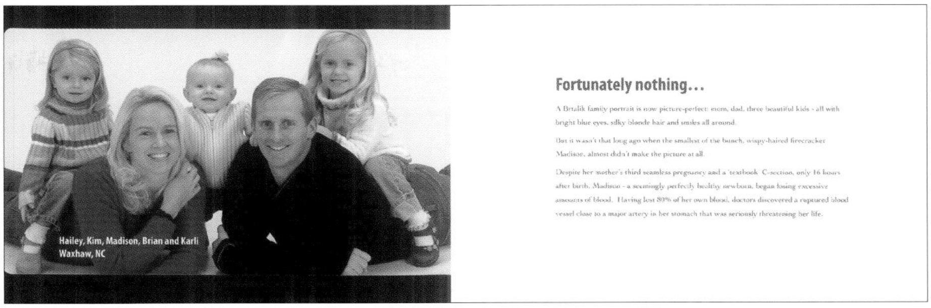
Fortunately nothing...
Hailey, Kim, Madison, Brian and Karli
Waxhaw, NC

What are the odds?

Moonlight Creative Group – Charlotte, North Carolina
Designers : Dawn Newsome, Jesse Weser
Client : Community Blood Center of the Carolinas

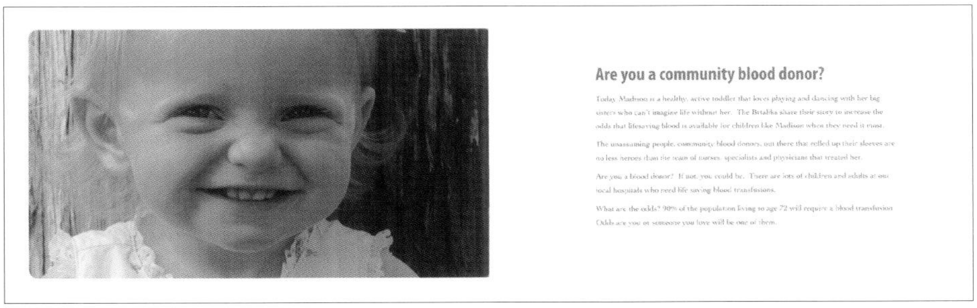
Are you a community blood donor?

TFI Envision, Inc. – Norwalk, Connecticut
Designer : Elizabeth P. Ball
Client : Connecticut Grand Opera & Orchestra

An In-Depth Look at: SUTTON STUDIOS

David Sutton is a photographer who loves dogs—a lot. And he wants to share that love among people, animals, and organizations. So every fall he chooses some of his favorite families, and has Augusta Toppins, senior designer at Chicago's SGDP, develop a calendar showcasing the best images of the year for the following twelve months.

"It features actual people who've come in and done portraits with him," Toppins says of the calendar, which is replete with black-and-white images of soulful eyes and multispecies families against simple backdrops. "He specializes in [pet] portraits. People have even brought in horses." And lest the horses feel excluded from his annual "Dog Days" piece, the canines depicted within don't have the last word, either. "It's not just dogs, but the people too," she says. "They tell the story and about how they met their dogs. A lot of the people have rescue stories."

With respect to the dignity of the dogs—some foppish, some floppy—and the integrity of the photographs themselves, Toppins personally makes sure that the wall calendar conveys the love that Sutton puts into every image. "We also handle the printing process and make sure it looks right," Toppins says. And right it is on another level—the front of each calendar states "100% of the suggested donation price of $10 directly benefits animal welfare organizations."

"People purchase [the calendars] from pet stores or their vets," Toppins explains, "and the proceeds go to animal protection leagues and humane societies. It's unique as a promotional piece in that it's a promotion for one person, but the proceeds go to various nonprofits around town. It's a fundraiser." Not only are the calendars a hit with animal lovers who might hang the calendars in their kitchens or offices, but with mainstream media: *The Chicago Tribune* featured the 2008 calendar in a list of excellent holiday gifts.

Doing this pro bono job is a simple joy for Toppins, who lives with a basset hound named Riley. "I'm a huge animal fan," she says. "They give me these projects to make me happy."

SGDP – **Chicago, Illinois**
Designer : Augusta Toppins
Client : Sutton Studios

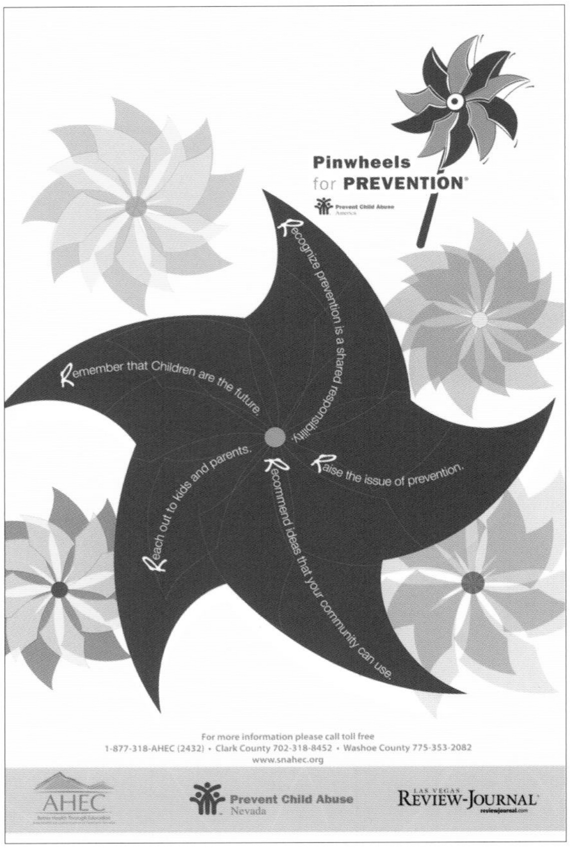
Pinwheels
for PREVENTION®
Prevent Child Abuse America
Recognize prevention is a shared responsibility.
Remember that Children are the future.
Raise the issue of prevention.
Reach out to kids and parents.
Recommend ideas that your community can use.
For more information please call toll free
1-877-318-AHEC (2432) • Clark County 702-318-8452 • Washoe County 775-353-2082
www.snahec.org
AHEC
Prevent Child Abuse
Nevada
LAS VEGAS
REVIEW-JOURNAL®
reviewjournal.com

Sutton Watkins Advertising & Marketing – Las Vegas, Nevada
Designers : Jennifer Green, Kathy Watkins
Client : Area Health Education Center of S. Nevada

Subcommunication – Montréal, Canada
Designers : Valérie Desrochers
Client : Youtheatre

THE NEW MOTHER
BY KATHLEEN MCDONNELL
Everybody loves a good secret, Turkey and Blue-Eyes included. But how far will they go to uncover what a bewitching stranger won't tell them? Will they cross the line and jeopardize their happy home life? Or will they stay true to their promise to never be disobedient? In THE NEW MOTHER, children learn that there are consequences to their actions and that life is never quite as it seems.
« A wonderfull children's play... the audience sat spellbound ».
– K. Greenaway, The Gazette, 2005 –
Conseil des Arts du Canada
Canada Council for the Arts
Conseil des arts et des lettres Québec
CONSEIL DES ARTS DE MONTRÉAL
YOUTHEATRE
FOR CHILDREN AGES: 6-12
SCHOOL TOUR:
OCTOBER 30 – DECEMBER 22, 2006
NEW! MATINÉES PERFORMANCES AT THÉÂTRE CALIXA-LAVALLÉE: NOVEMBER 9 & 10, 2006.
15 MONT-ROYAL O. BUR. 125 / MONTRÉAL (QC) H2T 2R9 / T. 514.844.8781 • F. 514.844.2330
INFO@YOUTHEATRE.CA / WWW.YOUTHEATRE.CA

Directory

2creativo
C.Llull, 63-69, 2º 7ª
Barcelona 08005 Spain
www.2creativo.net

2nd Floor Design
228 North Street
Portsmouth, VA 23704
757-393-9580

3 Dogz Creative Inc.
255 Duncan Mill Road, Suite 609
Toronto, Ontario M3B 3H9
416-510-0066

3rd Edge Communications
162 Newark Ave. 3rd Floor
Jersey City, NJ 07302
201-395-9960

21 Skye Design
5915 Mason Blvd.
Prospect, KY 40059
502-593-4784

Aaron Design, Inc.
7 West 20th Street, Suite 2F
New York, NY 10011
212-414-1522

A Blue Moon Arts LLC
3939 S. Harvard, Suite 190
Tulsa, OK 74135
918-742-3136

Active Ingredients, Inc.
12 E. Sir Francis Drake Blvd., Suite D
Larkspur, CA 94939
415-497-6759/415-464-1060

Alexander Egger
Satellites Mistaken for Stars
1170 Vienna, Austria
www.satellitesmistakenforstars.com

Alexander Isley Inc.
9 Brookside Place
Redding, CT 06896
203-544-9692 x10

Ambient Creative Arts studio
Vista, CA 92081
760-631-9515
www.scottmosher.com

Anderson Design Group
116 29th Ave. N
Nashville, TN 37203
615-327-9894

Andigo New Media
150 W. 25th St. #904
New York, NY 10001
212-727-8445

And Partners
158 West 27th Street Floor 7
New York, NY 10001
(212) 414 4700

Andrij Shevchenko
25 Posztamt
Berdyansk 71112 Ukraine
+380674505645

angryporcupine*design
1720 Creekside Lane
Park City, UT 84098
435-655-0645

Animal Legal Defense Fund
170 East Cotati Avenue
Cotati, CA 94931
707-795-7280

Anthem Worldwide
77 Maiden Lane
San Francisco, CA 94108
800-413-9120

Art Chantry
PO Box 9216
Tacoma, WA 98490
253-310-3993

Arvids Baranovs
Slokas 36-4a
Riga LV-1048 Latvia
+371029755745

Atomic Design
1048 Blueberry Court
Crowley, TX 76036
817-939-2445

Avive Design
10400 SW Ridgeview Lane
Portland, OR 97219
503-977-5597

Baker Creative
386 Main Street
Groveport, OH 43125
614-836-3845

BBMG
200 Park Avenue South, Suite 1516
New York, NY 10003
212-473-4902 x204

BBR Creative
444 Jefferson St.
Lafayette, LA 70501
337-233-1515

Belyea
1809 7th Avenue, Suite 1250
Seattle, WA 98101
206-682-4895

Bill Weber Studios
PO Box 39 - Planetarium Station
New York, NY 10024
917-679-7583

biz-R
35a Fore Street
Totnes, Devon TQ9 5HN
+44 1803 868989

Black Eye Design
1701 Marie Anne East, Suite 1
Montreal, QC, H2J 2E2
514-940-2121

Bleu Sky Creative
2 Church Street, Suite 2B
Burlington, VT 05401
802-864-8224

BLIK
655 G Street Suite E
San Diego, CA 92101
619-234-4434

Bluewater Advertising & Design
51 Ascot Drive
Ocean, NJ 07712
732-922-2269

Bohnsack Design
13996 E. Plactia Marlinda
Vail, AZ 85641
602-999-1147

Brady Communications
16th Floor, Four Gateway Center
Pittsburgh, PA 15222-1207
412-288-9300

Brand RAVE, Inc.
6354 Old Wood
Buford, GA 30518
678-640-6159

Bronson Ma Creative
17706 Copper Sunset
San Antonio, TX 78232
214-457-5615

Bruketa & Zinic Om
Zaurtnica 17
Zagreb, 10000 Croatia
+385 1 6064 000

Büro North
Level 1/35 Little Bourke Street
Melbourne 3000, Australia
03-9654 3259

Calagraphic Design
523 Stahr Rd.
Elkins Park, PA 19027
215-782-1361

Cala/Krill Design
5 Myrtle Avenue
Claymont, DE 19703
alyssa@littleutopia.com

Carbon Studio
14 Hafod Street, Grangetown
Cardiff, UK
www.carbonstudio.co.uk

CDI Studios
2215a Renaissance Drive
Las Vegas, NV 89119
702-876-3316

Coalesce Marketing & Design, Inc.
4321 West College Ave., Suite 475
Appleton, WI 54914
920-380-4444

Connie Hwang Design
815 NE 5th Street
Gainesville, FL 32601
352-328-6549

Contact Jupiter
5 Laurier ST.,
Steustache, Quebec J7R 2E5
450-491-3883

Content Solutions
1413 E. McKinney St.
Denton, TX 76209
940-384-9407 x227

cornbeefwindstorm designs
116 29th Ave. N
Nashville, TN 37203
615-327-9894

Cosmic
200 2nd Ave S Ste 150
St. Petersburg, FL 33701
727-421-1996

Crawford Design
57 East Washington St.
Chagrin Falls, OH 44022
440-893-0070

Curiosity Group
119 SE Main St.
Portland, OR 97214
503-797-0016

d-10.net
13a St. Peter Street
Dundee, Angus, Scotland, DD1 4JJ
+44 7974 704860

Delphine Keim-Campbell
1415 Pine Cone Rd. No. 8
Moscow, ID 83843
208-882-5140

Dept. of Art, Sam Houston State Univ.
PO Box 2089, 1028 21st St.
Huntsville, TX 77341
936-294-4762

Design 446
2411 Atlantic Ave., Suite 4
Manasquan, NJ 08736
732-859-3521

Design about Town
18 Bartol St.
San Francisco, CA 94133
415-205-8488

design hoch drei GmbH + Co. KG
Hallstr. 25a
Stuttgart, BW, 70376 Germany
oliver.biwer@design-hoch-dri.de

Design Management RUFFNEKK Oy
Rajamännynahde 3 E
02710 Espoo, Finland
www.ruffnekk.com

Designs on You!
813 Rogers Ct.
Ashland, KY 41101
606-329-0077
http://designs-on-you.net

dezinegirl creative studio, LLC
5752 Oberlin Dr., Suite 106
San Diego, CA 92121
858-350-4527

Digital Dimensions 3
8 Colony Drive East
West Orange, NJ 07052
973-868-0343

DK Design
2121 Peralta St. #121
Oakland, CA 94607
415-944-8541

Dotzero Design
208 SW Stark St. #307
Portland, OR 97204
503-892-9262

Drexel University,
Antoinette Westphal
College of Media Arts & Design,
Graphic Design Program
33rd & Market St. Nesbitt Floor 2
Philadelphia, PA 19104
215-895-0268

EBD
2500 Walnut Street #401
Denver, CO 80205
303-830-8323

Elasticbrand, LLC
8 Second Street
Brooklyn, NY 11231
413-652-1146

elf design, inc.
951-2 Old County Road
#171
Belmont, CA 94002
650-358-9973

Elixiron
El. Venizelou 49
Thessaloniki, 546 31 Greece
info@elixirion.gr

EMdash Design
123 Makefield Road
Yardley, PA 19067
215-337-9192

EP designworks
2505 Devils Glen Rd. #2008
Bettendorf, IA 52722
563-332-5559

Exhibit A: Design Group
2-25 East Sixth Avenue
Vancouver, BC V5T 1J3
www.exhibitadesigngroup.com

Factor Design
580 Howard Street, Suite 303
San Francisco, CA 94105
415-896-6051

Fleming Design
128 W. 8th Ave.
Vancouver, BC, Canada
info@flemingdesign.com

foxnoggin - thinking design
3242 E. Indian School Road
Phoenix, AZ 85008
602-808-8820

Frangipanni Communications
31A Cantonment Road
Singapore 089747
www.frangipanni.com.sg

Fresh Oil
251 Cottage Street
Pawtucket, RI 02860
401-709-4656

Gemini 3D
380, Route Principale, Suite 201
Cap-aux-Meules, Quebec G4T 1C9
www.gemini3d.com

Get A Clue
14 3rd Ave NE Suite 250
Hickory, NC 28601
828-261-0075

GHL Design
2410 Stafford Ave.
Raleigh, NC 27607
919-270-6244

Glitschka Studios
1976 Fitzpatrick Ave. SE
Salem, OR 97306
971-223-6143

Goodform Design
611 Carroll Street
Brooklyn, NY 11215
347-546-5980

Gough Graphics
65A South Pleasant Street
Bradford, MA 01835
978-457-5217

Gouthier Design : A Brand Collective
245 W. 29th Street, Suite 1304
New York, NY 10001
212-244-7430

Graham Hanson Design
60 Madison Avenue Floor 11
New York, NY 10010
212-481-2858

GreenLeaf MeDia
2040 Winnebago Street
Madison, WI 53704
608-240-9611

Group Fifty-Five Marketing
3011 West Grand Blvd., 329 Fisher Bldg.
Detroit, MI 48072
313-875-1155

Hansen Design Group
123 S. Main Street
Woodruff, SC 29388
864-476-6493

Hatch Design
353 Broadway St.
San Francisco, CA 94133
415-398-1650

Hebsandfish
25 Tateman Street
Worcester, MA 01607
www.hebsandfish.com

Helena Seo Design
1000 Escalon Ave. Suite 1012
Sunnyvale, CA 94085
408-830-0086

Hello Design
8684 Washington Blvd.
Culver City, CA 90232
310-839-4885

Hitz Studio
1079 Samsonville Road
Kerhonkson, NY 12446
845-626-7730

Holohan Design
6760 Germantown Avenue
Philadelphia, PA 19119
215-621-6559

Hornall Anderson
710 2nd Avenue Suite 1300
Seattle, WA 98104
206-467-5800

Hull Creative Group
7 Harvard Street
Brookline, MA 02445
617-232-3544

IE Design + Communications
422 Pacific Coast Highway
Hermosa Beach, CA 90254
310-376-9600

Infinite Studio
Via Casarino, 127
Albisola (Savona) 17011, Italy
www.infinitestudio.it

Insight Marketing Design
401 East 8th St., Suite 304
Sioux Falls, SD 57103
605-275-0011

Jacob Tyler Creative Group
1501 Front Street, Unit 107
San Diego, CA 92101
619-573-1061 x605

James Marsh Design
8 Cannongate Road
Hythe, Kent CT21 5PX
+44 (0) 1303 263118

JGA
29110 Inkster Rd., Suite 200
Southfield, MI 48034
248-355-0890

Jill Bell Brandlettering
9001 Pawnee Lane
Leawood, KS 66206
913-649-4505

Jill Lynn Design
400 17th St., NW Unit 1335
Atlanta, GA 30363
770-313-9343

JM Design Studio, Inc.
7116 Colony Club Dr. #202
Lake Worth, FL 33463
561-596-9071

John Sposato Design + Illustration
179 Hudson Terrace
Piermont, NY 10968
845-365-1940

John Wingard Design
925 Bethel St., Suite 306
Honolulu, HI 96813
808-529-8833

Jonathan Yuen
81 Tiong Poh Rd. #02-65A
Singapore 160081
www.jonathanyuen.com

Joni Rae and Associates
16500 Alyse Court
Encino, CA 91436
818-783-8080

Joven Orozco Design
2810 Villa Way
Newport Beach, CA 92663
949-723-1898

JPL Productions
471 JPL Wick Dr.
Harrisburg, PA 17111
800-421-7697

j. riley creative LLC
2671 Marilee Lane
Houston, TX 77057
713-785-1828

Kalico Design
PO Box 1574
Frederick, MD 21702
240-446-9765

Karoo Design
2 Venture Road
Southampton, Hampshire, 50167NP
info@karoodesign.com

Katie Cusack Illustration
125 West Hubbard Ave. Apt A
Columbus, OH 43215
912-844-1608

Kelly-Anne Leyman Design
2803 Stanbridge Street, Apt. B111
East Norriton, PA 19401
215.219.1103

Kelsey Advertising & Design
133 Main Street Suite A
LaGrange, GA 30240
706-298-3781

Kendra Spencer Design
393 East MacArthur Street
Sonoma, CA 95476
707-338-4624

Kenton Smith Adv. & PR, Inc.
330 E. Central Blvd.
Orlando, FL 32801
407-856-6680 x236

Knowlton Multimedia
9154 Anasazi Trail
Highlands Ranch, CO 80129
303-683-3308

Kristyn Kalnes Studio
818 Sheridan Street
Madison, WI 53715
608-441-5316

Krug Creative
428 A Haywood Road
Asheville, NC 28806
828-285-7100

Lebow
31 Menin Road
Toronto, ON M6C 3J1
416-784-9789

Leibold Associates, Inc.
983 Ehlers Rd.
Neenah, WI 54956
920-725-5328

Levine & Associates, Inc.
1090 Vermont Ave., NW, Suite 440
Washington D.C. 20005
202-842-3660 x112

Liquid Pixel Studio
162 Camden Avenue
Staten Island, NY 10309
917-319-0413

Los Alamos National Laboratory
PO Box 1663, MS:K491
Los Alamos, NM 87545
505-667-3764

LTD Creative
103 S. Carroll St., Suite 2D
Frederick, MD 21701
301-682-4293

Lucie M. Rice Illustration
4107 Kimbark Drive
Nashville, TN 37215
615-269-6530

Mad Dog Graphx
1443 W Northern Lights Blvd., Suite U
Anchorage, AK 99503
907-276-5062

McKinney
318 Blackwell Street
Durham, NC 27701
919-313-0802

MDG Strategic Branding
13 Water Street
Holliston, MA 01742
508-429-0755

Melanie Marder Parks
5 Broadview Lane
Red Hook, NY 12571
845-758-0656

Melvin Ng
8 Dover Rise #08-02 Heritage View
Singapore 138679
ngmel@singnet.com.sg

Michael Doret Graphic Design
6545 Cahuenga Terrace
Hollywood, CA 90068
323-467-1900

Michelle Roberts Design
PO Box 32
Barneveld, NY 13304
315-269-7732

Minds on Marketing
8864 Whitney Drive
Lewis Center, OH 43035
740-548-1645

MiresBall
2345 Kehner Blvd.
San Diego, CA 92101
619-234-6631

Miriello Grafico
1660 Logan Avenue
San Diego, CA 92113
619-234-1124

Moonlight Creative Group
1705 East Blvd., Suite 100
Charlotte, NC 28203
704-358-3777

Morgan Gaynin, Inc.
194 Third Avenue
New York, NY 10003
212-475-0440

MSLK Graphic Design
23-23 33rd Road
Long Island, NY 11106
718-545-0075

NALINDESIGNô
Georg Goebel Strasse 19
58809 Neuenrade, Germany
www.nalindesign.com

Nassar Design
11 Park Street
Brookline, MA 02446
617-264-2862

Octavo Designs
8 N. East Street, Suite 100
Frederick, MD 21701
301-695-8885

Open Creative Group
28 Olmsted Street
Birmingham, AL 35242
205-437-3395

Open Studio Design
449 W. 56 Street 5B
New York, NY 10019
917-499-5242

OrangeSeed Design
901 N 3rd Street, Suite 305
Minneapolis, MN 55401
612-252-9757 x205

Paragon Marketing Communications
PO Box 6097
Salmiya, 22071 Kuwait
www.paragonmc.com

Passing Notes, Inc.
200 2nd Street No. 201
Oakland, CA 94607
510-835-8035

Pensaré Design Group
1313 F Street NW, Third Floor
Washington D.C. 20004
202-638-7700

Phototransformations
29 Bartlett Street
Beverly, MA 01915
978-395-1292

Pi Design
760 Las Posas Road, Suite A2
Camarillo, CA 93010
805-383-0054

pierpoint design + branding
6714 N Pittsburg
Spokane, WA 99217
509-466-1565

Poul Lange Design
71 Saint Marks Place #10
New York, NY 10001
212-254-3306

Q
Sonnenberger Strabe 16
65193 Wiesbaden, Germany
www.q-home.de

Randi Wolf Design
18 Cypress Ct.
Glassboro, NJ 08028
856-582-8181

RDormann Design
76 Kuhlthau Avenue
Milltown, NJ 08850
732-247-4459

Reactor
3111 Wyandotte, Suite 203
Kansas City, MO 64111
816-841-3682

Rickabaugh Graphics
384 W. Johnstown Rd.
Gahanna, OH 43230
614-337-2229

Right-Hemisphere Laboratory
7940 W. Chestnut Dr.
Littleton, CO 80124
303-972-3168

Rob Dunlavey Illustration
8 Front Street
South Natick, MA 01760
508-651-7503

Rock, Paper, Scissors
178 E. Crogan Street, Suite 220
Lawrenceville, GA 30045
678-442-1825

Rotor
836 40th Avenue NE
Minneapolis, MN 55405
763-706-3906

Roycroft Design
7 Faneuil Hall Marketplace 4th Floor
Boston, MA 02109
617-720-4506

Rubin Cordaro Design
115 N 1st Street
Minneapolis, MN 55401
612-343-0011

Rule29 Creative, Inc.
303 West State Street
Geneva, IL 60134
630-262-1009

Saba Dö Graphix
461 Aragon Ave
White Rock, NM 87544
505-672-2250

Sabingrafik, Inc.
7333 Seafarer Place
Carlsbad, CA 92011
760-431-0439

Sayles Graphic Design
3701 Beaver Ave.
Des Moines, IA 50310
515-279-2922

Scott Adams Design Associates
290 Marlot Street #803
Minneapolis, MN 55405
612-236-1146

SGDP
314 W. Superior Suite 300
Chicago, IL 60610
312-376-0360

Shimokochi-Reeves
832 Cole Avenue
Los Angeles, CA 90038
323-957-9055

Simpatico Design Studio, LLC
529 E Bellefonte Ave.
Alexandria, VA 22301
703-837-0584

Skidmore
301 W. 4th Street, Suite 300
Royal Oak, MI 48067
248-591-2600

Softpill
3953 Cerrito Ave.
Oakland, CA 94611
grace@softpill.com

Sol Design Group
2700 J Street, 2nd Floor
Sacramento, CA 95816
916-448-3265

Soloflight Design Studio
126 Sloan Street
Roswell, GA 30075
770-925-1115

Somewhat Awesome Design
523 Stahr Rd.
Elkins Park, PA 19027
215-782-1361

Speedy Motorcycle Studio
PO Box 456
Medford, NJ 08055
617-875-1871

Splash:Design
106-1441 Ellis St.
Kelowna, BC Canada
250-868-1059

Srijan Advertising
202 Princess Centre, 2nd Floor
Indore (M.P.) 452 003, India
nitin.srijan@gmail.com

Stephen Burdick Design
20 Piedmont Street
Boston, MA 02116
617-695-1400

Sterling Cross Creative
15 W. MacArthur St.
Sonoma, CA 95476
707-939-8886

Studio 33 Design
710 Arroyo Drive #1
South Pasadena, CA 91030
626-799-0246

Studio International
Buconjiceva 43
Zagreb, 10000 Croatia
boris@studio-international.com

Studio QED, Inc.
205 DeAnza Blvd. #148
San Mateo, CA 94402
650-804-6564

Subcommunication
24 Avenue Mont-Royal West, Suite 1003
Montréal, Québec, H2T 2S2
514-845-9423

Sue Todd Illustration
146 Alameda Ave.
Toronto, Ontario M6C 3X2
416-784-5313

Sungrafx
9435 Provost Rd., NW, Suite #205
Silverdale, WA 98383
360-692-3021

Sutton Watkins Advertising
5844 S. Pecos Rd., Suite A
Las Vegas, NV 89120
702-270-2147

Symbiotic Solutions
26A Kresge Art Center
East Lansing, MI 48824
517-862-2337

Synthetic Infatuation
488 Wabasha N St #302
St. Paul, MN 55102
312-203-6267

TFI Envision, Inc.
111 Westport Avenue
Norwalk, CT 06951
203-845-0700

The College of Saint Rose
432 Western Avenue
Albany, NY 12203-1490
518-454-5102

The Id Entity
5709 Cambridge Drive
Fredericksburg, VA 22407
540-834-0151

The Partners
Albion Courtyard,
Greenhill Rents, Smithfield,
London, Ecim 6PQ
freya@thepartners.co.uk

Theyhatemydesign Studio
Perum Permata Hijau kav.15
Bangunharjo,Sewon
Bantul, Yogyakarta, 55187, Indonesia
+62 8562856685

Th!nkCreative Advertising
813 W. Saint Germain St.
St. Cloud, MN 56301
320-259-9400

Tim Goldman Illustration Design
35-16 85th Street 6E
Jackson Heights, NY 11372
718-965-9110

Tomato Graphics
517 N. Shore Drive
Amarillo, TX 79118
806-367-8086

Top Design
2284 Moreno Drive.
Los Angeles, CA 90039
323-202-4611

Tread Creative
15495 Los Gatos Blvd.,
Suite 1
Los Gatos, CA 95032
408-358-3077

TrueBlue
1215 Latta Street
Chattanooga, TN 37406
423-624-0040

Type E Design
600 North Henry Street
Alexandria, VA 22314
703-567-4540

Urban Gecko, Inc.
4695 MacArthur Court,
Suite 1100
Newport Beach, CA 92660
949-798-6150

USA TODAY Brand Marketing
7950 Jones Branch Drive
McLean, VA 22108
703-854-5369

Velocity Design Works
52 Ellen St.
Winnipeg, Manitoba, Canada
204-475-0514

Ventress Design Group
3310 Aspen Grove Drive,
Suite 303
Franklin, TN 37067
615-727-0155

Viadesign
3911 Hanney Street
San Diego, CA 92110
619-220-0470

Wallace Church, Inc.
330 East 48th Street
New York, NY 10017
212-755-2903

WAX
320-333 24th Avenue SW
Calgary, Alberta T2S 3E6
403-262-9323

Wildlife & Whimsy
345 Livingston Avenue
Missoula, MT 59801
406-531-6253

www.loredanastudio.com
264 5th Avenue #3A
New York, NY 10001
646-228-1781

xo Create!
1320 Union Hill Industrial Court,
Suite C
Alpharetta, GA 30004
678-319-4242

Yellobee Studio
1349 West Peachtree Street,
Suite 2000
Atlanta, GA 30309
404-249-6407

Zc Creative
1007 Serpentine Lane
Wyncote, PA 19095
215-576-0722

Zerofractal Studio
250 The Esplanade,
Suite 401A
Toronto, Ontario, M5A 1J2

Zunda Group, LLC
41 North Main Street
South Norwalk, CT 06890
203-853-9600